Something
Tastes Funny

SEAN DONNELLAN

Something
Tastes
Funny

WARNER BOOKS

A Time Warner Company

Warner Books, Inc. 1271 Avenue of the Americas, New York, NY 10020
Visit our Web site at
http://pathfinder.com/twep

 A Time Warner Company

Printed in the United States of America
First Printing: June 1997
10 9 8 7 6 5 4 3 2 1

Library of Congress Cataloging-in-Publication Data
Donnellan, Sean.
   Something Tastes Funny / Sean Donnellan
     p. cm.
   Includes Index.
   ISBN 0-446-67322-6
   1. Cookery. 2. Cookery—Humor. I. Title.
   TX714.D64 1997
   641.5—dc21   97-1836
                                   CIP

Photos by Max S. Gerber
Recipes by Naidre Miller
Illustrations by Sean Donnellan
Cover and Interior Design by Spinning Egg Design Group, Inc.

To the loving memory of
Helen V. Partridge and Paul L. Kaminski—
their creative spirit lives on in all whom they touched.

Acknowledgments

Sean wishes to thank:

My beautiful wife, Jay, for keeping my heart warm even when this business is cold. Thank you, my love, for all the things you do to keep me going.

My manager, Arlyne Rothberg, for being my incredible guide through this madness and making this book happen.

Mom and Dad, for all the love and support and always letting me choose my own path. Deborah Partridge (Mom), thanks for my artistic eye.

Jerry Donnellan (Dad), thanks for my never-ending drive.

Tom Partridge, for letting your little nephew be a part of you and your friends' creative insanity.

Anna Donnellan, thank you for being the incredible woman that you are and lending your super model talents to this book.

Naidre Miller, thank you for your patience and great work making my half-baked ideas a delicious reality.

Max S. Gerber, your endless energy and brilliant work made my job easy.

Marc Unger, for your trusted opinion that helped keep my stories on track.

Warner Books: Mel Parker for believing in this project; and my editor, Rob McMahon, for helping me pull it all together

Celeste Bantz and Dan Potash at Spinning Egg Design Group for stepping in and working with my concepts.

TV Food Network: former president Reese Schonfeld and Jonathan I. Lynne, thank you both for giving me a great start.

Michael G. Leonard, for reading this when it was an unedited mess.

Amy MacWilliamson, Jay Donnellan, Jerry Donnellan, and Danielle Gerber for helping out behind the camera.

Rosemarie Raccioppi, for teaching me that believing in yourself can overcome more obstacles than good grades can.

Robert D. Uttrich, for always helping out.

Paul Pacheco, for being there in the early days.

To the pioneers of the early part of my career, Hy Schuster, Bob Delaney, Chris Thiesing, and Frank LoBuono. Thank you for giving me a chance.

Glenn Farrington, for hanging in there and lending a hand.

The Comedy Pub on America Online, keyword: LOL.

Ron Grove and Louise Contreras, for being my West Coast office when I didn't have one.

Phil Cross at OD's in Nyack, New York, thanks for caring about what we eat.

Lock, Stock & Barrel in Bardonia, New York.

All the schoolteachers I never got along with—yes, you did have a comic in your class and thanks for the stage time.

Naidre Miller would like to thank her mom, Jeri Penning-Buxton, for giving her a love of food and for teaching her how to cook. Without her guidance and unflagging support, none of this would be possible.

The Ingredients

Introduction

This is my story. The story of how my childhood dream turned into a glorious career that made me the first lady of the American theater. Wait. I'm sorry. That was Helen Hayes. My story is about a rosy-cheeked kid who overcame a reading disability by dropping out of college. I'm not even writing my story! I'm writing a cookbook. Yep, a cookbook. OK, it's a cookbook filled with stories and half-baked ideas, but a cookbook just the same.

I always wanted to write a book, but I didn't think anybody would let me. In my high school yearbook I was voted the guy most likely to be in the yearbook the following year. I used to tell my wife, Jay, that if I ever got a chance to write a book, it was going to be titled *My Grandmother's Brain Is Larger Than Mine*. The book would set out to prove that my grandmother, Anna Donnellan, was smarter than all of her children and grandchildren put together. You see, nobody ever wants to tell Anna the truth about what's going on. If somebody is sick, getting a divorce, or in trouble of any kind, they always hide it from my grandmother. My cousin Adam and I joke that no one has yet told her that my father fought in the Vietnam war. But, unbeknownst to the rest of the family, she never misses a trick. I haven't been given a chance to write that book yet, so it's the cookbook for now.

If you told me three years ago that I would author my own cookbook, I would have said, "But everybody knows how to open Spam." Since then my food world has changed quite a bit. In April 1995, the third rendition of *How To Boil Water* aired on the TV Food Network, with me as the host. At the time, my being asked to host a show about cooking was the equivalent of Julia Child's being asked to host a show about kickboxing. But TVFN felt that the intended audience of novice cooks was not being reached by the previous hosts—perhaps because they were intimidated by a real chef's trying to teach them culinary basics. So in their search for a guy who could fill a half hour of airtime without a script and didn't know much about cooking, they found me. And thus was born a cooking show for people who don't know how to cook, hosted by a guy who doesn't know how to cook. Learning together. That's basically the whole idea behind *How To Boil Water*. I'm not a cook, so if I can do it, you can do it. With 260 episodes completed, the concept obviously worked. The success of *How To Boil Water* currently has me in negotiations with The Learning Channel for my own surgery show. Fine by me, because either way I get to work with liver.

This book is designed to give hope and inspiration to those poor souls who feel a night of fine dining means delving into the jerky rack at the 7-Eleven. The recent college grad, the young professional, or anyone who's gotten to the point where he or she is tipping the delivery guy more than Jim Carrey makes for starring in a movie can use this book as a trusty guide.

This is your culinary Rand McNally. Consider every white plate a blank canvas and break free from your life of the "Warhol Soup Can" as you take your palette to new heights. The steps are here for you to follow. Climb these stairs at your own steady pace. When you reach the top, you will be met by yourself, but you will sense that this new you is a little different. At first you will not be sure what is so different about this other you. Then you will notice that the new you has a greater sense of confidence and pride. Extending his or her arms, the new you will offer the old you a gift in the form of a fresh baked meat loaf. The old you will ask, "Where did you get this?" The new you will respond by saying, "You made it; your journey is now complete." Take each step one at a time and you will reach the top sooner than you think. Whenever you doubt that you are ready to progress to the next level, look in the mirror and repeat this statement: "I'm not a bad cook. I'm a good cook, a caring and loving cook. At this time I am the best cook I can be and each day the cook inside me grows to new heights." You can do it. Frequent flyer miles don't build up if you take the bus. All of us are capable of making good food. There is an old adage that says, "If you teach a man how to caulk his own windows, he will save up to 35 percent on his heating bill." This book is the torch I pass along to you my friends. Read it. Enjoy it. Above all, eat well from it.

Something Tastes Funny

Sean and Naidre first met on the set of *How To Boil Water* when Naidre was working for the TV Food Network as a cook and food stylist. In addition to her career as a recipe tester and developer for cookbooks and magazines, Naidre teaches cooking privately and has worked with Martha Stewart, Emeril Lagasse, Dean Fearing, David Rosengarten, Mary Sue Milliken, and Susan Feniger. Sean and Naidre have created a menu that will delight the taste buds without monopolizing all of your time. Within each recipe, we have listed the caloric content and nutritional information of the dish. If, at first glance, the numbers seem high, it is because we have based them on realistic portions and not on the small servings that most cookbooks list. The recipes are user-friendly and flexible. Don't feel threatened by quantities. You don't need to hire a specialist from the Bureau of Weights and Measures. With most recipes (baking requires precision), feel free to add and subtract as you see fit. Following a recipe for a pasta dish is not supposed to be like working with high explosives in the laboratory. If you add a pinch too much basil or a tad too little egg whites, you're not going to end up hanging from the rafters like Grandpa Munster. Most of all, this book is a guide to help you create delicious, uncomplicated food.

KITCHEN
BASICS

Tools

wooden spoons—an assorted set of three

vegetable peeler (can also be used to make chocolate curls)

balloon whisk—thinner and wider spokes get more air into whatever you are beating

ladle—preferably heat-resistant plastic

rolling pin *without* handles—makes it easier to detect how much pressure you are using

colander (metal)—for straining pasta, cleaning lettuce, myriad other uses

metal mesh strainer—for straining small things, like angel hair pasta, beans, vegetables

collapsible metal steamer—for steaming vegetables, fish, dumplings

small paring knife—for cutting small things, like shallots and fruit

8- or 10-inch chef's knife—whichever is more comfortable in your hand; I prefer Wusthof knives—they are well balanced and well made

serrated bread knife—great for slicing tomatoes, too

set of graduated glass bowls—not metal; they react with acid (i.e., lemon juice, vinegar)

cutting board—wood harbors too much bacteria, so get a plastic one

stainless steel measuring spoons and cups—plastic holds odors and bacteria and melts in dishwashers

refrigerator thermometer—to make sure your refrigerator is cold enough (33-40°F). Any warmer than 40°F and bacteria grow at alarming rates!

oven thermometer—to make sure that your oven is properly calibrated; if it isn't as most aren't, you can make the necessary adjustments to make sure that your oven is at the proper temperature

parchment paper—indispensable for rolling out dough, making cookies, chopping nuts, etc.

Pots and Pans

small sauté pan—I prefer *not* to use a nonstick pan

large sauté pan

8- or 10-inch nonstick sauté pan

6- or 8-quart pot for pasta or soup (large sauce/stock pot)—new ones have a pasta strainer and a steamer insert included, and are a great purchase

2-quart pot (small saucepan)

cast-iron grill pan

roasting pan—nonstick preferably

cookie sheets—one with sides, one without

nonstick loaf pan

9-inch nonstick pie pan

Staples, Spices and Herbs, Condiments

extra-virgin olive oil—use the best quality that you can afford. High price does not always equal high quality. Buy small bottles and experiment to see which brand or region you like best. All extra-virgin oils are cold pressed, meaning that heat was not used to extract the oil and therefore did not affect the taste or break down the molecular structure and integrity of the oil. Use extra-virgin for dressing a dish, for dishes that do not require high heat for cooking, and in salad dressings. Many stores now sell other cold-pressed oils, so when possible, go for them.

vegetable oil or canola oil—best for dishes that will be cooked at higher heat or pan-fried. They have a higher smoking point, so they can be heated hotter without breaking down and burning.

flavored oils—there are many flavored oils on the market now that are interesting and fun to play with and can really make a difference in a dish. I love *Consorzio's* oils—they come in terrific flavors like roasted garlic and basil.

balsamic vinegar—there are different grades; some are aged for years before being bottled and range in flavor from very sharp to very sweet. Buy small bottles and experiment to find the flavor you like best.

cumin—provides a familiar Mexican flavor.

garlic powder—indispensable! An easy way to add garlic if you are too lazy or out of fresh garlic.

crushed red pepper—a quick way to add spice to any dish, especially pizza.

bay leaf—adds a depth to stews and soups that is hard to describe, but you know when it is missing.

rosemary—a must when roasting potatoes or cooking with tomatoes.

oregano—Greek and Italian are both sold—Greek is more pungent, Italian is softer. Try both and see which you prefer.

thyme—lemony flavored herb that is indispensable for vegetable cooking.

curry powder—not an herb, but a complex blend of many different spices, varying from brand to brand, in both heat level and depth of flavor. It is made up of turmeric (for color), cumin, fenugreek, coriander, celery seed, pepper, garlic, and ginger in differing formulas.

ground ginger—great to add to marinades and barbecue sauce.

Bell's Seasoning—a terrific blend of spices for chicken dishes, sold in a paper box.

chile powder—pure ground red chile peppers—not *chili* powder, which is a mix of cumin, chile powder, oregano, cayenne pepper, garlic, and allspice.

cinnamon—a must in all apple dishes, not to mention in any type of chili.

mustard—there are a million in the stores now. Grey Poupon is still a great mustard, but explore the others!

canned tomatoes—always use whole, peeled tomatoes in juice. The quality varies from brand to brand, so experiment. A staple in every kitchen.

Liquid Smoke—a liquid that captures the taste of smoked foods perfectly. Very concentrated, so use only a drop or two at a time.

peppermill and whole peppercorns—don't cheat yourself on flavor by using preground pepper. Some people prefer the mixed color peppercorns, but I prefer regular black.

kosher salt—good for a million things, including putting out fires. I just prefer the taste, and since it does not have iodine added it is lower in sodium.

table salt—iodized and has a saltier flavor and higher sodium. Use when baking, since the grains are finer.

frozen pizza dough—most grocery stores have this in their freezer sections. Also, don't be too shy to ask your local pizzeria if you can buy dough from them and freeze it for later use. It tastes better than store-bought. Just remember to leave enough time for it to defrost!

frozen pie dough—most storebought pie crust dough is inedible. It really is worth it to take 5 minutes (literally!) and make a batch or two of pie dough, wrap it up well, and freeze it. You can even roll it out, place it in the pie pan, cover it, and freeze it.

chicken and vegetable broth or stock—Chinese restaurants are a good source for chicken stock. Canned broth will do, but try not to use bouillon cubes—they just have too many chemicals in them. Another option is to cook down canned chicken or vegetable broth to concentrate the flavor.

Asian roasted sesame oil—very concentrated, rich flavor. Try a drop or two in chicken soup.

Asian fish sauce (nam pla)—gives that Thai flavor.

soy sauce or tamari—regular or sodium reduced. Great to use as a marinade with other seasonings for beef and chicken.

butter—always cook with unsalted butter. Salted butter is generally inferior butter that is salted to mask its "off" taste. Salted also burns easier than unsalted.

chocolate—because quality chocolate is an integral part of any recipe, spend the extra money and buy the good stuff! Valrhona is a special favorite, but on the whole, any European chocolate is going to be better than any American chocolate. Do not store in refrigerator; just keep well wrapped in a cool, dark spot.

Note: During the late summer, when herbs are at their peak, I buy a couple of bunches of my favorites: rosemary, thyme, oregano, lemon verbena (for tea), and mint (for tea) and hang them upside down to dry. Then I put the dried leaves in glass canning jars to use during the winter. The flavor is so much better, and using herbs that you dried yourself really makes a difference.

Storage Techniques

Knowing how to properly store foods is just as important as knowing how to cook. Keep a thermometer in your fridge to check the temperature. It should always be between 33 and 40°F.

lettuce—never use a knife on lettuce because the knife releases chemicals in the lettuce that hasten browning. Rip off the bottom (heart), to cause the leaves to separate. Place in a large bowl, or preferably the sink, full of very cold water. Let sit for 2 minutes, then agitate the water slightly to get any remaining dirt off of the leaves. Gently shake the water off the leaves and let drain for a moment. Rip the leaves into the desired size and place them on a flat dish towel or paper towel. Don't pile too high or crowd the leaves together. Then roll up the towel full of leaves. Put in a plastic bag or wrap in plastic wrap. It sounds complicated, but it really only takes about 4 minutes and guarantees that your lettuce won't rot before you get to eat it.

fresh herbs—most green herbs will last a week if you cut the stem ends a bit, stick the herbs upright in a glass of water like cut flowers, and cover with a plastic bag. Don't put on top shelf of fridge, as they are sensitive to cold and might freeze.

foods in general—never place hot food in the refrigerator; it brings down the temperature of the refrigerator to an unsafe level. Cool the hot food to room temperature, and then place in refrigerator. Wrap well, and consume leftovers within two days. Freezing food does not make food that is going bad suddenly safe to eat.

dried fruit and nuts—nuts should always be stored, tightly wrapped, in the freezer unless you plan to use them quickly. Nuts are very high in oils that easily go rancid. To defrost, just quickly toast the nuts in a 375°F oven for 10 minutes or in a dry sauté pan before using. Dried fruit should be stored in airtight jars or containers. Again, I suggest glass canning jars. If the fruit gets too dry, soak in water or fruit juice for an hour or so until softer, or simmer for 5 minutes.

bread—slice first, wrap tightly, and place in freezer. Toast as needed.

bagels—slice first, then put in a resealable bag and freeze. Toast as needed.

Note: **If in doubt, throw it out!** Never eat anything that you are not sure about. Follow your instincts. A good rule of thumb is *two* days for leftovers, then throw them out.

What Are You Eating?

Cooking is one of the most important skills for maintaining your health. In this world of preservatives and prepackaging, the opportunity to have total control over the ingredients you ingest is a great asset. We live in a time when there is actually a demand for Twinkies Light! What I wonder about is the sad physical state one must be in to switch from a regular Twinkies to low-cal Twinkies and think that you are doing yourself some good. It's not as if the person is switching over to organic produce—it's still a Twinkie! The same goes for those who are addicted to low-fat frozen yogurt. It's only low in fat until you hit the toppings section and the guy asks, "Do you want any toppings on that?" The response is, like, "Yeah, why don't you give me some of the Nestle's Crunch bar, some of the gummy bears, some of the coconut, some of the peanut . . . Aww . . . what the heck—throw a roast beef on there and, while you're at it, be a dear and put some whipped cream on top!"

As a whole we eat horribly in this country. We even load up our Olympic athletes with McDonald's, Snickers bars, and Coca-Cola and wonder why we still can't luge. You don't need me to point this out, because television does it for us. Thirty percent of the ads on TV today are for antacids, stomach tablets, and digestive aids.

The commercials are ridiculous. The wife is always cooking dinner and the husband walks in like the moron that all husbands are in commercials, and so goes the conversation:

Wife: "Honey, I'm making your favorite—rat's asses and Tabasco!"

Husband: "Ummm . . . sounds great, but you know what rat's asses and Tabasco does to my stomach. I won't be able to breathe all night and I'll be on the can until Wednesday."

Wife: "No, you won't, because the first course is this little pill called Forget What Your Body Is Trying to Tell You! Take just one little Forget What Your Body Is Trying to Tell You! and you can eat rat's asses and Tabasco for the next twelve hours."

Husband: "Well I just might. . . . Golly, honey, you must really love me."

It's very clear why we have these products. Americans spend $1 billion a year on over-the-counter antacids. So, that proves that the people of this great land have a lot of trouble figuring out what they should and shouldn't eat. If you eat something that lights you up like Las Vegas and keeps you open all night, don't eat it! Don't take some drug that alters your system from doing its job of keeping you alive! Frustration sets in after a while when I hear people say things like, "I can't figure out why the spicy sausage doesn't sit well in my tummy." It's rather simple: intestines don't break down other intestines very well—it's called professional courtesy.

I'm not here to tell you what you should and shouldn't eat. Truly, eat what you like and eat what you love—just be smart and know what you're eating.

1
APPETIZERS

Black Bean and Corn Salsa

Serves
4

1	16-OUNCE CAN BLACK BEANS
1	CUP COOKED CORN KERNELS
3	PLUM TOMATOES, CHOPPED
1	SMALL JALAPEÑO PEPPER, SEEDED AND MINCED
3	SCALLIONS, THINLY SLICED
1	SMALL RED ONION, FINELY CHOPPED
2	TABLESPOONS CHOPPED FRESH CILANTRO
2	TABLESPOONS RED WINE VINEGAR
2	TABLESPOONS VEGETABLE OIL
1	TEASPOON SALT

NUTRITION

Per Serving
Calories (kcal): ----------306.2
Total Fat (g): ------------8.4
Saturated Fat (g): ---------1.1
Cholesterol (mg): ---------0
Carbohydrate (g): ---------48.4
Dietary Fiber (g): ---------10.8
Protein (g): --------------13.7
Sodium (mg): ------------556
Calcium (mg): ------------98
Iron (mg): ----------------4.0
Vitamin C (mg): -----------58
Vitamin A (i.u.): ----------836

Drain liquid from beans and rinse in cool water. Place in a large bowl with the corn, tomatoes, jalapeño, scallions, onion, and cilantro.

In a small bowl, combine vinegar, oil, and salt. Pour over other ingredients, toss, and refrigerate. Stir well before serving.

Tip: This is especially great if made at least 6 hours ahead.

Note: Great as a topping for grilled chicken or shrimp, as well as a side salad.

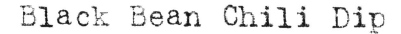

Black Bean Chili Dip

Serves
8

4	SMALL CHORIZO SAUSAGES, HALVED AND SLICED
6	GARLIC CLOVES, MINCED
1	CUP FINELY CHOPPED ONION
6	RADISHES, HALVED AND THINLY SLICED
1	TEASPOON MINCED CANNED CHIPOTLE PEPPER
1	POUND GROUND PORK, OR CHICKEN, BEEF, OR TOFU
6	14-OUNCE CANS BLACK BEANS, RINSED AND DRAINED
$\frac{1}{2}$	CUP FRESH LIME JUICE
	SALT
1	CUP GREEN SALSA
1	TEASPOON FRESH OREGANO
$\frac{1}{2}$	POUND MONTEREY JACK CHEESE, SHREDDED
$\frac{1}{4}$	CUP CHOPPED CILANTRO

NUTRITION

Per Serving Not Including Chips

Calories (kcal):	871.7
Total Fat (g):	31.0
Saturated Fat (g):	12.9
Cholesterol (mg):	89
Carbohydrate (g):	95.2
Dietary Fiber (g):	22.8
Protein (g):	55.6
Sodium (mg):	456
Calcium (mg):	438
Iron (mg):	8.7
Vitamin C (mg):	12
Vitamin A (i.u.):	527

In a large, heavy saucepan, heat chorizo slices over medium-high heat just until they release their oil. Add garlic, onion, radishes, and chipotle pepper and sauté until soft. Add meat and continue to cook, breaking up meat with a spoon, for 5 to 10 minutes or until cooked through. Add beans, lime juice, and salt to taste. Reduce heat, cover, and simmer for 10 minutes. Pour in salsa, oregano, and half of the cheese, and continue to simmer until cheese melts.

Pour chili into a serving dish, and sprinkle with remaining cheese and the cilantro. Serve warm with tortilla chips.

Bruschetta

Serves
4

N U T R I T I O N	
Per Serving Including Bread	
Calories (kcal):	460.5
Total Fat (g):	17.9
Saturated Fat (g):	2.9
Cholesterol (mg):	0
Carbohydrate (g):	64.2
Dietary Fiber (g):	5.2
Protein (g):	11.4
Sodium (mg):	6.76
Calcium (mg):	21
Iron (mg):	4.2
Vitamin C (mg):	27
Vitamin A (i.u.):	856

4	LARGE, RIPE TOMATOES, COARSELY CHOPPED
2	SCALLIONS, THINLY SLICED
4	GARLIC CLOVES, 3 CRUSHED AND 1 HALVED
$\frac{1}{4}$	CUP EXTRA-VIRGIN OLIVE OIL
1	BUNCH FRESH BASIL, $\frac{1}{2}$ CUP TORN INTO PIECES, $\frac{1}{2}$ CUP LEFT WHOLE
	SALT AND PEPPER
	SLICED ITALIAN BREAD

In a large glass bowl, combine the tomatoes, scallions, crushed garlic, olive oil, torn basil leaves, and a little salt and pepper. Let sit 30 minutes.

Toast the slices of bread and then rub the halved garlic clove on each to perfume the slices.

Place the slices of toasted bread on a platter. Top each with about 2 tablespoons of the tomato mixture. Garnish each slice with a whole basil leaf. (Or pile the toast in a pretty basket or on a plate, and let people assemble their own.)

Note: Everyone has his or her version of this—this is mine. Make more than you think you need; it goes fast.

Calzone

Serves
4

1	POUND PIZZA DOUGH, DEFROSTED IF PREVIOUSLY FROZEN
2	CUPS RICOTTA CHEESE, WHOLE OR SKIM MILK
1	10-OUNCE PACKAGE FROZEN SPINACH LEAVES, THAWED AND DRAINED
$\frac{1}{2}$	CUP DICED FRESH MOZZARELLA CHEESE
	SALT AND PEPPER
2	TABLESPOONS OLIVE OIL

NUTRITION	
Per Serving Using Whole Milk Ricotta	
Calories (kcal):	570.5
Total Fat (g):	29.1
Saturated Fat (g):	13.7
Cholesterol (mg):	75
Carbohydrate (g):	52.5
Dietary Fiber (g):	1.0
Protein (g):	24.2
Sodium (mg):	177
Calcium (mg):	361
Iron (mg):	4.0
Vitamin C (mg):	4
Vitamin A (i.u.):	1,671

Preheat oven to 450°F. Grease a baking sheet. Lightly flour your hands and a rolling pin and roll dough out to a $\frac{1}{3}$-inch-thick rectangle. Cut dough into 4 squares.

In a large bowl, combine the ricotta, spinach, mozzarella, and salt and pepper to taste. Place one fourth of the stuffing mixture on half of each dough piece, leaving a 1-inch border free of stuffing, and fold over the other half. Roll edge into itself, creating a seal, then press to make a tight seal.

Place calzone on greased sheet pan, brush with oil, and cut a small slit in top of each to let steam escape. Bake 20 minutes or until the dough is golden brown. Let sit for 5 minutes before serving. Note: The filling possibilities are endless—see Fast Homemade Pizza, page 18.

Classic Steamed Mussels

Serves
4

4	TABLESPOONS OLIVE OIL
1	MEDIUM RED ONION, FINELY CHOPPED
4	GARLIC CLOVES, THINLY SLICED
2	POUNDS MUSSELS, SCRUBBED AND DEBEARDED
$\frac{1}{2}$	CUP DRY VERMOUTH
$\frac{1}{2}$	CUP WATER
2	CUPS CHOPPED RIPE TOMATOES
	SALT AND PEPPER
4	SCALLIONS, THINLY SLICED

NUTRITION	
Per Serving Not Including Bread	
Calories (kcal):	394.4
Total Fat (g):	19.0
Saturated Fat (g):	2.9
Cholesterol (mg):	64
Carbohydrate (g):	20.1
Dietary Fiber (g):	2.3
Protein (g):	28.8
Sodium (mg):	668
Calcium (mg):	94
Iron (mg):	10.0
Vitamin C (mg):	43
Vitamin A (i.u.):	1,001

In a large sauté pan, heat oil until very hot, and sauté onion and garlic until softened but not colored. Add the mussels, vermouth, water, and tomatoes. Raise heat and bring to a boil, cook for 1 minute at boil, then cover and steam for 2 minutes, or until mussels are open. Discard any mussels that do not open. Season broth with salt and pepper to taste. Bring to table in same pot, or divide into 4 serving bowls with a slotted spoon and pour broth over mussels. Sprinkle on scallions and serve with a lot of bread.

Creamless Mushroom Soup

Serves
6

2	TABLESPOONS UNSALTED BUTTER
1	CUP PEELED AND SLICED CARROTS
1	CUP SLICED ONION
1	CUP SLICED LEEKS
$\frac{1}{2}$	CUP SLICED CELERY
2	POUNDS WHITE MUSHROOMS, SLICED
1	TEASPOON FRESH THYME LEAVES
6	CUPS CHICKEN OR VEGETABLE STOCK
	SALT AND PEPPER
4	TEASPOONS MINCED FRESH PARSLEY

NUTRITION

Per Serving Using Chicken Stock

Calories (kcal): ----------140.3
Total Fat (g): -------------6.3
Saturated Fat (g): ---------3.0
Cholesterol (mg): ---------11
Carbohydrate (g): ---------14.2
Dietary Fiber (g): ---------3.3
Protein (g): ----------------9.1
Sodium (mg): -------------904
Calcium (mg): -----------63
Iron (mg): -----------------3.7
Vitamin C (mg):-----------12
Vitamin A (i.u.): ---------5,531

Melt butter over medium-high heat in a large soup pot. Add carrots, onion, leek, and celery, and cook until tender but not browned, about 10 minutes. Stir in the mushrooms and thyme, and cook until mushrooms have softened, about 5 minutes. Add stock and salt and pepper to taste and simmer, covered, for 30 minutes.

Puree the soup in small batches in a food processor, or with an upright blender. Adjust seasonings, and serve in bowls with a sprinkle of parsley.

Chore Boy

My life in the culinary world was not always as glamorous as it is now. You don't just wake up one day and begin to hobnob with Emeril Lagasse. It just doesn't work that way. Kids, what I'm trying to say is that you don't start off in the food industry drinking margaritas with Robin Leach. That stuff is years away, and you must accept that the dawn of that day may never come.

My beginnings were at the bottom of the food chain, so to speak, working at a place called Lock, Stock & Barrel. I know what you're thinking—waiter, bus boy . . . No, no, no. Those were the jobs I dreamed of. Oh, how I longed to bring bread and empty ashtrays. I, my friends, was a dishwasher—the lowest rung on the restaurant ladder. I could be fired by the coat-check girl.

Being a dishwasher didn't just mean washing dishes. There was more to the job than smelling like wet food for three days. I prepped the salad and shrimp, maintained the pickle stock, and occasionally cleaned up vomit. This wasn't a union job, so forget health benefits . . . although there were a few small perks. Speaking of which, let's talk about the employee meal. I could have anything on the menu for free as long as it didn't have any value. My first day, the owner came up to me, put his arm around my shoulder, and said, "Yous can have any ding on da' house, except for da' specials, da' seafood, and any ding wit' meat in it." Sodas were also free and this I took full advantage of. In one shift I would toss back enough cola to keep the Philippines up for a week.

Sometimes I washed alone, but when it was busy I had a partner. My partner was critical. If he sucked at his job, so did the next eight hours of my life. In the early days my partner was Don Basso. Don got me my primo position at Lock, Stock & Barrel and showed me the ropes. He and I had cheated on many Spanish exams together in high school, so he knew I could be trusted with the dirty little secrets of the dishwashing trade. He taught me, for instance, that it is much easier to break a mustard-encrusted plate than to wash it. And onion soup crocks? Forget it! Those we buried out back. It's easier to buy a shovel, dig a hole, throw in the crocks, refill the hole, and plant shrubbery to hide the evil doings than it was to wash those crocks. Don also taught me a variety of ways to help pass the time. He introduced me to the wonders of throwing cucumber slices into a box fan, and how a soggy baked potato to the head was the best way to stifle a cranky waitress in need of a fork. The job didn't pay very well. I could've made more stitching pants in Guatemala. But I was sixteen and all I needed was gas money for my car. (Well, okay, that wasn't the only thing I needed at sixteen. There was something else I badly needed, but children might be reading this.)

So that was my first experience in the world of fine cuisine. I worked there for six months before moving on to the far more lucrative and creatively satisfying field of car washing. However, I won't get into that right now. I'll save that story for my next book on auto repair, which will be titled *Something Sounds Funny and It's Going to Cost You.*

Fast Homemade Pizza

Serves
6

1	POUND PIZZA DOUGH, DEFROSTED IF PREVIOUSLY FROZEN
1 $\frac{1}{2}$	CUPS TOMATO SAUCE
2	CUPS THINLY SLICED FRESH MOZZARELLA CHEESE

NUTRITION	
Per Serving	
Calories (kcal):	304.5
Total Fat (g):	11.3
Saturated Fat (g):	6.1
Cholesterol (mg):	34
Carbohydrate (g):	37.3
Dietary Fiber (g):	1.2
Protein (g):	13.6
Sodium (mg):	530
Calcium (mg):	233
Iron (mg):	2.6
Vitamin C (mg):	8
Vitamin A (i.u.):	941

Preheat oven to 450°F. Lightly grease a large baking sheet.

Using a lightly floured rolling pin and surface, roll out the dough to approximately a 10 x 14-inch rectangle. (You can also just gently stretch the dough with your hands.) Transfer the dough to the greased sheet and press out to the edges. Top with tomato sauce and sprinkle evenly with the cheese. Bake for 15 to 20 minutes, until dough is golden brown. You may need to turn pizza around in oven so that it browns evenly.

Note: The topping possibilities are endless. Sautéed mushrooms, sun-dried tomatoes, olives, any vegetables, roasted peppers, ricotta cheese, fresh tomatoes, goat cheese, shrimp, thinly sliced zucchini, spinach, onions—go wherever your mind (or tongue) takes you. If you are a vegetarian, use tofu squares or seitan as a topping. Have fun with this!

Also, this is great for a party—just cut into 2-inch squares before serving.

Garbanzo and Eggplant Dip

Serves
4

2	SMALL EGGPLANTS
1	15-OUNCE CAN GARBANZO BEANS (CHICK-PEAS), DRAINED
$\frac{1}{4}$	CUP PLAIN YOGURT, STRAINED
1	TEASPOON LIME ZEST, GRATED
2	TABLESPOONS FRESH LIME JUICE
1	GARLIC CLOVE, CRUSHED
2	TABLESPOONS EXTRA-VIRGIN OLIVE OIL
$\frac{1}{4}$	TEASPOON CAYENNE PEPPER OR PAPRIKA

NUTRITION

Per Serving Not Including Bread

Calories (kcal):	202.9
Total Fat (g):	8.4
Saturated Fat (g):	1.4
Cholesterol (mg):	2
Carbohydrate (g):	29.2
Dietary Fiber (g):	8.5
Protein (g):	5.9
Sodium (mg):	193
Calcium (mg):	55
Iron (mg):	1.5
Vitamin C (mg):	9
Vitamin A (i.u.):	271

Broil the eggplants for about 15 minutes, turning occasionally, until charred on all sides. Let sit until cool enough to handle, then remove the skin, squeeze out the juice, and let drain on a paper towel.

Place drained eggplant and all remaining ingredients except cayenne in food processor, and process until smooth. Place in a serving bowl and sprinkle with a little cayenne for garnish. Serve with oil-cured black olives and toasted pita bread. Cut bread into eighths.

Hummus Bi Tahina

Serves
8

2	15-OUNCE CANS GARBANZO BEANS (CHICK-PEAS), UNDRAINED
3	GARLIC CLOVES
$\frac{1}{4}$	CUP TAHINI (SESAME SEED PASTE)
$\frac{1}{4}$	CUP FRESH LEMON JUICE
3	TABLESPOONS WATER

Drain the beans, reserving $\frac{1}{4}$ cup of the liquid. In the bowl of a food processor, combine beans with liquid, garlic, tahini, lemon juice, and water. (Or, for a thicker consistency, mash by hand with a fork.)
Serve chilled with warm pita bread.

NUTRITION	
Per Serving Not Including Bread	
Calories (kcal):	233.2
Total Fat (g):	7.1
Saturated Fat (g):	0.9
Cholesterol (mg):	0
Carbohydrate (g):	33.4
Dietary Fiber (g):	9.2
Protein (g):	11.2
Sodium (mg):	13
Calcium (mg):	132
Iron (mg):	4.7
Vitamin C (mg):	6
Vitamin A (i.u.):	39

Lentil Soup

Serves
8

$\frac{1}{4}$	CUP VEGETABLE OIL
1	LARGE CARROT, PEELED AND DICED
1	LARGE YELLOW ONION, CHOPPED
6	GARLIC CLOVES, MINCED (OR MORE IF SMALL)
2	TEASPOONS CHOPPED FRESH THYME
2	TEASPOONS CHOPPED FRESH ROSEMARY
3	TABLESPOONS BALSAMIC OR RASPBERRY VINEGAR
1	HEAD ESCAROLE, COARSELY CHOPPED
$\frac{1}{4}$	POUND MUSHROOMS, CHOPPED
1	POUND BROWN LENTILS
4	CUPS CHICKEN OR VEGETABLE STOCK
12	CUPS WATER
1	28-OUNCE CAN TOMATOES
	SALT AND PEPPER
$\frac{1}{4}$	CUP CHOPPED FRESH ITALIAN FLAT-LEAF PARSLEY

NUTRITION	
Per Serving Using Chicken Stock	
Calories (kcal):	293.4
Total Fat (g):	8.3
Saturated Fat (g):	1.1
Cholesterol (mg):	0
Carbohydrate (g):	37.7
Dietary Fiber (g):	18.3
Protein (g):	19.4
Sodium (mg):	413
Calcium (mg):	59
Iron (mg):	6.0
Vitamin C (mg):	12
Vitamin A (i.u.):	2,848

Heat oil in a large stockpot or soup pot. Add carrot, onion, garlic, thyme, and rosemary. Sauté for 10 minutes, but do not brown. Add vinegar and let cook down, then add escarole and mushrooms and sauté for 5 more minutes.

Add lentils, stock, water, tomatoes, and pinch of salt and pepper. Stir well, bring to a boil, reduce heat to a low simmer, cover, and cook for 2 hours, stirring often. Sprinkle with parsley and serve.

Note: A friendly, warm soup guaranteed to make you feel good. Tastes better the next day, like all soups.

Mango Salsa

Serves
4

3	LARGE MANGOES, OR **1** PAPAYA
1	GREEN JALAPEÑO PEPPER, SEEDED AND MINCED
4	TABLESPOONS FRESH LIME JUICE
1$\frac{1}{2}$	TABLESPOONS FINELY CHOPPED FRESH MINT
1	TEASPOON GRATED FRESH GINGER
	SALT

Peel mangoes with a small, sharp knife. Cut the flesh from the center pit and cut into small cubes. Combine the mangoes with the jalapeño, lime juice, mint, ginger, and salt to taste. Stir, cover, and refrigerate for about 1 hour. Serve with chicken, shrimp, or pork. Makes 2 cups.

NUTRITION

Per Serving

Calories (kcal):	109.9
Total Fat (g):	0.5
Saturated Fat (g):	0.1
Cholesterol (mg):	0
Carbohydrate (g):	28.9
Dietary Fiber (g):	3.0
Protein (g):	1.1
Sodium (mg):	4
Calcium (mg):	20
Iron (mg):	0.4
Vitamin C (mg):	75
Vitamin A (i.u.):	6,134

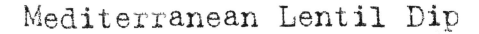

Mediterranean Lentil Dip

Serves
4

$\frac{2}{3}$	CUP GREEN OR BROWN LENTILS
$1\frac{1}{4}$	CUPS COLD WATER
1	TEASPOON GROUND CUMIN
1	GARLIC CLOVE, CRUSHED
1	TABLESPOON LEMON ZEST, GRATED
3	TABLESPOONS FRESH LEMON JUICE
3	TABLESPOONS EXTRA-VIRGIN OLIVE OIL
$\frac{1}{4}$	CUP CHOPPED FRESH MINT
	SALT AND PEPPER
	ADDITIONAL CHOPPED MINT AND LEMON ZEST

NUTRITION	
Per Serving Not Including Bread	
Calories (kcal):	204.1
Total Fat (g):	10.6
Saturated Fat (g):	1.4
Cholesterol (mg):	0
Carbohydrate (g):	20.0
Dietary Fiber (g):	10.0
Protein (g):	9.2
Sodium (mg):	5
Calcium (mg):	28
Iron (mg):	3.4
Vitamin C (mg):	10
Vitamin A (i.u.):	22

Rinse lentils, put them in a medium saucepan, cover with cold water, and bring to a boil. Lower heat and simmer for 5 minutes or until tender, then drain.

Place lentils in a food processor and add the cumin, garlic, lemon zest and juice, olive oil, and mint and process until smooth. Add salt and pepper to taste. Spoon into a serving bowl and garnish with a little chopped mint and lemon zest. Serve with toasted pita bread, cut into eighths.

Note: Regular brown lentils work great, but if you can find green Puy lentils, try them. They have better flavor, but are hard to find.

Taco Pie

I'm ten years old and my dad got tickets to a Mets game. No big deal, right? It's 1980 and the Mets stink. So, of course, during rain delays they are still milking the highlights of when they won the 1973 pennant. Yes, these were the years before Bill Buckner rejuvenated the franchise. I didn't care. I was a young American boy out to take in the national pastime. A summer evening under the stars. The roar of 747s just clearing Shea Stadium. It was a weeknight game and that was big—out late with Dad and it wasn't even the weekend.

Plus, these weren't just tickets; these were box seat tickets. My first box seat experience! A tremendous rite of passage for any true sports fan. I had never seen a major-league diamond up close before. I could see the bases. I could smell the grass. (The only grass you could smell in the upper deck was sold in plastic baggies.) The players were huge and I could easily see all the action. I got to see the Mets screw up almost as if I were standing on the field. I could see their so-called best pitcher hang a curveball like it was a Salem witch. I was able to determine that it wasn't so much bad hops as bad fielding that caused balls to shoot past the Met infielders. Basically, I got to see them stink—up close and personal.

That night I also learned that the stadium fare is much more varied when you're sitting in the elite sections. But, better than varied was that it existed at all. I was accustomed to the life of a peasant, sitting in the upper deck with all the other undesirables. There were no foul balls up there, no yearbooks sold, and no oxygen. The camera never panned your section and food vendors didn't go that far north. You had a better shot of a bag of peanuts falling out of a passing jumbo jet right into your lap than you did of making a purchase from a stadium vendor. And you can forget Cracker Jacks—they only exist in the song, pal.

But "down under," the vendor was my best buddy. I asked for things and they appeared. By the fourth inning, with the Mets down 9-2 and the Lindy having a better shot of making a comeback, I was tearing up my autographs of Steve Henderson and Ed Kranepool in favor of Joe the hot dog guy and Eddie the peanut man. All I could ever need was brought right to my side—hot dogs, soda, popcorn, pretzels, cotton candy, premium ice cream, and oh, yes, you better believe Cracker Jacks. And when I found myself bored with the stadium vendors and their offerings, it was only a short walk, between innings, to the vending mother ship—the stadium concession stand. Here were the specialty items. In plain English, this was where they sold the good stuff. It was on such a stroll in the sixth inning that night that I discovered something the vendors did not bring: taco pie! Yes, *taco pie!* Two of the greatest foods known to mankind had been joined together to better serve the human race. How could I not have heard of this before? All the warm, sweet happiness of pie with all the spicy zest of a taco. The world had not seen that much warm, happy, spicy-sweet zest since the Village People. I raced back to my dad to get his opinion on this find . . . and get the much-needed cash.

My dad, ever the wise father, strongly advised against my eating any food called taco pie, particularly since it had originated from Shea Stadium, a place not known for its culinary prowess. But I would not be thwarted. I refused to believe that anything called taco pie could be evil in any way. Was it the price that bothered him? I know he had already spent a lot of money, but that had never been an issue before. Just in case, I said, "It's only ten dollars, Dad." To which he replied, "Sure you don't want a batting helmet instead? They probably taste better." "No, Dad, it's taco pie!" He gave me the cash and the taco pie was mine.

The Mets didn't win the game that night and neither did my gastrointestinal tract, because that taco pie didn't stay in my ball park. It came up high and inside and took me downtown.

Taco Pie

Serves
6

2	15-OUNCE CANS BLACK BEANS
2	EARS CORN, KERNELS CUT OFF, OR 8-OUNCE FROZEN CORN KERNELS
1	TEASPOON GROUND CUMIN
1	TEASPOON CHILI POWDER
	SALT AND PEPPER
1	SMALL RED ONION, MINCED
1	MEDIUM RED BELL PEPPER, FINELY CHOPPED
8	OUNCES SHREDDED CHEDDAR CHEESE
1	15-OUNCE JAR SALSA, MEDIUM OR HOT
4	TABLESPOONS SOUR CREAM
1	MEDIUM AVOCADO, SLICED INTO STRIPS
4	TABLESPOONS FINELY CHOPPED BLACK OLIVES

N U T R I T I O N

Per Serving Not Including Chips

Calories (kcal):	587.3
Total Fat (g):	30.2
Saturated Fat (g):	12.0
Cholesterol (mg):	46
Carbohydrate (g):	57.1
Dietary Fiber (g):	14.6
Protein (g):	26.6
Sodium (mg):	47.5
Calcium (mg):	111
Iron (mg):	5.0
Vitamin C (mg):	39
Vitamin A (i.u.):	3,103

Drain and rinse beans; pour into a large, shallow bowl. Scatter corn kernels over beans. Sprinkle with half of the cumin and chili powder and a little salt and pepper. Sprinkle chopped onion and red pepper next, then shredded cheddar cheese on top. Pour salsa around the outside edge of the circle.

Make a crater in the center using your fingers or a spoon, and fill with sour cream. Fan the avocado slices around the sour cream, scatter with the olives, and sprinkle on the remaining cumin and chili powder. Serve with plenty of tortilla chips. Note: A slightly refined version, great for parties. But make more than you think that you will need; it goes fast! Can be made ahead and refrigerated.

Roasted Portabella Mushrooms

Serves
8

1	POUND PORTABELLA MUSHROOM CAPS, WIPED CLEAN
2	TABLESPOONS OLIVE OIL
2	ROASTED RED PEPPERS, THINLY SLICED
$\frac{1}{2}$	POUND SMOKED MOZZARELLA CHEESE, THINLY SLICED
1	TABLESPOON DRIED ROSEMARY
	SALT AND PEPPER

NUTRITION

Per Serving

Calories (kcal):	143.4
Total Fat (g):	10.7
Saturated Fat (g):	4.9
Cholesterol (mg):	25
Carbohydrate (g):	5.4
Dietary Fiber (g):	1.3
Protein (g):	7.6
Sodium (mg):	121
Calcium (mg):	174
Iron (mg):	1.0
Vitamin C (mg):	56
Vitamin A (i.u.):	1,887

Preheat the broiler (or grill). Brush the mushrooms lightly with oil, and place bottom side up on sheet pan. Broil for 2 minutes, or until softened. Flip mushrooms over, place a slice of red pepper and a slice of cheese on top of each in a decorative manner, sprinkle with rosemary, and place under broiler again. Cook for 2 more minutes, or until the cheese is well melted.

Place on a serving platter, and sprinkle with salt and pepper to taste.

Note: The cheese can be omitted for strict vegetarians. Great as an hors d'oeuvre or as a side dish. Can be made and assembled in advance and heated when needed.

Smoky Baba Ghanouj

Serves
6

2	MEDIUM EGGPLANTS, CUT IN HALF LENGTHWISE
$\frac{1}{4}$	CUP TAHINI (SESAME SEED PASTE)
3	TABLESPOONS FRESH LEMON JUICE
$\frac{1}{2}$	TEASPOON SALT
1	GARLIC CLOVE
	PAPRIKA
6	PITA BREADS, SPLIT IN HALF

NUTRITION	
Per Serving	
Calories (kcal):	270.8
Total Fat (g):	6.4
Saturated Fat (g):	0.9
Cholesterol (mg):	0
Carbohydrate (g):	46.2
Dietary Fiber (g):	5.4
Protein (g):	9.0
Sodium (mg):	505
Calcium (mg):	166
Iron (mg):	4.0
Vitamin C (mg):	6
Vitamin A (i.u.):	135

Preheat oven to 400°F.

Place eggplants, cut side up, in a pan and bake 20 minutes, or until tender. Let cool slightly, then peel and chop.

In a food processor or by hand, mix eggplant with tahini, lemon juice, salt, and garlic. Mix until a smooth paste. Cover and chill. Sprinkle paprika on top and serve with pita bread.

Mussel Bisque

Serves
6

$1\frac{1}{2}$	POUNDS MUSSELS, IN SHELL
$\frac{2}{3}$	CUP DRY WHITE WINE
$1\frac{2}{3}$	CUPS WATER
2	TABLESPOONS UNSALTED BUTTER
1	SMALL RED ONION, DICED
1	SMALL LEEK, THINLY SLICED
1	MEDIUM CARROT, PEELED AND DICED
2	RIPE MEDIUM TOMATOES, PEELED, SEEDED, AND CHOPPED
2	GARLIC CLOVES, CRUSHED
1	CELERY STALK, DICED
$\frac{1}{2}$	MEDIUM RED BELL PEPPER, SEEDED AND DICED
1	CUP HEAVY CREAM
1	TABLESPOON CHOPPED FRESH PARSLEY
	SALT AND WHITE PEPPER

NUTRITION	
Per Serving	
Calories (kcal):	286.9
Total Fat (g):	16.6
Saturated Fat (g):	9.1
Cholesterol (mg):	77
Carbohydrate (g):	15.1
Dietary Fiber (g):	2.0
Protein (g):	15.8
Sodium (mg):	360
Calcium (mg):	98
Iron (mg):	5.5
Vitamin C (mg):	36
Vitamin A (i.u.):	4,705

Scrub mussels and pull off beards. Discard any that are broken or that do not close when tapped. Place mussels in a large pan with $\frac{1}{3}$ cup of wine and $\frac{1}{3}$ cup of water. Cover and cook over high heat only until mussels open. With a slotted spoon, remove mussels to another dish and let cool. Discard any that do not open.

Remove most mussels from shells, leaving a few in shells as garnish. Strain the mussel broth through a piece of cheesecloth, and set aside.

Heat butter in a large, heavy saucepan and add the onion, leek, carrot, tomatoes, and garlic. Cook over medium-high heat for 2 to 3 minutes, until softened. Add the remaining $\frac{1}{3}$ cup wine and cook for an additional 2 minutes. Lower the heat, add the broth, remaining $1\frac{1}{3}$ cups water, and the celery and simmer for 10 minutes. Add the mussels, red pepper, cream, parsley, and salt and pepper to taste, heating just until hot—do not boil. Serve hot or let cool and serve chilled.

2
SALADS

- ✪ Caesar Salad
- ✪ Fresh Vegetable and Couscous Salad
- ✪ Salad Bars
- ✪ Hot Goat Cheese Salad
- ✪ Salade Niçoise
- ✪ Sautéed Mushrooms over Greens
- ✪ Tabbouleh Salad
- ✪ The Big Walk
- ✪ Thai Chicken Salad
- ✪ Tomato Basil Salad
- ✪ Tropical Fruit Salad
- ✪ White Salad

Caesar Salad

Serves
4

3	TABLESPOONS WHITE WINE VINEGAR
1	TEASPOON LEMON ZEST, FINELY GRATED
2	TABLESPOONS FRESH LEMON JUICE
2	GARLIC CLOVES, MINCED OR PRESSED
1	TEASPOON DIJON MUSTARD
1	TEASPOON ANCHOVY PASTE, OR 1 2-OUNCE CAN ANCHOVIES, DRAINED
2	HARD-BOILED EGGS, FINELY CHOPPED
4	TABLESPOONS FRESHLY GRATED PARMESAN CHEESE
	BLACK PEPPER
$\frac{1}{2}$	CUP EXTRA-VIRGIN OLIVE OIL
1	HEAD ROMAINE LETTUCE, RINSED AND DRAINED
2	CUPS CROUTONS

NUTRITION

Per Serving

Calories (kcal):	393.0
Total Fat (g):	32.7
Saturated Fat (g):	5.7
Cholesterol (mg):	110
Carbohydrate (g):	16.7
Dietary Fiber (g):	4.2
Protein (g):	9.8
Sodium (mg):	256
Calcium (mg):	147
Iron (mg):	2.7
Vitamin C (mg):	37
Vitamin A (i.u.):	3,680

Place vinegar, lemon zest and juice, garlic, mustard, anchovy paste, eggs, 2 tablespoons of cheese, and pepper to taste in a bowl and mix well. While whisking, slowly drizzle in the oil and continue beating until it is well combined.

Tear the lettuce leaves into bite-size pieces and place into a serving bowl with the croutons. Pour the dressing around the outside of the bowl and toss to coat. Sprinkle the remaining cheese over the salad and serve immediately.

Tip: Make sure that the lettuce is dry, or the dressing will not stay on the lettuce and you'll have a watery salad.

Note: Everyone has a version of this famous salad, but this is a healthier and easier version than the traditional. To make it even better, prepare your own croutons by dicing any bread into 1-inch cubes. Toss cubes lightly with olive oil, salt, and garlic and toast in a low oven until croutons are dried out. Homemade croutons are *much* better!

Fresh Vegetable and Couscous Salad

Serves
4

1	10-OUNCE PACKAGE QUICK-COOKING COUSCOUS
1	SMALL ZUCCHINI, HALVED AND THINLY SLICED
1	SMALL RED BELL PEPPER, CORED, SEEDED, AND CUT INTO STRIPS
1	SMALL YELLOW BELL PEPPER, CORED, SEEDED, AND CUT INTO STRIPS
1	SMALL RED ONION, CUT INTO LONG SLICES
1	CUP PEAS, COOKED (USE FRESH IF POSSIBLE)
$\frac{1}{2}$	CUP EXTRA-VIRGIN OLIVE OIL
$\frac{1}{4}$	CUP FRESH LEMON JUICE
1	GARLIC CLOVE, MINCED
$\frac{1}{2}$	TEASPOON CHOPPED FRESH THYME
	SALT AND PEPPER

NUTRITION

Per Serving

Calories (kcal):	577.9
Total Fat (g):	27.9
Saturated Fat (g):	3.8
Cholesterol (mg):	0
Carbohydrate (g):	70.6
Dietary Fiber (g):	6.3
Protein (g):	12.5
Sodium (mg):	181
Calcium (mg):	51
Iron (mg):	2.1
Vitamin C (mg):	140
Vitamin A (i.u.):	1,514

Prepare the couscous according to directions on box. In a large serving bowl, combine all vegetables. In a small bowl, combine the olive oil, lemon juice, garlic, and thyme. Toss the couscous with the vegetables and drizzle on the dressing, gently tossing to mix. Season to taste with salt and pepper.

Note: A fresh, clean salad, great as a side dish for chicken or fish, or as a light main dish. Add any vegetables that you like or that are in season, such as asparagus. It is best served at room temperature.

Salad Bars

The restaurant salad bar is one of the greatest inventions in the food world. You pay one price and whatever you can fit on one plate is yours, no questions asked, free and clear. This is no easy task, of course, because the plate they give you is the size of a bottle cap. All those leafy greens, the croutons, the garbanzo beans—the real trick is stacking and placing everything in the right spot. It's the closest common man comes to performing surgery. Using tongs, working through a sneeze guard (which is a polite way of saying disease shield), one cherry tomato in the wrong place and you could lose the patient. A true salad bar master can get a sample of everything the bar has to offer in one trip—even the toppings he or she does not care for. This is done to maximize the dollar. In America we go by one code and that is this: "I don't like it, I don't want it, I have no room for it, oh, it's free! I'll take two."

The consummate salad bar patron will first circle the bar as an eagle does its prey, waiting to swoop down and pounce on the helpless Waldorf salad. If supplies are low, these predators of mid-range dining will demand a restocking of the baby corn and stand at the bar, arms folded in silent protest, until that demand is met. These people are pros and would sooner shut a restaurant down than be denied an extra dinner roll.

In an effort to capitalize on the greed of the nation, some restaurateurs have added peel-and-eat-shrimp to the salad bar station. Once again, for a fixed price the avaricious can gorge themselves on all the shrimp they can peel and stuff themselves with. The idea is a sound promotion. Once in the restaurant, people will feel that the shrimp offer is such a great deal that they will order more drinks, an expensive entrée, coffee, and dessert. Word will soon spread and the restaurant will be filled beyond maximum fire code specification and the shrimp will pay for itself many times over. What restaurant owners do not work into the equation is the unsavory types—coupon cutters and mongers of the two-for-one world. These are the patrons who will drive a restaurant under. They will peel and eat until their fingers bleed, clean the wound with a Wet-nap, and start all over again. They will wash it all down with free water as the shrimp becomes the main course and table salt is the appetizer. A mint toothpick will cap off the meal nicely, as they leave behind nothing but a thirty-five-cent tip and a pile of crustacean carnage.

A cousin to the restaurant salad bar is the deli salad bar. Both contain tantalizing delights, but the deli salad bar charges you by the pound. I consider myself a master in the art of the one-trip restaurant salad bar. What I can fit onto a plate would amaze you. The deli salad bar is another beast altogether, the sucker punch of the salad bar industry.

A giant plastic container replaces the minuscule plate. The large plastic container offers a false sense of security and fools one into thinking: "I can fill this tub in my sleep." I look at a trip to the deli salad bar as a quick, economical meal. But time after time, I cram all I can into that plastic tub and end up with salad that costs me $11.50. The trick at the deli salad bar is to not select items by flavor but by girth. Potato salad, for instance, is yummy but very heavy. Everything is bathed in thick sauces, and I swear they put quarter pound sinkers in the olives just to weigh them down. To master the deli salad bar you must trade in your surgeon's mask for a physics degree. I'm not very good at physics, and when I am lightheaded from hunger, they've got me just where they want me. After getting cleaned out by too many deli salad bars, I realized for the same price as the oily mushroom salad on a bed of romaine I could have had a nice tuna steak on a bed of risotto.

Hot Goat Cheese Salad

Serves 4

DRESSING

$\frac{1}{4}$	CUP VEGETABLE OIL
$\frac{1}{4}$	CUP TARRAGON OR WINE VINEGAR
1	TABLESPOON HAZELNUT OR WALNUT OIL
1	TABLESPOON DIJON MUSTARD
1	TABLESPOON WATER

PATTIES

1	EGG
1	TABLESPOON WATER
2	TABLESPOONS FINE YELLOW CORNMEAL
1	TABLESPOON FINE BREAD CRUMBS
1	TABLESPOON SESAME SEEDS
1	TABLESPOON GRATED PARMESAN CHEESE
8	OUNCES GOAT CHEESE
2	TABLESPOONS UNSALTED BUTTER OR VEGETABLE OIL
4	CUPS MESCLUN SALAD OR MIXED GREENS
$\frac{1}{2}$	CUP NIÇOISE OR OTHER OLIVES
4	OIL-PACKED SUN-DRIED TOMATOES, SLICED OR DICED
1	SCALLION, SLICED

For the dressing: combine vegetable oil, vinegar, walnut or hazelnut oil, mustard, and water in a screw-top jar. Shake to combine and chill.

For the patties: combine egg and water in a small bowl. Stir the cornmeal, bread crumbs, sesame seeds, and Parmesan cheese in another small dish. Divide the goat cheese into 8 equal portions. (If it comes in a log, just slice in half, then the halves in half, then each of those pieces in half.) Dip each slice in the egg and water mixture, then into the coating, making sure to cover completely. You can make these ahead, put on a plate, cover, and refrigerate. Make sure that they are not eggy.

Melt butter or oil in a large nonstick pan and heat to medium-hot. Add goat cheese patties and cook until golden brown, then flip and cook till golden on other side.

In a bowl, toss mesclun with olives, tomatoes, and scallion. Arrange greens on plates and place 2 goat cheese patties on top of the greens (or put greens on large platter and place all patties on top). Sprinkle dressing over greens lightly and serve immediately, while cheese is still hot. Serve with crusty bread.

Note: To save time, clean greens and veggies and shape goat cheese patties ahead of time, then just quickly sear goat cheese and assemble when you are ready. A great way to start a meal.

NUTRITION			
Per Serving			
Calories (kcal):	788.0	Protein (g):	27.4
Total Fat (g):	63.6	Sodium (mg):	797
Saturated Fat (g):	22.5	Calcium (mg):	650
Cholesterol (mg):	129	Iron (mg):	6.3
Carbohydrate (g):	36.5	Vitamin C (mg):	123
Dietary Fiber (g):	1.7	Vitamin A (i.u.):	3,212

Salade Niçoise

Serves
4

DRESSING

$\frac{1}{4}$	CUP EXTRA-VIRGIN OLIVE OIL
$\frac{1}{4}$	CUP WHITE WINE OR HERBED VINEGAR
$\frac{1}{2}$	TEASPOON SUGAR
1	TEASPOON MINCED FRESH TARRAGON
$\frac{1}{2}$	TEASPOON DIJON MUSTARD
	SALT AND PEPPER TO TASTE

SALAD

$\frac{1}{2}$	POUND FRESH GREEN BEANS, TRIMMED
$\frac{3}{4}$	POUND TINY NEW POTATOES, THICKLY SLICED
1	HEAD BOSTON OR BIBB LETTUCE
2	6-OUNCE CANS CHUNK WHITE TUNA IN WATER
2	MEDIUM TOMATOES, CUT INTO WEDGES
2	HARD-BOILED EGGS, SLICED
$\frac{1}{2}$	CUP BLACK OR NIÇOISE OLIVES
2	SCALLIONS, SLICED
4	ANCHOVY FILLETS (OPTIONAL)

NUTRITION	
Per Serving	
Calories (kcal):	401.3
Total Fat (g):	19.5
Saturated Fat (g):	3.2
Cholesterol (mg):	133
Carbohydrate (g):	29.1
Dietary Fiber (g):	5.6
Protein (g):	30.3
Sodium (mg):	487
Calcium (mg):	128
Iron (mg):	4.6
Vitamin C (mg):	51
Vitamin A (i.u.):	2,379

For the dressing: assemble ingredients in a screw-top jar and shake to combine.

Bring a large pot of water to a boil. Wash and trim beans. Wash and slice potatoes. Cook potatoes till tender; in same water, cook beans till tender. Drain and set aside to cool. (Or make ahead of time.)

Line plates or large serving bowl with lettuce. Arrange beans, potatoes, tuna, tomato wedges, egg slices, and olives in a decorative manner on top. Sprinkle with scallions. Top salad with anchovy fillets and drizzle dressing on top.

Note: This is a great summer main dish. A nice change is to grill or broil fresh tuna steaks or salmon fillets and use in place of the canned tuna.

Sautéed Mushrooms over Greens

Serves
4

$\frac{3}{4}$	POUND ASSORTED MUSHROOMS
6	TABLESPOONS EXTRA-VIRGIN OLIVE OIL
3	TABLESPOONS FRESH LEMON JUICE
2	GARLIC CLOVES, CRUSHED
3	TABLESPOONS FINELY CHOPPED FRESH ITALIAN FLAT-LEAF PARSLEY
1	TEASPOON FINELY CHOPPED FRESH DILL
4	CUPS MIXED SALAD GREENS OR MESCLUN
	SALT AND PEPPER

NUTRITION

Per Serving

Calories (kcal):	283.3
Total Fat (g):	27.6
Saturated Fat (g):	3.7
Cholesterol (mg):	0
Carbohydrate (g):	8.8
Dietary Fiber (g):	2.4
Protein (g):	3.5
Sodium (mg):	31
Calcium (mg):	54
Iron (mg):	4.8
Vitamin C (mg):	21
Vitamin A (i.u.):	2,204

Slice mushrooms $\frac{1}{3}$-inch thick. (If using oyster mushrooms, leave whole.)

In a large bowl, mix 2 tablespoons of oil and 2 tablespoons lemon juice with a fork. Place greens on top, and toss to cover with dressing. Set aside.

Heat remaining 4 tablespoons oil in a large sauté pan and add mushrooms. Add garlic, parsley, dill, and remaining tablespoon lemon juice. Cook over medium-high heat until they are tender and mushroom liquid has evaporated, but there is still oil in the pan.

Place dressed greens in center of plate, and top with sautéed mushrooms. Drizzle onto plate any liquid from pan and season to taste with salt and pepper. Serve immediately.

Tabbouleh Salad

Serves
6

2	CUPS HOT WATER
1	CUP BULGUR WHEAT
1	SMALL RED ONION, FINELY CHOPPED
$\frac{1}{2}$	CUP CHOPPED FRESH MINT
$\frac{1}{2}$	CUP CHOPPED FRESH PARSLEY
1	TABLESPOON LEMON ZEST, GRATED
3	TABLESPOONS EXTRA-VIRGIN OLIVE OIL
1	SMALL CUCUMBER, PEELED, SEEDED, AND CHOPPED

NUTRITION	
Per Serving	
Calories (kcal):	159.2
Total Fat (g):	7.3
Saturated Fat (g):	0.9
Cholesterol (mg):	0
Carbohydrate (g):	22.0
Dietary Fiber (g):	5.4
Protein (g):	3.8
Sodium (mg):	11
Calcium (mg):	34
Iron (mg):	1.3
Vitamin C (mg):	13
Vitamin A (i.u.):	368

In a large glass bowl, combine hot water and bulgur wheat, cover with plastic wrap, and let steam for at least 15 minutes, or until bulgur is completely softened.

Fluff the bulgur with a large fork, separating the grains well. Gently add in the remaining ingredients, and toss well.

Note: Perfect on a hot summer day. This salad travels well for a picnic, and it holds well, too, so it can be made a day ahead. Feel free to add absolutely anything that strikes you—you can't mess this one up!

The Big Walk

Throughout life, food is used as a reward. Ice cream and cake on birthdays or a favorite dinner to celebrate a good report card. I never received a good report card, but I heard stories about what went on with kids who did. Certain foods at certain times give us comfort and trigger fond memories. One such food reminds me of the first time I ever felt confident.

I was five years old. After school, my mom took me to my friend Andrew's house. Andrew didn't live too far away, but the block he lived on had tons of kids running all over the place. This was very cool because only two kids lived across the street from me, and after school they always did the same thing—piano lessons and homework. Their mom just did not understand that you must play when it's light out and leave that indoor cerebral stuff for when it's dark. Whiffle ball is just not as much fun when you have to wear a mining helmet. So spending a late autumn afternoon at Andrew's sounded like a refreshing plan, as well as a delightful break from the mundane.

What I did not bargain for was Andrew's older brother messing up my day. It seems that this was the day of the week that Andrew's brother beat the crap out of him. I guess Andrew didn't have it written down in his day planner and double-booked my visit. His brother was in the third grade at the time, so to us he was like forty. He wanted nothing to do with me, but he was hell-bent on treating his little brother like a POW. So with all the excitement going on, I explained to Andrew while he was enduring one of his beatings that if he didn't play with me, I was going home. Not having a brother myself, I did not understand that this situation was totally out of his control.

Well, Andrew getting pushed came to Andrew getting shoved, and I announced I was going home. The only snag in this bold social move was that my mom was not due to pick me up for another hour and a half. But I had to stick to my plan, so I started walking. Now, mind you, Andrew's house was only three-quarters of a mile from

my house, but to a five-year-old that is most of the world. I was Magellan circumnavigating the Earth. And besides, I had never really done anything by myself before. At that age everything is still done for you—somebody else picks out your clothes, someone makes your food, and someone drops you off and picks you up wherever you go. This was the first time I truly did something on my own.

Twenty minutes later I set foot on my property without a scratch. I didn't get lost, I didn't get hurt, and most of all, I didn't have a way to explain to my mother and grandmother how the hell I got home. I remember my mom's eyes almost shooting out of her head when she saw me walk in the door. "How did you get home?" she asked. I straightened up and, in a booming voice that would've made Patton proud, said, "I walked." I then very calmly moved past her into the kitchen, grabbed a big Butterfinger candy bar, took it into the living room, and sat down. My mother and grandmother yelled at me for the next four hours, ranting and raving and finding more synonyms for the word *disappointing* than Roget could've ever imagined. But I was unfazed. I just smiled the whole time, eating my Butterfinger and knowing I made it home and nobody could take that away from me. To this day, when I see a Butterfinger, I swell with confidence because, deep down, I know little Sean made it home.

Thai Chicken Salad

Serves
4

$\frac{1}{4}$	CUP FRESH CILANTRO LEAVES
3	TABLESPOONS SOY SAUCE OR TAMARI
1	TABLESPOON WATER
1	TABLESPOON THAI FISH SAUCE (NAM PLA)
2	GARLIC CLOVES, MINCED
$\frac{1}{2}$	TEASPOON FRESHLY GROUND PEPPER
2	SKINLESS AND BONELESS CHICKEN BREAST HALVES, CUT INTO SMALL CUBES
4	OUNCES CELLOPHANE NOODLES
3	TABLESPOONS FRESH LIME JUICE
1	TEASPOON SUGAR
1	HEAD ROMAINE LETTUCE, TORN IN BITE-SIZE PIECES
2	PLUM TOMATOES, CUT INTO WEDGES
1	MEDIUM CUCUMBER, PEELED AND CHOPPED
4	SCALLIONS, THINLY SLICED
2	TABLESPOONS CHOPPED DRY-ROASTED PEANUTS

Mix cilantro, $1\frac{1}{2}$ tablespoons soy sauce, the water, fish sauce, garlic, and pepper in a shallow bowl. Add chicken cubes and mix to coat, cover, and marinate in refrigerator for at least 30 minutes but up to 24 hours.

Soak the cellophane noodles for 20 minutes in enough water to cover, and then drain and gently squeeze out extra moisture with a dish towel. Cut into 2-inch pieces.

Preheat broiler. Drain the chicken from the marinade (discard the marinade), place in a baking dish, and broil for 10 minutes or until cooked through.

While chicken is cooking, make dressing. Combine lime juice, remaining $1\frac{1}{2}$ tablespoons soy sauce, and the sugar in a screw-top jar, cover, and shake.

Line plates with lettuce, arrange noodles on top, and place the chicken, tomatoes, and cucumber cubes over noodles. Drizzle dressing on top, then sprinkle scallions and peanuts over all.

Note: Look for cellophane noodles and Thai fish sauce in the ethnic foods aisle of the supermarket or in an Asian market. Feel free to substitute shrimp, beef, or tofu for the chicken.

NUTRITION	
Per Serving	
Calories (kcal):	327.5
Total Fat (g):	10.4
Saturated Fat (g):	2.6
Cholesterol (mg):	47
Carbohydrate (g):	36.2
Dietary Fiber (g):	6.9
Protein (g):	23.8
Sodium (mg):	1,248
Calcium (mg):	102
Iron (mg):	3.6
Vitamin C (mg):	57
Vitamin A (i.u.):	4,219

Tomato Basil Salad

Serves
4

4	LARGE, VERY RIPE TOMATOES, PREFERABLY BEEFSTEAK OR HEIRLOOM
$\frac{1}{4}$	CUP EXTRA-VIRGIN OLIVE OIL
	KOSHER SALT
	FRESHLY GROUND PEPPER
1	GARLIC CLOVE, MINCED
$\frac{1}{2}$	CUP FRESH BASIL LEAVES, SLICED IN RIBBONS

Slice the tomatoes $\frac{3}{4}$-inch thick and lay them on a platter. Drizzle with the olive oil, then sprinkle with salt, pepper, and garlic. Add basil on top and serve immediately.

Tip: This salad can sit out to marinate for up to 2 hours, if desired.

Note: There is nothing better on a hot summer night than this salad, served with a big crusty loaf of bread and maybe a sprinkling of balsamic vinegar. Or add slices of fresh mozzarella or ricotta salata cheese for a more substantial dish.

NUTRITION

Per Serving

Calories (kcal): 147.7

Total Fat (g): 14.0

Saturated Fat (g): 1.9

Cholesterol (mg): 0

Carbohydrate (g): 6.2

Dietary Fiber (g): 1.4

Protein (g): 1.2

Sodium (mg): 11

Calcium (mg): 16

Iron (mg): 0.8

Vitamin C (mg): 25

Vitamin A (i.u.): 971

Tropical Fruit Salad

Serves
4

DRESSING

$\frac{1}{4}$	TEASPOON FINELY SHREDDED ORANGE PEEL
2	TABLESPOONS FRESH ORANGE JUICE
1	TABLESPOON VEGETABLE OIL
2	TEASPOONS HONEY
$\frac{1}{4}$	TEASPOON POPPY SEEDS

SALAD

1	MEDIUM PAPAYA, PEELED, SEEDED, AND SLICED
1	MEDIUM MANGO, PEELED, SEEDED, AND SLICED
1	LARGE ORANGE, PEELED AND SECTIONED
2	KIWIFRUIT, PEELED AND SLICED
1	PINT RASPBERRIES
	FRESH MINT SPRIGS, FOR GARNISH

NUTRITION

Per Serving

Calories (kcal):	177.2
Total Fat (g):	4.3
Saturated Fat (g):	0.5
Cholesterol (mg):	0
Carbohydrate (g):	36.7
Dietary Fiber (g):	8.6
Protein (g):	2.1
Sodium (mg):	5
Calcium (mg):	64
Iron (mg):	0.7
Vitamin C (mg):	135
Vitamin A (i.u.):	2,460

For the dressing: combine orange peel and juice, oil, honey, and poppy seeds in a screw-top jar, shake to combine, and chill.

For the salad: arrange papaya slices, mango slices, orange sections, kiwi slices, and raspberries in a decorative manner on individual plates or on a platter. Drizzle dressing on top, and garnish with mint sprigs.

Note: A nice way to start a meal or to end one. Substitute any fruits that are ripe and in season—this is just a guideline. Try some of the new exotic fruits like starfruit or uglifruit. The fruits in this recipe won't discolor because of their high acid content. A nice touch is to serve the dressing on the side of the plate in a hollowed out piece of orange peel, like a little cup.

White Salad

Serves
4

$\frac{1}{3}$	CUP DRY-ROASTED HAZELNUTS
1	SMALL FRISÉE LETTUCE OR ESCAROLE
2	BELGIAN ENDIVE
1	SMALL FENNEL BULB
1	CELERY STALK
2	TABLESPOONS CHAMPAGNE VINEGAR
$\frac{1}{2}$	TEASPOON DIJON MUSTARD
	SALT AND PEPPER
3	TABLESPOONS VEGETABLE OIL
3	TABLESPOONS HAZELNUT OIL

NUTRITION	
Per Serving	
Calories (kcal):	311.5
Total Fat (g):	27.5
Saturated Fat (g):	2.6
Cholesterol (mg):	0
Carbohydrate (g):	15.9
Dietary Fiber (g):	8.4
Protein (g):	5.2
Sodium (mg):	105
Calcium (mg):	195
Iron (mg):	3.2
Vitamin C (mg):	27
Vitamin A (i.u.):	5,623

Toast hazelnuts in a 350°F oven just till they start to turn golden. Rub off skins, coarsely crush, and set aside.

Tear frisée into bite-size pieces. Slice bottom $\frac{1}{2}$ inch off of endive and separate leaves. Cut the fennel into quarters and slice as thin as possible. Slice celery paper thin on the diagonal.

In a small bowl, beat together the vinegar, mustard, and salt and pepper to taste. Very slowly whisk in the oils.

Arrange greens on plates, drizzle with dressing, and sprinkle with nuts.

Note: Buy a small can of hazelnut oil and use in salad dressings. It gives a distinctive but subtle flavor to salads. This is a nice crisp, clean salad.

3
BREAKFAST

Basic Muffin Recipe

Makes
12
Muffins

1	CUP FRESH OR FROZEN BERRIES
$1\frac{1}{3}$	CUPS ALL-PURPOSE FLOUR
$\frac{3}{4}$	CUP WHOLE WHEAT FLOUR
6	TABLESPOONS SUGAR
1	TABLESPOON BAKING POWDER
$\frac{1}{2}$	TEASPOON SALT
$\frac{1}{4}$	TEASPOON BAKING SODA
1	CUP SKIM MILK
3	TABLESPOONS VEGETABLE OIL
1	LARGE EGG
$1\frac{1}{2}$	TEASPOONS VANILLA EXTRACT
1	TEASPOON LEMON ZEST, GRATED

NUTRITION

Per Muffin

Calories (kcal):	148.3
Total Fat (g):	4.2
Saturated Fat (g):	0.6
Cholesterol (mg):	18
Carbohydrate (g):	24.5
Dietary Fiber (g):	1.2
Protein (g):	3.8
Sodium (mg):	222
Calcium (mg):	119
Iron (mg):	1.2
Vitamin C (mg):	7
Vitamin A (i.u.):	71

If using fresh fruit, dice into pieces the size of peas. If using frozen fruit, defrost partially and dry on paper towels.

Preheat oven to 425°F, and place rack in upper third of oven.

In a large bowl, sift together the flours, sugar, baking powder, salt, and baking soda. In a separate small bowl, whisk together the milk, oil, egg, vanilla, and lemon zest. Gently add the berries to the flour, stirring until well distributed.

Stir in the milk mixture, and blend just until the ingredients are combined. *Do not* overmix.

Spray 12 muffin cups with nonstick cooking spray, and pour $\frac{1}{4}$ cup of batter into each cup. Bake about 15 minutes, until golden on top and springy to the touch. Let cool on a rack for 5 minutes before serving.

Note: These muffins are lower in fat (4 grams) than usual muffins, and they certainly taste better than storebought.

Best Bran Muffins

Makes
12
Muffins

4	TABLESPOONS UNSALTED BUTTER, IN BITS
$\frac{1}{2}$	CUP BOILING WATER
$1\frac{1}{4}$	CUPS WHEAT BRAN (NOT CEREAL)
$\frac{3}{4}$	CUP ALL-PURPOSE FLOUR
$\frac{1}{2}$	CUP WHOLE WHEAT FLOUR
$\frac{2}{3}$	CUP RAISINS
$\frac{2}{3}$	CUP SUGAR
$1\frac{1}{4}$	TEASPOONS BAKING SODA
$\frac{1}{4}$	TEASPOON SALT
$1\frac{1}{3}$	CUPS BUTTERMILK
1	LARGE EGG
2	TABLESPOONS MOLASSES
	BRAN FLAKES CEREAL FOR TOPPING

NUTRITION

Per Muffin

Calories (kcal):	188.2
Total Fat (g):	5.2
Saturated Fat (g):	2.9
Cholesterol (mg):	30
Carbohydrate (g):	34.8
Dietary Fiber (g):	3.6
Protein (g):	4.2
Sodium (mg):	213
Calcium (mg):	22
Iron (mg):	1.6
Vitamin C (mg):	1
Vitamin A (i.u.):	189

Preheat oven to 400°F.

In a large mixing bowl, combine butter and boiling water. Add bran and mix well. Stir in both flours, raisins, sugar, baking soda, salt, buttermilk, egg, and molasses. Mix just until combined. *Do not* overmix.

Spoon into 12 greased or papered muffin cups and sprinkle with bran flakes. Bake 22 to 24 minutes, or until a toothpick inserted in the centers comes out clean. Cool on a rack for 5 minutes before serving.

Note: Batter can be made up to 3 weeks in advance and refrigerated.

Weekend Breakfast

For most of my youth I spent my weekends with my dad. Yes, I'm from a broken home: "Oh, help me, Jerry Springer! How can I go on?" I never understood the term "broken home" because there was nothing actually broken in my house, with the exception of a few hurled dishes. I wish I only came from a broken home. If all of my childhood woes could've been solved with a toolbelt and a case of Meister Bräu, I wouldn't need to spend most of the profits from this book on senseless gym equipment designed to tone my body when it's my ego that needs definition.

My parents got divorced when I was fairly young, and my father would always pick me up on Saturday morning, after I had just watched the latest episode of H.R. Pufnstuf or *Land of the Lost*, or whatever twisted Saturday morning insanity I was into at the time. First order of business was to go to my grandparents' house, where my grandmother would make a late morning breakfast and my grandfather would fall asleep in a La-Z-Boy with the TV on and an AM radio blaring out the local gardening call-in show on WRKL.

Breakfast consisted of the usual fare of pancakes, bacon, eggs, and on occasion, hash. I remember a time when my dad became fixated on scrapple. All I know is that it's a meat substance that comes from Pennsylvania. I'll bet you dollars to pig snouts that if you asked a native Pennsylvanian, he wouldn't be able to tell you exactly what it is, either. I do remember the first day Dad had it. He picked me up, and before I had a chance to say hello, he exclaimed, "Guess what I got?" Now, I'm a kid so I'm thinking if I'm supposed to be as excited as he was it could be one of only three things: A Shogun Warrior, the six-inch *Star Wars* action figure of Hammer Head (who was featured in the Creature Cantina), or a baseball autographed by Dave Kingman. Jumping up and down, I screamed "What, Daddy, what?" "Scrapple," he said. "I got it." OK, I thought, this was not on my list of wonderful surprises, but I'll play along since Dad seemed so happy about this treat. "I found it and we're having it for breakfast." He had this look on his face like he had just got his hands on the rarest of Cuban cigars, but I looked as any young child would when threatened with an industrially packaged block of gray breakfast meat—uneasy. I could go into an elaborate account of the taste, texture, and consistency of scrapple, or I could tell you its taste reminded me of the finest sirloin steak, but that would be an absolute lie. The only thing fine about scrapple are some of the random bone shavings. I didn't have any use for scrapple then and you will not find any scrapple recipes in this book now. I guess if scrapple has any use at all, it's as grout for my "broken home."

Breakfast Burritos

Serves
4

1	TEASPOON VEGETABLE OIL
6	SCALLIONS, GREEN AND WHITE PARTS SEPARATED AND THINLY SLICED
1	CUP CANNED BLACK BEANS, DRAINED AND RINSED
4	LARGE EGGS
1	LARGE TOMATO, SEEDED AND DICED
	SALT AND PEPPER
1	TEASPOON SEEDED AND MINCED JALAPEÑO PEPPER
4	CORN OR FLOUR TORTILLAS
2	TABLESPOONS CHOPPED FRESH CILANTRO
$\frac{1}{4}$	CUP GRATED SHARP CHEDDAR CHEESE

N U T R I T I O N

Per Serving Using Corn Tortillas

Calories (kcal):	408.7
Total Fat (g):	11.9
Saturated Fat (g):	3.8
Cholesterol (mg):	220
Carbohydrate (g):	54.1
Dietary Fiber (g):	9.6
Protein (g):	22.4
Sodium (mg):	285
Calcium (mg):	203
Iron (mg):	5.0
Vitamin C (mg):	13
Vitamin A (i.u.):	729

In a large nonstick skillet, heat oil over medium heat. Add the white part of the scallions and the beans and heat. While beans are heating, in a small bowl, beat eggs with a fork until frothy and light, then set aside. Add tomato to beans and cook for 1 minute. Add salt and pepper.

Add eggs to pan and let set for 1 minute. Add jalapeño and stir the egg mixture, cooking until desired doneness. Divide the egg mixture among the 4 tortillas, sprinkle with cilantro, scallion tops, and cheddar cheese, then fold bottom up and roll to close.

Note: This is one of the best ways to clean out your refrigerator! The ingredients here are a guideline, but feel free to use *anything* that you want or have in the house. You can't mess this one up. You can also make the burritos ahead of time, refrigerate them and then reheat in the oven or microwave.

Healthy Pancakes

Serves
4

1	CUP ALL-PURPOSE FLOUR
$\frac{1}{2}$	CUP QUICK-COOKING ROLLED OATS
1	TABLESPOON BAKING POWDER
$\frac{1}{2}$	TEASPOON SALT
$1\frac{1}{2}$	CUPS BUTTERMILK
2	TABLESPOONS VEGETABLE OIL
3	LARGE EGGS, SEPARATED
$\frac{1}{2}$	TEASPOON CINNAMON
	MAPLE SYRUP

NUTRITION	
Per Serving Not Including Syrup	
Calories (kcal):	287.6
Total Fat (g):	12.0
Saturated Fat (g):	2.6
Cholesterol (mg):	163
Carbohydrate (g):	32.9
Dietary Fiber (g):	0.7
Protein (g):	11.7
Sodium (mg):	683
Calcium (mg):	520
Iron (mg):	2.7
Vitamin C (mg):	1
Vitamin A (i.u.):	274

In a large bowl, combine flour, oats, baking powder, and salt. Beat in the buttermilk, oil, and egg yolks.

In a separate bowl, beat the egg whites until stiff and gently fold them into the batter.

Heat a heavy-bottomed skillet or griddle over medium heat until hot. Grease lightly with butter, and pour about $\frac{1}{4}$ cup of batter (for each pancake) into the skillet. Cook until the top edges have bubbles and the bottom is golden, about $1\frac{1}{2}$ minutes. Flip and cook pancake for 1 minute, or until golden on other side.

Remove to a platter, and keep warm in a 225°F oven while you finish cooking the rest of the pancakes. Sprinkle with cinnamon and serve with maple syrup.

Tip: Feel free to add up to 1 cup of any fillings that you like, such as mixed berries, pecans, walnuts, diced apples, peaches, nectarines, bananas, or dried fruit mix.

Note: It really is worth it to take the extra 3 minutes and make pancakes from scratch, instead of using a boxed mix.

Master Scone Recipe

Serves
4

2	CUPS ALL-PURPOSE FLOUR
1	TEASPOON CREAM OF TARTAR
$\frac{1}{2}$	TEASPOON BAKING SODA
$\frac{1}{2}$	TEASPOON SALT
$1\frac{1}{2}$	TABLESPOONS SUGAR
4	TABLESPOONS UNSALTED BUTTER, CHILLED, IN BITS
$\frac{3}{4}$	CUP WHOLE MILK

Preheat oven to 450°F.

Sift the flour, cream of tartar, baking soda, salt, and sugar into a large bowl. Cut in the butter until mixture resembles coarse meal. Make a well in the center, add milk, and quickly blend together. Turn out onto a well-floured surface.

Quickly either roll to $\frac{1}{2}$-inch thickness and cut out 3-inch biscuits or place on a greased baking sheet, form into 1 large disk, cut into 8 wedges, and separate the wedges a bit. Bake 10 to 12 minutes, until tops are golden. Serve fresh from the oven with butter and jam. Makes 8 scones.

Note: It is worth it to try making this recipe. Though scones can be made plain, it is best to add 1 cup filling, such as fruit, nuts, or cheese. Fresh from the oven, nothing tastes better. Top the scones with some terrific strawberry preserves, and you are in heaven.

Scrambled Eggs with Smoked Salmon and Cream Cheese

Serves
4

4	LARGE EGGS
	FRESHLY GROUND PEPPER
1	TABLESPOON UNSALTED BUTTER
1	SMALL RED ONION, DICED SMALL
$\frac{1}{4}$	POUND SMOKED NOVA SALMON OR LOX
$\frac{1}{4}$	CUP CREAM CHEESE, SOFTENED
2	TABLESPOONS CHIVES, THINLY SLICED

NUTRITION

Per Serving
Calories (kcal): ----------199.7
Total Fat (g): ------------14.3
Saturated Fat (g): ---------6.8
Cholesterol (mg): ---------243
Carbohydrate (g): ---------4.5
Dietary Fiber (g): ---------0.8
Protein (g): ----------------13.1
Sodium (mg): ------------329
Calcium (mg): -----------49
Iron (mg): -----------------1.3
Vitamin C (mg): -----------3
Vitamin A (i.u.): ----------725

In a medium bowl, beat eggs until frothy. Add pepper.
In a large, heavy-bottomed skillet, heat butter over medium heat.
Add onion and sauté for 1 minute. Pour in eggs, and let set for
30 seconds. Add salmon and stir the eggs, add cream cheese bits,
cover, and let set for 30 seconds. Cook until eggs are cooked to
desired doneness, then spoon onto plates, sprinkle with chives,
and serve immediately.
Note: Great to serve with very dark rye or pumpernickel bread
and a nice fruit salad.

Hector Lives

Let me begin by saying that I love my wife more than anything in the world. I truly do. She is bright and sweet and warm and loving, and everything else you could ask from a soulmate. She also happens to be a FITNESS FANATIC! To say she enjoys working out is to say that Albert Einstein kind of liked math. When we got married, this was fine. However, I've come to learn that my beautiful wife is actually two people. There's Jay, the supportive wife who cares for me and loves me, and with whom I plan to share my world, and then there's Hector, the fitness freak who's never met a Nautilus machine she didn't like and whose idea of a romantic evening at home is a couple of PowerBars and an arm-wrestling competition with yours truly.

My wife has worked as a personal trainer for years. Do you know what that can be like at those times when you are not at your personal best? Dropping little hints like, "Oh, you're back to eating that, are you?" I'll be lying on the couch watching *My Child Is Missing Again* on Lifetime, starring Victoria Principal, with a wine spritzer in one hand and a can of cashew clusters in the other, while Hector's in the corner isolating her obliques. Sometime at the end of the day she will just come right out and ask, "Did you get to the gym today?" I'll plead, "Gosh, no, pooky bear, today was crazy. I worked twenty hours." And she'll argue, "Well, that leaves four more hours, then, doesn't it?" Now, don't get the wrong idea. It's not as if she checks her heart rate while she's brushing her teeth or yells out things like "No pain, no gain" while vacuuming the carpet. She's capable of leading a normal life. It's just that at certain times, Hector rears her bandanna-wrapped head.

Hector can come out at any time. Hector may visit when we're hanging out in a hotel room together on a road gig. I may be going over my material for the show that evening, Jay will be aimlessly flipping through the cable channels asking me if I'm ready, encouraging me to have a good show. Then she comes upon the World's Strongest Man competition on ESPN, at which time Hector starts screaming, "Flip that car, Claus. Lift with the legs, you pansy!" I don't understand how she can become captivated by some Icelandic bovine, hormone-laden freak dragging a boat anchor around or squat-lifting a group of school kids for prize money. But that's her—Doctor Jay and Mister Hector. What I have come to realize is that the lovely woman I married is not just some cute girl who likes to do cute girl things. Cute girls look up to Meg Ryan, take an aerobics class once in a while, and watch *Melrose Place*. My cute girl looks up to Franco Columbo, could bench-press Meg Ryan fifteen times, and watches strong man competitions on ESPN.

Sean's Scrambled Tofu

Serves 2

1	POUND FIRM TOFU
1	POUND SOFT TOFU
2	TEASPOONS VEGETABLE OIL
1	LARGE WHITE ONION, DICED
1/2	TEASPOON TURMERIC
3	GARLIC CLOVES, MINCED
6	MEDIUM MUSHROOMS, SLICED
1/2	TEASPOON DRIED OR FRESH BASIL
	DASH OF CAYENNE PEPPER
2	LARGE CARROTS, PEELED AND GRATED
2	LARGE SCALLIONS, SLICED
4	SPRIGS CILANTRO, FINELY CHOPPED
	SALT AND PEPPER

NUTRITION

Per Serving

Calories (kcal):	454.4
Total Fat (g):	25.5
Saturated Fat (g):	3.5
Cholesterol (mg):	0
Carbohydrate (g):	27.5
Dietary Fiber (g):	10.2
Protein (g):	39.6
Sodium (mg):	345
Calcium (mg):	594
Iron (mg):	27.0
Vitamin C (mg):	38
Vitamin A (i.u.):	20,785

Drain tofu and rinse with cold water. Pat dry. Heat oil in a large sauté pan over medium heat and add onion, stir, and add turmeric. Add garlic and mushrooms, being sure not to burn the garlic. Sauté for 2 minutes, then crumble the tofu into the pan. Stir to combine, add the basil and cayenne, then the carrots and scallions. Let cook for 3 more minutes to evaporate the water that will come out of the tofu. Sprinkle with cilantro, add salt and pepper to taste, and serve immediately.

Note: Here's a really healthy alternative to eggs for breakfast. It really is good—so good, in fact, that you won't miss the eggs. Be careful with the turmeric, however. It stains things like countertops and fingers.

Spanish Frittata

Serves
2

$\frac{1}{3}$	CUP OLIVE OIL
1	LARGE POTATO, PEELED AND THINLY SLICED
	SALT AND PEPPER
1	LARGE ONION, THINLY SLICED
4	LARGE EGGS
2	MEDIUM TOMATOES, SEEDED AND CHOPPED
2	SCALLIONS, CHOPPED

NUTRITION	
Per Serving	
Calories (kcal):	557.8
Total Fat (g):	46.6
Saturated Fat (g):	8.1
Cholesterol (mg):	425
Carbohydrate (g):	21.4
Dietary Fiber (g):	3.7
Protein (g):	15.7
Sodium (mg):	418
Calcium (mg):	107
Iron (mg):	3.0
Vitamin C (mg):	41
Vitamin A (i.u.):	1,478

Heat the oil in a large sauté pan, and add the potato. Season with salt and pepper, and cook over medium-high heat until golden and crisp, about 10 minutes.

Add the onion as soon as the potato begins to brown, and turn the potato and onion so that they brown evenly. It will take about 5 minutes more for them to brown.

Beat the eggs with a bit of salt and pepper and pour the potato-onion mixture into the bowl. Pour the egg mixture back into the pan and cook over low heat until the bottom sets and starts to brown, about 5 minutes.

Invert a plate over top of pan, flip omelet onto it, then slide omelet back into pan so that the uncooked side now faces the bottom. Cook until the eggs are set, 3 more minutes. Serve slices of the frittata, and garnish with the tomatoes and scallions.

4
GRAINS

Barley and Greens

Serves
4

2	TABLESPOONS UNSALTED BUTTER OR VEGETABLE OIL
1	MEDIUM ONION, FINELY CHOPPED
2	GARLIC CLOVES, MINCED
2	CUPS CHOPPED ARUGULA LEAVES, OR OTHER GREEN LIKE KALE OR CHARD, OR A COMBINATION
1	CUP PEARL BARLEY
3	CUPS CHICKEN OR VEGETABLE STOCK
	DASH OF GRATED NUTMEG
2	TABLESPOONS CHOPPED FRESH PARSLEY
2	SCALLIONS, CHOPPED
	SALT AND PEPPER

NUTRITION

Per Serving Using Butter
and Chicken Stock

Calories (kcal):	302.7
Total Fat (g):	8.0
Saturated Fat (g):	4.0
Cholesterol (mg):	15
Carbohydrate (g):	47.4
Dietary Fiber (g):	8.8
Protein (g):	12.7
Sodium (mg):	824
Calcium (mg):	267
Iron (mg):	5.5
Vitamin C (mg):	24
Vitamin A (i.u.):	3,508

In a large saucepan or small soup pot, melt butter over medium heat. Add onion and cook for 2 minutes, then add garlic and cook for 2 more minutes, being careful not to brown the garlic. Add arugula and toss, then add barley, stock, and nutmeg. Bring to a boil, then lower heat to a simmer and cover. Cook for 35 minutes, or until barley is tender and all of the liquid has been absorbed.

Stir in parsley and scallions, season to taste with salt and pepper, and serve immediately.

Note: A natural combination—delicious, fast, and healthy. If you like this, try the Sautéed Bulgur with Escarole (page 71).

Grain and Cheese Burgers

Serves
4

1	TABLESPOON UNSALTED BUTTER OR VEGETABLE OIL
$\frac{1}{2}$	POUND MUSHROOMS, THINLY SLICED
$1\frac{1}{2}$	CUPS SCALLIONS, FINELY CHOPPED
$\frac{1}{2}$	CUP OLD-FASHIONED ROLLED OATS
$\frac{1}{2}$	CUP COOKED BROWN RICE
$\frac{1}{3}$	CUP CHEDDAR CHEESE, SHREDDED
$\frac{1}{4}$	CUP MOZZARELLA CHEESE, SHREDDED
3	TABLESPOONS CHOPPED WALNUTS
3	TABLESPOONS LOW-FAT COTTAGE CHEESE OR RICOTTA CHEESE
1	LARGE EGG
2	TABLESPOONS CHOPPED PARSLEY
	SALT AND PEPPER

NUTRITION	
Per Serving Using Butter	
Calories (kcal):	245.1
Total Fat (g):	13.7
Saturated Fat (g):	5.7
Cholesterol (mg):	78
Carbohydrate (g):	20.3
Dietary Fiber (g):	3.2
Protein (g):	12.7
Sodium (mg):	193
Calcium (mg):	191
Iron (mg):	4.1
Vitamin C (mg):	12
Vitamin A (i.u.):	964

Preheat broiler.

In a medium sauté pan (preferably nonstick), heat the butter and sauté the mushrooms and scallions until they are softened, about 5 minutes. Add the oats and cook, stirring for 2 more minutes. Remove from heat and let cool a bit.

Stir in the rice, shredded cheeses, walnuts, cottage cheese, egg, and parsley. Season with salt and pepper. Shape mixture into 4 patties, $\frac{1}{2}$ inch thick, and place on an oiled baking sheet. Broil 3 minutes per side until golden. Or sauté in a well-heated nonstick sauté pan, flipping once, until golden on both sides. Serve with buns and your favorite fixings.

Note: These burgers were inspired by the Columbia Bar and Grill in Los Angeles and were a customer favorite. You can get cooked brown rice from a Chinese restaurant, or buy the quick cooking kind to save time.

Grain Burgers

Serves
4

4	TEASPOONS SESAME SEEDS
1	TABLESPOON GROUND CORIANDER
1	TABLESPOON GROUND CUMIN
$\frac{1}{2}$	TEASPOON PURE CHILE POWDER
$1\frac{1}{2}$	CUPS CANNED GARBANZO BEANS (CHICK-PEAS), DRAINED (A $15\frac{1}{2}$-OUNCE CAN)
1	CUP COOKED RICE (PREFERABLY BROWN)
$\frac{2}{3}$	CUP WHEAT GERM
2	TEASPOONS CANOLA OIL
4	SCALLIONS, FINELY CHOPPED
3	GARLIC CLOVES, MINCED
$\frac{1}{2}$	TEASPOON SALT
$\frac{1}{2}$	TEASPOON FRESHLY GROUND PEPPER

Toast the sesame seeds for 2 minutes in a hot skillet, taking care not to burn them. Add the coriander, cumin, and chile powder and cook for 10 seconds longer, so that all spices are aromatic. Turn onto a plate to cool.

In a large bowl, mash the beans with a potato masher or fork, then add the rice and half the wheat germ.

In a medium skillet, heat the oil over medium heat, and add the scallions, garlic, and toasted spices. Cook until softened, then remove from heat and add to the mashed bean mixture. Add salt and pepper, and mix well with hands. Shape into four $\frac{3}{4}$-inch-thick patties.

Pour remaining $\frac{1}{3}$ cup wheat germ on a plate and press patties in it, coating both sides. Grill, broil, or sauté patties for about 3 minutes per side, or until nicely golden. Serve on pita breads or buns, topped with tomato slices and lettuce or spinach leaves.

Note: You can even grill these without them crumbling on the grill!

NUTRITION	
Per Serving Using White Rice	
Calories (kcal):	294.3
Total Fat (g):	7.6
Saturated Fat (g):	0.8
Cholesterol (mg):	0
Carbohydrate (g):	47.5
Dietary Fiber (g):	7.4
Protein (g):	11.6
Sodium (mg):	552
Calcium (mg):	94
Iron (mg):	5.1
Vitamin C (mg):	8
Vitamin A (i.u.):	248

Zucchini Wheat Germ Burgers

Serves
4

2	LARGE EGGS
$\frac{3}{4}$	CUP WHEAT GERM, TOASTED
$\frac{1}{2}$	CUP SHREDDED MONTEREY JACK CHEESE
$\frac{1}{4}$	CUP CHOPPED MUSHROOMS
$\frac{1}{2}$	SMALL ONION, MINCED
$\frac{1}{2}$	TEASPOON CRUMBLED THYME
$\frac{1}{2}$	TEASPOON CRUMBLED ROSEMARY
$1\frac{1}{2}$	CUPS SHREDDED ZUCCHINI
	SALT AND PEPPER
1	TABLESPOON VEGETABLE OIL

NUTRITION

Per Serving

Calories (kcal):	199.5
Total Fat (g):	12.1
Saturated Fat (g):	4.2
Cholesterol (mg):	119
Carbohydrate (g):	12.7
Dietary Fiber (g):	3.4
Protein (g):	11.8
Sodium (mg):	179
Calcium (mg):	145
Iron (mg):	2.2
Vitamin C (mg):	5
Vitamin A (i.u.):	469

In a large mixing bowl, beat the eggs. Stir in wheat germ, cheese, mushrooms, onion, thyme, rosemary, and zucchini. Add salt and pepper to taste. Shape into 4 patties, $\frac{3}{4}$ inch thick.
In a nonstick sauté pan, heat the oil, place in patties, and cook until golden, about 4 minutes. Flip, and cook other side until golden too, about 3 minutes more. Serve with buns and your favorite fixings.

Tip: Try roasted red peppers as a topping!
Note: Don't let the wheat germ scare you away! These are a delicious and healthy alternative to beef burgers, and can easily be translated for a strict vegetarian by using a cheese and egg substitute.

Lack of Guidance

Recently I received a phone call regarding my ten-year high school reunion, and I started thinking about those glorious, wonderful high school days. In fact, I thought about my glorious, wonderful high school days for a full three seconds before realizing I didn't have any glorious, wonderful high school days—not unless you consider acne, sexual frustration, and intense anxiety glorious and wonderful. I began to think about the first meeting I had with my high school guidance counselor, a tall thin man who bore a striking resemblance to film director John Waters. I thought about all the advice he gave me about what to expect during my next four years at Clarkstown South High School and how out of touch with reality he actually was. I recall our conversation. It was early September 1983 [insert cheesy flashback music here]. "Come in, Sean. Have a seat. If you don't already know, I'm Ted Mather, but I want you to think of me as your buddy Ted. I'm your friend, your confidant. I want you to feel like you can come by my office any time, any day, and . . . make an appointment. Just come by and say, 'Mr. M., is Thursday at 11:15 good?' And sure enough, Thursday at 11:15 I'll be nothing but ears and a cup of coffee, 'cause you know, I got to have my coffee.

"I'm your sounding board for anything, not just school stuff. Hey, I got my finger on the pulse. I know there is more on the minds of today's young adults than just academia. I know what it's like to have your head racing with excitement. Heck, I was in your shoes once, too.

"You're thinking about when the next school mixer is, or who has the latest keen 45. Yes, music is such a big part of youth. It's the rhythm of our hearts. It can put a spring in your stride when you're down. It can take you to the top of the highest mountain, but you know there ain't no mountain high enough, right Sean? Diana Ross said that.

"What musical albums do you fancy, Sean? . . . Iron who? . . . Iron Maiden? . . . No, can't say I've heard of them. Have they ever been on *American Bandstand*? . . . No, well, I'll keep my ear out for them. Anyway, the point is you really can confide in me. I want you to think of me as your loyal Gunga Din and this office as your very own Hoover Dam.

"I'd like to take a couple of moments here to explain to you what my role is going to be in preparing you for the bright future that lies ahead. As your guidance counselor, my primary job is to organize long meetings between your teachers and your parents. This is nothing to be afraid of because it's *not* like we're going to sit around on plastic furniture and drink coffee and analyze you like the troubled chimp at the zoo who just won't feed at the right time like the others. It's *not* like your teachers will begin by saying: 'Sean is a friendly kid and a pleasure to have in class,' causing your parents to beam with pride only to be hit with 'He also happens to be one of the most pathetic students we've seen in recent memory.' Don't think for a second that your teachers will paste on a phony smile as they say 'We're here to help,' which of course you'll realize is false because true help would require effort on our part.

"And rather than put forth that effort, we'll choose to subject you to a battery of tests normally reserved for the criminally insane. I can further assure you that when those tests are completed there will *not* be another parent-teacher 'pow-wow' called at which your fate will be decided by a small cadre of trained professionals, dressed in fashions that date back to the McCarthy hearings, whose minds are clouded by lukewarm caffeine and glazed fried dough hoops. At this meeting there will *not* be an unveiling of the master plan by the tribal elder, or as we like to refer to him around here, the school principal. A man so wise he knows the definition of almost every word in the dictionary with the exception of one . . . *alcoholic.* He will *not* expound on the brilliance of standardized testing and its ability to pinpoint precisely the reason for your scholastic woes, before blaming the fact that you can't spell properly on the psychological trauma caused by the divorce of your parents when you were two years old.

"This will of course *not* lead us to classify someone like you, who actually has a high IQ, as a lazy underachiever, thus taking all the heat off of us and putting all the blame on you and your parents. Even though we realize by attaching the blame to your family rather than the school system we are furthering the troubles that are already running rampant throughout your life. We can't afford to usurp the integrity of the web of bureaucracy that has led so many to the uniformed path of this student assembly line we love so much. Sure, we may completely miss the fact that the reason why someone in his junior year of high school has the reading comprehension level of a first grader has nothing to do with problems at home, but has every-thing to do with dyslexia. Because you see Sean, dyslexia is a learning disability, and we don't believe in learning disabilities, in the same way we don't believe in three-headed fairies or wiping the chalk off our pants. We only know one way to teach, and we expect you to know only one way to learn, and that's our way, Sean. The fact that you will probably graduate from this fine institution having never read a book will not be looked on as an amazing feat of brilliance, but will instead be viewed as another glaring example of your total disregard for the sanctity of the educational system. You feel better, Sean? You're feeling a lot more optimistic about the whole high school experience, aren't you buddy?

"Good, now let's talk about the SATs. No, that's not venereal disease. If you would like to talk about that, go see the school nurse. I'm talking about placement exams, Sean—that's what it's all about. Now, I know they are still three years away, but those years will go by quicker than you know. So I'd start thinking about courses, tapes, and practice tests. The SATs are the foundation for your future. They pave the way to college, and college is the trial to your career, and your career leads to success. You could be like me, relaxing at home buying two-for-one Haggar slacks out of the back of *Reader's Digest.* Because that's hassle-free quality shopping and that comes with success.

"Well, it's been great talking to you, Sean . . . but I have to meet with everybody from A to F and of course I'm still in D. See ya soon . . . OK . . . best of luck . . . bye, bye . . . God, this is good coffee."

Malaysian Scented Rice

Serves
4

2	CUPS LONG-GRAIN RICE
2	TABLESPOONS VEGETABLE OIL
1	CINNAMON STICK, 2 INCHES LONG
2	WHOLE CLOVES
$\frac{1}{4}$	TEASPOON CARDAMOM SEEDS
6	SHALLOTS, THINLY SLICED
$1\frac{1}{2}$	TABLESPOONS GRATED FRESH GINGER
2	GARLIC CLOVES, MINCED
$\frac{1}{2}$	TEASPOON TURMERIC
3	CUPS CHICKEN OR VEGETABLE STOCK

NUTRITION

Per Serving Using Chicken Stock

Calories (kcal):	478.2
Total Fat (g):	9.3
Saturated Fat (g):	1.4
Cholesterol (mg):	0
Carbohydrate (g):	86.7
Dietary Fiber (g):	4.3
Protein (g):	11.7
Sodium (mg):	601
Calcium (mg):	114
Iron (mg):	6.6
Vitamin C (mg):	7
Vitamin A (i.u.):	4,805

Wash the rice in a strainer until the water runs clear. Drain for 30 minutes.

Heat oil in a deep saucepan, and add cinnamon, cloves, and cardamom and cook for 1 minute, stirring. Add shallots, ginger, garlic, and turmeric and cook for another minute, or until softened, but not brown.

Add rice and cook for 2 minutes so that each grain of rice has been coated with oil. Add stock and bring to a boil. Reduce heat, cover, and cook over low heat for 16 minutes, or until all liquid has been absorbed. Only take cover off to peek toward the end of cooking time. Remove from heat and let sit for 10 minutes.

Fluff gently and serve hot.

Note: A special rice dish from Malaysia, usually served on a wedding day. Don't save it for a special occasion, though. Make it for no reason besides the fact that it tastes delicious!

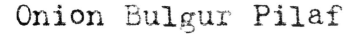

Onion Bulgur Pilaf

Serves **4**

3	TABLESPOONS UNSALTED BUTTER OR VEGETABLE OIL
1	TEASPOON OLIVE OIL
1	MEDIUM ONION, FINELY CHOPPED
2	MEDIUM LEEKS, CLEANED AND FINELY CHOPPED
2	SMALL SHALLOTS, FINELY CHOPPED
2	GARLIC CLOVES, FINELY CHOPPED
1	CUP BULGUR WHEAT
2 $\frac{1}{2}$	CUPS CHICKEN OR VEGETABLE STOCK
$\frac{1}{4}$	CUP CHOPPED FRESH PARSLEY
	SALT AND PEPPER
$\frac{1}{4}$	CUP FRESHLY GRATED PARMESAN CHEESE

NUTRITION
Per Serving Using Butter and Chicken Stock
Calories (kcal): 309.7
Total Fat (g): 12.8
Saturated Fat (g): 6.8
Cholesterol (mg): 27
Carbohydrate (g): 40.5
Dietary Fiber (g): 8.2
Protein (g): 11.3
Sodium (mg): 824
Calcium (mg): 155
Iron (mg): 3.0
Vitamin C (mg): 16
Vitamin A (i.u.): 2,203

Heat butter and oil in a large, heavy saucepan with a tight-fitting lid over medium-high heat. Add onion and cook for 1 minute. Add leeks, shallots, and garlic, reduce heat to low, and cook, covered, for 20 minutes or until onions are richly caramelized, but not browned.

Add bulgur and mix well to coat the flakes. Add the stock, raise heat to high, and bring to a boil. Lower heat to a simmer and cover. Cook for 20 to 25 minutes or until all of the liquid has been absorbed. Do not keep peeking!

Turn off heat, add parsley, and re-cover the pan. Let stand for 10 minutes. Season with salt and pepper and fluff with a fork. Top with a sprinkling of cheese.

Note: This ricelike dish goes particularly well with any poultry dish, but can also be served with soup and a salad for a satisfying vegetarian meal.

Risotto with Mushrooms and Rosemary

Serves
4

2	OUNCES DRIED MUSHROOMS (PORCINI, SHIITAKE)
2	CUPS VEGETABLE BROTH OR CHICKEN STOCK
2	TABLESPOONS UNSALTED BUTTER
2	TABLESPOONS VEGETABLE OIL
1	SMALL ONION, FINELY CHOPPED
1½	CUPS ARBORIO RICE
	SALT AND PEPPER
1	TEASPOON MINCED FRESH ROSEMARY

NUTRITION

Per Serving Using Vegetable Broth

Calories (kcal):	495.6
Total Fat (g):	15.1
Saturated Fat (g):	5.1
Cholesterol (mg):	18
Carbohydrate (g):	80.6
Dietary Fiber (g):	3.7
Protein (g):	9.7
Sodium (mg):	979
Calcium (mg):	38
Iron (mg):	1.3
Vitamin C (mg):	4
Vitamin A (i.u.):	2,363

Soak the mushrooms in boiling water to cover until very soft, about 30 minutes. Drain and save the water. Measure and add enough water to equal 3 cups.

In a medium pot, bring the broth and water to a simmer. In a large, heavy-bottomed wide pan, heat butter and oil. Add onion and sauté until transparent. Add mushrooms and rice and stir well so that each grain of the rice has been tossed in the butter and oil mixture.

Add 1 cup of the hot stock to the rice and stir as it is absorbed by the rice. Continue to add stock, 1 cup at a time, stirring well as it is absorbed until rice is tender but not mushy, about 25 minutes. You may not need all of the stock—use your judgment. Add salt and pepper to taste and the rosemary, and serve immediately.

Note: I don't know why risotto has developed a reputation for being difficult to make—it is among the easiest things to do. And it's very versatile; you can put just about anything in it and it always tastes great, especially served with Parmesan cheese.

Sautéed Bulgur with Escarole

Serves
4

2	TABLESPOONS VEGETABLE OIL
1	SMALL ONION, FINELY CHOPPED
2	GARLIC CLOVES, MINCED
1	HEAD ESCAROLE, THICKLY SLICED
1 $\frac{1}{2}$	CUPS CHICKEN OR VEGETABLE STOCK
1	CUP BULGUR WHEAT
	SALT AND PEPPER

N·U·T·R·I·T·I·O·N

Per Serving Using Chicken Stock

Calories (kcal): ----------206.3

Total Fat (g): -------------7.8

Saturated Fat (g): ---------1.0

Cholesterol (mg): ----------0

Carbohydrate (g): ---------29.4

Dietary Fiber (g): ---------6.9

Protein (g): ----------------6.8

Sodium (mg): -------------437

Calcium (mg): ------------42

Iron (mg): ----------------1.2

Vitamin C (mg):----------3

Vitamin A (i.u.): ---------258

In a large saucepan with a tight-fitting lid, heat oil over medium heat. Add onion and cook for 1 minute. Add garlic and cook for 4 more minutes. Add escarole and stock, raise heat to high and bring to a boil. Stir in the bulgur, reduce heat to a simmer, cover, and cook over low heat for 20 to 25 minutes, or until all liquid is absorbed. Turn off heat and let stand, covered, for 10 minutes. Season with salt and pepper, and fluff with a fork.

Note: Similar to Barley and Greens (page 62), yet different enough to get its own recipe.

Tall Grass

Growing up. I lived in a big, old house with my mother, my mother's younger brother Tom (better known as my uncle), and her mother, my grandmother Helen. A house requires a certain amount of maintenance, but unfortunately Tom and myself were not what you might consider "handy"–particularly Tom. I. at least, had a certain knack for fixing electronic things and Tom, well, he had a knack for sitting in front of them. My grandmother was the real family wizard. There was nothing she couldn't fix, sew, mend, cook, dissect, or teach. She was gifted at woodworking, reupholstering furniture, making Halloween costumes, barbecuing, gardening, throwing a curveball, painting, swimming the backstroke, baking cookies, spelunking, performing open-heart surgery, and administering last rites to a terminally ill parakeet. I hate to admit it, what with my now being an author and all, but my grandmother wrote every one of my book reports when I was in school. If she was still around today, my grandmother would be writing this entire book and would complete it in the time it takes to watch *As the World Turns*. All I would have to do is make a lovely cover with some markers and paste, and I'd be done with it and would get an A+. My grandmother could get more done before 9:00 A.M. than the U.S. Army did in the 1980s.

Yard work provided my grandmother with her greatest high. Some people reach for heavy narcotics, but Helen reached for the rake. A fresh raking took her places Timothy Leary only dreamed of. However, when it came to the actual mowing, the responsibility was passed to my uncle Tom and me. It's not that Grandma wouldn't have done it herself (who do you think installed the TV antenna up on the roof?), it's just that our lawn was fairly large and our push mower was an unwieldy contraption that cut grass with all the efficiency of a pair of scissors.

Tom and I were always looking for a better way to keep the grass in check. We would push along on a hot, sunny day and pretend we were riding atop a state-of-the-art Toro—shiny red with an adjustable blade and a big, cushy seat. This fantasy would last a good ten to twelve seconds before we would stumble back to reality as the mower clogged up yet again. With the time I spent cleaning out the blade, I could've mowed Versailles. We prayed for that new mower for years. We could see it clearly in our minds' eyes. And, as Zen teaches, voice a vision to the universe and your vision will soon appear.

One morning my grandmother's sister, Vicki, showed up at our house with their old mower. She explained that she had decided to employ a lawn service and had no further use for it. It was a beauty to behold: a bright red Toro, with an adjustable blade and a cushy seat. Tom and I felt a joy that day that we hadn't felt since they took the TV show *Alice* off the air. (We hated *Alice*. Boy, did we hate *Alice*. We hated every character on *Alice*. We hated Flo, Vera, Mel, everybody. Even now, just thinking about it I get . . . all right, I'm sorry, I'll get back to the lawn mower saga.) Finally, we could look forward to a pleasant day of mowing. But that day never came because Grandma Helen took one look at the thing and hopped on it like it was Clark Gable, and off she rode. From that day on she mowed the lawn. We were not to touch the new mower. My grandmother felt that we just didn't possess the skill to operate it. We didn't put up a fuss because, deep down, Tom and I knew we weren't handy people, and drinking lemonade in the pool was a better deal, anyway.

Lemongrass Coconut Rice

Serves
6

1	CUP LONG-GRAIN RICE
1	STALK LEMONGRASS, BOTTOM **6** INCHES ONLY
1 $\frac{3}{4}$	CUPS COCONUT MILK
2	BAY LEAVES
$\frac{1}{2}$	TEASPOON TURMERIC
	SALT

NUTRITION	
Per Serving	
Calories (kcal):	163.6
Total Fat (g):	16.8
Saturated Fat (g):	14.8
Cholesterol (mg):	0
Carbohydrate (g):	4.5
Dietary Fiber (g):	1.7
Protein (g):	1.7
Sodium (mg):	11
Calcium (mg):	17
Iron (mg):	1.5
Vitamin C (mg):	2
Vitamin A (i.u.):	37

Wash the rice under running cold water until water runs clear. Bruise the lemongrass stalk by hitting it with the blunt end of a knife.

Place coconut milk, rice, lemongrass, bay leaves, turmeric, and a pinch of salt in a medium saucepan. Slowly bring to a boil, stirring once in a while. Once it boils, lower heat to a low simmer, cover, and cook for 25 minutes, or until all liquid is absorbed.

Remove bay leaves and lemongrass and serve hot.

Note: This is an amazingly fragrant and flavorful rice dish.

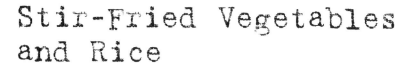

Stir-Fried Vegetables and Rice

Serves **4**

1 ½	CUPS LONG- OR SHORT-GRAIN BROWN RICE
3	CUPS WATER
2	TABLESPOONS VEGETABLE OIL
1	TABLESPOON ASIAN ROASTED SESAME OIL
3	LARGE GARLIC CLOVES, MINCED
2	TABLESPOONS GRATED FRESH GINGER
1	BUNCH SCALLIONS, CHOPPED
2	MEDIUM CARROTS, COARSELY CHOPPED
1	BOK CHOY, COARSELY CHOPPED
¼	POUND FRESH GREEN BEANS, TRIMMED AND CHOPPED
½	POUND SHIITAKE MUSHROOMS
2	TABLESPOONS TAMARI
1	TABLESPOON CURRY POWDER
2	TABLESPOONS SESAME SEEDS, BLACK IF AVAILABLE

Rinse rice in a colander under cold water until water runs clear, then drain. Place in a medium pot with tight-fitting lid, add water, cover, and bring to a boil. Reduce heat to low and cook, covered (no peeking), for 30 minutes. Turn off heat and let sit, covered.

Heat oils in a wok or large skillet. Add garlic and ginger and cook for 30 seconds over high heat. Add remaining vegetables (reserve 2 tablespoons of scallions) and cook for 3 minutes. Add tamari and curry powder, and cook for 3 minutes more. Add rice to pan and toss together. Transfer to a platter or plates, and sprinkle with sesame seeds and reserved scallions.

Note: The veggies listed here are a guide—use what you like and what is fresh. You cannot mess this recipe up, no matter what you do!

NUTRITION	
Per Serving	
Calories (kcal):	585.4
Total Fat (g):	15.7
Saturated Fat (g):	2.2
Cholesterol (mg):	0
Carbohydrate (g):	106
Dietary Fiber (g):	9.5
Protein (g):	14.3
Sodium (mg):	450
Calcium (mg):	89
Iron (mg):	4.0
Vitamin C (mg):	20
Vitamin A (i.u.):	10,876

5

PASTA

- ✪ Asparagus and Red Pepper Fusilli
- ✪ Cold Sesame Noodles
- ✪ Late-Night Shopper
- ✪ Emergency Pasta
- ✪ Grown-Up Macaroni and Cheese
- ✪ Linguine with Clam Sauce
- ✪ Perfect Tomato Sauce
- ✪ No-Frills Soda
- ✪ Sean's Cream Substitute
- ✪ Spaghetti alla Carbonara
- ✪ Summer Pasta
- ✪ Wild Mushroom Linguine

Asparagus and Red Pepper Fusilli

Serves
4

1	POUND FUSILLI, SPAGHETTI, OR PENNE
1	POUND ASPARAGUS, TRIMMED AND CUT ON DIAGONAL INTO BITE-SIZE PIECES
1	MEDIUM RED BELL PEPPER, CORED, SEEDED, AND CUT INTO 1-INCH SQUARES
4	TABLESPOONS EXTRA-VIRGIN OLIVE OIL
	SALT AND PEPPER
1	TABLESPOON CHOPPED FRESH OREGANO
1	TABLESPOON CHOPPED FRESH THYME
1	LEMON, JUICED
	FRESHLY GRATED PARMESAN CHEESE

NUTRITION

Per Serving Not Including Cheese

Calories (kcal):	579.6
Total Fat (g):	15.7
Saturated Fat (g):	2.2
Cholesterol (mg):	0
Carbohydrate (g):	94.5
Dietary Fiber (g):	5.6
Protein (g):	17.7
Sodium (mg):	12
Calcium (mg):	77
Iron (mg):	6.0
Vitamin C (mg):	71
Vitamin A (i.u.):	1,770

Bring water for pasta to a boil. Add pasta and cook according to package directions. Preheat oven to 475°F.

In a large bowl, toss asparagus and red pepper with oil, salt, and pepper. Place on a baking sheet and roast for about 5 minutes, depending on how thick the pieces are. They should be just tender, but not soft. Return to bowl and top with fresh herbs and lemon juice.

When pasta is done, drain well and pour on top of hot vegetables; toss to mix. Taste for salt and pepper and serve with cheese.

Note: You can use any pasta shape that you like, but short pastas work best here. You can add chicken for a fuller dish, or serve as is for a side dish.

Cold Sesame Noodles

Serves
8

$\frac{2}{3}$	CUP PEANUT BUTTER
$\frac{2}{3}$	CUP ASIAN ROASTED SESAME OIL
$\frac{1}{2}$	CUP SOY SAUCE
$\frac{1}{2}$	CUP STRONG BREWED TEA
3	TABLESPOONS DARK BROWN SUGAR, PACKED
$2\frac{1}{2}$	TABLESPOONS CHILI OIL
2	TABLESPOONS RED WINE VINEGAR
4	GARLIC CLOVES, CHOPPED
1	2-INCH PIECE FRESH GINGER, CHOPPED
$1\frac{1}{2}$	POUNDS SPAGHETTI, COOKED, RINSED, AND DRAINED
3	SCALLIONS, GREEN PARTS THINLY SLICED
2	MEDIUM CARROTS, PEELED AND SHREDDED
1	LARGE CUCUMBER, SHREDDED

NUTRITION	
Per Serving	
Calories (kcal):	675.6
Total Fat (g):	34.7
Saturated Fat (g):	4.9
Cholesterol (mg):	0
Carbohydrate (g):	75.7
Dietary Fiber (g):	4.6
Protein (g):	17.7
Sodium (mg):	947
Calcium (mg):	44
Iron (mg):	4.4
Vitamin C (mg):	5
Vitamin A (i.u.):	5,155

In a food processor, combine the peanut butter, sesame oil, soy sauce, $\frac{1}{4}$ cup of tea, brown sugar, chili oil, vinegar, garlic, and ginger. Process until smooth. Add tablespoons of the remaining tea until the dressing is the consistency of soup. In a large bowl, gently toss together the dressing, pasta, and scallion greens. Place on platter, and garnish with carrots and cucumber.

Note: If desired, add 2 cups cooked chicken, either shredded or cubed, or 1 pound cooked shrimp.

Late-Night Shopper

I like to shop at large grocery stores late at night. In fact, I like to go to giant suburban supermarkets almost as much as Pat Buchanan likes to go to gun rallies. Late at night there are usually only half a dozen customers in a store that takes up four acres of land, so I'm able to shop at my own pace. I can stare at row after row of endless crap for as long as I wish. If I feel the need to take twenty minutes in the international section in a quest for premium chutney, then so be it. Even if I'm only after razors, I'll hit all seventy-three aisles. I feel it's critical that I familiarize myself with the store's layout because, in the event of catastrophic disaster, I want to know where they keep the bunker items. I mean, look, if Ned the electrician-"weekend" neo-Nazi-amateur videographer should ever declare on his local cable access show that he's come into some uranium-234 and plans on using it next Tuesday, I don't want to spend Monday in a grocery store wondering where the hell they keep the Vienna sausages.

Shopping late at night relaxes me. Walking slowly down the aisles, just me and my cart, whistling along to the Muzak version of "Do You Know the Way to San Jose" while quietly pondering the nutritional drawbacks of choosing Count Chocula over Mueslix cereal soothes my restless soul. I'm not sure if it's the walking or the Muzak. And if it is the Muzak, I'm not sure whether it's soothing my soul or sucking it out. If you hang out in supermarkets long enough, you can hear Muzak versions of songs you never thought were possible. I once heard a Muzak version of the Talking Heads' "Psycho Killer," and I started fantasizing about Eddie Vedder walking in on a late-night Ding Dong run, only to be smacked in his little "artist's" head by a scrubbed-down, medicinal version of "Jeremy" and watching his body start to twitch with all the grunge angst of a generation as he comes to the painful realization that there is an evil even greater than Ticketmaster.

Late at night I enjoy the beauty and pageantry of the various point-of-purchase displays. During the day I rush past these displays, never really appreciating the evil machinations that went into creating a vision so glorious that I'm compelled to pick up an entire gross of Brawny paper towels. The vibrance of the packaging, the careful stacking that defies all known laws of gravity—these displays deserve to be admired for the beacons of pop culture that they are. Like it or not, the supermarket is the truest representation of our life in the good old U.S.A. Anyone choosing to study our culture need only examine an A & P to do it. It would take all of 10 minutes for any sociologist to unravel the mysteries of our diet, ailments, vices, currency, journalistic tastes (*The Enquirer, The Globe, The Weekly World News*), and fashion trends and celebrity scandals we find so captivating. It's all right there by the BreathAsure. Someone should make a grocery store into a museum display right now. Right after the treasures of ancient Egypt and the vases of the Ming dynasty should be a complete replica of the Pathmark in Nanuet, New York. If King Tut were buried today, he would be entombed in a Wal-Mart with a tanning bed as his sarcopha-gus. For his journey into the next life, he'd have a six-pack of Bud in a Playmate cooler by his side.

If you have yet to experience the bliss of a late-night stroll through a supermarket, give it a try. However, please be advised that some supermarkets are not for the late-night shopping novice. I once went to one in Hollywood, California, on a Sunday night back in 1995 and I saw more freaks in this place than you would find in a movie about P. T. Barnum directed by Federico Fellini. This Hollywood grocery store made PeepWorld in Times Square (before it was knocked down by the Disney corporation and replaced with Goofy's Family Fun Palace) look like a Christian gift shop. Thankfully, I can handle myself in these situations. If things start getting weird, my strategy is to blend in with the surroundings, much like one of those chameleons you see on the Discovery Channel, by clinging to the shelf and pretending to have an animated conversation with a box of Mrs. Paul's Fish Sticks. If you do not feel you can pull off such an act—or something similar, like, for instance, reenacting the Spanish American War with an avocado and canned ham—stay out of Hollywood. The rest of the country's supermarkets are yours for the taking—your time, that is.

Emergency Pasta

Serves
4

1	POUND LINGUINE, OR ANY OTHER SHAPE PASTA
2	TABLESPOONS EXTRA-VIRGIN OLIVE OIL
4	GARLIC CLOVES, MINCED
1	CUP OIL-CURED OLIVES, PITTED
1	4-OUNCE JAR ROASTED RED PEPPERS
1	4-OUNCE JAR MARINATED ARTICHOKE HEARTS
2	SUN-DRIED TOMATOES, CHOPPED
$\frac{1}{4}$	CUP FRESHLY GRATED PARMESAN CHEESE
	CRUSHED RED PEPPER FLAKES

NUTRITION

Per Serving
Calories (kcal): ----------629.9
Total Fat (g): --------------14.5
Saturated Fat (g): ---------2.7
Cholesterol (mg): ----------4
Carbohydrate (g): ---------106.3
Dietary Fiber (g): ---------7.5
Protein (g): ----------------21.7
Sodium (mg): -------------978
Calcium (mg): ------------164
Iron (mg): -----------------8.4
Vitamin C (mg):-----------38
Vitamin A (i.u.): ----------1,155

Bring water for pasta to a boil. Add pasta and cook according to package directions. Heat oil in a large skillet. Add garlic and gently sauté 2 minutes. Do not brown. Add olives, red peppers, artichoke hearts, and tomatoes. Sauté while pasta cooks.

Drain pasta well, add to vegetables in skillet, add cheese and red pepper flakes, and toss well to mix.

Note: You can run into the grocery store, get what you need in four minutes, get home again, and make dinner in ten minutes! Or, better yet, keep this stuff on hand and you will always be prepared for an emergency dinner.

Grown-Up Macaroni and Cheese

Serves
4

2	CUPS WHOLE MILK
2	TABLESPOONS UNSALTED BUTTER
2	TABLESPOONS ALL-PURPOSE FLOUR
	SALT
	FRESHLY GROUND WHITE PEPPER
	GRATED NUTMEG
1	POUND PENNE OR ELBOW MACARONI
$\frac{1}{4}$	POUND GORGONZOLA CHEESE, CRUMBLED
$\frac{1}{2}$	CUP FRESHLY GRATED PARMESAN CHEESE

NUTRITION

Per Serving

Calories (kcal):	430.8
Total Fat (g):	25.7
Saturated Fat (g):	16.0
Cholesterol (mg):	73
Carbohydrate (g):	31.6
Dietary Fiber (g):	0.6
Protein (g):	18.4
Sodium (mg):	745
Calcium (mg):	437
Iron (mg):	1.6
Vitamin C (mg):	1
Vitamin A (i.u.):	803

Heat milk to just warm in a small saucepan.

In a large saucepan over low heat, combine the butter and the flour, stirring until the butter melts and is completely mixed with the flour. Continue cooking the mixture for 3 minutes, taking care not to brown it. Gradually add the warmed milk, whisking in a little at a time, until smooth. Season with salt, pepper, and nutmeg. Cook until well thickened and smooth. Remove from heat.

Preheat oven to 350°F. Bring water for pasta to a boil. Add penne and cook until half tender. Drain well. Transfer to a buttered 6 x 12-inch baking dish. Pour white sauce over top, sprinkle with gorgonzola, and mix gently. Sprinkle top with Parmesan. Place in oven and bake for 20 minutes, or until golden on top. Serve immediately.

Note: Definitely a grown-up version of a classic. To make it more traditional, use sharp cheddar cheese instead of the gorgonzola.

Linguine with Clam Sauce

Serves
4

$1\frac{3}{4}$	POUNDS LITTLENECK OR MANILLA CLAMS
$\frac{1}{2}$	CUP DRY WHITE WINE
$\frac{1}{2}$	CUP WATER
1	TABLESPOON EXTRA-VIRGIN OLIVE OIL

SAUCE

2	TABLESPOONS EXTRA-VIRGIN OLIVE OIL
$\frac{1}{3}$	CUP FINELY CHOPPED ONION
1	GARLIC CLOVE, MINCED
1	14-OUNCE CAN TOMATOES
$\frac{1}{2}$	TEASPOON SALT
	FRESHLY GROUND PEPPER
$\frac{3}{4}$	POUND LINGUINE OR BUCATINI
2	TABLESPOONS CHOPPED FRESH PARSLEY

NUTRITION	
Per Serving	
Calories (kcal):	743.5
Total Fat (g):	15.6
Saturated Fat (g):	2.0
Cholesterol (mg):	133
Carbohydrate (g):	79.2
Dietary Fiber (g):	3.3
Protein (g):	62.8
Sodium (mg):	710
Calcium (mg):	237
Iron (mg):	59.7
Vitamin C (mg):	62
Vitamin A (i.u.):	1,829

Scrub the clams under cold running water, discarding any open or broken ones. Place them in a large pot and add wine, water, and oil; heat until clams open. Discard any that do not open. Remove clams from the pot with a slotted spoon. Let the liquid settle for a few minutes, then strain and set aside.

For the sauce: heat the oil in a large saucepan over medium heat and add onion and garlic. Sauté over medium-low heat till translucent, then add tomatoes and the reserved clam liquid. Season with salt and pepper, and simmer for 30 minutes or until liquid is reduced by half.

Heat a pot of water for the pasta and cook just till al dente. Drain well, and add pasta to sauce, toss thoroughly, sprinkle with parsley, and serve immediately.

Note: This is a red clam sauce but it's not too tomatoey. I use canned tomatoes here, but really ripe plum tomatoes would make a difference.

Perfect Tomato Sauce

Serves
4

$\frac{1}{4}$	CUP EXTRA-VIRGIN OLIVE OIL
4	GARLIC CLOVES, MINCED
$\frac{1}{2}$	CUP DRY WHITE WINE
$1\frac{1}{2}$	POUNDS RIPE PLUM TOMATOES, PEELED AND CHOPPED
1	WHOLE RED CHILE PEPPER
	SALT AND WHITE PEPPER

In a large sauté pan over medium heat, heat oil. Add the garlic, reduce the heat to very low, and very slowly and gently cook garlic so that it does not burn or brown, about 5 minutes. Carefully add the wine, raise the heat to medium-high, and cook off the alcohol, about 2 minutes. Add the tomatoes, whole chile pepper, salt, and pepper. Cook, uncovered, about 5 minutes, stirring often. Serve immediately over pasta of choice, making sure to remove chile pepper beforehand.

Note: This is best made when tomatoes are in season. You can also use canned tomatoes, however. You don't even need cheese, it is so good!

NUTRITION	
Per Serving	
Calories (kcal):	180.9
Total Fat (g):	14.1
Saturated Fat (g):	1.9
Cholesterol (mg):	0
Carbohydrate (g):	9.4
Dietary Fiber (g):	1.9
Protein (g):	1.7
Sodium (mg):	18
Calcium (mg):	17
Iron (mg):	1.0
Vitamin C (mg):	41
Vitamin A (i.u.):	1,370

No-Frills Soda

Sometimes I lay awake and ponder, "Do I have what it takes? Do I possess the same drive and determination as those who came before me? Will I ever be able to step up to the plate and mold the youth of America? Could I be a Little League coach?"

I was a good baseball player, and sometimes that helps make a great coach. But is it that simple? Of course not. To be a good Little League coach, it takes more than having a bat bag in your trunk. It is not the clipboard or the whistle that turns spastic pre-teens into winners. Rather, it's the psychological games the coach plays that gets the team cheap no-frills soda after a big win. For it is widely known, but rarely publicized, that the best way to help a kid who is having trouble with hitting an inside fastball is to tell him he sucks.

* AFTER TASTE THAT COULD KILL A GOAT !

* PERFECT FOR SCHOOL MIXERS

COLA

* GUARANTEED NOT TO RESEMBLE THE FLAVOR OF ANY TOP NAME BRAND

* GREAT FOR WHEN YOU JUST DON'T CARE WHAT YOUR GUESTS ARE DRINKING

For decades, dehumanization has been the method of choice for many coaches. A well-placed insult can turn a .200 hitter into an all-star overnight. Kids respond well to phrases like, "Hey, Mary, if you keep swinging like that, I'm gonna take away your batting helmet and give you a bonnet!" And when a small child lets a ground ball roll through his legs, it's pointless to explain that he must learn to keep his glove down and his eyes on the ball. Better to rifle scorchers at him from ten feet away while screaming, "Bed wetter! Bed wetter!"

You can't really blame the coach for these humiliating verbal assaults, because I'm sure that they suffer through the same indignities at their places of employment. I'm sure a day doesn't go by when someone's not screaming, "You call that a spreadsheet, Timmy? Do you have your head up your butt? Do ya!? You know, Timmy, I just don't think you're giving this your all. So how about you and the rest of these wimps in your department go outside and run twenty-five laps around the building."

Okay, look, I don't really believe anything I've just written. Most Little League coaches are evil. They've never gotten over the fact that they weren't talented enough to play ball in the pros, or even at a family barbecue. Personally, I don't feel the need to take out my frustrations on a bunch of kids. All these kids want to do is pretend that they're Ken Griffey Jr. for a few hours a week. I'm not saying I don't snap at people. I just try to reserve it for whatever Comedy Shack I'm at that weekend, when the hammered troll up front, who has three beepers 'cause "you know he's got his own business," tries to be witty. I have no problem with this because I think if you're old enough to buy a drink, you're old enough to know better.

You probably think I'll never let my kids play Little League baseball or that I'll never subject my own flesh and blood to the torment of these half-crazed, suburban Casey Stengels. The truth is I will. Because the greatest lessons in life are learned on the Little League baseball diamond. I'm not talking about teamwork and sportsmanship—not that those aren't valuable lessons. It's just that I seldom see them applied in the real world. No, the lesson I'm talking about is one of the greatest lessons the human race has ever known. I'm speaking of the vital importance of nepotism. Once you realize that the coach's son will play every out of every inning, no matter how much he blows, the sooner you understand it is not what you know, but who you know. Nepotism will rule this earth until the day it freezes over again, and even then if you kiss the ass of the right guy, I bet you could get a luxury hut near the equator.

Sean's Cream Substitute

Serves
5

1	10½-OUNCE PACKAGE LOW-FAT SILKEN TOFU
1	CUP PLAIN RICE DREAM
1	TEASPOON CRUSHED RED PEPPER FLAKES
2	TEASPOONS DRIED BASIL
2	PINCHES SALT

NUTRITION

Per Serving

Calories (kcal):	67.3
Total Fat (g):	3.4
Saturated Fat (g):	0.7
Cholesterol (mg):	2
Carbohydrate (g):	3.8
Dietary Fiber (g):	0.8
Protein (g):	6.5
Sodium (mg):	82.4
Calcium (mg):	135.4
Iron (mg):	3.5
Vitamin C (mg):	1.4
Vitamin A (i.u.):	228

Place everything in a blender and process until smooth. Can be refrigerated. Adjust seasonings for other dishes. Makes $2\frac{1}{2}$ cups for $\frac{1}{2}$-cup servings.

Tip: Add this "cream" to tomato sauce for a great pink sauce.

Note: Sean came up with this great recipe as a healthy substitute for the cream in most soups and pasta sauces.

Spaghetti alla Carbonara

Serves
4

$\frac{1}{2}$	POUND PANCETTA OR BACON
2	TABLESPOONS VEGETABLE OIL
1	GARLIC CLOVE, BRUISED
4	LARGE EGGS
$\frac{3}{4}$	CUP FRESHLY GRATED PARMESAN CHEESE
	SALT AND FRESHLY GROUND PEPPER
1	POUND SPAGHETTI

NUTRITION	
Per Serving	
Calories (kcal):	736.0
Total Fat (g):	22.8
Saturated Fat (g):	7.0
Cholesterol (mg):	264
Carbohydrate (g):	86.4
Dietary Fiber (g):	2.7
Protein (g):	42.8
Sodium (mg):	1,880
Calcium (mg):	258
Iron (mg):	5.9
Vitamin C (mg):	0
Vitamin A (i.u.):	423

Cut the pancetta into strips. Heat the oil in a large saucepan and fry the pancetta and garlic until the pancetta starts to crisp, about 5 minutes.

Break the eggs into a bowl, add the cheese, and beat thoroughly. Season with salt and pepper. Meanwhile, cook the spaghetti, drain well, and add to the pan with the pancetta. Remove the pan from the heat, add the egg and cheese mixture, and stir well. The heat from the pasta will cook the egg, creating a creamy, rich sauce. Serve immediately.

Note: This is a completely evil dish, but so delicious that once in a while, you just have to go for it! Serve with a light green salad and some crusty bread.

Summer Pasta

Serves
4

$\frac{1}{4}$	CUP EXTRA-VIRGIN OLIVE OIL
1	POUND PACKAGE PENNE PASTA
1	PINT CHERRY TOMATOES, HALVED, OR REGULAR TOMATOES, CUBED
$\frac{1}{2}$	CUP OIL-CURED OLIVES, PITTED AND HALVED
4	TABLESPOONS COARSELY RIPPED FRESH BASIL
2	GARLIC CLOVES, MINCED
$\frac{1}{2}$	POUND RICOTTA SALATA CHEESE, CRUMBLED
	SALT AND PEPPER

NUTRITION

Per Serving

Calories (kcal):	680.2
Total Fat (g):	24.8
Saturated Fat (g):	7.1
Cholesterol (mg):	29
Carbohydrate (g):	92.4
Dietary Fiber (g):	3.7
Protein (g):	22
Sodium (mg):	209
Calcium (mg):	164
Iron (mg):	5.7
Vitamin C (mg):	18
Vitamin A (i.u.):	1,008

Bring a large pot of salted water to a boil. Add 1 tablespoon of the olive oil to the water. Add pasta to water and cook according to package directions.

In a large serving bowl, place halved tomatoes, olives, basil, garlic, the rest of the olive oil, cheese, and salt and pepper to taste.

When pasta is finished cooking, drain very well and place on top of ingredients in the bowl. Let sit for 30 seconds, toss well to combine, and serve hot or at room temperature.

Note: This is a pasta that I make all summer long, and even during the winter when I want a reminder of summer. It's great the next day for lunch, or for a party. Sometimes I add cubed chicken breast pieces, or instead of the ricotta salata, I use smoked mozzarella. Try all the variations you can—it's so good and so easy.

Wild Mushroom Linguine

Serves
4

1	CUP NONFAT PLAIN YOGURT
$\frac{1}{2}$	CUP DRIED PORCINI MUSHROOMS
1	TABLESPOON OLIVE OIL
1	POUND OYSTER MUSHROOMS, QUARTERED
1	POUND SHIITAKE MUSHROOMS, QUARTERED
1	LARGE CARROT, PEELED AND JULIENNED
$\frac{3}{4}$	POUND LINGUINE
5	MEDIUM SHALLOTS, SLICED
3	GARLIC CLOVES, MINCED
$\frac{1}{2}$	CUP DRY WHITE WINE
$1\frac{1}{2}$	TEASPOONS FRESH THYME
$\frac{1}{4}$	CUP PARMESAN CHEESE
$\frac{1}{4}$	CUP CHOPPED FRESH ITALIAN FLAT-LEAF PARSLEY

Bring a large pot of salted water to a boil.

Drain yogurt in a strainer lined with cheesecloth or a coffee filter overnight in refrigerator.

Soften the porcinis in boiling water to cover, about 20 minutes. Drain and strain soaking liquid.

Heat half the oil in sauté pan until very hot, then add oyster mushrooms, cover, and cook for 2 minutes. Stir and continue to cook till slightly browned. Remove oyster mushrooms and add shiitakes to same pan, repeating process. Add porcinis to pan, cook for 1 minute,

then put oysters back in pan.

Cook carrot, in strainer, in boiling water for 3 minutes. Add linguine to pasta pot and cook according to package directions.

While the pasta is cooking, heat the remaining oil, add shallots, and cook until translucent, then add garlic and cook for 1 minute. Raise the heat to high, add wine, and boil for 2 minutes. Add mushroom water, carrot, and thyme and cook for 2 minutes. Stir in yogurt and heat just till heated through; do not boil.

Drain linguine and put back in pot. Add yogurt mixture as well as mushrooms. Toss with Parmesan and parsley, and season with salt and pepper to taste.

NUTRITION	
Calories (kcal):	856.6
Total Fat (g):	8.5
Saturated Fat (g):	2.1
Cholesterol (mg):	5
Carbohydrate (g):	176.0
Dietary Fiber (g):	18.4
Protein (g):	32.3
Sodium (mg):	192
Calcium (mg):	305
Iron (mg):	11.8
Vitamin C (mg):	18
Vitamin A (i.u.):	9,924

6

VEGETABLES

- ❂ JERRY'S TAKE-OUT OMELETS
- ❂ Black and White Vegetarian Chili
- ❂ Green Beans with Shallots, Lemon, and Thyme
- ❂ Mediterranean Tofu Sauté
- ❂ Ratatouille
- ❂ Roasted Garlic Mashed Potatoes
- ❂ Gingered Carrots
- ❂ GIVE IT AWAY!
- ❂ Roasted Vegetables
- ❂ Sautéed Broccoli Rabe
- ❂ Summer Vegetable Sauté
- ❂ Tofu Cacciatore

Jerry's Take-Out Omelets

"Are there any more egg rolls?" is a phrase that is never uttered when my father, Jerry, does the ordering. I still can't figure out what causes him to order so much food. Maybe it's a result of his training as a platoon sergeant in Vietnam or maybe it was his years touring the world with Frank Sinatra. He's not sure which experience gives him worse flashbacks.

When I was a kid, after a long Saturday of father and son activities, my dad and I would often pick up take-out Chinese food, and my dad always ordered enough food so we could stuff ourselves, and so could the Harlem Globetrotters if they happened to come by (hey, it happened to Gilligan). My dad never pulled any portion punches. Because of his extravagant ordering, Saturday's dinner often became Sunday's breakfast. Not to worry, though, because this man always had a plan for everything. When shopping for Christmas presents at the local mall, he first performed a recon mission where he mapped out his plan of attack. And then on "P-day," he barked out his commands: "Okay, Sean, at 1300 hours you rush the Swiss Colony for the processed meat and cheese gift sets. I'll pull a flanking maneuver on the Radio Shack and pick up the cordless phone. We'll rendezvous at Mr. Pretzel. If you get into trouble, here's a poncho and some flares. Good luck, son."

The leftovers plan for the Chinese food was simple. In his never-ending quest to create the ultimate omelet, my dad would load them up with leftover Chinese food or pizza. I never knew exactly what would be in my omelet until I cut into it, because my dad ran his kitchen like the o'mighty Zeus, never letting mere mortals into his gastronomic Olympus. I would stand outside curious but would not interrupt because, as he put it, "The longer you're in here, the longer it will be before you eat. Now out of my kitchen." His Chinese food omelets and pizza omelets were not unpleasant surprises. However, his drumstick and coleslaw topped with cranberry sauce supreme was not much of a hit. And his holiday theme dishes—a jelly-bean omelet comes to mind—were valiant attempts but untouchable just the same.

Black and White Vegetarian Chili

Serves
6

2	CUPS DRIED BLACK BEANS, SOAKED OVERNIGHT
$\frac{3}{4}$	CUP DRIED NAVY BEANS, SOAKED OVERNIGHT
2	TABLESPOONS OLIVE OIL
2	MEDIUM ONIONS, FINELY CHOPPED
2	GARLIC CLOVES, FINELY CHOPPED
2	MEDIUM RED BELL PEPPERS, CORED, SEEDED, AND CUT INTO $\frac{1}{2}$-INCH DICE
1	TEASPOON CUMIN POWDER
1	TEASPOON GROUND CORIANDER
2	TEASPOONS DRIED OREGANO
$\frac{1}{2}$	TEASPOON PURE CHILE POWDER
2	14-OUNCE CANS TOMATOES, CHOPPED
3	TABLESPOONS TOMATO PASTE
1	TEASPOON SUGAR
	SALT TO TASTE
$2\frac{1}{2}$	CUPS VEGETABLE BROTH
$\frac{1}{4}$	CUP FRESH CILANTRO LEAVES

Drain beans, put in separate saucepans, cover with cold water, and boil for 15 minutes, then lower heat and simmer for about 30 minutes, until tender but not mushy. They will cook at different speeds, so check both. Drain and set aside. Heat the oil in a large saucepan and add onion, garlic, and red pepper. Sauté over medium heat for 5 minutes, until vegetables are soft but not browned. Add cumin, ground coriander, oregano, and chile powder. Add chopped tomatoes, tomato paste, sugar, salt, beans, and broth. Stir to combine, bring to a boil, lower heat, and simmer for 45 minutes, stirring once in a while. Ladle into bowls, and garnish with fresh cilantro. Note: A light vegetarian chili. You can add cooked diced chicken breast for a heartier meal, or serve as a side dish. Great served with fresh tortillas or cornbread. To make at the last minute, use drained and rinsed canned beans and just simmer until beans are heated through.

NUTRITION	
Per Serving	
Calories (kcal):	462.8
Total Fat (g):	7.9
Saturated Fat (g):	1.4
Cholesterol (mg):	1
Carbohydrate (g):	77.4
Dietary Fiber (g):	20.1
Protein (g):	24.2
Sodium (mg):	1,018
Calcium (mg):	197
Iron (mg):	7.2
Vitamin C (mg):	68
Vitamin A (i.u.):	4,014

Green Beans with Shallots, Lemon, and Thyme

Serves
4

1	POUND FRESH GREEN BEANS
2	TABLESPOONS UNSALTED BUTTER
2	SMALL SHALLOTS, MINCED
1	TEASPOON FRESH OR DRIED THYME LEAVES
	SALT AND PEPPER TO TASTE
	JUICE OF HALF A LEMON

NUTRITION

Per Serving

Calories (kcal):	98.3
Total Fat (g):	6.3
Saturated Fat (g):	3.8
Cholesterol (mg):	16
Carbohydrate (g):	10.3
Dietary Fiber (g):	3.9
Protein (g):	2.5
Sodium (mg):	9
Calcium (mg):	50
Iron (mg):	1.4
Vitamin C (mg):	20
Vitamin A (i.u.):	2,580

Wash beans in cold water. Trim ends of beans, either using a sharp knife or snap them off.

Heat a large skillet over medium heat and add butter. Add shallots and sauté for 30 seconds. Add beans, sprinkle with thyme, salt, and pepper, and cover. Cook for 3 to 4 minutes, shaking pan once in a while to prevent them from burning or sticking. Check to see if tender; if not, recover and cook until desired doneness. They should still have snap, but rawness should be cooked out. Add lemon juice, toss, and serve. Note: So simple to make, and people love it!

Mediterranean Tofu Sauté

Serves
4

3	TABLESPOONS OLIVE OIL
1	CUP FIRM TOFU
$\frac{1}{2}$	CUP THINLY SLICED RED ONION
$\frac{1}{2}$	CUP QUARTERED SHIITAKE MUSHROOMS
	OR WHITE MUSHROOMS
2	GARLIC CLOVES, SLIVERED
1	CUP COOKED ARTICHOKE HEARTS (NOT MARINATED)
$1\frac{1}{2}$	CUPS CANNED TOMATOES WITH JUICE
1	TABLESPOON DRAINED CAPERS
$\frac{1}{4}$	CUP OLIVES, OIL-CURED OR KALAMATA
	SALT AND PEPPER

NUTRITION	
Per Serving	
Calories (kcal):	246.3
Total Fat (g):	15.8
Saturated Fat (g):	2.2
Cholesterol (mg):	0
Carbohydrate (g):	20.1
Dietary Fiber (g):	5.7
Protein (g):	11.4
Sodium (mg):	288
Calcium (mg):	159
Iron (mg):	6.8
Vitamin C (mg):	20
Vitamin A (i.u.):	734

Heat 2 tablespoons of olive oil in a large nonstick skillet or wok, and gently stir-fry the tofu until golden brown on all sides. Remove and set aside. Heat the remaining oil and add the onion, mushrooms, and garlic and sauté until slightly softened and colored. Add the artichokes, tomatoes, capers, and olives and cook for 4 minutes. Add salt and pepper to taste. Carefully put the tofu back into the pan, heat through, and serve immediately, with rice and Parmesan cheese.

Tip: Artichoke hearts are available in the frozen food section of most supermarkets.

Note: Most people prefer a "meatier" consistency for the tofu, so either cube, freeze, and then thaw it, or press it with a weight in the fridge for a couple of hours. Either method will remove excess water, and as a result the tofu will have a firmer texture.

Ratatouille

Serves
6

1	LARGE EGGPLANT, CUT INTO 1-INCH CHUNKS
4	LARGE ZUCCHINI, CUT INTO 1-INCH CHUNKS
	SALT
6	TABLESPOONS OLIVE OIL
2	MEDIUM GREEN BELL PEPPERS OR 5 LONG ITALIAN PEPPERS, CORED, SEEDED, AND ROUGHLY CHOPPED
1	LARGE ONION, CUT INTO EIGHTHS
4	LARGE TOMATOES, ROUGHLY CHOPPED
1	BAY LEAF
	FRESHLY GROUND PEPPER
2	GARLIC CLOVES, MINCED
$\frac{3}{4}$	TEASPOON FRESH OR DRIED THYME
2	TABLESPOONS CHOPPED FRESH PARSLEY
1	TEASPOON CHOPPED FRESH BASIL

NUTRITION

Per Serving

Calories (kcal):	183.3
Total Fat (g):	14.2
Saturated Fat (g):	2.0
Cholesterol (mg):	0
Carbohydrate (g):	14.3
Dietary Fiber (g):	4.8
Protein (g):	3.1
Sodium (mg):	105
Calcium (mg):	45
Iron (mg):	1.6
Vitamin C (mg):	50
Vitamin A (i.u.):	1,122

Place the eggplant and zucchini chunks on a towel-lined plate, sprinkle with salt, and weigh them down to drain for at least 30 minutes.

Rinse the eggplant and zucchini in cold water, gently squeeze, then pat dry with paper towels. Heat 4 tablespoons of the olive oil in a large skillet and lightly brown the eggplant and zucchini over medium-high heat. Transfer the vegetables to a large bowl.

Lightly sauté the peppers in the same oil, and then add the eggplant back to the skillet. Top with the onion, tomatoes, bay leaf, and remaining 2 tablespoons oil. Sprinkle with salt and pepper, and simmer uncovered for 20 minutes, stirring frequently. Add the garlic and thyme, and cook 20 more minutes. Garnish with the parsley and basil. Remove bay leaf and serve hot or cold.

Note: Usually tastes even better the second day, so make in advance, or make extra!

Roasted Garlic Mashed Potatoes

Serves
4

4	HEADS OF GARLIC
1	TABLESPOON OLIVE OIL
6	LARGE POTATOES, PEELED AND CUT INTO QUARTERS
1	TEASPOON SALT
1	CUP WHOLE MILK
2	TABLESPOONS UNSALTED BUTTER
	SALT AND PEPPER TO TASTE

NUTRITION

Per Serving

Calories (kcal):	254.7
Total Fat (g):	11.3
Saturated Fat (g):	5.3
Cholesterol (mg):	24
Carbohydrate (g):	34.1
Dietary Fiber (g):	2.8
Protein (g):	5.7
Sodium (mg):	631
Calcium (mg):	92
Iron (mg):	1.4
Vitamin C (mg):	35
Vitamin A (i.u.):	291

Preheat oven to 400°F. Slice garlic heads in half, and place halves on foil. Drizzle with olive oil, wrap up, and bake about 20 minutes, until heads are soft and caramelized. This can be done in advance, and the garlic refrigerated.

Place potato chunks in a large pot of cold water, add the salt, bring to a boil, and cook just until potatoes are tender. *Do not* overcook!

Heat milk and butter together in a saucepan, but do not boil. When potatoes are cooked, drain and return to the pot. Cook for a moment over medium heat to evaporate any water. Remove pot from heat, begin to mash, then add hot milk and butter mixture, garlic, and salt and pepper to taste. Mash to desired smoothness.

Note: To add more vitamins and minerals—not to mention color and texture!—leave the potatoes unpeeled, but wash them well.

Gingered Carrots

Serves
6

12	MEDIUM CARROTS, PEELED AND JULIENNED
4	TABLESPOONS UNSALTED BUTTER
$\frac{1}{4}$	CUP LIGHT BROWN SUGAR
$1\frac{1}{2}$	TEASPOONS GROUND OR GRATED FRESH GINGER
	SALT

NUTRITION

Per Serving

Calories (kcal):	156.3
Total Fat (g):	8.4
Saturated Fat (g):	5.1
Cholesterol (mg):	22
Carbohydrate (g):	20.5
Dietary Fiber (g):	4.3
Protein (g):	1.6
Sodium (mg):	54
Calcium (mg):	46
Iron (mg):	0.9
Vitamin C (mg):	13
Vitamin A (i.u.):	40,812

Place carrots in a medium pot of cold water and bring to a boil. Drain carrots as soon as tender, maybe 2 minutes.

In a medium sauté pan, melt butter and add brown sugar, ginger, and a pinch of salt. Cook over low heat until well combined and soft.

Add carrots and cook over low heat for 2 minutes so that all flavors combine. Serve immediately.

Note: Makes even a carrot hater smile.

Give It Away!

I have to admit something: I love junk. Junk clothes, junk toys, junk appliances. Pretty much junk anything. And I know I'm not alone in my passion for acquiring useless items. On any given Sunday, on a walk through a flea market, you will be engulfed in a veritable "red-tag" sea of bargain hunters. Antique stores, second-hand novelty shops, and thrift

stores have found their way into every nook and cranny of America. Some people focus their energies on the acquisition of specific things. For these obsessives, the thought of not owning every single *Star Trek* whiskey decanter can cause sleeplessness and a profound sense of inadequacy. My affliction may be worse because I'm not even junk specific. I'll buy anything, any time, for any reason. Or, worse, for no reason. I've never actually found a use for my avocado press, yet I own one nonetheless. My Bobby Goldsboro album sits alone at the very far end of my album rack, yet it is comforting to know that if a houseguest should develop a sudden hankering to listen to "Honey," I've got it. My house has become haunted by these items. If you listen closely, when the sun sinks low and the full moon slowly rises in the night sky, you can hear their baleful wail emanating from my closet: "Use us, let us out, use us . . . I'm still a bargain at $19.95, *use us, use us, use us.*"

Eventually, the trinkets take control of my home and I am forced to exorcize the demons by sacrificing them to the charity gods. Or, if I had the guts, I could have a yard sale. Although some view the yard sale as a cute thing to do on a weekend to make a few extra bucks, I think of a yard sale as an invasive procedure whereby neighbors come to pick through your personal belongings and formulate psychological profiles of you based on your taste in dishes. They look down at things, bewilderment written all over their faces, and I am forced to admit, "Yes, Mrs. Johnson, I thought I could achieve the same abdominal splendor as Ms. Charlene Tilton with my purchase of the

Abdominizer. but now I'm willing to let you have it for $3.50." I just don't know if I have the courage to run my own shopping Believe It Or Not freak show.

I prefer the anonymity of the local charity bin. Nobody knows who put what in there, and volunteers can find people in need of most of these items. Goodwill, the Salvation Army, and the Police Athletic League are just some of the charities with donation bins. They are usually located in shopping center parking lots to remind us that if you just bought some more crap, you must have some extra crap at home for somebody in need.

Recently, while packing to move, I discovered that my wardrobe was in need of serious downsizing, so in an effort to keep my apparel at least within the present decade, I placed my old garments in a plastic bag and set off for the nearest Goodwill bin. I felt pretty good about myself. I'm not saying I was John the Baptist,

but I did have a sense that I was doing something benevolent for someone else. And I felt strongly about the people at Goodwill and their quest to provide the unfortunate among us with adequate clothing. However, as I approached the bin, I noticed a warning posted on the side that read:

"Removal of items from this bin is a crime and you will be prosecuted." They had rules! Rules? Correct me if I'm wrong, but if a guy is desperate enough to crawl into this bin at three in the morning to pull out a pair of plaid pants and a Fonzie T-shirt, shouldn't we let him have it?

I've learned that men are much worse than women when it comes to collecting junk. Not that women don't collect equal amounts. It's just that, occasionally, they hit on something that's aesthetically pleasing while a man is more apt to come home with an AC-DC mirror tucked under his arm. I think we like to buy these things because it's reassuring to know that, in the event the marriage should fail and we are forced into divorce court, we will at least be left with a couple of items. No woman will ever fight for 50 percent of the Old Milwaukee clock. Sure, she may get the kids, the house, and the car, but the plastic trinkets, knickknacks, and promotional give-aways are yours. In the end you can gather your bric-a-brac and put on those boxer shorts she hated as you reenact the movie *The Jerk* for all the neighborhood to see. Don't worry; you'll have your Old Milwaukee clock, along with enough dignity to fit into your Atlantic City shot glass.

Roasted Vegetables

Serves
4

2	LARGE POTATOES, PEELED AND COARSELY CHOPPED
2	LARGE BEETS, PEELED AND COARSELY CHOPPED
1	LARGE ONION, COARSELY CHOPPED
2	LARGE CARROTS, PEELED AND COARSELY CHOPPED
2	TABLESPOONS EXTRA-VIRGIN OLIVE OIL
1	TEASPOON CHOPPED FRESH ROSEMARY LEAVES
	SALT AND PEPPER

N U T R I T I O N

Per Serving

Calories (kcal):	145.2
Total Fat (g):	7.0
Saturated Fat (g):	1.0
Cholesterol (mg):	0
Carbohydrate (g):	19.4
Dietary Fiber (g):	3.6
Protein (g):	2.5
Sodium (mg):	185
Calcium (mg):	37
Iron (mg):	1.0
Vitamin C (mg):	18
Vitamin A (i.u.):	10,142

Heat oven to 425°F. In a roasting pan, place chopped vegetables and drizzle with oil and rosemary. Toss to coat evenly. Place pan in oven and roast for 40 minutes, or until vegetables are cooked through and tender. Sprinkle with salt and pepper and serve.

Tip: Wear plastic gloves to peel the beets.
Note: Other vegetables to try roasting are sweet potatoes, parsnips, celery, fennel, leeks, turnips, shallots, and squash. Try alone or in combinations.

Sautéed Broccoli Rabe

Serves
4

2	BUNCHES BROCCOLI RABE
4	TABLESPOONS EXTRA-VIRGIN OLIVE OIL
4	GARLIC CLOVES, MINCED
$\frac{1}{2}$	CUP WATER
	SALT AND PEPPER

NUTRITION	
Per Serving	
Calories (kcal):	136.1
Total Fat (g):	13.7
Saturated Fat (g):	1.9
Cholesterol (mg):	0
Carbohydrate (g):	3.3
Dietary Fiber (g):	1.4
Protein (g):	1.5
Sodium (mg):	13
Calcium (mg):	27
Iron (mg):	0.5
Vitamin C (mg):	42
Vitamin A (i.u.):	678

Rinse broccoli well, and discard tough stems and leaves. Chop coarsely.

Heat oil in a large, heavy skillet that has a lid, add garlic, and sauté for 30 seconds. Add broccoli and sauté for 3 minutes. Add water, cover, and cook for 4 minutes, or until all water has evaporated. Add salt and pepper to taste. Serve immediately.

Note: Since broccoli rabe is available year-round, it makes a great staple dish.

Summer Vegetable Sauté

Serves
4

$\frac{1}{2}$	CUP FRESH CILANTRO LEAVES
3	TABLESPOONS VEGETABLE OIL
$\frac{1}{4}$	POUND FRESH GREEN BEANS
$1\frac{1}{2}$	TABLESPOONS UNSALTED BUTTER
1	MEDIUM ZUCCHINI, CUT INTO $\frac{1}{2}$-INCH DICE
1	MEDIUM YELLOW SQUASH, CUT INTO $\frac{1}{2}$-INCH DICE
3	EARS CORN, KERNELS CUT OFF
1	SCALLION, FINELY CHOPPED
	SALT AND PEPPER
2	TEASPOONS FRESH LIME JUICE

N U T R I T I O N

Per Serving

Calories (kcal):	211.7
Total Fat (g):	15.7
Saturated Fat (g):	4.4
Cholesterol (mg):	12
Carbohydrate (g):	17.9
Dietary Fiber (g):	4.1
Protein (g):	4.1
Sodium (mg):	21
Calcium (mg):	73
Iron (mg):	2.6
Vitamin C (mg):	38
Vitamin A (i.u.):	718

Bring a medium pot of salted water to a boil. Put 6 tablespoons of cilantro leaves into a small sieve and immerse it in the boiling water for 5 seconds. Drop into cold water and squeeze dry. Leave the water boiling. Combine the blanched cilantro with the oil in a mini processor or grind with a mortar and pestle. Shred the remaining cilantro.

Toss the beans into the boiling water, and cook just till the raw edge is off, about 3 minutes. Drop into cold water and cut into $\frac{1}{2}$-inch pieces.

Melt the butter in a large sauté pan and add the zucchini and squash. Sauté over high heat for 2 minutes, until softened, then add the corn, scallion, and salt and pepper to taste, and sauté for 3 more minutes. Add the beans, and toss to heat the beans 1 more minute.

Stir the lime juice and remaining shredded cilantro into the vegetables, and drizzle the cilantro oil around the plate's edge. Serve hot or at room temperature.

Note: You can substitute oil for butter for sautéing, if you wish.

Tofu Cacciatore

Serves
6

2	POUNDS FIRM TOFU, CUT INTO BITE-SIZE PIECES
1	LEMON, JUICED
1	CUP ALL-PURPOSE FLOUR
	SALT AND PEPPER
6	TABLESPOONS OLIVE OIL
1	MEDIUM ONION, CHOPPED
6	GARLIC CLOVES, CRUSHED
1	LARGE RED BELL PEPPER, CORED, SEEDED, AND CUT INTO BITE-SIZE PIECES
1	POUND MUSHROOMS, HALVED
$\frac{1}{4}$	CUP RED OR WHITE WINE
1	2-POUND CAN TOMATOES, COARSELY CHOPPED
1	TABLESPOON DRIED OREGANO
$\frac{1}{4}$	CUP FRESH ITALIAN FLAT-LEAF PARSLEY
1	CUP FRESHLY GRATED ROMANO CHEESE

Place tofu cubes in a large bowl and toss with lemon juice. In a separate bowl, season flour with a little salt and pepper. Toss tofu in the flour to coat, a couple of pieces at a time, and set aside.

Heat a large skillet over medium-high heat and add 2 to 4 tablespoons of oil, as needed, to heat. Carefully place tofu in skillet, as much as will fit on bottom of pan, but not crowded. Cook till golden and flip over to cook other side. Continue flipping until all sides are browned and remove to a platter. This will probably take 3 batches.

After all tofu is cooked, in the same pan heat remaining 2 tablespoons of oil, add onion and garlic, and sauté for 4 minutes or until very soft. Add red pepper and cook for 4 more minutes. Add mushrooms, wine, tomatoes, herbs, and a pinch of salt and pepper. Raise heat to high to burn off alcohol, then lower to a simmer, cover pan, and cook for $\frac{1}{2}$ hour.

Add tofu cubes, replace cover, and simmer for 10 minutes. Serve over grain of your choice and sprinkle with cheese.

Note: This dish is an excellent alternative to the traditional chicken cacciatore. You can easily substitute diced chicken breast for the tofu and serve over pasta (orzo works well) or rice.

NUTRITION

Per Serving

Calories (kcal):	540.1
Total Fat (g):	32.6
Saturated Fat (g):	7.0
Cholesterol (mg):	19
Carbohydrate (g):	33.8
Dietary Fiber (g):	5.7
Protein (g):	34.8
Sodium (mg):	409
Calcium (mg):	571
Iron (mg):	19.0
Vitamin C (mg):	52
Vitamin A (i.u.):	1,490

1

7

S E A F O O D

- ✪ Baked Bass with Fennel
- ✪ Basil-Scallop Linguine
- ✪ Broiled Swordfish in a Ginger Marinade
- ✪ Cioppino
- ✪ A Bit off the Top
- ✪ Coriander Shrimp in Coconut Milk
- ✪ Poached Salmon with Ginger and Cilantro
- ✪ Sautéed Lemon Shrimp with Orzo
- ✪ Seared Sesame Tuna
- ✪ The Bus
- ✪ Spanish Shrimp in Garlic Sauce
- ✪ Steamed Salmon Steaks, Thai Style
- ✪ Trout with Lemon and Capers
- ✪ Whole Baked Bass with Fresh Thyme

Baked Bass with Fennel

Serves
4

1	MEDIUM FENNEL BULB, WITH LEAVES
$\frac{1}{4}$	CUP EXTRA-VIRGIN OLIVE OIL
3	GARLIC CLOVES, MINCED
	SALT AND PEPPER
$\frac{1}{4}$	CUP CHOPPED FRESH ITALIAN FLAT-LEAF PARSLEY
1	3-POUND WHOLE STRIPED BASS, HEAD AND TAIL ON, BACKBONE REMOVED
$\frac{1}{4}$	CUP FRESH LEMON JUICE
$\frac{1}{2}$	CUP DRY WHITE WINE OR VERMOUTH

NUTRITION	
Per Serving	
Calories (kcal):	505.4
Total Fat (g):	21.7
Saturated Fat (g):	3.5
Cholesterol (mg):	272
Carbohydrate (g):	8.5
Dietary Fiber (g):	0.5
Protein (g):	62.2
Sodium (mg):	284
Calcium (mg):	143
Iron (mg):	7.1
Vitamin C (mg):	19
Vitamin A (i.u.):	1,263

Preheat oven to 425°F.

Cut the fennel bulb into thin slices, reserving the feathery leaves. Heat oil in a large skillet and sauté fennel and half the garlic until tender but not browned, about 10 minutes. Using a slotted spoon, transfer cooked fennel to a bowl and add salt and pepper to taste and parsley. Keep the oil. Place the bass in a shallow oiled baking dish, open up the fish and put the cooked fennel mixture down the middle. Sprinkle with lemon juice and a few of the fennel leaves, and close the fish. Rub the top outside of the fish with the remaining garlic and some salt and pepper. Pour the fennel oil on top, along with the wine and the remaining fennel leaves. Place in middle of oven and bake for 10 minutes per inch of thickness of fish (about 20 minutes). Baste frequently with pan juices. Serve right out of pan, or transfer to a serving platter.

Tip: I prefer using a whole fish; however, 2 large fillets, placed on top of each other, work just as well.

Note: Very upscale taste with a minimum of effort! Try it with snapper, trout—just about any white fish will do.

Basil-Scallop Linguine

Serves
6

1	TABLESPOON OLIVE OIL
2	GARLIC CLOVES, MINCED
2	SHALLOTS, MINCED
2	TABLESPOONS MINCED FRESH BASIL LEAVES
2	TABLESPOONS MINCED FRESH ITALIAN FLAT-LEAF PARSLEY, PLUS ADDITIONAL FOR GARNISH
	SALT
$\frac{1}{4}$	TEASPOON CRUSHED RED PEPPER FLAKES
$\frac{1}{8}$	TEASPOON PEPPER
1	16-OUNCE CAN TOMATOES
$\frac{1}{2}$	CUP DRY WHITE WINE
2	TABLESPOONS TOMATO PASTE
1	POUND PACKAGE LINGUINE OR SPAGHETTI
1	TABLESPOON VEGETABLE OIL
1	POUND SEA SCALLOPS
1	10-OUNCE PACKAGE FROZEN ARTICHOKES, THAWED AND DRAINED
2	TABLESPOONS PINE NUTS

In a medium saucepan over medium heat, heat olive oil. Add garlic and shallots and cook, stirring constantly with a wooden spoon, until they are tender but not browned. Remove from heat.

Add basil, parsley, 1 teaspoon salt, red pepper flakes, black pepper, tomatoes, wine, and tomato paste to saucepan. Return to heat and bring to a boil, stirring to break up large pieces of tomatoes. Cover, reduce heat, and simmer for 20 minutes.

Cook linguine with 2 teaspoons of salt and vegetable oil in a large pot of boiling water.

While pasta cooks, place scallops in a colander and rinse in cold water. Drain thoroughly and cut each in half crosswise. Add scallops and artichokes to pan and cook 5 minutes or until scallops are tender and artichokes are hot. Set aside.

Place pine nuts in a small skillet over moderately high heat and toast in the pan—do not add oil. Set aside.

Drain pasta and place on a large serving platter or plates. Spoon tomato mixture on top and toss gently. Sprinkle with pine nuts and more parsley.

Note: A very light Italian white, like Gavi or Pino Grigio, goes well with this.

NUTRITION	
Per Serving	
Calories (kcal):	446.5
Total Fat (g):	8.3
Saturated Fat (g):	1.1
Cholesterol (mg):	25
Carbohydrate (g):	65.2
Dietary Fiber (g):	3.6
Protein (g):	24.7
Sodium (mg):	149
Calcium (mg):	52
Iron (mg):	206
Vitamin C (mg):	13
Vitamin A (i.u.):	1,263

Broiled Swordfish in a Ginger Marinade

Serves
4

4	SWORDFISH STEAKS, ABOUT 6 OUNCES EACH
1	LARGE LEMON, JUICED
2	TABLESPOONS GRATED FRESH GINGER
2	TABLESPOONS ASIAN ROASTED SESAME OIL
3	TABLESPOONS SOY SAUCE
1	GARLIC CLOVE, MINCED

NUTRITION	
Per Serving	
Calories (kcal):	278.8
Total Fat (g):	13.7
Saturated Fat (g):	2.9
Cholesterol (mg):	66
Carbohydrate (g):	4.2
Dietary Fiber (g):	0.1
Protein (g):	34.6
Sodium (mg):	776
Calcium (mg):	27
Iron (mg):	1.8
Vitamin C (mg):	23
Vitamin A (i.u.):	211

In a pan large enough to hold all the fish steaks, mix the remaining ingredients and add fish. Cover well, refrigerate, and turn fish a couple of times. Let marinate at least 2 hours.

Heat broiler and place fish on a broiling pan. Cook 3 minutes, then flip fish over and cook 2 minutes. The fish should be cooked through, but be very moist. *Do not* overcook fish!

Note: One of the simplest ways to cook fish. It works great with salmon and snapper, too. A marinating shortcut is to put everything in a resealable bag and turn the bag to coat.

Cioppino

Serves
6

$\frac{1}{2}$	CUP OLIVE OIL
1	LARGE ONION, CHOPPED
3	GARLIC CLOVES, CHOPPED
1	MEDIUM GREEN BELL PEPPER, CORED, SEEDED, AND CHOPPED
1	28-OUNCE CAN TOMATOES, CHOPPED
1	28-OUNCE CAN TOMATO PUREE
2	CUPS RED WINE
$\frac{1}{2}$	CUP CHOPPED FRESH ITALIAN FLAT-LEAF PARSLEY
	CAYENNE PEPPER
	SALT AND PEPPER
1	POUND MONKFISH OR OTHER FIRM FISH FILLETS
3	POUNDS MUSSELS, CLEANED AND DEBEARDED
1	POUND FRESH SHRIMP, PEELED AND DEVEINED

NUTRITION	
Per Serving	
Calories (kcal):	598.7
Total Fat (g):	25.3
Saturated Fat (g):	3.8
Cholesterol (mg):	211
Carbohydrate (g):	20.4
Dietary Fiber (g):	2.3
Protein (g):	58.4
Sodium (mg):	931
Calcium (mg):	212
Iron (mg):	17.0
Vitamin C (mg):	58
Vitamin A (i.u.):	2,469

Heat the olive oil in a large soup pot and sauté onion, garlic, and bell pepper for 2 minutes until softened. Add tomatoes, tomato puree, wine, parsley, a pinch of cayenne, and salt and pepper to taste, then simmer for 15 minutes to cook out some of the alcohol.

While sauce is simmering, cut the fish into 2-inch chunks. Place the fish and mussels into the simmering liquid, and simmer for 3 minutes. Add the shrimp and cook for 4 more minutes. Check seasoning: it should be a little spicy. Serve with a big bowl of Italian bread.

A Bit off the Top

Most of us have an obsession with our hair. Hairstyling is a source of endless worry for many individuals. It is the one act of grooming that continually perplexes us. I have three different hairstyles in this book alone. By the way, whichever one you like the best is the one I'm sticking with—the rest are just a phase. We get a handle on everything else very early in life. For instance, by the age of seven we have mastered the acts of teeth brushing, ear cleaning, and body washing.

But unlike a hairstyle, your method of flossing is rarely modified to suit the latest fashion trend. You'll never hear this report on *Entertainment Tonight*: "George Clooney has just switched to a waxed mint floss by Versace. When asked why the sudden switch, George simply said, 'I like to eat a lot of corn. Both on the cob and popped, and my old Donna Karan unwaxed white . . . just let me down.' "

The upkeep of our hair is so terrifying because it is totally out of our control. We put the most identifying aspect of our heads in the hands of some smock wearers with licenses, a pair of scissors, and vats of blue mystery fluid. Every one of us accepts the fact that when we get our hair cut, it will not be right for at least two weeks. The following two weeks is hair bliss, but by the tail end of week five, the honeymoon begins to end. The final two weeks become a steady ritual of blow drying, gelling, and wearing a hat. In the end we reluctantly return to the barber's chair with a false expectation of hope and we leave looking like a sickly hedgehog.

We must learn to admit that we are powerless over our hair. This quest for power over our own locks has made the Flow-Bee an infomercial king. People are fascinated by the idea that the perfect haircut may come from a device that is a mutated marriage between a Shop Vac and a pool hose, with a Garden-Weasel on the end of it. In all of us lies a little Vidal Sassoon waiting to open shop, but with this power comes responsibility. The idea of being the only Floyd in your personal Mayberry weighs heavy on the mind. No longer are you able to blame the putz at Supercuts when your friends ask, "Hey, who gave you the hatchet job, Helmet Head?"

I know this all too well because I once paid the greatest price for a free haircut. I was eight years old and had the week off from school. All week long my mother tried to get me into a barber's chair. I finally decided on Sunday that I was ready for my haircut, to which my mom replied, "No way! You had your chance." Figuring "How hard could it be?" I grabbed my mom's cosmetic mirror and a pair of cuticle scissors. Yes, that's right—those weird, curved, miniature scissors. My uncle Tom was the first to spot me as I removed a divot of hair from the area known as the bangs.

The next day at school was officially dubbed "Taunt and Ridicule Sean Monday." An impromptu assembly was held, and I was brought out on the stage by the school principal, who explained the do's and don'ts of personal grooming. After school it was off to the mall to see if Paulie the barber could work some magic, but Paulie worked for Mario's barber shop, not Siegfried and Roy, so there wasn't much that he could do. I didn't speak much Italian and he didn't speak any English, but his bucket of lollipops told me he cared. A man who sat in the corner of the barber shop served as an interpreter between Paulie and my mom. As my mother stood sobbing, the interpreter explained to her that I would look like a moron only for the next two weeks. My mom perked up and quipped, "That's great. I thought it would be a month."

Little did she know that, self-inflicted bad haircut or no self-inflicted bad haircut, puberty would set in and I would look like a moron until I was twenty.

Coriander Shrimp in Coconut Milk

Serves
4

1	TABLESPOON OLIVE OIL
2	GARLIC CLOVES, MINCED
1	MEDIUM JALAPEÑO PEPPER, SEEDED AND MINCED
1	CUP WHITE WINE
1½	CUPS UNSWEETENED COCONUT MILK
1	TABLESPOON MINCED FRESH GINGER
2	TEASPOONS KOSHER SALT
	FRESHLY GROUND PEPPER
1	POUND LARGE SHRIMP, PEELED AND DEVEINED
1	TEASPOON LEMON ZEST, GRATED
1	TABLESPOON FRESH LEMON JUICE
¼	CUP FRESH CILANTRO LEAVES, CHOPPED

NUTRITION	
Per Serving with Rice	
Calories (kcal):	405.4
Total Fat (g):	26.8
Saturated Fat (g):	19.9
Cholesterol (mg):	173
Carbohydrate (g):	8.6
Dietary Fiber (g):	2.3
Protein (g):	25.5
Sodium (mg):	1,126
Calcium (mg):	86
Iron (mg):	4.6
Vitamin C (mg):	35
Vitamin A (i.u.):	321

Heat a large skillet over medium-high heat and add oil, garlic, and jalapeño, and sauté for 15 seconds. Add wine, raise the heat to high, and simmer until the liquid is reduced to one fourth its original amount.

Lower heat to medium and stir in coconut milk, ginger, and salt and pepper to taste. Simmer slowly for 2 minutes, then lower the heat to barely simmering. Add the shrimp and cook until just cooked through, about 4 minutes.

Stir in the lemon zest, lemon juice, and cilantro and serve immediately over white rice.

Poached Salmon with Ginger and Cilantro

Serves
2

2	6-OUNCE SALMON FILLETS OR STEAKS
4	TABLESPOONS COARSELY CHOPPED FRESH CILANTRO
1	1-INCH PIECE FRESH GINGER, GRATED
2	GARLIC CLOVES, MINCED
$\frac{1}{4}$	CUP DRY WHITE WINE, OR WATER WITH LEMON
2	TABLESPOONS WATER

In a small, heavy-bottomed pan, place salmon, skin side down.
Top with half of the cilantro, the ginger, garlic, wine, and water.
Cover and simmer, allowing 8 minutes per inch of thickness, until
cooked through.
Serve the salmon with pan juices and remaining fresh cilantro.
Note: So fast, so easy, such a great way to cook salmon!

NUTRITION	
Per Serving	
Calories (kcal):	233.9
Total Fat (g):	6.1
Saturated Fat (g):	1.0
Cholesterol (mg):	88
Carbohydrate (g):	3.6
Dietary Fiber (g):	0.5
Protein (g):	35.0
Sodium (mg):	124
Calcium (mg):	76
Iron (mg):	3.0
Vitamin C (mg):	22
Vitamin A (i.u.):	201

Sautéed Lemon Shrimp with Orzo

Serves
4

1	CUP UNCOOKED ORZO
2	TABLESPOONS PLUS **1** TEASPOON OLIVE OIL
	SALT AND PEPPER
2	GARLIC CLOVES, MINCED
20	LARGE FRESH SHRIMP, PEELED AND DEVEINED, TAILS ON
$\frac{1}{4}$	CUP FRESH ITALIAN FLAT-LEAF PARSLEY, FINELY CHOPPED
1	CUP DRY WHITE WINE
1	LEMON, ZESTED AND JUICED
3	TABLESPOONS UNSALTED BUTTER
1	TABLESPOON CAPERS, RINSED AND DRAINED

NUTRITION

Per Serving

Calories (kcal):	355.4
Total Fat (g):	18.7
Saturated Fat (g):	7.0
Cholesterol (mg):	123
Carbohydrate (g):	22.1
Dietary Fiber (g):	0.9
Protein (g):	17.3
Sodium (mg):	139
Calcium (mg):	120
Iron (mg):	6.5
Vitamin C (mg):	27
Vitamin A (i.u.):	1,344

Bring a medium pot of salted water to a boil, add orzo, and cook until al dente. Drain and toss with 1 teaspoon of olive oil and salt and pepper to taste.

While orzo is cooking, heat remaining 2 tablespoons olive oil in a large sauté pan, add garlic, and cook over low heat for 1 minute. Add shrimp, a pinch of salt and pepper, and 2 tablespoons of parsley and cook for 3 to 4 minutes, or until shrimp are opaque. Remove from pan and keep warm.

Bring sauté pan to high heat, add wine and lemon juice, and boil for 1 minute, or until liquid is reduced by half. Remove from heat, add remaining parsley, stir in butter, zest, and capers, and check for seasonings. Put shrimp back into sauce, and serve on a bed of orzo.

Seared Sesame Tuna

Serves
2

2	6-OUNCE YELLOWFIN TUNA STEAKS
2	TABLESPOONS ASIAN ROASTED SESAME OIL
2	TEASPOONS SOY SAUCE
4	TABLESPOONS SESAME SEEDS, TOASTED
1	TABLESPOON KOSHER SALT
	SPRIGS OF CILANTRO FOR GARNISH

NUTRITION	
Per Serving	
Calories (kcal):	417.0
Total Fat (g):	25.5
Saturated Fat (g):	3.8
Cholesterol (mg):	77
Carbohydrate (g):	2.2
Dietary Fiber (g):	0.0
Protein (g):	45.0
Sodium (mg):	3,167
Calcium (mg):	53
Iron (mg):	2.8
Vitamin C (mg):	2
Vitamin A (i.u.):	113

Rub tuna steaks with sesame oil and soy sauce, cover, and return them to the refrigerator for 30 minutes.

Pour sesame seeds onto a plate and pat tuna steaks onto seeds to coat evenly. Heat an iron skillet (or other heavy-bottomed pan) to medium-high, add the salt, and place sesame crusted tuna steaks on top of salt. Cook for 2 minutes per side, being careful not to burn the sesame seeds.

Serve immediately, garnished with cilantro sprigs, and serve with sautéed snow peas or asparagus.

Note: A really easy, fast dish that always impresses! Also great to do as an appetizer—just slice cooked tuna thinly and serve on toast points with an avocado slice.

The Bus

I don't like buses. I know we need mass transit to cut down on pollution and save energy, but we also need peace in our daily lives. And, unfortunately, traveling by bus provides all the serenity of a leisurely stroll through the Golan Heights. Let's start with the drivers, or as I like to call them, Satan's little chauffeurs. I've never met one who wasn't evil. I realize that trying to maneuver a forty-seat vehicle through Manhattan's busy streets is a strenuous, nerve-racking experience, but, hey, we all got it rough. So how about saving that disinterested, icy cold stare for your next tax audit? I am not the reason you took this thankless municipal job, so I shouldn't be the focus of your wrath. I'm sorry if I had to reach into my pocket for an extra nickel, but is that any reason to go from zero to hyperspeed smiling malevolently as I am knocked four rows back and land on some elderly woman's hip? Also, why is it that when you show a bus driver your transfer and ask, "Is this transfer still valid?" he looks at you as though you had just asked, "Excuse me, is this my hand?" Maybe the answer is obvious to a seasoned driver, but my college didn't offer a major in bus management.

Have you ever tried to decipher a bus schedule? I could read a copy of *War and Peace* written backward and in Sanskrit more effortlessly. Likewise, bus drivers act as though they are annoyed by having to stop and pick up passengers. I could be wrong about this, but I think that's why they were hired. I don't think they were told at orientation, "Okay, I just want you to drive from Houston Street up to 196th Street and then turn around." Picking up passengers and taking them to their appointed destinations is your job, so try to be polite! Okay? You are a *civil* servant. You are there to serve the needs of the citizens. Remember that, you horn-headed fare takers!

New York City bus drivers are not the only ones to blame. I've been emotionally abused on charter buses, school buses, and buses that took me from the airport to my rental car. It just seems to go with the territory. I guess maybe part of my bus problem is that I've taken buses only when I had to go someplace miserable, such as school, on a lousy field trip, to a bad comedy gig, to Atlantic City etc., etc. I hate the bus so much, I wrote a poem.

TAKE THE BUS

TAKE THE BUS
IT'S MASS-IRRITATION-TRANSPORTATION
TO YOUR DESTINATION

TANGLED IN AN AUTOMOTIVE SEA
THAT AROMA IN THE AIR I AM SURE IT'S PEE
FELLOW TRAVELER NEXT TO ME
IS HE DEAD OR RESTING?
THE WOMAN TO MY LEFT
HER GUM CHEWING IS QUITE TESTING

NOT A BLOCK GOES BY THAT'S NOT A STOP
PICK UP, LET OFF, TRAFFIC LIGHT
SLOW DOWN AND STOP IT GOES ON ALL NIGHT
I THINK TO MYSELF MAN I COULD HAVE
DRAGGED A DEAD COW CROSS TOWN FASTER
I DON'T HAVE CHANGE!
I NEED A TRANSFER!

THE BUS GETS YOU NOWHERE VERY QUICK
THE TAXI OR TRAIN IS WHERE I'LL STICK
HOURGLASS TELLS ME I'M OUT OF HERE
INTO A YELLOW CHEVY,
LET THE MAN WITH THE METER STEER

THIS BUCK'S FOR YOU, WITHOUT A MINUTE TO SPARE
JUST HOW YOU GOT THERE, THE MAN DOESN'T CARE.

All right, I'm no Robert Frost, but then I'd like to see him try to
make baked apples funny.

Spanish Shrimp in Garlic Sauce

Serves
2

$\frac{1}{4}$	CUP OLIVE OIL
5	LARGE GARLIC CLOVES, FINELY CHOPPED
1	BAY LEAF
1	SMALL HOT DRIED CHILE PEPPER, SEEDED AND CRUMBLED
$\frac{3}{4}$	POUND MEDIUM SHRIMP
1	TEASPOON PAPRIKA
$\frac{1}{2}$	LEMON, JUICED
	SALT AND PEPPER
	CHOPPED FRESH PARSLEY

NUTRITION

Per Serving
Calories (kcal): 224.9
Total Fat (g): 15.2
Saturated Fat (g): 2.1
Cholesterol (mg): 129
Carbohydrate (g): 5.9
Dietary Fiber (g): 0.3
Protein (g): 18.1
Sodium (mg): 129
Calcium (mg): 73
Iron (mg): 2.7
Vitamin C (mg): 32
Vitamin A (i.u.): 847

In an 8-inch sauté pan, over moderate heat, heat the oil till hot but not smoking. Stir in the garlic, bay leaf, and chile pepper and cook, stirring, until the garlic just begins to turn gold. Immediately add the shrimp, paprika, lemon juice, and salt and pepper to taste, and cook, stirring constantly, until the shrimp is just cooked through, being careful not to overcook. Remove bay leaf. Sprinkle with chopped parsley and transfer to a serving dish. Serve immediately with good crusty bread.

Note: If you don't mind getting your hands dirty, leave the shells on—it adds great flavor. Otherwise, remove the shells before cooking for a neater presentation.

Steamed Salmon Steaks, Thai Style

Serves
4

1	TABLESPOON VEGETABLE OR CANOLA OIL
2	SHALLOTS, SLICED THINLY
1	2-INCH PIECE FRESH GINGER, JULIENNED
4	GARLIC CLOVES, SLIVERED
$\frac{1}{4}$	CUP LIGHT BROWN SUGAR
$\frac{1}{4}$	CUP THAI FISH SAUCE (*NAM PLA*)
4	SALMON STEAKS, ABOUT 6 OUNCES EACH
	FRESH CILANTRO LEAVES

NUTRITION	
Per Serving	
Calories (kcal):	381.0
Total Fat (g):	11.9
Saturated Fat (g):	1.4
Cholesterol (mg):	88
Carbohydrate (g):	28.9
Dietary Fiber (g):	0.4
Protein (g):	38.9
Sodium (mg):	128
Calcium (mg):	85
Iron (mg):	3.0
Vitamin C (mg):	2
Vitamin A (i.u.):	1,798

In a medium skillet, heat the oil until very hot but not smoking, and add the shallots, ginger, and garlic. Cook for 1 minute, until very aromatic but not browned. Add the brown sugar and fish sauce and cook for 5 minutes.

Spread half of the sauce on a lightly oiled plate that will fit into a steamer, and place the steaks on top of the sauce. Pour the other half of the sauce on top of the steaks, and let marinate for 20 minutes.

Fill steamer with enough water to sit below, but not touch, the steamer basket, and bring to a high simmer. Place the plate in the basket, cover, and steam for approximately 10 minutes, or until the meat is opaque.

Carefully remove the steaks with a spatula to a serving plate, and spoon any remaining sauce over steaks. Garnish with cilantro leaves. Serve with cold beer.

Note: This a very delicious low-calorie way to serve salmon—or just about any fish. Serve with fluffy rice and a crisp green vegetable.

Trout with Lemon and Capers

Serves
2

	OIL FOR SAUTÉING
2	RAINBOW TROUT FILLETS, PIN BONES REMOVED
	SALT AND PEPPER
	FLOUR FOR DREDGING
3	TABLESPOONS UNSALTED BUTTER, CUT INTO SMALL CUBES
2	LEMONS, HALVED AND JUICED
1	TEASPOON CAPERS, RINSED AND DRAINED
1	TEASPOON CHOPPED FRESH PARSLEY

NUTRITION

Per Serving
Calories (kcal): ----------361.7
Total Fat (g): --------------22.9
Saturated Fat (g): ---------11.8
Cholesterol (mg): ---------140
Carbohydrate (g): ---------11.6
Dietary Fiber (g): ---------0.0
Protein (g): ---------------34.1
Sodium (mg): -------------239
Calcium (mg): -----------178
Iron (mg): ----------------1.9
Vitamin C (mg): ----------88
Vitamin A (i.u.): ----------806

Heat oil in a large sauté pan. Season the fish with salt and pepper and dredge in the flour, shaking off any excess flour. Place the trout flesh side down in the pan and cook for 2 minutes. Flip and cook for 2 more minutes. Remove the fish from the pan and place on a plate and keep warm in the oven.

Add the butter to the same pan—it will begin to brown and foam. Add the lemon juice and shake the pan to incorporate the juices. Remove from the heat, and add the capers and parsley. Remove the fish from the oven, pour the sauce over the fish and serve.

Note: Any type of white fish fillet will work equally well—don't limit yourself to trout!

Whole Baked Bass with Fresh Thyme

Serves **4**

2	TABLESPOONS WHITE OR RED WINE VINEGAR
$\frac{3}{4}$	CUP FINELY CHOPPED SHALLOTS
1	5-POUND BASS (OR RED SNAPPER), CLEANED
	SALT AND PEPPER
2	TEASPOONS FRESH THYME LEAVES
$\frac{1}{4}$	CUP FRESH ITALIAN FLAT-LEAF PARSLEY, CHOPPED
1	TABLESPOON OLIVE OIL
2	BAY LEAVES
1	LEMON, CUT INTO THIN RINGS

NUTRITION	
Per Serving	
Calories (kcal):	709.4
Total Fat (g):	24.6
Saturated Fat (g):	4.9
Cholesterol (mg):	386
Carbohydrate (g):	9.3
Dietary Fiber (g):	0.4
Protein (g):	108.3
Sodium (mg):	404
Calcium (mg):	497
Iron (mg):	9.7
Vitamin C (mg):	40
Vitamin A (i.u.):	4,571

Preheat oven to 375°F.

In a small sauté pan, heat vinegar and add shallots. Sauté for about 5 minutes or until transparent.

Rinse and dry the fish. Sprinkle salt, pepper, and half the thyme and parsley inside, then spread shallots inside. Close fish, sprinkle outside with salt, pepper, remaining thyme and parsley, and olive oil. Place fish on a large piece of foil or parchment paper, place 1 bay leaf and half the lemon slices under the fish and 1 bay leaf and remaining lemon on top. Wrap and seal the edges, place on cookie sheet, and bake for 35 minutes.

Open wrapping by cutting open at table for a dramatic presentation. Serve immediately.

Note: So easy, it's a wonder that people don't cook in foil or paper more often.

8

POULTRY

- Chicken Chili
- Chicken Stew
- Chicken with Saffron Rice and Peas
- Chile-Cornmeal Crusted Chicken Breasts
- Sea-Monkey Do
- Ginger Chicken
- Italian Hunters' Chicken
- Roast Chicken
- Thai Roasted Duck
- Grade School Birthday
- Turkey Burgers
- Turkey Meat Loaf

Chicken Chili

Serves
4

2	TEASPOONS VEGETABLE OIL
3	MEDIUM ONIONS, CHOPPED
2	GARLIC CLOVES, MINCED
1	POUND SKINLESS AND BONELESS CHICKEN BREASTS
2	15-OUNCE CANS WHITE BEANS
1	JALAPEÑO PEPPER
1	TEASPOON GROUND CORIANDER
1	TEASPOON GROUND CUMIN
2	14-OUNCE CANS WHOLE TOMATOES
2	LIMES
1	BUNCH CILANTRO, CHOPPED
1	SMALL RED ONION, FINELY CHOPPED
8	OUNCES SOUR CREAM
2	CUPS CORN KERNELS, FROZEN OR FRESH
	SALT AND PEPPER
	TORTILLA CHIPS OR TORTILLAS

RED KIDNEY (handwritten note next to white beans)

Heat a large stockpot over medium heat, add oil, then add onions and sauté for 2 minutes. Add garlic, and while onions and garlic are cooking, cube chicken breasts and rinse beans. Add chicken to the pot and brown on all sides. While chicken is browning, seed and mince the jalapeño.

Once chicken is browned, add coriander, cumin, tomatoes, and beans. Reduce heat and simmer for 10 minutes. Squeeze 1 lime into chili. Cut other lime into wedges and put on a plate with cilantro, red onion, and sour cream.

Stir in corn and cook for 5 more minutes, till all flavors are blended. Season to taste with salt and pepper. Serve hot with assorted garnishes and tortilla chips or warm tortillas.

Note: A lighter take on a standard. It doubles easily without any extra work, and is a crowd pleaser. The chili really will taste better if made a day in advance—or double so that you have plenty of leftovers! It also freezes very well.

NUTRITION	
Per Serving Without Tortilla Chips	
Calories (kcal):	781.5
Total Fat (g):	18.3
Saturated Fat (g):	8.7
Cholesterol (mg):	91
Carbohydrate (g):	97.3
Dietary Fiber (g):	21.5
Protein (g):	57.1
Sodium (mg):	558
Calcium (mg):	428
Iron (mg):	13.5
Vitamin C (mg):	67
Vitamin A (i.u.):	1,074

Chicken Stew

Serves
4

1	5–6-POUND CHICKEN, CUT INTO EIGHTHS
$\frac{1}{4}$	CUP ALL-PURPOSE FLOUR
4	TABLESPOONS VEGETABLE OIL
1	MEDIUM ONION, CHOPPED
4	SMALL CARROTS, PEELED AND CHOPPED
4	SMALL POTATOES, PEELED AND CHOPPED
4	SMALL PARSNIPS, PEELED AND CHOPPED
	SALT AND PEPPER TO TASTE
1	TEASPOON DRIED THYME
$\frac{1}{4}$	CUP DRY SHERRY (OPTIONAL)
12	OUNCES MUSHROOMS, COARSELY CHOPPED
$\frac{3}{4}$	CUP CHICKEN STOCK OR BROTH
$\frac{1}{4}$	CUP MINCED FRESH PARSLEY

NUTRITION

Per Serving Including Sherry

Calories (kcal):	854.5
Total Fat (g):	33.1
Saturated Fat (g):	6.7
Cholesterol (mg):	185
Carbohydrate (g):	67.0
Dietary Fiber (g):	12.4
Protein (g):	68.9
Sodium (mg):	515
Calcium (mg):	146
Iron (mg):	6.9
Vitamin C (mg):	61
Vitamin A (i.u.):	20,578

Remove skin from chicken and dredge chicken in flour so that the pieces are thoroughly coated (use a plastic bag). Heat oil in a large casserole or pot until hot. Add chicken in batches, turning once, cooking over high heat until lightly browned on all sides. Remove to a paper towel-lined plate. Add onion to pot and stir to loosen bits from bottom. Add carrots, potatoes, and parsnips. Sprinkle with salt and pepper and thyme, and stir. Cover, lower heat to medium, and cook for 3 minutes. Place chicken back into pot with vegetables. If desired, add sherry and raise heat to burn off alcohol. Cook until liquid is reduced by half, about 1 minute.

Add mushrooms to pot, then pour in stock, cover, and cook at a low simmer for 45 minutes. Just before serving, sprinkle with parsley.

Note: What is more comforting than a bowl of stew? Feel free to improvise with vegetable choices—you can't mess up stew!

Chicken with Saffron Rice and Peas

Serves
4

2	TABLESPOONS VEGETABLE OIL
	SALT AND PEPPER
2½	POUNDS CHICKEN, CUT INTO EIGHTHS
1	SMALL ONION, FINELY CHOPPED
2	TABLESPOONS PAPRIKA
1	GARLIC CLOVE, CRUSHED
1	28-OUNCE CAN TOMATOES
2½	CUPS RICE
2½	CUPS BOILING WATER
	PINCH OF SAFFRON OR TURMERIC
1	6-OUNCE PACKAGE FROZEN PEAS
2	TABLESPOONS CHOPPED FRESH PARSLEY

NUTRITION

Per Serving

Calories (kcal):	747.4
Total Fat (g):	23.2
Saturated Fat (g):	5.1
Cholesterol (mg):	155
Carbohydrate (g):	72.5
Dietary Fiber (g):	5.1
Protein (g):	59.4
Sodium (mg):	450
Calcium (mg):	127
Iron (mg):	9.0
Vitamin C (mg):	23
Vitamin A (i.u.):	3,297

Heat oil in a large skillet. Season chicken parts with salt and pepper and place in the hot oil, skin side down. Cook over medium heat, turning the parts to brown lightly on all sides. Set the chicken aside.

Add the onion to the same pan and cook slowly until softened, but not colored. Add the paprika and cook, stirring, for 2 minutes, then add the garlic and tomatoes.

Cook the mixture over high heat for about 5 minutes to evaporate liquid so the mixture is no longer soupy. Add the rice, water, and saffron, and mix well. Return the chicken parts to the dish, bring to a boil over high heat, then reduce to a simmer, cover, and cook for 20 minutes. Remove chicken and add peas and parsley, and cook 5 more minutes. Combine with chicken and serve.

Note: If using fresh peas, use 1 pound (in pods) and add peas with rice to pot.

Chile-Cornmeal Crusted Chicken Breasts

Serves
2

$\frac{1}{2}$	CUP FINELY GROUND YELLOW CORNMEAL
1	TABLESPOON PURE CHILE POWDER, OR TO TASTE
$\frac{1}{2}$	TEASPOON GROUND CORIANDER
1	TEASPOON GROUND CUMIN
1	TEASPOON DRIED OREGANO
	SALT AND PEPPER
12	OUNCES CHICKEN CUTLETS
1	LARGE EGG, BEATEN
2	TABLESPOONS VEGETABLE OIL

N U T R I T I O N	
Per Serving	
Calories (kcal):	537.8
Total Fat (g):	30.4
Saturated Fat (g):	6.1
Cholesterol (mg):	193
Carbohydrate (g):	30.3
Dietary Fiber (g):	4.1
Protein (g):	35.2
Sodium (mg):	159
Calcium (mg):	65
Iron (mg):	4.7
Vitamin C (mg):	4
Vitamin A (i.u.):	1,795

Mix cornmeal with the dried spices. Rinse and dry chicken breasts, dip in egg, then in cornmeal mixture, making sure to evenly cover with cornmeal.

Heat oil in large skillet over medium heat, and add chicken. Cook until browned, about 4 minutes, then gently turn over to brown other side.

Note: It is the flavorful, crusty coating that seals in the juices. Serve with rice for a traditional hearty dinner.

You can also bake the cutlets on a sheet pan at 375°F for 10 minutes.

Sea-Monkey Do

My wife and I lived in New York City for two years in a quintessential New York City apartment: a fourteen hundred dollar a month walk-in closet. I'm sorry, did I say closet? Cubbyhole is more accurate. We bought our carpeting by the inch. (Why do I sound like Shecky Donnellan all of a sudden?) Anyway, we're both animal lovers, and we really wanted to get a pet, but with space being so tight we couldn't rationalize getting a dog. I suppose we could've gotten one of those tiny dogs that people seem to love dressing up in sweaters, but to me a dog that can fit in a change purse isn't actually a dog. I don't want a pet that I can dress up without a struggle. The miniature, sweater-wearing dogs always have this sullen look on their faces that says, "If I were a real dog I could have stopped this canine L. L. Bean fashion accident." A true Jack London, *Call of the Wild* dog isn't going to put up with any sweaters. You try putting a real dog in a cashmere cardigan, and not only will it bite the hand that feeds it, it'll rip the whole arm out of the socket.

We could've opted for a cat, except I'm allergic and if we shared the same living space, I wouldn't be able to breathe. They have managed to breed hairless cats. Have you seen one? They look pathetic. Some drunken geneticist had the idea of crossing a Persian with an inner tube. The poor thing would start dealing nip just to keep itself in Rogaine. I don't want my pet to look like Jackie Coogan. I just can't see a hairless cat being an uplifting experience at the end of a hard day. No matter what, I'd look down at my bald cat and think, "Oh dear, Morris is on chemo."

So that knocks out the top two pet choices. What's left? A bird. I'm not really into birds. I know they can turn on you—I've seen the Alfred Hitchcock movie. Of course, if I did own a bird it would finally give me a use for the pseudo-intellectual, it's hip to be homeless, New York City rag known as the *Village Voice* because I could line the bottom of the cage with back issues. (By the way, guys, thanks for the glowing review.)

I thought about getting a ferret, but being in the entertainment industry, I've met my share of weasels. A big snake. Nope. I just don't see myself as one of those "walking around town with big snake" kind of guys. Plus, I couldn't put up with people always saying, "Hey, look, snake guy is getting coffee," "Snake guy was on the subway today," and "Snake guy in-line skates with his snake—isn't that neat?" If I walked around with a big snake I'd have to wear leather shorts and change my name to Octavio.

So we settled for Sea-Monkeys. Yes, the same Sea-Monkeys you ordered out of a comic book when you were a kid. Some of you might think that collecting the bacteria from between bathroom tiles and sticking it in a jar might be more captivating, but you're wrong. We grew very attached to those spunky little translucent brine shrimp. So much so, that when we lost one, it felt as if a member of our own family were gone. It was just before Christmas 1995, and at the time we had five Sea-Monkeys still swimming strong. During the week between Christmas and the New Year, our five monkeys became four. We didn't know how it happened. Could it have been natural causes even though he was young and healthy? We ruled out drowning and traffic accident immediately. Murder? No way. Because, to borrow a line from *Battle for the Planet of the Apes*, "Sea-Monkeys don't kill Sea-Monkeys." It looked like another sad case of Sea-Monkey suicide. The other four monkeys were getting it on, waiting to bring in 1996, Sea-Monkey style. Number five, on the other hand, had no number six. They say that the holidays are the hardest time of year to get through when you're alone, but I didn't think he'd do a foolish thing like that. Maybe he just couldn't cope. The office parties, family TV specials, and living in a fish bowl with all eyes on him! Childhood lasted only about twelve hours. His mother was a packet of powder, and his father was me. He must've felt alone. There are no Sea-Monkey singles bars, personal ads, computer chat rooms, or outreach programs. So the way I figure it, one night, while the other two couples were playing Pictionary, he excused himself from the game, swam to the bottom, and finished himself off with an overdose of . . . whatever it is Sea-Monkeys OD on.

Ginger Chicken

Serves
6

4	WHOLE SKINLESS AND BONELESS CHICKEN BREASTS
1	TABLESPOON VEGETABLE OIL
1	BUNCH BROCCOLI, IN FLORETS
2	CUPS SNOW PEA PODS
2	CUPS CHICKEN STOCK
1	2-INCH PIECE FRESH GINGER, GRATED
1	TABLESPOON CORNSTARCH
$\frac{1}{3}$	CUP COLD WATER
$\frac{1}{3}$	CUP SOY SAUCE
$\frac{1}{3}$	CUP DRY SHERRY
1	TEASPOON ASIAN ROASTED SESAME OIL
2	SCALLIONS, THINLY SLICED

N U T R I T I O N

Per Serving
Calories (kcal): ------------223.2
Total Fat (g): --------------5.5
Saturated Fat (g): ----------1.0
Cholesterol (mg): ----------64
Carbohydrate (g): ----------8.2
Dietary Fiber (g): ----------2.2
Protein (g): -----------------30.3
Sodium (mg): --------------1,187
Calcium (mg): ------------53
Iron (mg): ------------------2.6
Vitamin C (mg): -----------41
Vitamin A (i.u.): ----------349

Cut chicken breasts into 1-inch cubes, and stir-fry in the vegetable oil over high heat until the outside is golden, but the inside is barely cooked, about 2 minutes. Remove the chicken and set aside. Steam broccoli in the wok for 2 minutes, then add snow peas and cook for 1 minute, and remove them. Lower the heat to medium-high and add the stock and ginger to wok and cook for 3 minutes. Combine the cornstarch with the cold water and stir it into the wok and boil until the sauce has thickened. Add the soy sauce, sherry, and sesame oil. Add the chicken and vegetables, and cook for 2 minutes or until the chicken is heated through. Scatter on scallions. Serve with rice.

Note: Lots of ingredients, but don't let the list scare you off. This is better than any Chinese restaurant in your neighborhood.

Italian Hunters' Chicken

Serves
4

1	5–6-POUND CHICKEN, CUT UP, OR CHICKEN PIECES OF CHOICE
3	GARLIC CLOVES, SMASHED
1	TABLESPOON ROSEMARY, FRESH IF POSSIBLE
1	TABLESPOON THYME, FRESH IF POSSIBLE
1	TABLESPOON SAGE, FRESH IF POSSIBLE
1	BOTTLE DRY WHITE WINE
	SALT AND PEPPER
1	OUNCE DRIED PORCINI MUSHROOMS (OPTIONAL)
1	28-OUNCE CAN TOMATOES

NUTRITION	
Per Serving Including Mushrooms	
Calories (kcal):	629.7
Total Fat (g):	18.8
Saturated Fat (g):	5.0
Cholesterol (mg):	185
Carbohydrate (g):	21.0
Dietary Fiber (g):	3.3
Protein (g):	63.2
Sodium (mg):	514
Calcium (mg):	93
Iron (mg):	6.3
Vitamin C (mg):	32
Vitamin A (i.u.):	1,411

Place the chicken pieces in an ovenproof pot or roasting pan along with the garlic, herbs, and enough wine to cover. Sprinkle with salt and pepper and let marinate in the refrigerator for at least 30 minutes, but preferably 2 hours. If you are using porcinis, add to the marinade and let soak, too.

Preheat oven to 375°F.

Place the pot or roasting pan over medium-high heat and cook chicken just till skin colors and some of the alcohol evaporates, turning once in a while. Add tomatoes, cover, and put the pot in the oven. Cook about 1 hour, or until chicken is tender. Bring straight to table with plenty of bread for sopping up sauce.

Note: This is an amazingly simple, yet foolproof and delicious way to cook chicken. Try it! Make extra for great leftovers.

Roast Chicken

Serves
4

1	6-POUND ROASTING CHICKEN
1	LARGE ONION
2	MEDIUM POTATOES
3	GARLIC CLOVES, HALVED
2	TABLESPOONS OLIVE OIL
1	TABLESPOON ROSEMARY, FRESH IF POSSIBLE
1	TABLESPOON THYME, FRESH IF POSSIBLE
	KOSHER SALT AND PEPPER
1	LEMON

NUTRITION

Per Serving
Calories (kcal): ------------556.6
Total Fat (g): -------------25.1
Saturated Fat (g): ---------5.8
Cholesterol (mg): ---------185
Carbohydrate (g): ---------19.7
Dietary Fiber (g): ---------1.8
Protein (g): ----------------62.3
Sodium (mg): -------------322
Calcium (mg): ------------105
Iron (mg): ------------------5.0
Vitamin C (mg): -----------35
Vitamin A (i.u.): ----------191

Preheat oven to 425°F.

Rinse chicken under cold water, making sure to rinse cavity and remove giblet package. Pat dry with paper towels. Let sit and dry.

Coarsely chop onion (but reserve the scraps), potatoes, and garlic, put in roasting pan, and toss with 1 tablespoon oil, half the rosemary and thyme, and salt and pepper to taste. Put chicken on top of potatoes, rub with remaining 1 tablespoon

oil, sprinkle with remaining rosemary and thyme, and more salt and pepper. Cut lemon in half and put in cavity with onion scraps. Place roasting pan in hot oven and cook for about 1 hour.

When done, juices will run clear when chicken is pierced below the leg. Carve and serve with roasted potatoes and onion.

Note: The most basic and delicious way to roast a chicken.

Thai Roasted Duck

Serves
4

1	5-POUND DUCK
1	TEASPOON SALT
1	TEASPOON RED CURRY PASTE
2	GARLIC CLOVES, MINCED
1	TEASPOON ASIAN ROASTED SESAME OIL
1	TABLESPOON GRATED FRESH GINGER
3	TABLESPOONS SOY SAUCE OR TAMARI
3	TABLESPOONS HONEY
1	LEMON, JUICED

N·U·T·R·I·T·I·O·N

Per Serving

Calories (kcal):	1,725.2
Total Fat (g):	162.1
Saturated Fat (g):	54.2
Cholesterol (mg):	311
Carbohydrate (g):	17.9
Dietary Fiber (g):	0.4
Protein (g):	48.1
Sodium (mg):	1,414
Calcium (mg):	70
Iron (mg):	10.5
Vitamin C (mg):	33
Vitamin A (i.u.):	700

Preheat oven to 350°F.

Rinse duck under cold water and discard excess fat around cavities. In a small bowl, mix salt, curry paste, and garlic. Place duck on a rack in a large roasting pan and rub salt mixture evenly all over the duck. Place in oven and bake for 1 hour. (If not using a rack, carefully and frequently remove fat from bottom of pan with a baster.)

In a small bowl, mix sesame oil, ginger, soy sauce, honey, and lemon juice. After 1 hour, pour over duck. Bake for 1 more hour, basting every 15 minutes.

Remove duck from oven and let sit for 10 minutes, then carve and serve immediately.

Tip: Red curry paste is available in Asian markets and ethnic foods sections of supermarkets.

Note: For some reason, everyone is afraid to cook duck. Be afraid no longer—your fears are unfounded! This is a great first-time duck recipe, one sure to become a favorite if you give it a shot! Since the duck gives off a lot of fat, it is best to cook it on a rack or to remove the fat with a baster every 15 minutes when you baste it.

Grade School Birthday

My birthday parties in elementary school were out of hand. My mother and grandmother would let me invite the entire second grade—about forty or fifty kids. Growing up as an only child, that's a lot of little visitors. If one kid came over, I was ecstatic, so having forty to fifty was like winning the "only child lotto"! I didn't know who to play with first. I didn't know who would have the privilege of being the first to check out my collection of Big Jim action figures and accessories. And, trust me, I had them all. I had the Big Jim camper, the Big Jim Olympic ski-jump, the Big Jim safari set, the Big Jim disco palace, the Big Jim flower shop, the Big Jim halfway house. I was the mayor of Big Jim land. The problem was, every toy I played with I had to play with alone. Now, with Big Jim or army figures this was fine, but board games like Battleship were a much sadder story. Picture me at about seven years old. I look at one board and yell out "B-5." Then I slide across my bedroom carpet, look at the other board, and yell "Miss." I would do this for so long I had to have knee replacement surgery at age nine.

Steve Rubino was always the first kid to arrive. All decked out in my maroon velour V neck, I played it cool as I greeted Steve at the top of the steps as if I were some kind of second-grade Hugh Hefner, letting him know he was about to get a taste of my party style. The next few kids were no sweat for "Little Hef." Then came the slam! Before I knew it, there would be a brigade of boys and girls running amuck on my turf, chowing down ice cream, and swigging orange soda. I was Nero and Rome was falling apart. After a couple of hours of this, my friends would start to become restless as seven-year-olds are wont to do. And from the corner of the yard the chants would begin: "We want the clown! We want the clown! Bring on the pointless children activities!" Every year my playmates (get it, I was "Little Hef") would expect clowns and balloon twisting and pin-the-tail-on-the-donkey or maybe a magic show. Instead, every year they got my teenage uncle Tom and his friend Terence performing songs and skits on the front porch like it was some kiddy U.S.O. show. They didn't just perform. They worked it! I don't know why they wanted to perform for a bunch of kids. It seemed silly at the time, but I guess, looking back, art transcends all ages. The songs they wrote were about themselves and the angst of growing up as teenagers in West Nyack, New York—topics sure to please any grade-school audience. My personal favorite was a song entitled "Mommy Won't Let Me Drink at the Prom." I could really relate. For the grand finale, Tom and Terence would wear these turkey costumes that Mom had made from brown paper bags. The turkey theme had to do with my birthday being so close to Thanksgiving. Then they would run around the yard in their gray corduroys as every kid chased them trying to pull the tail off the giant turkey. The kid who won got a little plastic gift from Mom and a nice lecture from my uncle on the joys of oversleeping.

Turkey Burgers

Serves
4

1½	POUNDS GROUND TURKEY
1	LARGE EGG, BEATEN
½	CUP FINELY CHOPPED ONION
1	GARLIC CLOVE, MINCED
1	TEASPOON THYME, FRESH IF POSSIBLE
	SALT AND PEPPER
2	TABLESPOONS VEGETABLE OIL

NUTRITION	
Per Serving	
Calories (kcal):	338.4
Total Fat (g):	22.2
Saturated Fat (g):	5.0
Cholesterol (mg):	188
Carbohydrate (g):	1.4
Dietary Fiber (g):	0.4
Protein (g):	31.5
Sodium (mg):	250
Calcium (mg):	45
Iron (mg):	2.8
Vitamin C (mg):	1
Vitamin A (i.u.):	102

Place turkey in a large bowl, add remaining ingredients, except oil and mix well but quickly. Form into 4 patties, place on a plate, and put back in refrigerator for 30 minutes.

Heat oil in heavy-bottomed pan (cast-iron is great) and place patties gently in pan. Cook over medium heat for 5 minutes. Carefully flip and cook for 4 more minutes.

Note: You can also use ground chicken. Another option is to add ½ cup bread crumbs to the mixture—it will make a slightly lighter burger.

Turkey Meat Loaf

Serves
6

1 $\frac{1}{2}$	POUNDS GROUND TURKEY
1	SMALL ONION, FINELY CHOPPED
1	MEDIUM CARROT, PEELED AND FINELY CHOPPED
1	SMALL RED BELL PEPPER, CORED, SEEDED, AND FINELY CHOPPED
1	CUP BREAD CRUMBS
2	EGG WHITES
1	TEASPOON SALT
1	TEASPOON PEPPER
1	TEASPOON GROUND SAGE
3	TABLESPOONS KETCHUP

NUTRITION	
Per Serving	
Calories (kcal):	270.1
Total Fat (g):	10.7
Saturated Fat (g):	2.9
Cholesterol (mg):	90
Carbohydrate (g):	18.7
Dietary Fiber (g):	2.1
Protein (g):	23.7
Sodium (mg):	791
Calcium (mg):	50
Iron (mg):	2.5
Vitamin C (mg):	27
Vitamin A (i.u.):	4,130

Preheat oven to 375°F.

Mix all ingredients except ketchup together in a bowl, making sure that they are well combined. Shape into a loaf and place on a foil-covered cookie sheet with sides. Spread ketchup on top, and bake for 45 minutes. Let sit for 5 minutes before slicing.

Note: Serve with Roasted Garlic Mashed Potatoes (page 100) for the ultimate comfort food dinner!

9
MEAT

- ⊛ Barbecued Flank Steak
- ⊛ Beef Stew
- ⊛ Country-Style Barbecued Spareribs
- ⊛ Lamb Shanks in Guinness
- ⊛ HAVE IT YOUR WAY
- ⊛ Perfect Burgers
- ⊛ Not Mom's Meat Loaf

- ⊛ Mexican Roast Pork
- ⊛ Pork Chops with Caramelized Onions and Apples
- ⊛ "HEY, BIG GUY!"
- ⊛ Roast Leg of Lamb with Spinach and Goat Cheese
- ⊛ Standing Rib Roast

"Barbecued" Flank Steak

Serves
2

4	TABLESPOONS OYSTER SAUCE OR HOISIN SAUCE
2	TABLESPOONS SOY SAUCE
2	GARLIC CLOVES, MINCED
1	12-OUNCE FLANK STEAK

Mix oyster sauce, soy sauce, and garlic. Pour into a resealable bag and add flank steak. Shut bag and let marinate for 30 minutes to 2 hours in refrigerator.

Preheat broiler. Place steak on foil-lined broiling pan or cookie sheet with sides, and top with marinade. Broil 3 minutes, then flip meat and broil 2 minutes on other side. Let sit for 2 minutes before slicing into thin slices on an angle.

Note: Everyone will think that you have a grill in your kitchen. An extremely fast, satisfying dish.

NUTRITION	
Per Serving Using Oyster Sauce	
Calories (kcal):	336.2
Total Fat (g):	17.8
Saturated Fat (g):	7.5
Cholesterol (mg):	87
Carbohydrate (g):	7.3
Dietary Fiber (g):	0.2
Protein (g):	35.0
Sodium (mg):	2,196
Calcium (mg):	24
Iron (mg):	4.3
Vitamin C (mg):	1
Vitamin A (i.u.):	0

Beef Stew OK

Serves
4

ADD EXTRA SALT AT THE END OF 1ST HOUR

$\frac{1}{4}$	CUP ALL-PURPOSE FLOUR
	SALT AND PEPPER
2	POUNDS BEEF STEW MEAT, TRIMMED
3	TABLESPOONS VEGETABLE OIL
1	TABLESPOON SUGAR
2	CELERY STALKS, DICED
4	PARSLEY SPRIGS, CHOPPED
1	GARLIC CLOVE, MINCED
1	BAY LEAF
2	CUPS CANNED TOMATOES
4	CUPS BEEF BOUILLON
1	TABLESPOON TOMATO PASTE
4	MEDIUM CARROTS, PEELED AND CHOPPED
3	MEDIUM POTATOES, PEELED AND CHOPPED
12	SMALL WHITE BOILING ONIONS, PEELED

NUTRITION

Per Serving

Calories (kcal):	1,002.9
Total Fat (g):	58.6
Saturated Fat (g):	20.0
Cholesterol (mg):	227
Carbohydrate (g):	47.1
Dietary Fiber (g):	7.5
Protein (g):	70.5
Sodium (mg):	2,868
Calcium (mg):	180
Iron (mg):	9.8
Vitamin C (mg):	53
Vitamin A (i.u.):	21,190

Season flour with salt and pepper to taste. Dredge meat in flour. In a large soup pot, brown meat in hot oil. Add sugar, celery, parsley, garlic, bay leaf, tomatoes, bouillon, and tomato paste. Bring to a boil, reduce heat, and simmer 1 hour. Taste and season with additional salt and pepper, or herbs of your choice, if desired. Add carrots and potatoes and continue to simmer until vegetables are tender. Add onions and simmer until onions are tender, about 5 minutes. Remove bay leaf before serving. Note: This is a flavorful, but not highly seasoned stew. Additions may include *fines herbes*, wine, or your choice of spice and herb combinations. Customize it according to your taste.

$1/_2 t$

Country-Style Barbecued Spareribs

Serves
4

SAUCE

2	GARLIC CLOVES, MINCED
$\frac{1}{4}$	CUP VEGETABLE OIL
$\frac{1}{4}$	CUP MOLASSES
$\frac{1}{4}$	CUP SOY SAUCE
1	TABLESPOON DIJON MUSTARD
$\frac{1}{4}$	CUP CIDER VINEGAR
$\frac{1}{4}$	CUP MAPLE SYRUP
4	DASHES WORCESTERSHIRE SAUCE
	HOT PEPPER SAUCE, TO TASTE
3	POUNDS COUNTRY-STYLE PORK OR BEEF RIBS

NUTRITION	
Per Serving Using Pork Ribs	
Calories (kcal):	947.4
Total Fat (g):	65.1
Saturated Fat (g):	20.7
Cholesterol (mg):	207
Carbohydrate (g):	30.3
Dietary Fiber (g):	0.3
Protein (g):	57.9
Sodium (mg):	1,033
Calcium (mg):	134
Iron (mg):	4.7
Vitamin C (mg):	2
Vitamin A (i.u.):	20

Combine all sauce ingredients except pepper sauce in a small sauce pan and heat to a simmer. Cook until the garlic is softened, about 10 minutes, then remove from heat. Add pepper sauce and let cool. Place ribs in a shallow pan and coat with cooled sauce. Cover with plastic wrap and let marinate at least 2 hours, but preferably overnight.

Allow meat to come back to room temperature and grill or broil (reserving the remaining marinade) the ribs for about 10 minutes per side, or until meat is firm to the touch when poked with your finger. While meat is cooking, pour remaining marinade in a small saucepan and bring to a boil. Simmer for 5 minutes. Pour extra sauce over cooked ribs and serve immediately.

Note: You could buy storebought sauce, but why? I recommend making the sauce in advance, then marinating the meat overnight and just throwing it on the grill or broiling it when you are ready.

Lamb Shanks in Guinness

Serves
6

4	TABLESPOONS VEGETABLE OIL
6	LAMB SHANKS, ABOUT $\frac{3}{4}$ POUND EACH
	SALT AND PEPPER
$\frac{1}{2}$	CUP ALL-PURPOSE FLOUR
5	CUPS COARSELY CHOPPED ONIONS
4	CUPS BEEF STOCK
2	12-OUNCE BOTTLES GUINNESS STOUT
4	MEDIUM CARROTS, PEELED AND COARSELY CHOPPED
2	LARGE PARSNIPS, PEELED AND COARSELY CHOPPED
2	SMALL RUTABAGAS, PEELED AND COARSELY CHOPPED
$\frac{1}{2}$	CUP PITTED PRUNES

NUTRITION

Per Serving

Calories (kcal):	901.3
Total Fat (g):	50.6
Saturated Fat (g):	18.8
Cholesterol (mg):	203
Carbohydrate (g):	42.2
Dietary Fiber (g):	8.2
Protein (g):	61.5
Sodium (mg):	1,476
Calcium (mg):	145
Iron (mg):	7.0
Vitamin C (mg):	47
Vitamin A (i.u.):	13,788

Heat oil in a large, heavy stockpot over high heat. Season lamb with salt and pepper and coat in flour. Shake off excess and reserve. Add lamb to pot in batches, browning well, and transfer to a bowl. Reduce heat, add onions, and cook, scraping up browned bits, until translucent. Add remaining flour and cook for 1 minute. Return lamb and juices to pot, raise heat, add stock and Guinness, and bring to a boil. Reduce heat and simmer 1 hour.

Add carrots, parsnips, and rutabagas and simmer, uncovered, until tender, about 45 minutes. Add prunes and cook for 10 more minutes.

The guy next to me is Phil Cross, chef at O'Donoghues in Nyack, New York. He is the creator of the best beef and veggie burgers I have ever tasted.

Have It Your Way

Everybody loves a burger. It is a simple joy. Burgers are loved so much that vegetarians came up with their own meatless creations in order to satisfy their craving. I would be hard pressed to think of someone who doesn't have a hankering for a burger of some kind every now and then. A good burger is an explosion of flavor resulting from how you build it. I don't care what you make it from, be it beef, turkey, vegetable, tempeh, lentil, or tofu—it's all a burger to me. The ritual is the same. Pile on the lettuce, onions, tomatoes, and pickles and have a good time.

Fast-food joints have come up with a way to use this burger ritual against us. They have what is known as the "fixings bar." This may seem like a harmless and reasonable attempt to placate those among us who must have the burger a certain way every time or they become like Rainman, "Lettuce, definitely lettuce." If they take off the bun and see no lettuce, they start to scream and bang their heads on the counter. Have you ever been stuck behind one of those Goof-troupe rejects who's making more demands than a terrorist with a plane full of hostages because he thinks he's getting his burger and side of chicken flickins at Le Cirque? Sometimes you feel like smacking the guy and saying, "Hey, who told you to come out in public . . . No, no, no, you need to go back home. You're obviously not done incubating yet. This Roy Rogers day trip is way too much for you to handle right now."

But they have not incorporated the fixings bar for the benefit of mankind. No, it's all about profits. Because, you see, the real brilliance of the fixings bar is that you are doing the work! That's right, you are now a fast-food restaurant employee. You see, somebody used to do that for you—it was once part of the service you paid for. They canned the guy who used to do that and now you're that guy! Don't you get it? The whole reason any of us go to any of these places is that we don't want to screw around making anything at home. But if you are going to do the work anyway, do it at home where you'll do a much better job. It's hard to imagine that we got duped by this meat-marketing plan, but don't feel bad. Just think of the poor kid who got replaced by a pair of tongs.

Perfect Burgers

Serves
4

$1\frac{1}{2}$	POUNDS GROUND SIRLOIN
1	SMALL ONION, FINELY DICED
1	TEASPOON KOSHER SALT
1	TEASPOON GROUND PEPPER
3	DASHES WORCESTERSHIRE SAUCE
3	DROPS LIQUID SMOKE FLAVORING
	VEGETABLE OIL
1	MEDIUM TOMATO, SLICED
1	SMALL RED ONION, THINLY SLICED

NUTRITION

Per Serving

Calories (kcal):	448.2
Total Fat (g):	25.5
Saturated Fat (g):	10.0
Cholesterol (mg):	109
Carbohydrate (g):	19.2
Dietary Fiber (g):	2.3
Protein (g):	34.1
Sodium (mg):	837
Calcium (mg):	67
Iron (mg):	5.1
Vitamin C (mg):	10
Vitamin A (i.u.):	193

In a large mixing bowl, place beef, diced onion, $\frac{1}{2}$ teaspoon salt, pepper, Worcestershire sauce, and Liquid Smoke. Using hands, quickly but thoroughly combine ingredients. Divide meat in half in the bowl, then divide those halves in half and pat into burgers. Place on a plate and refrigerate if not using immediately.

Brush grill with vegetable oil, or add 1 tablespoon oil to skillet and heat over medium-high heat. Sprinkle the remaining $\frac{1}{2}$ teaspoon salt into the pan, and then add burgers. Cook until desired doneness. 3 minutes per side for rare, 4 minutes per side for medium-rare, 5 minutes per side for medium, 6 minutes per side for medium-well, and 7 minutes per side for well. Serve with sliced tomatoes, red onion slices, and buns.

Note: Grill or, for best indoor taste, use a cast-iron skillet. Grill the burgers about 5 inches from the flame and only flip them once!

Not Mom's Meat Loaf

Serves
6

2	TABLESPOONS UNSALTED BUTTER
3	GARLIC CLOVES, MINCED
2	SMALL ONIONS, MINCED
1	LARGE CELERY STALK, MINCED
$1\frac{1}{2}$	POUNDS GROUND CHUCK OR ROUND
8	OUNCES HOT SAUSAGE
$\frac{3}{4}$	CUP SOFT BREAD CRUMBS
2	LARGE EGGS
$\frac{1}{4}$	CUP KETCHUP
2	TABLESPOONS MILK
$1\frac{1}{2}$	TEASPOONS WORCESTERSHIRE SAUCE
$\frac{3}{4}$	TEASPOON SALT
$\frac{1}{4}$	TEASPOON CAYENNE PEPPER

NUTRITION	
Per Serving	
Calories (kcal):	648.6
Total Fat (g):	46.4
Saturated Fat (g):	18.5
Cholesterol (mg):	193
Carbohydrate (g):	25.2
Dietary Fiber (g):	2.2
Protein (g):	30.5
Sodium (mg):	1,120
Calcium (mg):	82
Iron (mg):	3.9
Vitamin C (mg):	6
Vitamin A (i.u.):	408

Preheat oven to 375°F.

Heat butter in large sauté pan, and add garlic, onions, and celery. Add meat, sausage, bread crumbs, eggs, ketchup, milk, Worcestershire sauce, salt, and cayenne. Shape into a loaf, place in a 9 x 13-inch pan, and bake for 1 hour, 10 minutes.

Mexican Roast Pork

Serves
6

1	2½-POUND BOSTON BUTT
	VEGETABLE OIL
2	TEASPOONS SALT
2	TEASPOONS PEPPER

MARINADE

2	ANCHO CHILE PEPPERS, SEEDED
4	GARLIC CLOVES, COARSELY CHOPPED
1	MEDIUM ONION, COARSELY CHOPPED
2	TABLESPOONS COARSELY CHOPPED FRESH GINGER
¼	CUP CIDER VINEGAR
¼	CUP SWEET VERMOUTH
½	TEASPOON DRIED THYME
½	TEASPOON DRIED OREGANO
1	TEASPOON GRATED NUTMEG
2	TEASPOONS SWEET PAPRIKA
1	TEASPOON SUGAR

Rub the meat with a few teaspoons of oil. Pierce all over with the tip of a small knife. Rub salt and pepper in all over.

Place chiles in a small bowl and cover with boiling water to soften, about 5 minutes. Drain. In a blender, puree the chiles, garlic, onion, and ginger, then add vinegar, vermouth, and seasonings and sugar. Rub the meat all over with the sauce, making sure to get some in the holes. Reserve remaining marinade. Place meat in the refrigerator and let marinate for at least 2 hours or up to 24 hours.

Preheat oven to 325°F. Place the meat in a roasting pan and put in oven. Baste every 20 minutes and roast for 1 hour and 45 minutes, or until a meat thermometer reads 155°F. Let sit for 10 minutes before carving. A nice gravy can be made with the drippings. Follow procedure for Standing Rib Roast (page 157).

Note: This is a great way to cook pork, and it's delicious! Serve with Mexican rice, beans, and tortillas.

NUTRITION

Per Serving

Calories (kcal):	640.2
Total Fat (g):	46.0
Saturated Fat (g):	16.7
Cholesterol (mg):	169
Carbohydrate (g):	6.4
Dietary Fiber (g):	1.4
Protein (g):	44.9
Sodium (mg):	1,362
Calcium (mg):	44
Iron (mg):	2.8
Vitamin C (mg):	50
Vitamin A (i.u.):	1,901

Pork Chops with Caramelized Onions and Apples

Serves
4

$\frac{1}{2}$	CUP UNSALTED BUTTER
6	LARGE YELLOW ONIONS, SLICED $\frac{1}{4}$-INCH THICK
$\frac{1}{4}$	CUP RED WINE OR SWEET VERMOUTH
1	TEASPOON SUGAR
	SALT AND PEPPER
2	LARGE APPLES, PEELED AND SLICED
4	THICK-CUT PORK CHOPS, ABOUT $3\frac{1}{2}$ POUNDS TOTAL

NUTRITION

Per Serving

Calories (kcal):	544.7
Total Fat (g):	37.9
Saturated Fat (g):	19.3
Cholesterol (mg):	135
Carbohydrate (g):	24.8
Dietary Fiber (g):	4.6
Protein (g):	25.2
Sodium (mg):	295
Calcium (mg):	64
Iron (mg):	1.5
Vitamin C (mg):	14
Vitamin A (i.u.):	901

Heat butter in a large sauté pan over medium heat. Add onions and cook for 5 minutes. When softened, raise heat to high to brown slightly. Add wine, sugar, and salt and pepper, raise heat, and bring to a boil. Lower heat to very low, cover pan, and cook for 20 minutes. Add apple slices, and continue cooking for 10 more minutes so that onions and apples are really soft.

Place chops on a foil-covered baking sheet, sprinkle with salt and pepper, and broil 4 minutes per side, making sure that they are nicely browned. You can also pan-fry or grill them. Place onion and apple mixture on a platter and put chops on top. Serve immediately.

Note: Yellow onions slowly sautéed in butter with apples. Yum! Better than regular old pork chops with applesauce. Sort of a grown-up version.

"Hey, Big Guy!"

I'm six foot three, so it is safe to say that I'm tall. I'm no pituitary freak, but on average, I'm taller than most. Overall, I like being tall just fine. Sure, airplanes are a hassle and movie seats are too close together, but nothing in life is perfect. Sometimes it's hard to get those nifty slacks I want in the right size. (By the way, I hate the word *slacks* almost as much as I hate the TV show *Alice*. In fact, if I saw a commercial for slacks featuring Vic Tayback, there might be a blood bath.) But there are a couple of things about being tall that really bother me. The first one is this, and I'm going to say it for all to hear: *No, I do not play basketball.* Just because we're closer to the basket doesn't mean we're good at the game! The other thing that gets to me is that when you are tall, everybody likes to point that fact out.

If you walk the streets of New York City, you are constantly bombarded by street vendors, all of whom have set up storefront businesses in front of other people's stores. These street merchants love calling out to you to grab your attention, as if the T-shirt depicting two Barneys humping isn't enough. The phrase I'm hit with constantly is, "Hey, Big Guy." "Hey, big guy." Well isn't that charming? I just don't know how to deal with the "Hey, big guy." I don't like having my entire existence reduced to a physical characteristic by somebody selling used magazines and gutted electronics off a bridge table for five bucks a pop. It's all I can do to restrain myself from firing back with, "What do you want, you short, unwashed petty thief?" Tall people are the only ones for whom it is socially acceptable to label by physical attribution. You never hear anyone yell out, "Hey, bald guy, need Knicks tickets?" or "Yo, cross-eyed girl, how about a nice pair of Ray•Bans?" and it would just be plain mean for someone to exclaim, "I got incense . . . Tubby!"

The point is that there's no need to call me "Big Guy." What's wrong with "Hey, Buddy" or a nice "Yo, brother" or the ever-popular "My friend"? Or better yet, don't yell out anything. If I need incense or stolen watches or the November '89 issue of *Playboy*, I'll find you.

Roast Leg of Lamb with Spinach and Goat Cheese

Serves
8

2	TABLESPOONS OLIVE OIL
1	SHALLOT, MINCED
2	LEEKS, WHITE PART ONLY
	SALT AND PEPPER
4	CUPS FRESH SPINACH, CLEANED
2	GARLIC CLOVES, MINCED
$1\frac{1}{2}$	CUPS GOAT CHEESE
1	5-POUND LEG OF LAMB, BONED AND BUTTERFLIED
3	TABLESPOONS CHOPPED FRESH ROSEMARY
$\frac{1}{2}$	CUP CRACKED BLACK PEPPER CORNS

NUTRITION

Per Serving

Calories (kcal):	687.1
Total Fat (g):	49.7
Saturated Fat (g):	22.4
Cholesterol (mg):	177
Carbohydrate (g):	10.9
Dietary Fiber (g):	3.0
Protein (g):	48.8
Sodium (mg):	231
Calcium (mg):	290
Iron (mg):	7.5
Vitamin C (mg):	12
Vitamin A (i.u.):	2,437

Preheat the oven to 425°F.

In a sauté pan, heat 1 tablespoon oil. When the pan is very hot, sauté the shallot and leeks, adding a pinch of salt and pepper. Sauté for 1 minute, then add the spinach and garlic and sauté until the spinach has wilted. Remove from heat and turn into a mixing bowl. Add the cheese to the mixture, and combine well.

Lay the lamb on the counter and rub with the remaining 1 tablespoon olive oil, rosemary, salt to taste, and a pinch of the peppercorns. Spread the spinach filling evenly over meat, then roll meat up lengthwise and tie with butcher's twine. Roll the rolled roast in the remaining peppercorns and place in a shallow roasting pan. Cook for 1 hour, 20 minutes or until a meat thermometer reads 150°F. Let the roast rest for 10 minutes before slicing.

Note: Don't be intimidated—roasting a leg of lamb is one of the easiest things that you can do, and people are always impressed!

Standing Rib Roast

$\frac{1}{2}$	TEASPOON SALT
$\frac{1}{4}$	TEASPOON PEPPER
$\frac{1}{4}$	TEASPOON DRIED BASIL
$\frac{1}{4}$	TEASPOON DRIED MARJORAM
$\frac{1}{4}$	TEASPOON DRIED THYME
$\frac{1}{4}$	TEASPOON DRIED SAGE
1	9-POUND RIB ROAST, TRIMMED
$\frac{1}{2}$	CUP RED WINE

GRAVY

$\frac{1}{2}$	CUP RED WINE
$\frac{1}{4}$	CUP ALL-PURPOSE FLOUR
$\frac{1}{2}$	TEASPOON SALT
	PEPPER
1	10-OUNCE CAN BEEF BROTH

Preheat oven to 325°F. Mix salt, pepper, and herbs in a small bowl and rub it all over and into beef on all sides. Stand roast, fat side up, on a rack in a shallow roasting pan. Insert a meat thermometer through the fat into the thickest part of the meat, but not near the bone. Pour wine over roast and place in oven. Baste several times, and cook for about 3 hours for rare—120° on thermometer. (Twenty minutes per pound for medium-rare is a good guide.)

When roast is done, transfer it carefully to a carving platter and cover with foil. Let it stand in a warm place and it will continue to cook while you make the gravy.

Remove as much of the fat from the roasting pan as possible, leaving browned bits behind. Place on a medium burner and pour in the wine, making sure to loosen any bits from the pan. Let cook for 1 minute. Add flour, salt, and pepper to make a paste and cook for 2 minutes, smoothing out any lumps with a whisk. Gradually add the broth, whisking to keep it smooth. Bring to a boil, then lower heat and simmer for 3 minutes.

Using a large sharp knife, carve meat across roast toward the bone. Cut along the bone to remove slices, or cut through bone and serve with bone. Serve with gravy on side.

Tip: Unless you want an entirely well-done roast, remove from oven when roast is 120° in the middle. It will continue to cook to medium-rare (125°) in the center while it cools and rests.

Note: Sounds hard, but is actually really easy. Great for a holiday dinner or for entertaining a bunch of meat lovers.

N U T R I T I O N	
Per Serving	
Calories (kcal): ------752.6	Protein (g): ---------114.7
Total Fat (g): ---------25.4	Sodium (mg): -------798
Saturated Fat (g): ----8.7	Calcium (mg): ------29
Cholesterol (mg): ----297	Iron (mg): ----------11.5
Carbohydrate (g): ----3.9	Vitamin C (mg): ----0
Dietary Fiber (g): ----0.0	Vitamin A (i.u.): ----9

10
DESSERTS

- ✪ Big Apple Pie
- ✪ Chocolate Decadence
- ✪ Comforting Baked Apples
- ✪ First Prize Chocolate Fudge Cake
- ✪ Fruit Pizza
- ✪ Nectarine and Raspberry Pie
- ✪ ICE CREAM SAVES THE WORLD!
- ✪ Perfect Chocolate Cake
- ✪ Plum and Blueberry Crisp
- ✪ The Best Chocolate Chip Cookies
- ✪ Grandma Helen's Pie
- ✪ THE GREAT DIET PIE CAPER

Big Apple Pie

Serves
8

	PASTRY FOR 2-CRUST 9-INCH PIE
6	CUPS PEELED AND THINLY SLICED GRANNY SMITH APPLES
$\frac{3}{4}$	CUP SUGAR
2	TABLESPOONS ALL-PURPOSE FLOUR
1	TABLESPOON LEMON JUICE
$\frac{3}{4}$	TEASPOON GROUND CINNAMON
$\frac{1}{4}$	TEASPOON SALT
$\frac{1}{8}$	TEASPOON GRATED NUTMEG

NUTRITION	
Per Serving	
Calories (kcal):	118.2
Total Fat (g):	0.1
Saturated Fat (g):	0.0
Cholesterol (mg):	0
Carbohydrate (g):	30.1
Dietary Fiber (g):	1.7
Protein (g):	0.5
Sodium (mg):	69
Calcium (mg):	7
Iron (mg):	0.3
Vitamin C (mg):	4
Vitamin A (i.u.):	1

Place bottom crust in a 9-inch pie pan. Preheat oven to 425°F. In a large bowl, combine all remaining ingredients and toss to coat. Spoon into pastry-lined pan. Top with remaining pastry, seal edges (crimp decoratively), and cut 6 slits radiating from the center. Bake until the crust is golden brown, about 45 minutes. Serve with vanilla ice cream, if desired.

Note: You can substitute the apples for just about any fruit you like—berries, peaches, pears—experiment!

Chocolate Decadence

Serves
12

5	OUNCES BITTERSWEET OR SEMISWEET CHOCOLATE
1	LARGE EGG, AT ROOM TEMPERATURE
1	LARGE EGG YOLK, AT ROOM TEMPERATURE
1	TEASPOON VANILLA EXTRACT
$\frac{1}{2}$	CUP PLUS $1\frac{1}{2}$ TEASPOONS UNSWEETENED DUTCH-PROCESS COCOA POWDER
$\frac{2}{3}$	CUP PLUS $\frac{1}{4}$ CUP SUGAR
2	TABLESPOONS ALL-PURPOSE FLOUR
$\frac{3}{4}$	CUP LOW-FAT MILK
2	LARGE EGG WHITES
$\frac{1}{8}$	TEASPOON CREAM OF TARTAR

Preheat oven to 350°F. Lightly coat the sides of an 8 x 2-inch round cake pan with vegetable oil cooking spray. Line the bottom with parchment or wax paper. Place the chocolate in a large bowl. In a small bowl, lightly beat the whole egg, yolk, and vanilla.

In a heavy medium saucepan, combine the cocoa with $\frac{2}{3}$ cup sugar and the flour. Gradually whisk in enough milk to form a smooth paste. Whisk in the remaining milk. Bring to a simmer over moderate heat, stirring constantly with a wooden spoon. Simmer very gently, stirring constantly for $1\frac{1}{2}$ minutes. Pour the hot cocoa mixture over the chocolate and let sit for 30 seconds, then whisk until completely smooth. Whisk in the egg mixture.

Using an electric mixer, beat the egg whites at medium speed until foamy and then add the cream of tartar and beat until soft peaks form. Gradually add the remaining $\frac{1}{4}$ cup sugar, increase the speed to high, and beat until whites are stiff but not dry.

Using a large rubber spatula, fold one fourth of the whites into the chocolate mixture. Fold in the remaining whites.

Scrape the batter into the prepared pan and smooth the top. Set the cake pan in a large baking pan and place in lower third of oven. Pour enough boiling water into the baking pan to reach half way up the sides of the cake pan. Bake for 30 minutes, or until the cake springs back when very gently pressed. It will still be very soft inside, but it will firm up as it sits.

Remove the cake pan from the water bath and set aside on a rack to cool. Cover with plastic wrap and refrigerate overnight or for up to 2 days. You can also unmold it, wrap well, and freeze for up to 2 months. To serve, run a thin, sharp knife around the edge of the pan to loosen the cake. Invert the cake on a plate covered with wax paper. Peel off the paper and turn the cake right side up on a serving plate. Slice the cake with a thin, sharp knife, dipping it in hot water and drying between slices.

NUTRITION

Per Serving

Calories (kcal): 151.0	Protein (g): 3.2
Total Fat (g): 5.2	Sodium (mg): 25
Saturated Fat (g): 2.8	Calcium (mg): 32
Cholesterol (mg): 37	Iron (mg): 1.1
Carbohydrate (g): 26.7	Vitamin C (mg): 0
Dietary Fiber (g): 2.0	Vitamin A (i.u.): 88

Comforting Baked Apples

Serves
6

8	LARGE McINTOSH APPLES, QUARTERED
2	TABLESPOONS UNSALTED BUTTER
$\frac{1}{4}$	CUP PURE MAPLE SYRUP
$\frac{1}{4}$	CUP LIGHT BROWN SUGAR, PACKED
1	TEASPOON GROUND CINNAMON
	PINCH OF SALT

NUTRITION

Per Serving

Calories (kcal):	202.5
Total Fat (g):	4.8
Saturated Fat (g):	2.6
Cholesterol (mg):	11
Carbohydrate (g):	43.1
Dietary Fiber (g):	5.2
Protein (g):	0.4
Sodium (mg):	4
Calcium (mg):	33
Iron (mg):	0.8
Vitamin C (mg):	11
Vitamin A (i.u.):	251

Preheat oven to 325°F. Butter an 11 x 14-inch baking pan, and put apples in.

In a small pan, melt butter, then add maple syrup, brown sugar, cinnamon, and salt. Mix well and pour over apples.

Bake for 30 to 45 minutes, basting often. Serve warm, in bowls.

Note: If you are feeling especially needy, add a scoop of vanilla ice cream on top. Yikes!

First Prize
Chocolate Fudge Cake

Serves
12

1	12-OUNCE PACKAGE SEMISWEET
	CHOCOLATE CHIPS
5	TABLESPOONS WATER
2	TABLESPOONS INSTANT COFFEE POWDER
1½	CUPS UNSALTED BUTTER, SOFTENED
2	CUPS GRANULATED SUGAR
6	LARGE EGGS, SEPARATED
1	CUP ALL-PURPOSE FLOUR
	CONFECTIONERS' SUGAR

NUTRITION	
Per Serving	
Calories (kcal):	474.6
Total Fat (g):	29.6
Saturated Fat (g):	17.4
Cholesterol (mg):	168
Carbohydrate (g):	50.9
Dietary Fiber (g):	0.8
Protein (g):	5.2
Sodium (mg):	266
Calcium (mg):	27
Iron (mg):	1.4
Vitamin C (mg):	0
Vitamin A (i.u.):	1,018

Heat oven to 350°F. Butter a 9-inch springform pan and wrap outside of pan, extending up behind rim, securely with foil to insulate and prevent edges from burning. Heat chocolate with water and coffee powder in medium saucepan over very low heat, stirring occasionally, just until chocolate is melted. Cool to room temperature. Beat butter with electric mixer until creamy. Beat in sugar until light and fluffy, about 5 minutes. Beat in yolks, one at a time, beating well after each. On low speed, gradually add flour. Stir in cooled chocolate mixture.

In a clean bowl, beat whites until foamy. Gradually increase speed and beat until stiff, but not dry. Fold one fourth of the whites into chocolate mixture and once incorporated, fold in the rest. Pour batter into prepared pan. Bake 60 to 65 minutes, or until toothpick inserted in cake about 1 inch from edge comes out clean. Do not worry if top cracks. Cool in pan on a rack. Cover and then refrigerate overnight. Remove sides of pan. Sift confectioners' sugar lightly over top. Use a stencil for an extra touch.

Fruit Pizza

Serves
6

	PASTRY FOR **1**-CRUST **10**-INCH PIE
2	TABLESPOONS UNSALTED BUTTER, MELTED
1	MEDIUM PLUM, PITTED AND SLICED $\frac{1}{4}$-INCH THICK
1	MEDIUM PEACH, PITTED AND SLICED $\frac{1}{4}$-INCH THICK
$\frac{1}{2}$	CUP STRAWBERRIES, HALVED
$\frac{1}{2}$	CUP BLUEBERRIES
1	TABLESPOON ALL-PURPOSE FLOUR
$3\frac{1}{2}$	TABLESPOONS SUGAR
	WHIPPED CREAM FLAVORED WITH A LITTLE GROUND GINGER

NUTRITION

Per Serving Without Whipped Cream

Calories (kcal):	147.2
Total Fat (g):	7.7
Saturated Fat (g):	4.5
Cholesterol (mg):	19
Carbohydrate (g):	19.2
Dietary Fiber (g):	1.1
Protein (g):	1.3
Sodium (mg):	22
Calcium (mg):	7
Iron (mg):	0.5
Vitamin C (mg):	11
Vitamin A (i.u.):	383

Preheat oven to 450°F.

On a lightly floured surface, roll out dough into a 10-inch round. Fold in half and transfer to an ungreased baking sheet. Unfold the dough and gently smooth. Using a pastry brush, lightly brush on some of the melted butter. Arrange the fruit decoratively on top, leaving a 1-inch border free of fruit. Sprinkle the flour and remaining butter on the surface and then $2\frac{1}{2}$ tablespoons of the sugar. Fold up the edge of the dough, forming a crust.

Bake the "pizza" for about 20 minutes, or until the bottom is golden brown. Remove from oven and turn on the broiler. Sprinkle remaining 1 tablespoon of sugar on top and then broil for just 1 minute, until the juice begins to bubble. Slide onto a cooling rack to cool slightly, and serve warm with flavored whipped cream.

Nectarine and Raspberry Pie

Serves
6

2 $\frac{3}{4}$	CUPS ALL-PURPOSE FLOUR
$\frac{1}{2}$	TEASPOON SALT
6	TABLESPOONS UNSALTED BUTTER, CHILLED, IN BITS
$\frac{1}{2}$	CUP VEGETABLE SHORTENING
$\frac{1}{2}$	CUP ICE WATER

FILLING

6	CUPS HALVED AND SLICED NECTARINES
2	TABLESPOONS FRESH LEMON JUICE
$\frac{1}{2}$	CUP SUGAR
2	TABLESPOONS ALL-PURPOSE FLOUR
1	TEASPOON GROUND CINNAMON
1	PINT RASPBERRIES
2	TABLESPOONS UNSALTED BUTTER, IN BITS
1	LARGE EGG, BEATEN
1	TABLESPOON SUGAR

Preheat oven to 425°F.

In a large bowl, combine flour with salt. Add butter and shortening and toss to coat with your fingers. Rub the mixture between your fingers, bringing up flour from the bottom to the top, until the mixture looks like coarse meal. Sprinkle with ice water, 1 tablespoon at a time, stirring with a fork, until dough comes together

and holds. Sprinkle the work surface with a little flour and turn dough out onto the surface. Gather it into a ball, then flatten into a disk. Wrap in plastic and refrigerate at least 30 minutes.

Make the filling: In a large bowl, combine nectarine slices, lemon juice, sugar, flour, and cinnamon. Toss, and let sit for 30 minutes while dough rests.

Sprinkle work surface with a little flour, flatten the dough slightly by hitting with rolling pin, and roll dough out to $\frac{1}{4}$-inch thickness. Line a buttered 9-inch square or round baking pan with dough, but do not trim overhang. Evenly distribute nectarine mixture, scatter on berries, and dot with butter. Close overhanging flaps of dough over fruit—they won't touch and will be uneven, but that's the whole idea. Brush the crust with beaten egg, sprinkle with sugar, and bake until the crust is golden and the juice is bubbling, about 40 minutes. Cool on a rack and serve cool or warm.

Note: Any assortment of fruits will work here, but I like the combination of stone fruit and berries best!

NUTRITION	
Per Serving	
Calories (kcal):	566.0
Total Fat (g):	23.7
Saturated Fat (g):	10.1
Cholesterol (mg):	57
Carbohydrate (g):	81.3
Dietary Fiber (g):	2.4
Protein (g):	8.6
Sodium (mg):	191
Calcium (mg):	27
Iron (mg):	3.0
Vitamin C (mg):	10
Vitamin A (i.u.):	1,228

Ice Cream Saves the World!

Newspapers, books, and magazines constantly remind us that the rain forests are being destroyed. Television documentaries on the subject have almost surpassed Hitler documentaries as the most popular form of cable programming. The only conclusion I've drawn from watching these programs is that both Hitler and rain forest destruction are evil! The big difference is that Hitler was stopped. I'm not comparing the horror of Hitler's reign to the plight of the rain forests on any level, but what I'm getting at is if our government really wants to stop something or someone it most certainly can.

Let me put it this way. If Hitler were back in power today, our first act of aggression would not involve Sting and Don Henley storming the beaches at Normandy (although playing Twisted Sister really loud did cause a certain pox-marked Panamanian dictator to run screaming into the arms of U.S. Marines). I don't see any musicians joining forces with Jim Brown or Charles Bronson as part of the New Dirty Dozen. I'm all for rock stars lending support to good causes. I just don't understand why rock stars can't teach us something useful. We are constantly bombarded by musicians on VH-1 and MTV telling us about the atrocities of humankind. It's always about a great injustice here or a horrible oppression there. I believe rock stars genuinely want to help, because people who are forced to live under the stranglehold of oppression don't buy many albums. Americans are conditioned to buy this to fix that. It's all on the consumer's shoulders to pull the world together. Let's be real. How much Ben & Jerry's Rain Forest Crunch do I have to consume to stop the destruction? If I balloon up to twelve hundred pounds, maybe then I'll have done my part to save the planet. Only then I'll need Dick Gregory to save me.

The rain forest tragedy has only human greed to blame. It's out of control. Thousands and thousands of acres are eliminated each day. We are so smart and technologically advanced that we can download nude photos of silicone-infested wonder Pamela Lee—I mean Anderson—I mean Lee—I mean Puente. (Hey, she loves drummers. Just check the tabloids after you buy the book.) Yet we can't save the rain forests. Blowing money on albums, concerts, ice cream, T-shirts, pledge drives, fancy peanut brittle, and theme restaurants is not going to do the trick. The only real solution is to simply pull the plug on the butthead with the bulldozer. All the United Nations forces would have to do is ask him nicely.

UN FORCES: "Hey, Carlo, how about no bulldozing today?"

CARLO: "What do you mean? Do you realize how many acres I destroy in a second?"

UN FORCES: "Yes, we all do, and that's why we're here."

CARLO: "No."

UN FORCES: "Come on."

CARLO: "No. If I stop, everybody will be able to breathe."

UN FORCES: "We'll buy you some ice cream."

CARLO: "What kind?"

UN FORCES: "Ben and Jerry's."

CARLO: "You got that Chunky Monkey?"

UN FORCES: "Yep."

CARLO: "Can I get that in one of those tasty waffle cones?"

UN FORCES: "Sure, just give me the keys."

CARLO: "OK."

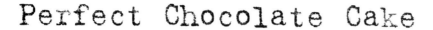
Perfect Chocolate Cake

<table>
<tr><td rowspan="11" valign="top">Serves
12</td></tr>
</table>

2 2/3	CUPS ALL-PURPOSE FLOUR
1	CUP UNSWEETENED COCOA POWDER
1	TABLESPOON BAKING SODA
1/2	TEASPOON SALT
1/2	TEASPOON GROUND CINNAMON
1	CUP UNSALTED BUTTER, SOFTENED
3	CUPS BROWN SUGAR, FIRMLY PACKED
4	LARGE EGGS
1	TABLESPOON VANILLA EXTRACT
1 1/3	CUPS SOUR CREAM
1 1/3	CUPS HOT WATER

FROSTING

4	OUNCES UNSWEETENED CHOCOLATE
2	OUNCES SEMISWEET CHOCOLATE
1/2	CUP UNSALTED BUTTER, CUT INTO SMALL CUBES
5	CUPS CONFECTIONERS' SUGAR
1	CUP SOUR CREAM
2 1/2	TEASPOONS VANILLA EXTRACT
1/4	TEASPOON GROUND CINNAMON

Heat oven to 350°F. Grease three 9-inch round cake pans. Line bottoms with wax paper, then grease and flour paper.

Combine flour, cocoa, baking soda, salt, and cinnamon in a medium bowl. Set aside. Beat butter in mixer bowl until creamy. Beat in brown sugar. Beat in eggs, one at a time, beating well after each. Add vanilla. At low speed, add dry ingredients alternately with sour cream, beginning and ending with dry ingredients. Stir in hot water; beat at low speed just until blended.

Pour batter into prepared cake pans and bake 30 to 35 minutes, or until a toothpick inserted in center comes out clean. Cool in pans on a rack for 10 minutes. Unmold and cool completely.

Make the frosting: Heat chocolate and butter over very low heat, stirring occasionally, just until melted. Cool to room temperature. Combine confectioners' sugar, sour cream, vanilla, and cinnamon in mixer bowl. Beat in cooled chocolate mixture until creamy. Frost cake.

Note: This is a great birthday cake or other special-occasion cake. The cinnamon adds a nice level of depth.

NUTRITION

Per Serving

Calories (kcal):	844.1
Total Fat (g):	41.7
Saturated Fat (g):	25.0
Cholesterol (mg):	152
Carbohydrate (g):	118.3
Dietary Fiber (g):	4.2
Protein (g):	9.2
Sodium (mg):	699
Calcium (mg):	122
Iron (mg):	4.1
Vitamin C (mg):	0
Vitamin A (i.u.):	1,327

Plum and Blueberry Crisp

Serves
6

6	CUPS PITTED AND QUARTERED PLUMS
1	PINT BLUEBERRIES
1	TABLESPOON LEMON JUICE
2	TABLESPOONS ALL-PURPOSE FLOUR
$\frac{1}{4}$	CUP GRANULATED SUGAR

TOPPING

1	CUP ALL-PURPOSE FLOUR
$\frac{1}{2}$	CUP FINELY CHOPPED WALNUTS
$\frac{1}{2}$	CUP LIGHT BROWN SUGAR
6	TABLESPOONS UNSALTED BUTTER, CHILLED, IN BITS

NUTRITION	
Per Serving	
Calories (kcal):	452.2
Total Fat (g):	19.5
Saturated Fat (g):	8.1
Cholesterol (mg):	33
Carbohydrate (g):	67.8
Dietary Fiber (g):	4.3
Protein (g):	6.7
Sodium (mg):	10
Calcium (mg):	33
Iron (mg):	1.9
Vitamin C (mg):	23
Vitamin A (i.u.):	1,071

Preheat oven to 375°F.

In a large bowl, combine the fruit, lemon juice, flour, and sugar. Set aside.

Make the topping: In a medium bowl, combine the flour, walnuts, and brown sugar. Add the butter and combine by rubbing the flour and butter mixture through your fingers, breaking up the mixture till it looks like large crumbs.

Spread the fruit mixture in an 8-inch square glass baking dish or casserole and sprinkle the topping evenly over the fruit. Bake in the upper third of the oven until the topping is golden and the juice is bubbling. Cool on a rack, and serve room temperature or warm.

The Best Chocolate Chip Cookies

Makes
25

1	CUP UNSALTED BUTTER
1	TEASPOON SALT
2	TEASPOONS VANILLA EXTRACT
$\frac{1}{4}$	CUP GRANULATED SUGAR
$\frac{3}{4}$	CUP LIGHT BROWN SUGAR, FIRMLY PACKED
2	LARGE EGGS
$2\frac{1}{4}$	CUPS ALL-PURPOSE FLOUR
1	TEASPOON BAKING SODA
1	TEASPOON HOT WATER
2	CUPS WALNUTS
1	POUND SEMISWEET CHOCOLATE, CUT INTO $\frac{1}{2}$-INCH PIECES

In large bowl of an electric mixer, beat the butter until soft, then add the salt, vanilla, and sugars and beat until smooth. Add eggs and mix. On low speed, add half the flour, scraping the sides down.

In a small cup, stir the baking soda into the hot water, then add to the dough. Add the rest of the flour and beat only until combined. Do not overmix. Remove the bowl from the mixer and stir in the nuts and chocolate by hand. Refrigerate the dough for at least 2 hours, or even overnight.

Preheat oven to 375°F, and adjust the racks so that the oven is divided in thirds. Line cookie sheets with parchment or foil, shiny side up.

Place a piece of foil or parchment on the counter, and put rounded tablespoons of the dough on it. Wet your hands with cold water and shake off, but don't dry. Roll a piece of the dough between your damp hands into a ball, then flatten it between your hands so they are $\frac{1}{2}$-inch thick. Place on lined cookie sheets, 2 inches apart. Bake for 12 minutes, or until golden brown and crisp. If necessary, reverse sheets in oven so that they all get evenly browned. *Do not* underbake. Let cookies sit for a moment, then transfer them to a cooling rack with a spatula.

Note: My mom's cookies are the best.

NUTRITION

Per Serving

Calories (kcal):	216.8
Total Fat (g):	11.3
Saturated Fat (g):	4.3
Cholesterol (mg):	18
Carbohydrate (g):	28.4
Dietary Fiber (g):	2.0
Protein (g):	3.9
Sodium (mg):	146
Calcium (mg):	23
Iron (mg):	1.5
Vitamin C (mg):	0
Vitamin A (i.u.):	43

Grandma Helen's Pie

Serves
6

2	CUPS ALL-PURPOSE FLOUR
	PINCH OF SALT
$\frac{2}{3}$	CUP VEGETABLE SHORTENING
	COLD WATER
6	MEDIUM APPLES (A VARIETY)
$\frac{1}{2}$	CUP SUGAR, OR MORE IF DESIRED
	DASH OF GROUND CINNAMON
	DASH OF GRATED NUTMEG

NUTRITION

Per Serving

Calories (kcal):	499.0
Total Fat (g):	23.7
Saturated Fat (g):	5.8
Cholesterol (mg):	0
Carbohydrate (g):	69.5
Dietary Fiber (g):	3.7
Protein (g):	4.6
Sodium (mg):	1
Calcium (mg):	16
Iron (mg):	2.2
Vitamin C (mg):	8
Vitamin A (i.u.):	73

Blend flour and salt in a medium bowl, add shortening and blend with a pastry blender or fork. When the mixture is crumbly, add just enough cold water for the dough to hold together. Separate dough into 2 large balls, dust 2 pieces of wax paper with flour, and place one ball between the 2 pieces. Roll out dough between the wax paper to a circle about 9 inches in diameter.

Peel off the paper on one side and place dough into an 8-inch pie plate. Peel off other piece of paper. Roll out the second piece of dough the same way, but make it slightly larger, about 10 inches. Place both in refrigerator.

Preheat oven to 425°F.

Peel, core, and slice apples, then place in a large mixing bowl. Toss with sugar, cinnamon, and nutmeg. Put the apple mixture in the bottom crust, cover with the top crust, and pinch edges together. Put a few fork holes in the top crust and brush with a little cream or melted butter. Bake for 20 minutes, then lower heat to 350° and bake for 40 minutes more, or until the crust is lightly browned and the apples are tender.

Note: This is Sean's mother's and grandmother's pie recipe.

The Great Diet Pie Caper

My grandmother Helen made the best pies I've ever eaten. Some people make good pies, but so often they specialize in just one kind of pie. Be it pecan or blueberry, the average pie baker's view is normally a myopic one—or in this case, a "pieopic" one. But not Helen. Apple, chocolate cream, and pumpkin were just a few of the howitzers

in her baking arsenal. And to top it off, she made the most delicious crust as well. Flaky and hearty, crispy yet yielding, Helen's pie crust was the embodiment of all that is exceptional in the world. Each year in the Northeast, the cool advances of the late September air blush the maple leaves a fiery gold. In my home this signaled the start of pie season. The commencement of pie season was always a tranquil time for me. The new school year was still in its infancy, and I had yet to blemish my academic slate. Even at my worst, I could support the flimsy facade that I was a competent student until Columbus Day. Arriving

home to the aromatic intoxication of the first apple pie of the season would lure my thoughts to those of a young Abraham Lincoln. I would think to myself, "Best tend to the wood pile before I take part in a piece of that mighty fine pie." Then I would sit by the hearth, do my homework on a rock, and play Atari by firelight. Such were the intrusive thoughts triggered by the scent of a fresh baked pie.

One year pie season hit our house with a baking fury never before seen. My grandmother's sister Wanda was living with us, and our oven became an endless fount of baked goods. Helen and Wanda tag-teamed the kitchen with no holds barred. The twin oven was held in a merciless headlock until it surrendered the tastiest of treats.

Pie season reached its apex on Thanksgiving Day. Thanksgiving was Helen's "Super Bowl Thursday." In addition to serving the traditional spread with all the trimmings, she topped it off by baking ten to fifteen pies, even though only ten family members attended the autumnal feast. The ratio of people to pies would lead you to believe that ten to fifteen pies would be overkill, but on the contrary, many relatives and family friends would make a pilgrimage to see Helen after their own family meal, just for a slice of pie nirvana. As the legend of her pies spread, the number of dessert hoppers grew.

Nearly twenty years ago, my mother proclaimed that she was on a diet and would not be taking part in the parade of pies on Thanksgiving Day. In my grandmother's eye, not to eat pie on Thanksgiving was a sin beyond forgiveness. So to meet with the demands of a changing world and a dieting daughter, Helen reached into her bag of tricks and concocted a diet pie. The days before Thanksgiving, as my mother and grandmother fought the battle of the pie bulge, Uncle Tom recruited a new devotee to Helen's "Temple of Pie." Tom's prospect was his friend Paul. Tom told Paul of the growing legend of Helen's pies and extended him an invitation, which Paul, a pastry junkie, quickly accepted. In years to come, Paul would prove to be a great friend of the family and a zealot when it came to ritualistic holiday celebration. (A showman never to be outdone, Paul would arrive unannounced on Christmas Eve, dressed as a holiday pine tree that lit up when you plugged him in. If the party was in his honor and no costumes were prepared, Paul would resort to acts of strength. At a soiree celebrating the completion of his MBA from Columbia

University, Paul split open a honeydew melon with his head. Paul would perform whenever there was a gathering. The only problem was no one knew what form the ubiquitous Paul would take.) Thanksgiving Day arrived and everything was in place. The house was buzzing with the anticipation of the holiday bounty. Steam fogged the windows, so the doors were open to cool down the house with crisp autumn air. The table was set and the mad rush was on to finish the final trimmings. In all the confusion we almost didn't notice a swift-moving teen in a blue-hooded sweatshirt dart in the side door and out the front door. I leapt up from my seat to catch a glimpse of the fleeing intruder, who was also a thief. His hot criminal hand cradled a pie as he fled down the road, and Helen immediately checked which pie had been stolen. After a quick inventory, Helen's worst fear was confirmed: "He stole the diet pie!" Helen was not concerned that her home was violated on this sacred day, but rather that her baking reputation might be destroyed now that the diet pie was out in public.

Paul soon called and admitted that he was the "pie perpetrator." When all was said and done, Helen had Paul over for a proper slice of her very undiet pie. By the time the low-cal pie was returned, my mom had already had a piece of regulation chocolate cream. On that strange day my grandmother and Paul became great friends, and Helen promised never to bake a diet pie again.

GENERAL INDEX

RECIPE INDEX

DICKENS' LONDON

DICKENS' LONDON
An Imaginative Vision

Introduced by Peter Ackroyd

Text by Piers Dudgeon

HEADLINE

Created and produced by
PILOT PRODUCTIONS LTD
59 Charlotte Street, London W1P 1LA

Copyright © Pilot Productions Ltd, 1987
Contributions by Peter Ackroyd
Copyright © Peter Ackroyd, 1987

First published in Great Britain in 1987 by
HEADLINE BOOK PUBLISHING PLC

This edition published in 1989
Reprinted in 1991

British Library Cataloguing in Publication Data

Dickens, Charles, 1812-1870
    Dickens' London
    1. Dickens, Charles, 1812-1870 – Homes and
    haunts – England – London 2. London (England)
    – Description
    I. Title
    823'.8 PR4528-9

Typeset by Dorchester Typesetting Limited, Dorset
Printed by Tien Wah Press (PTE.) Limited, Singapore

ISBN: 0-7472-7997-7

Pilot Productions wish to thank Jonathan Jones for his editorial
assistance and Anthea Zeman for her research assistance.

We would also like to thank the following picture sources for their
permission to include the photographs in the book:

The Dickens House Museum, Guildhall Library: City of London, Dr
Barnardo's, The Museum of London, London Borough of Camden
Local History Library, David Francis, BBC Hulton Picture Library,
The Science Museum of London, The Salvation Army, Greater
London Record Office, The Mansell Collection, The Fotomas Index,
The Victoria and Albert Museum, The National Maritime Museum,
Westminster City Library, Sir Benjamin Stone Collection, City of
Birmingham Libraries, Royal Commission on the Historical
Monuments of London

Contents

Introduction

London created Dickens, just as Dickens created London. He came to it as a small, nervous child but by the time of his death, in 1870, he had recreated that city for the generations that followed him. He found a city of brick, and left a city of people. London entered his soul; it terrified him and it entranced him. It became the material for his fantasy and the arena for his polemic. And, in the end, it was truly Dickens' London.

His family settled in the metropolis in 1822, when he was ten years old; 'settled' is hardly the word, however, since from the beginning they embarked upon a shiftless life which was to take them from house to house, from Camden Town to the Borough, from Gower Street to Somers Town, and it was not really until Dickens acquired fame as a novelist that these domestic wanderings came to an end. During the early years of his life London was for the novelist a place of precarious refuge, then, and yet the most profound shock was also one of the first: within less than two years of the family's arrival in the city John Dickens, the novelist's father, was arrested for debt and incarcerated in the Marshalsea Prison. It was at this time that Dickens himself was sent out to work in an old blacking-factory by Hungerford Stairs: 'No words,' he wrote later, 'can express the secret agony of my soul . . .' That warehouse, and his work there covering the tops of paste-blacking, never left his memory – he always recalled the rats, the dirt, the decay, and the old tumbling building lurching over towards the river, the river which was now bearing away the hopes of his childhood. The Thames always haunted his imagination, and it runs through his novels just as surely as it runs through the city itself. It became an emblem for his descent into London, his first awareness of its depths: for here was a child, eager, ambitious, with an equal thirst for learning and for applause, suddenly laid waste by the amorphous darkness of the city. 'I often forget in my dreams,' he wrote, 'that I have a dear wife and children; even that I am a man; and wander desolately back to that time of my life.'

And so this vision of London as a place of darkness, as a place of imprisonment and suffocation, never left him. In a way it is as if the city itself took on the shape of his fears so that for him it became an unreal city, a shadow play in which the various areas of darkness were cast by Dickens' own hands. So it is that in his fiction he returns again and again to the same areas – the Strand, the Borough, Covent Garden, Waterloo Bridge, Camden Town, all these places being the sites of his youthful anguish and

London as a place of imprisonment. In a way it is as if the city itself took on the shape of his fears.

7

'Draw but a little circle above the clustering housetops, and you shall have within its space everything, with its opposite extreme and contradiction close beside.' Master Humphrey's Clock

humiliation. The journey from the blacking factory to Lant Street (where for a short while he lodged near his father's prison) becomes a dolorous way with each street corner another bead on the rosary of his pain – 'My old way home by the Borough made me cry, after my eldest child could speak,' he wrote in the same autobiographical fragment, and it was in Covent Garden, close to the site of his childhood suffering, that Little Dorrit cries out, 'And London looks so large, so barren and so wild.'

Most of the areas which haunted him have now gone for ever – his first house in Bayham Street demolished, the warehouse gone, the Marshalsea Prison dismantled. And yet these places still live because of Dickens; they survive in the horror which he was able to impart to them – 'Mother! . . . bury me in the open fields – anywhere but in these dreadful streets . . . they have killed me.' And the London of his childhood has lived on, too, in the imagination of all those who have read his novels – the terrible London, the oppressive London, the destructive London which Henry James saw through the eyes of the greater novelist, 'packed to blackness with accumulations of suffered experience'.

And yet the London of the 1820s and 1830s was not simply a fulcrum of Dickens's own 'suffered experience', and indeed even for him it was much more than a place of sorrowful mysteries only: it was here that he learnt self-reliance, after all, and it was

in the city that he acquired that capacity for work and that determination to succeed which were eventually to triumph over all the circumstances of his early years. But, more importantly, this was the place which liberated his imagination and filled it with scenes and with characters that he would have discovered nowhere else on earth. Even as a child he became entranced with it and in a late essay, 'Gone Astray', he recalls a day when he was lost in London and when his enduring images were of the Giants of Guildhall, of a toyshop, of a City like a bazaar from *The Arabian Nights*, of a theatre – all of which comprised an 'enchanted spot', a glittering metropolis made up from memories of his childhood reading and from his own impassioned fantasies of a life quite different from any he had known before.

And what kind of city was it in those early days? It glittered only in Dickens' youthful imagination. It was only partly illuminated by gas (and that of a yellow and smokey sort, not the brilliant lighting of the 1890s), so that most of the streets were lit by infrequent oil lamps and there were linkboys bearing lights to escort late pedestrians home; there were watchmen known as 'Charlies' (the Metropolitan Police were not established until

1829). It was a more compact city than it was soon to become, and in part it still retained its eighteenth century rural aspects – just beyond the grime of the city there were strawberry fields at Hammersmith and Hackney, and in the aptly named Haymarket farmers still came to haggle over the price of that commodity. The great public buildings which are now associated with London had not yet been erected: until 1827, for example, Trafalgar Square was a patch of waste ground enlivened only by a coach-stand.

When old men looked back on this period, in the 1880s, they characteristically remembered the dog fights, the cock fights, the numerous public hangings, the pillory; but they also recalled the fact that London then enjoyed what was still essentially an eighteenth-century street life – the ballad singers, the theatres with their playbills put up in the local tobacco shop or pastry cook's, the brightly coloured caricatures displayed in the shop windows (around which crowds tended to congregate to see the latest engravings by Gillray or Cruikshank), the strolling peddlers with their penny dreadfuls and their 'last confessions', the beer shops, the gin palaces (there was no age limit for drinking and, before 1839, no licensing hours), the dancing saloons, the pleasure gardens, the free-and-easies, the penny gaffs, the unlicensed theatres. Even the streets themselves took on a theatrical character, and one contemporary noted how many houses 'had plastered and painted windows, which looked like scenes in pantomime'. And then there were the song books, the almanacs, the broadsides, the political ballads, the religious ballads, the criminal ballads. It was often said, at the end of the nineteenth century, that London had then been a more colourful place, a city where the absence of any standardised education (and indeed of any standardised social system) encouraged eccentricity and oddity of every kind. Certainly this is the metropolis which we find in Dickens; it would not be too much to say that this early London, this London with its heart in the eighteenth century and its mind in the nineteenth, this London which is now so distant, was the city which entranced him.

His own education in its way was extensive and peculiar. He went from the blacking factory to a school near Mornington Crescent and it seems that, when he emerged as a lawyer's clerk in his fifteenth year, he was already a Londoner *in excelsis*. One of his contemporaries said of him that, 'his knowledge of London was wonderful, for he could describe the position of every shop in the West End streets'. In addition, 'he could imitate, in a manner that I have never heard equalled, the low population of the streets of London in all their varieties.' Here we have the makings of the novelist, taking in to himself, as it were, the noises and the localities of the great city, turning himself into a simulacrum of its population. And he never ceased to write about

Covent Garden. 'Such stale and vapid rejected cabbage-leaf and cabbage-stalk dress, such damaged-orange countenance, such squashed pulp of humanity, are open to the day nowhere else.'
Our Mutual Friend

London – all of his novels, with the exception of *Hard Times*, are deeply invaded by the city. It is not just that he was never really able to write about life outside London – his excursions into the country are seen, as it were, through quintessentially Cockney eyes – it is simply that he needed the city. He needed its life; he

10

'. . . and so into Smithfield; from which place arose a tumult of discordant sounds that filled Oliver Twist with amazement.'

needed the streets of this 'magic lantern', as he called it. '. . . A day in London sets me up again and starts me,' he told his close friend John Forster, and one of his daughters remembers how he was often forced out into the noise and tumult 'to enable him to struggle through some difficult part of a long story . . . a long walk in the noisy streets would act upon him as a tonic.'

He was distracted and even soothed by the tumult but also, in the life of the streets, he found confirmation of, and sustenance

'The restlessness of a great city, and the way in which it tumbles and tosses before it can get to sleep, formed one of the first entertainments offered to the contemplation of us homeless people.'
The Uncommercial Traveller

for, his own teeming imagination. He wanted to know everything, to notice every aspect and detail of the urban multitude around him, and it was said soon after his death that 'when you talked to him you found out that his first thought is to find out something new about London life – some new custom or trade or mode of living – and his second thought is to imagine the people engaged in that custom or trade.' And we can find no better confirmation of his need for London than the fact that he lived in it for most of his life – in Doughty Street, in Devonshire Terrace and in Tavistock Square. Even after he had bought Gad's Hill Place in Kent, he still rented houses in London so that he was never more than a few steps away from the real world of his fiction.

London was his great subject. He was the first novelist clearly (if not necessarily consciously) to see that a new form of life was being created, and as a result he has justly been called 'the first great novelist of the industrial city'. He became the chronicler of London at a uniquely propitious moment: even as he wrote it was growing all around him and throughout the first half of the nineteenth century the 'great Oven', as he sometimes called it, was spreading through Bloomsbury, Islington and St John's Wood in the North and, in the West and South, through Paddington, Bayswater, South Kensington, Lambeth, Clerkenwell, Peckham, and elsewhere. It became the largest city in the world, just as Britain itself became the first urbanised society in the world; Dickens's art as a novelist thus coincides with an enormous change in the direction of human history and part of his great popularity must surely spring from the fact that he was able to offer an idealised image – a coherent report – of a phenomenon that was bewildering even those who were then taking up their places in a new society and under a new dispensation.

And there was much to bewilder the inhabitants of this burgeoning London. There were times when it seemed like a new Inferno, and *The Great Metropolis* (published in 1837) gives some impression of the sheer noise alone: 'To the stranger's ear, the loud and everlasting rattle of the countless vehicles which ply in the streets of London is an intolerable annoyance. Conversation with a friend whom one chances to meet in mid-day is out of the question . . . one cannot hear a word the other says.' There were the hansom cabs, the new omnibuses, the old stage coaches, the hackney coaches, the waggons, the growing railways (the line from London to Birmingham was built with the aid of some 20,000 labourers and has been described as 'the largest public work ever to be undertaken in the whole history of man'). It was calculated at the time that in 1850 'more than 5,000 horseman passed through Temple Bar in one day' and, in addition, omnibus drivers or conductors – known as 'cads' – kept up a constant shout about their various destinations. In some

11

ways London was a noisier, even more active, city than the one in which we live today and although the plethora of such things as advertising and street traffic might suggest some resemblance to the twentieth-century metropolis, this is an illusion. It was a quite different city. It was a city of small shops, of specialised workshops (such as the manufacture of clothing, machinery and consumer goods), and as a result it was a much more varied place, a more surprising place, a place of enormous heterogeneous bustle and energy.

And that is precisely what Dickens evokes within his novels – this quite new kind of human energy that was even then being created. As a result his novels embody the vigour and the disorder of the city, just as of course they reflect his interest in

'. . . not far from the open square in Clerkenwell, which is yet called, by some strange perversion of terms "The Green",' where Mr Brownlow is robbed and Oliver discovers (to his horror) the purpose of Fagin's training.

the urban mass as it struggled to find political and economic expression. He found one of his first great subjects in those crowds which he memorialised in *Nicholas Nickleby*: 'Streams of people apparently without end poured on and on, jostling each other in the crowd and hurrying forward . . .' In fact most Victorian artists came to love crowds – we see this particularly in the painters of the mid-century (Frith being the major example). Dickens and his contemporaries were celebrating the sheer spectacle of people gathered together, a celebration of human

Busy Holborn. There were the hansom cabs, the new omnibuses, the old stage coaches, the hackney coaches, the waggons. . . . In some ways London was a noisier, even more active, city than the one in which we live today.

It was calculated in 1850 that more than 5,000 horsemen passed through Temple Bar in a day.

energy at a time when its possibilities were just becoming apparent. This is the London of his imagination and in all of his novels we feel the chaos and the momentum of the great city, 'instinct with life and occupation' (*Pickwick Papers*). This is a world of mobility, of change, of speed, of clock time, of the discovery of electromagnetic forces, of the engine, of the steam pump – all of it coming and resounding together in the metropolis so that we have the vision of *Bleak House*: '. . . every noise is merged, this moonlight night, into a distant ringing hum, as if the city were a vast glass, vibrating.'

Of course other and more nebulous consequences emerge from this unique form of human organisation and it was Dickens, for example, who first realised the aesthetic possibilities of a strange new world. He became its chronicler at the right time:

London was as interesting to its own inhabitants then as it now is to us, and there is no doubt that they were eager to see, to read, and to learn all they could about their novel circumstances. In these conditions we find the growth of a more strident melodrama, in its dramatic contrasts mimicking the change and uncertainty of metropolitan life; there are new forms of comedy, particularly the comedy of shiftless street life; and a harsher kind of romanticism emerges – the romanticism which springs from the urban dark.

All of these elements are to be found in Dickens. It is the

13

'Cabs are all very well in cases of expedition, when it's a matter of neck or nothing, life or death, your temporary home or your long one.' Sketches

tumult of London, after all, that encourages the possibility of coincidence, of chance meetings: and in his novels there is a clear understanding of that conjunction of fates which can emerge from rapidity, movement, change and restless motion. But this rapidity means that, within the city, extremes of the human condition can meet, even touch and then move on – here where 'life and death went hand in hand; wealth and poverty stood side by side; repletion and starvation laid them down together' (*Nicholas Nickleby*) and were 'wealth and beggary, vice and virtue, guilt and innocence . . all treading on each other and crowding together . . .' (*Master Humphrey's Clock*). And so, even in these descriptions, the celebration of London is overshadowed by other forebodings; the resistless momentum of the great city leads some people they know not where, in directions which they do not wish to travel.

For Dickens, then, London can be a place of helplessness and anonymity. He once told a journalist that, 'in a city where 99 per cent are strangers to everybody, people would as soon read the Directory as stop and observe every new face they encountered.' So it can be a place of isolation and, therefore, of imprisonment – throughout Dickens' writings there are intimations of the metropolis as a great prison, and the journeys of the workers leaving it at the end of the day are described by him as those of 'prisoners departing from gaol'. As a child he had often

passed the walls of Newgate Prison, and it came for him to stand as an emblem of 'the guilt and misery of London', an emblem he was never able to forget. But London is also a place of secrets, each house enclosing its own so that at night it becomes a locked vault of whispered fears or confessions. And behind these images lies the spectacle of the crowd, of hurrying passers-by, of 'the eternal tread of feet upon the pavement' (*David Copperfield*). London itself becomes an emblem of forgetfulness – of a time that is moving forward with no sense of the past, a time for work and worry, a time that devours and ignores.

But this locale of secrets and of anonymity is perhaps best represented by the fog which is the most distinct atmospheric effect in nineteenth century London. There are several descriptions of fog in Dickens, most notably at the opening of *Bleak House*, but this was not some imagined and idealised obscurity. The London fog was very real indeed, and one contemporary talked of 'the vast city wrapt in a kind of darkness which seems neither to belong to the day nor the night . . .'. In November

Savage London: 'The amount of crime, starvation and nakedness and misery of every sort in the metropolis,' Dickens once said to a journalist, 'surpasses all understanding.'

This vision of London as a place of darkness, as a place of imprisonment and suffocation, never left him.

1844 this fog, a concatenation of chimneys and factories and steamboats and chemical works, turned London pitch black in the middle of the afternoon. But there was a sense in which Dickens loved it; he loved that unearthly darkness which made the city a place of fantasy and a harbinger of night. This was the city that harboured the grotesques and the monsters which he created, fashioning them as he did out of the mud and the dirt which he saw around him. Dickens loved the city of mist, the city of fog, the city of night, the city lit by scattered lights and one of the wonders of reading him is to be able to return to that world, to be able to stand with him on London Bridge and to see 'the red glare of the fires that burnt upon the small craft moored off the different wharfs, and rendering darker and more indistinct the murky buildings on the banks . . .' (*Oliver Twist*). To see with him once again the stuffy closed rooms, the clouds rolling across the sky, the mud, the streets, the mad, the afflicted.

Throughout his life Dickens was seen everywhere in London; it was almost as if he had become one of its presiding spirits, and a contemporary wrote soon after his death that 'the omnibus conductors knew him, the street boys knew him . . . he would turn up in the oddest places, and in the most inclement weather.' He was to be seen at 'lodging houses, station houses, cottages, hovels, Cheap Jack's caravans, workhouses, prisons, barbers' shops, schoolrooms, chandlers' shops, back attics, areas, back yards, dark entries, public houses, rag-shops, police courts, markets' – this topographical catalogue itself suggesting the endless diversity of London during the period, this city of small enclosed spaces butting upon each other, a London as heterogeneous and colourful as it was wide and wild. This was the London that Dickens walked in.

All his life Dickens walked. In many of his novels and journalistic sketches, there is an image of the narrator as

15

houses of Spitalfields, and the shabby 'artists' quarters around Fitzroy Square; he visited the old City churches and the dusty Inns around Holborn; he knew the carriage makers of Long Acre, the watch-makers of Clerkenwell, the news-vendors of Catherine Street and the old-clothes shops off Rosemary Lane. Even at the end of his life, worn out by nerves and dazed by fame, he continued his nocturnal perambulations; one friend remembers a walk with him to the opium dens of Limehouse, to observe a scene which he was later to employ in *The Mystery of Edwin Drood*. This was an area where he had first walked as a boy, when he visited his godfather there, and in this conjunction we see the continuities of his life. Indeed there is a sense in which these London walks consciously echoed those of his childhood, as if he realised that the source of his inspiration came from the London he had known in his earliest years and that he needed to keep fresh in his memory those childhood hours before he could bring the city fully to life.

An Opium Den. 'He is in the meanest and closest of small rooms. Through the ragged window-curtain, the light of the early day steals in from a miserable court. He lies, dressed, across a large unseemly bed, upon a bed-stead that has indeed given way under the weight upon it. Lying, also dressed and also across the bed, not longwise, are a Chinaman, a Lascar, and a haggard woman. The two first are in a sleep or stupor; the last is blowing at a kind of pipe, to kindle it. . . .' The Mystery of Edwin Drood

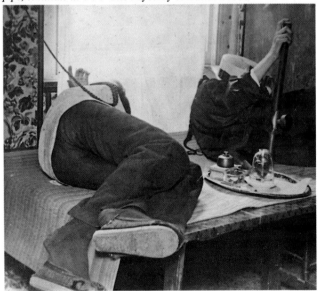

Dr Henry Dawson, an old school friend, described Dickens' delight in masquerading in the streets; 'I quite remember Dickens on one occasion heading us in Drummond Street in pretending to be poor boys, and asking the passers-by for charity – especially old ladies; one of whom told us she "had no money for beggar boys."' On these adventures the old ladies were quite staggered by the impudence of the demand, Dickens would explode with laughter and take to his heels.

wanderer and it is clearly one of great significance to him. The walker is a stranger; he passes through; he patrols those streets where the gas light or oil lamps throw strange shadows; he sees the solid mass of the city around him and yet, if he cares to look up, he sees the bright moon and all the stars (much brighter than any possible view from London today); he sees the rich and poor living within two or three streets of each other, and yet knowing very little of each other's existence; he sees the homeless and he sees the poor, and as he walks he slowly comes to perceive the nature of this city in which he finds himself. We have seen how in his childhood wanderings Dickens himself first came to understand London, but this was just the beginning of a lifetime of pilgrimages through the streets, alleys, rookeries and courts of the metropolis. He walked through grand Belgravia squares, through thick-set, red-brick City squares; he saw the weavers'

16

The brewery that was built at the corner of Tottenham Court Road and what is now New Oxford Street, and bounded on a third side by Bainbridge Street.

New Oxford Street cleared away some of the capital's worst slums – rookeries (crowded tenements) and lodging houses, where every type of crime was to be found.

And so London formed itself around him. But this was not just the city of Inns and Squares and endless bustling activity; it was not just the city of dioramas and waxworks and plays. There was another city, too, a darker city, which he commemorated in his fiction although even he could not bring himself to tell the precise and whole truth. For this was a savage London. He once told a journalist that, 'the amount of crime, starvation and nakedness and misery of every sort in the metropolis surpasses all understanding . . . I have spent many days and nights in the most wretched districts of the metropolis, studying the history of the human heart. There we must go to find it.' And it was in these mean streets that he did find the poverty and the desperation of the metropolis: he saw the skeletons outside the Whitechapel workhouse, wrapped in rags and dying of malnutrition, he saw the orphan children dying in the streets, he saw the boy in the Ragged School 'with burning cheeks and great gaunt eager eyes' who had nothing in the world except a 'bottle of physic' and who was gently led away to die. These were the human beings whom he observed on his journeys through

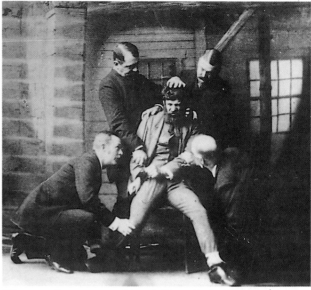

'We are not by any means devout believers in the old Bow Street Police. To say the truth, we think there was a vast amount of humbug about those worthies. Apart from many of them being men of very indifferent character, and far too much in the habit of consorting with thieves and the like, they never lost a public occasion of jobbing and trading the mystery and making the most of themselves. Continually puffed besides by incompetent magistrates anxious to conceal their deficiencies, and hand-in glove with the penny-a-liners of that time, they became a sort of superstition.'
The Uncommercial Traveller

London; they lived in the shadow that the city had cast, and perhaps we can only properly understand the nature of this place when we seek out its victims as Dickens had done.

The problem was that there were just too many people: the population of London had grown from one million at the beginning of the century to approximately 4.5 million by its close. They came in from outlying areas looking for work; they came from Ireland; they came from all the counties of England into the Great Wen, the Oven, the Fever Patch. So they were packed closer and closer together, and it seemed at times as if every inch of the clayey London soil had been built upon. Some found work, some were consigned to the workhouse (it was popularly believed that the London workhouses were the strictest in the country, well earning their nicknames as 'Bastilles') but there was also a floating population of vagrants and homeless drifters (it was

estimated that in 1850 there were some fifteen to twenty thousand of them) who slept in alleys or beneath the new railway arches. Dickens saw them, too, and knew that they were as integral a part of the city as the merchant of Bishopsgate or the hot-pieman of Houndsditch.

But it was as a direct result of these pressures from an enormously expanding population that wholly new fears and preoccupations sprang up within the city. There was, for example, a noticeable increase in crime. London had never been the safest of places but there had been nothing like the rate of crime which now afflicted the Victorians – one newspaper in 1867 estimated that in London there were '100,000 persons who live

'"Are those fever-houses, Darby?" Mr Bucket coolly asks, as he turns his bull's-eye on a line of stinking ruins.
'Darby replies that "all of them" are, and further that in all, for months and months, the people "have been down by dozens", and have been carried out, dead and dying "like sheep with the rot".'
Bleak House

by plunder'. In this huge city there were many 'no go' areas where the new Metropolitan Police force indeed never went; such areas were to be found in Bermondsey, Whitechapel, Stepney, Bethnal Green, Seven Dials, Lambeth, Southwark, Holborn and Westminster itself – the last site suggesting how, in nineteenth-century London, the extremes of vice and respecta-

18

bility might often meet.

And it was in these slums, with their rookeries and their lodging houses, that every type of crime and sexual deviancy was to be found. Here were incest and child prostitution on quite a large scale (to say nothing of the floating population of 'fallen women' who regularly patrolled the main thoroughfares and theatres of the city) – it was reported, for example, that a man had had sexual intercourse with the child he had begotten of his own daughter. This was indeed another country, and the good citizens of London lived in fear of an urban population who seemed literally to be beyond human civilization and who were often described as being no better than 'savages'. There were times, in fact, when many Londoners believed that there would be such a revolution, such an uprising, as to erase all marks of civilisation – Dickens himself hints at these fears both in *Barnaby Rudge* and in *A Tale of Two Cities*. But although there was to be no mass urban rebellion – in some ways London was too diverse, too much a congregation of separate locales, to allow any uniform or organised discontent – there was a deep uncertainty about the nature and the future of the city which had such people in it. No one was sure what kind of place London was, or what it might become.

But it was not just a question of a criminal or barbaric under-class who might terrify the residents of Golden Square or Lincoln's Inn Fields. There were more insidious threats emanating from the dark quarters of the city, the chief among them springing from the fact that until the mid-1860s London itself was a sanitary – or, rather, insanitary – nightmare. Half of the population relied upon water which was piped directly from the Thames – but this was a river into which 200 open sewers flowed, and which at times was described as a 'vast open cloaca'. And since this was the source from which the water came, untreated sewage was to be found emerging from the standing taps or out of the kitchen pipes – in water which was characteristically brown in colour. In addition mains drainage was not introduced into the capital until 1865, which meant that for most of Dickens' lifetime the water from the sinks and the closets ran down through old sewers and into the Thames or was allowed to drain into gigantic cesspools beneath the houses and the courts of the city.

Of course there was often very little water at all in the poorer quarters: in many districts it had to be taken from one standpipe for a short time each day or every alternate day. There was not enough water to wash, or to clean whatever small rooms they possessed, and one inspector in 1847 noted that 'the filth [by which he meant principally excrement] was lying scattered about the rooms, vaults, cellars, areas and yards, so thick, and so deep, that it was hardly possible to move through it.' The

In 1839 almost half the funerals in London were of children under the age of 10.

housing conditions for what might be described as the lower working-class are best summarised in this short official report on the death of one woman who lived with her husband and son in a small room, without bedstead or furniture, in Bermondsey: 'She lay dead beside her son upon a heap of feathers which were scattered over her almost naked body, there being neither sheet nor coverlet. The feathers stuck so fast over the whole body that the physician could not examine the corpse until it was cleansed, and then found it starved and scarred from the bites of vermin. Part of the floor of the room was torn up, and the hole used by the family as a privy.' This was London in 1843, at a time when houses were still being 'jerrybuilt' back to back, without ventilation or drainage, when old houses were still being filled with poor families and turned into stinking rookeries.

Dickens often took his friends on voyages through such slums, visiting some of the lodging houses as he did so: he would go in quite blithely but there are reports of his companions, overpowered by the stench within, who came out into the streets to be sick. But it has to be remembered that they were not simply offended by the smell; this was a period in which it was taken for granted that illness itself could be spread by pestiferous gases – Edwin Chadwick, the great sanitary reformer, believed that, 'all smell is disease'. As a result large parts of London were seen to be nothing other than a source of pestilence, a breeding ground of diseases which then permeated the entire capital. Londoners were not even safe from their dead: in 1856, in the poor houses

19

of Clerkenwell, 'when a death occurs the living and the dead must be together in the same room, the living must eat, drink and sleep beside a decomposing corpse.' Even when the dead were buried they simply became another source of contagion; the city burial grounds were so full that the corpses were piled on top of each other, often breaking through the ground and emitting what were then described as 'noxious gases'. In Clare Market by Drury Lane more than 1,200 bodies were buried in the same vault between 1823 and 1824, and one grave-digger at another site has described how 'I have been up to my knees in human flesh by jumping on the bodies so as to cram them into the least possible space at the bottom of the graves in which fresh bodies were afterwards placed.'

So the fear of disease was always present in Victorian London, and indeed the reality was quite as awful as any of the anxieties themselves. There were four occasions of cholera epidemic in Dickens' lifetime, and there were also regular outbreaks of such diseases as typhus, typhoid fever, scarlet fever, smallpox, and diphtheria. Between November and December of 1847 500,000 people were infected with typhus fever out of a total population of 2,100,000, for example, and it seemed to many people that London was indeed becoming what *The Lancet* described as a 'doomed city'. The average age of mortality in London was 27, while that for the working classes was 22, and in 1839 almost half the funerals in London were of children under the age of 10. Dickens is often criticised for the number of child-deaths which occur in his fiction, but he was reflecting no more than the truth – the children were dying around him. This is the forgotten side of Victorian London – that aspect which explains why city life was often described as 'feverish'. It was meant in a literal sense. In fact 'fever' was the predominantly diagnosed condition, and in fiction, too, human beings were often described as being 'in a fever'. Anxiety and demoralisation were widespread, and it was this general sense of imminent decay and prospective dissolution which marked the faces of the ordinary Londoners. So it is that in Dickens' own novels, also, there are often powerful intimations of the precariousness of civilisation. London was to him an 'unreal city' not necessarily because of his boyhood wanderings, but because it was conceivable that all that energy, all that industry, could die out, wither away, be destroyed in some ravaging illness. London, however sturdy it might seem, contained within itself the seeds of its own destruction.

And so in Dickens' novels there is a constant contrast between the well and the ill, between warmth and cold, between the domestic interior and the noisome streets, between the need for comfort and the anxiety about homelessness. Indeed in many Victorian London homes the exterior world seems literally to be kept at bay by a whole artillery of protective forces – screened by thick curtains and by lace inner curtains, muffled by patterned wallpaper and patterned carpets, held off by settees and ottomans and what-nots, mocked by wax fruit and wax flowers, its metaphorical and literal darkness banished by lamps and chandeliers and candles. The central idea is one of ferocious privacy, of shelter and segregation, and in fact by the latter half of the century the middle class and the working class were effectively divided from each other – the more fortunate members of the latter being placed in 'model flats' while the former migrated to the new London suburbs. Dickens himself was not immune to the need for domestic comfort but, unlike many of his middle-class contemporaries, he knew exactly what kind of London existed outside the confines of the private urban world – he knew what kind of city he dwelt in.

Of course he was not alone in his concerns – and, as the misery of the urban poor increased, so also did the number of philanthropic organisations designed to alleviate it; in 1851, there were some 536 such societies operating in the capital. In large part, their efforts were filling a vacuum, in the sense that no organised governmental or urban help was ever really available until the latter part of the century. Most of the problems of sanitation and disease arose from the fact that the administration of London until the mid-'50s comprised many different and conflicting authorities; there were poor law guardians, unions, parishes, vestries, improvement commissioners, turnpike trusts, water authorities, gas authorities, dock companies and a whole congerie of other bodies who took specific responsibility for only a small number of activities. The countervailing pressure for reform was almost as great, however, and as a counterpart to the host of metropolitan authorities there was also a vast panoply of statistical surveys, blue books, committees and inquiries designed both to inspect and to alleviate the problems of London. The first proper steps were taken when the Metropolitan Board of Works was established in 1855, primarily to establish a proper sewage system for the city, and by the mid-'60s there had been enormous improvements both in the administration and sanitary organisation of the city – a proper sewage system was built, the Thames was embanked, main drainage works were completed, railways were being extended, new roads built. Slowly even the worst of the rookeries were cleared – although the slums of the metropolis were never to be extirpated altogether. They exist still.

But, by degrees, London was transformed; it was no longer the city which Charles Dickens had known as a boy, and by the end of his life it was almost as if he had become a figure from another era. This was now the London of the music hall and the underground railway, the 'new woman' and the approaching fin-de-siècle. It was becoming the London of Oscar Wilde. The orderliness and relative symmetry of the old Georgian capital were slowly being displaced by the imperialist neo-Gothic and neo-classical architecture of Victorian public buildings. Something of the old compactness had gone for ever and with it, too, the particular gracefulness and particular colour of the eighteenth century. In its place was coming a London which was more massive, more closely controlled, more organised. The metropolis was much larger but it was also much more anonymous; it was a more public city but also a less human one. This was no longer the wild and barren place of Dickens' imagination, nor was it the extravagant and eccentric locale where all his characters had met and moved together.

And yet he never ceased to live in that old city. Its landscape filled his last novels, even when the lineaments of the new London were already apparent. But the old city was the one he loved. It was the city that made him. It was the city which almost destroyed him but which then raised him up. It was the city of his dreams and the city of his imagination. In Dickens' work, it is the city that will live for ever.

PETER ACKROYD
London, 1987

21

A Child's-Eye View

It was a chill, damp, windy night, when the Jew, buttoning his great-coat tight round his shrivelled body, and pulling the collar up over his ears so as completely to obscure the lower part of his face, emerged from his den. He paused on the step as the door was locked and chained behind him; and having listened while the boys made all secure, and until their retreating footsteps were no longer audible, slunk down the street as quickly as he could.

The house to which Oliver had been conveyed, was in the neighbourhood of Whitechapel. The Jew stopped for an instant at the corner of the street; and, glancing suspiciously round, crossed the road, and struck off in the direction of Spitalfields.

The mud lay thick upon the stones, and a black mist hung over the streets; the rain fell sluggishly down, and everything felt cold and clammy to the touch. It seemed just the night when it befitted such a being as the Jew to be abroad. As he glided stealthily along, creeping beneath the shelter of the walls and doorways, the hideous old man seemed like some loathsome reptile, engendered in the slime and darkness through which he moved: crawling forth, by night, in search of some rich offal for a meal.

He kept on his course, through many winding and narrow ways, until he reached Bethnal Green; then, turning suddenly off to the left, he soon became involved in a maze of the mean and dirty streets which abound in that close and densely-populated quarter.

The Jew was evidently too familiar with the ground he traversed to be at all bewildered, either by the darkness of the night, or the intricacies of the way. He hurried through several alleys and streets and at length turned into one, lighted only by a single lamp at the farther end. At the door of a house in this street, he knocked; having exchanged a few muttered words with the person who opened it, he walked upstairs.

A dog growled as he touched the handle of a room-door; and a man's voice demanded who was there.

'Only me, Bill; only me, my dear,' said the Jew, looking in.

OLIVER TWIST

Many of the routes followed by Dickens and his fictional characters can be traced on this map of 1832.

Scuttling vermin-like along the dark, dank corridors that separated the squalid slum-dwellings of the old East End, Fagin seems to embody the author's 'Kafkaesque' vision of the metropolis which has haunted his readers since the novel's first appearance in 1838. In fact a Gothic vision of London and tales of 'the merry old gentleman' (like Fagin, a personification of the devil) were already popular features of the street literature of the day.

Nobody wandering through London (as Dickens did, wide-eyed, as a boy) could have ignored the cheap newspapers and almanacks, 'penny dreadfuls', political or religious leaflets, and single sheet broadsides or ballads for sale. These publications had arisen in response to great new

23

'In that close corner where the roofs shrink down and cower together as if to hide their secrets from the handsome street hard by there are such dark crimes, such miseries and horrors, as could be hardly told in whispers.'
Master Humphrey's Clock

Right:
Dickens witnessed the advent of consumer advertising which transformed the streets of the City. In The Uncommercial Traveller, *he wrote: 'If I had an enemy whom I hated – which Heaven forbid! – and if I knew of something which sat heavy on his conscience, I think I would introduce that something into a Posting-Bill, and place a large impression in the hands of an active sticker. I can scarcely imagine a more terrible revenge.'*

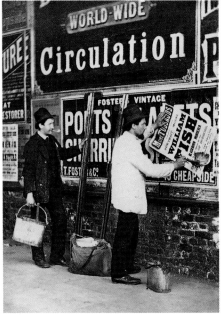

opportunities for communication presented by a massive influx of people to the capital city in the early nineteenth century; never before had so rapt an audience existed. Above the general hubbub of London's street traders, the cries of the distributors of the broadsheets – 'Three yards a penny!' or 'Two under fifty for a fardy!' – heralded the arrival of the city's very first mass-market reading public. Demand was especially strong for the ballad sheet, which wet many an appetite for the macabre and the sensational in both prose and verse. It appealed to the largest section of the community – the poor – because it was *short* (reading skills were not great amongst the nineteenth-century poor), *cheap*, and, like the tabloid newspaper that was to follow, concerned *popular* subjects such as sex, crime (especially murder) and Royalty.

But if a mass-market audience in London had been well primed to receive some elements of Dickens' stories (each published monthly in readably episodic form), his awareness of popular trends was not a critical influence on his description of the place. For that we must look to other, more deeply felt influences on Dickens' early life.

On February 20th, 1824, Dickens' father was arrested for debt and sent to the Marshalsea prison, the remains of which are situated near the

Chatham, the birthplace of Dickens' fancy, 'my hope of something beyond that place and time.'

corner of Borough High Street and Long Lane. Shortly afterwards Charles' mother, brothers and sisters (except for Fanny, older than Charles by 15 months, and a scholar and boarder at the Royal Academy of Music) joined John Dickens in prison. Charles, at twelve years of age, was left to survive as best he could on his own. Every day he would walk from his lodgings in Little College Street, Camden Town, to work in a rat-infested boot blacking factory called Warren's, situated down Craven Street off the Strand, where he was put to covering pots of paste-blacking with paper and string. He was so affected by this period that he told no-one about it during his lifetime, not even his wife, no-one save his closest friend and biographer, John Forster. 'The incidents,' wrote Forster, 'would probably never have been known to me, or indeed any of the occurrences of his childhood and youth, but for the accident of a question which I put to him one day in the March or April of 1847. . .' Fortunately we also have Dickens' own autobiographical writings about this time. Dickens' description of London is inextricably bound up with this period for two reasons: first because his abandonment provided an unrivalled opportunity for walking London's streets, where he developed a habit for noticing and remembering places, faces and odd goings on; and second, because the misery and despair with which he held this period of his life took on tragic proportions and inspired an imaginative transformation of what he saw, as well as a measure of the incredible motivation which drove him to share it with us.

The Journey to London

Charles Dickens was born at Mile End Terrace in Landport, Portsea, on February 7th, 1812. His father was a clerk in the Navy Pay Office there. A year later John Dickens' employment led the family to Southsea in Portsmouth (16 Hawk Street and at the end of 1813, 39 Wish Street). Then, briefly, in 1815 he transferred to the Admiralty Offices at Somerset House in London, and the family lodged in Norfolk Street (now the bottom end of Cleveland Street, near the Middlesex Hospital). At the beginning of 1817 John was again transferred, this time to the Navy Pay Office in Chatham, and thus the Dickens family found itself in Kent. After what had been a fairly hectic first five years for the boy, the next five – the period when the family was at Chatham – appear to have been very settled and by all accounts, significant in terms of the writer's artistic development. In Forster's words, Chatham was 'the birthplace of his fancy', and from the following passage we can appreciate that there were indeed important influences at work:

My father had left a small collection of books in a little room upstairs, to which I had access (for it adjoined my own) and which nobody else in our house ever troubled. From that blessed little room, Roderick Random, Peregrine Pickle, Humphrey Clinker, Tom Jones, the Vicar of Wakefield, Don Quixote, Gil Blas, and Robinson Crusoe, came out, a glorious host, to keep me company. They kept alive my fancy, and my hope of something beyond that place and time, – they, and the *Arabian Nights*, and the *Tales of the Genii*, – and did me no harm; for whatever harm was in some of them was not there for me; *I* knew nothing of it. It is astonishing to me now, how I found time, in the midst of my porings and blunderings over heavier themes, to read those books as I did. It is curious to me how I could ever have consoled myself under my small troubles (which were great troubles to me), by impersonating my favourite characters in them – as I did – and by putting Mr and Miss Murdstone* into all the bad ones – which I did too. I have been Tom Jones (a child's Tom Jones, a harmless creature) for a week together. I have sustained my own idea of Roderick Random for a month at a stretch, I verily believe. I had a greedy relish for a few volumes of Voyages and Travels – I forget what, now – what were on those shelves; and for days and days I can remember to have gone about my region of our house, armed with the centre-piece out of an old set of boot-trees – the perfect realization of Captain Somebody, of the Royal British Navy, in danger of being beset by savages, and resolved to sell his life at a great price. The Captain never lost dignity, from

---

*Murdstone was Copperfield's step-father who, with his sister, contrived David's mother's death.

Somerset House, 1857, where Dickens' father had a clerical post in the Navy Pay Office.

No 16 Bayham Street, demolished in 1910. Although the house was far from the worst to which the Dickens' family could have fallen, the Camden Town street made a stark contrast to the sweet meadows of Kent. In David Copperfield, *when David's young school-friend, Traddles, finds lodgings in London, it is 'in a little street near the Veterinary College at Camden Town' (very probably Bayham Street). 'I found that the street was not as desirable a one as I could have wished it to be, for the sake of Traddles.'*

having his ears boxed with the Latin Grammar. I did; but the Captain was a Captain and a hero, in despite of all the grammars of all the languages in the world, dead or alive.

This was my only and my constant comfort. When I think of it, the picture always rises in my mind, of a summer evening, the boys at play in the churchyard, and I sitting on my bed, reading as if for life. Every barn in the neighbourhood, every stone in the church, and every foot of the churchyard, had some association of its own, in my mind, connected with these books, and stood for some locality made famous in them. I have seen Tom Pipes go climbing up the church-steeple; I have watched Strap, with the knapsack on his back, stopping to rest himself upon the wicket-gate; and I *know* that Commodore Trunnion held that club with Mr Pickle, in the parlour of our little village alehouse.

DAVID COPPERFIELD

The passage is one of many in Dickens' auto-novel that since the author's death we know to be literally true. As Forster attests: 'Every word of this personal recollection had been written down as fact, some years before it found its way into *David Copperfield*; the only change in the fiction being his omission of the name of a cheap series of novelists then in course of publication. . .'. Robinson Crusoe, cast alone on his desert

28

island, provides an image constantly echoed in the novels, as in this description of David Copperfield's first and lonely, furnished set of rooms in the Adelphi:

It was a wonderfully fine thing to have that lofty castle to myself, and to feel, when I shut my outer door, like Robinson Crusoe, when he had got into his fortification, and pulled his ladder up after him. It was a wonderfully fine thing to walk about town with the key of my house in my pocket, and to know that I could ask any fellow to come home, and make quite sure of its being inconvenient to nobody, if it were not so to me. It was a wonderfully fine thing to let myself in and out, and to come and go without a word to anyone, and to ring Mrs Crupp up, gasping, from the depths of the earth, when I wanted her – and when she was disposed to come. All this, I say, was wonderfully fine; but I must say, too, that there were times when it was very dreary.

The influence of Fielding is equally clear – in *Oliver Twist,* innocence put through and exposed to the trials and temptations of the Evil City – and in so many others of his London stories. But these 'Chatham' tales – taken altogether a marvellous mixture of fantasy and brutal realism – were not the only ones to reach the impressionable young Dickens.

A young girl called Mary Weller who looked after him sometimes, would horrify him with stories about a certain Captain Murderer who killed his wife, cut her up, cooked her and then picked her bones; and Dickens recalled another story about a shipwright called Chips who sold his soul to the devil for a bizarre collection of utensils and a rat that could talk. Henceforth haunted by rats crawling over his body and infesting his ship, both Chips and the ship fell victim to their verminous appetite until all that remained of the poor man floated ashore, with one huge rat sitting, laughing, atop his head!

Chatham also saw in him the awakening of a real hunger for education, and Charles, who had been taught English and Latin by his mother every day from an early age, now emerged as a pupil of unusual promise at school.

It was quite natural, therefore, when his father was recalled to Somerset House in the summer of 1822, for Charles to remain in Chatham to finish the summer term in the care of his schoolmaster, Mr William Giles.

London

What Charles discovered when eventually he joined the family in London must have given him something of a jolt. In place of the three-storey house that they had enjoyed at 2 Ordnance Terrace in Chatham (one of a hill-top terrace of attractive buildings with pleasant gardens and plenty of fresh country air), he found a 'mean small tenement, with a wretched little back-garden abutting on a squalid court', the family's 'new' home at

The attic in No 16 Bayham Street.

Number 16, Bayham Street in Camden Town.

John Dickens had fallen badly into debt, and the situation proved so serious that it was decided that Charles should be taken out of school.

Although Bayham Street was far from the lowliest accommodation the family could have found in London at this time, its contrast with Chatham and the sudden thwarting of Dickens' academic aspirations were fiercely felt by the boy: 'As I thought in the little back garret in Bayham Street, of all I had lost in losing Chatham, what would I have given, if I had had anything to give, to have been sent back to any other school, to have been taught somewhere anywhere!' From an early age he had had a firm self-image that he was bright and going to go somewhere, an image very likely encouraged by both his parents, but certainly by his mother. When, a little later, he watched his sister Fanny receive a prize at the Royal Academy of Music, his despair was total and the experience left him with a bitter taste: 'I could not bear to think of myself – beyond the reach of all such honourable emulation and success. The tears ran down my face. I prayed, when I went to bed that night to be lifted out of the humiliation and neglect in which I was.'

John Dickens had always found it difficult to live within his means. By 1822 he had a large family (seven children of which two had died) and not an overly large salary; it is also possible that he was a small gambler. At any rate his impecuniousness was to dog him for most of his life, and his borrowing was to prove a perennial irritation both to his relations and, later, to Charles' publishers.

The boy bore his father no resentment for this critical turn of events – 'Everything that I can remember of his conduct to his wife, or children, or friends, in sickness or affliction, is beyond all praise.' John Dickens was a man possessed of an expansive and gregarious nature; perhaps this saved him from his son's recriminations (which somewhat unfairly were heaped, instead, by Charles upon his mother). Certainly the fictional recreation of John Dickens – as Wilkins Micawber in *David Copperfield* – displays a sympathy in its author for the theatrical nature of the man's personality, sufficient perhaps to forgive him more or less anything. Here, David meets Micawber at Murdstone and Grinby's (the fictional re-creation of Warren's blacking factory) for the very first time:

The counting-house clock was at half past twelve, and there was general preparation for going to dinner, when Mr Quinion tapped at the counting-house window, and beckoned to me to go in. I went in, and found there a stoutish, middle-aged person, in a brown surtout and black tights and shoes, with no more hair upon his head (which was a large one, and very shining) than there is upon an egg, and with a very extensive face, which he turned full upon me. His clothes were shabby, but he had an imposing shirt-collar on. He carried a jaunty sort of stick, with a large pair of rusty tassels to it; and a quizzing-glass hung outside his coat, – for ornament, I afterwards found, as he very seldom looked through it, and couldn't see anything when he did.

'This,' said Mr Quinion, in allusion to myself, 'is he.'

'This,' said the stranger, with a certain condescending roll in his voice, and a certain indescribable air of doing something genteel, which impressed me very much, 'is Master Copperfield. I hope I see you well, sir?'

I said I was very well, and hoped he was. I was sufficiently ill at ease, Heaven knows; but it was not in my nature to complain much at that time of my life, so I said I was very well, and hoped he was.

'I am,' said the stranger, 'thank Heaven, quite well. I have received a letter from Mr Murdstone, in which he mentions that he would desire me to receive into an apartment in the rear of my house, which is at present unoccupied – and is, in short, to be let as a – in short,' said the stranger, with a smile and in a burst of confidence, 'as a bedroom – the young beginner whom I have now the pleasure to –' and the stranger waved his hand, and settled his chin in his shirt-collar.

'This is Mr Micawber,' said Mr Chinion to me.

'Ahem!' said the stranger, 'that is my name.'

'Mr Micawber,' said Mr Quinion, 'is known to Mr Murdstone. He takes orders for us on commission, when he can get any. He has been written to by Mr Murdstone, on the subject of your lodgings, and he will receive you as a lodger.'

'My address,' said Mr Micawber, 'is Windsor Terrace, City Road. I – in short,' said Mr Micawber, with the same genteel air, and in another burst of confidence – 'I live there.'

I made him a bow.

'Under the impression,' said Mr Micawber, 'that your peregrinations in this metropolis have not as yet been extensive, and that you might have some difficulty in penetrating the arcana of the Modern Babylon in the direction of the City Road, – in short,' said Mr Micawber, in another burst of confidence, 'that you might lose yourself – I shall be happy to call this evening, and install you in the knowledge of the nearest way.'

I thanked him with all my heart, for it was friendly in him to offer to take that trouble.

'At what hour,' said Mr Micawber, 'shall I –'

'At about eight,' said Mr Quinion.

'At about eight,' said Mr Micawber. 'I beg to wish you good day, Mr Quinion. I will intrude no longer.'

So he put on his hat, and went out with his cane under his arm: very upright, and humming a tune when he was clear of the counting-house.

About this time – 'newly come out of the hop-grounds in Kent' – Dickens got lost in London. While staring up at the lion overlooking the gateway of Northumberland House (then on the corner of Trafalgar Square and the Strand), he is separated from his guardian (a family friend) with no thought of what an appropriate rehearsal this was for what was soon to happen to him.

The child's unreasoning terror of being lost, comes as freshly on me now as it did then. I verily believe that if I had found myself astray at the North Pole instead of in the narrow, crowded, inconvenient street over which the lion in those days presided, I could not have been more horrified. But, this first fright expended itself in a little crying and tearing up and down; and then I walked, with a feeling of dismal dignity upon me, into a court, and sat down on a step to consider how to get through life.

To the best of my belief, the idea of asking my way home never came into my head. It is possible that I may, for the time, have preferred the dismal dignity of being lost; but I have a serious conviction that in the wide scope of my arrangements for the future, I had no eyes for the nearest and most obvious course. I was but very juvenile; from eight to nine years old, I fancy.

I had one and fourpence in my pocket, and a pewter ring with a bit of red glass in it on my little finger. This jewel had been presented to me by the object of my affections, on my birthday, when we had sworn to marry, but had foreseen family obstacles to our union, in her being (she was six years old) of the Wesleyan persuasion, while I was devotedly attached to the Church of England. The one and fourpence were the remains of half-a-crown presented on the same anniversary by my godfather – a man who knew his duty and did it.

Armed with these amulets, I made up my little mind to seek my fortune. When I had found it, I thought I would drive home in a coach and six, and claim my bride. I cried a little more at the idea of such a triumph, but soon dried my eyes and came out of the court to pursue my plans. These were, first to go (as a species of investment) and see the Giants in Guildhall, out of whom I felt it not impossible that some prosperous adventure would arise; failing that contingency, to try

Northumberland House, demolished in 1874. The lion holding sway above the parapet held special significance for the young Dickens: 'When I was a very small boy indeed, both in years and stature, I got lost one day in the City of London. I was taken out by Somebody (shade of Somebody forgive me for remembering no more of their identity!), as an immense treat, to be shown the outside of Saint Giles's Church . . . 'We were conversational together, and saw the outside of Saint Giles's Church with sentiments of satisfaction, much enhanced by a flag flying from the steeple. I infer that we then went down to Northumberland House in the Strand to view the celebrated lion over the gateway. At all events, I know that in the act of looking up with mingled awe and admiration at the famous animal I lost Somebody.'

about the City for any opening of a Whittington nature; baffled in that too, to go into the army as a drummer.

So, I began to ask my way to Guildhall: which I thought meant, somehow, Gold or Golden Hall, I was too knowing to ask my way to the Giants, for I felt it would make people laugh. I remember how immensely broad the streets seemed now I was alone, how high the houses, how grand the mysterious everything. When I came to Temple Bar, it took me half an hour to stare at it, and I left it unfinished even then. I had read about the heads being exposed on the top of Temple Bar, and it seemed a wicked old place, albeit a noble monument of architecture and a paragon of utility. When at last I got away from it, behold I came, the next minute, on the figures of St Dunstan's! Who could see those obliging monsters

The famous 18th-century carvings of Gog and Magog resided at Guildhall until destroyed by a bombing raid in World War II. They were replaced in 1953. In the Old Testament (Ezekiel 38-9), Gog is a prince in the land of Magog, who leads the barbarian tribes of the North in an assault on Israel. In Genesis 10:2, Magog is a person – the son of Japheth and a member of the peoples that lived north of Israel. In the New Testament (Revelations 20:8) they reappear as nations that make war upon the Kingdom of Christ.

strike upon the bells and go? Between the quarters there was the toyshop to look at – still there, at this present writing, in a new form – and even when that enchanted spot was escaped from, after an hour and more, then Saint Paul's arose, and how was I to get beyond its dome, or to take my eyes from its cross of gold? I found it a long journey to the Giants, and a slow one.

I came into their presence at last, and gazed up at them with dread and veneration. They looked better-tempered, and were altogether more shiny-faced, than I had expected; but they were very big, and, as I judged their

Left:
'Thus I wandered about the City, like a child in a dream . . . roaming down into Austin Friars, and wondering how the Friars used to like it.'

34

Jo Toddyhigh in Master Humphrey's Clock *describes the giants: 'The Statues of the two giants, Gog and Magog, each above fourteen feet in height, those which succeeded to still older and more barbarous figures after the Great Fire of London, and which stand in the Guildhall to this day, were endowed with life and motion. These guardian genii of the City had quitted their pedestals, and reclined in easy attitudes in the great stained glass window. Between them was an ancient cask, which seemed to be full of wine; for the younger Giant, clapping his huge hand upon it, and throwing up his mighty leg, burst into an exulting laugh which reverberated through the hall like thunder.'*

pedestals to be about forty feet high, I considered that they would be very big indeed if they were walking on the stone pavement. I was in a state of mind as to these and all such figures, which I suppose holds equally with most children. While I knew them to be images made of something that was not flesh and blood, I still invested them with attributes of life – with consciousness of my being there, for example, and the power of keeping a sly eye upon me. Being very tired I got into the corner under Magog, to be out of the way of his eye, and fell asleep.

When I started up after a long nap, I thought the giants were roaring, but it was only the City. The place was just the same as when I fell asleep: no beanstalk, no fairy, no princess, no dragon, no opening in life of any kind. So, being hungry, I thought I would buy something to eat, and bring it in there and eat it, before going forth to seek my fortune on the Whittington plan.

I was not ashamed of buying a penny roll in a baker's shop, but I looked into a number of cooks' shops before I could muster courage to go into one. At last I saw a pile of cooked sausages in a window with the label. 'Small Germans, A Penny.' Emboldened by knowing what to ask for, I went in and said, 'If you please will you sell me a small German?' Which they did, and I took it, wrapped in paper in my pocket, to Guildhall.

The Giants were still lying by, in their sly way, pretending to take no notice, so I sat down in another corner, when what should I see before me but a dog with his ears cocked. He was a black dog, with a bit of white over one eye, and bits of white and tan in his paws, and he wanted to play – frisking about me, rubbing his nose against me, dodging at me sideways, shaking his head and pretending to run away backwards, and making himself good-naturedly ridiculous, as if he had no consideration for himself, but wanted to raise my spirits. Now, when I saw this dog I thought of Whittington, and felt that things were coming right; I encouraged him by saying, "Hi, boy!" "Poor fellow!" "Good dog!" and was satisfied that he was to be my dog for ever afterwards, and that he would help me to seek my fortune.

Very much comforted by this (I had cried a little at odd times ever since I was lost), I took the small German out of my pocket, and began my dinner by biting off a bit and throwing it to the dog, who immediately swallowed it with a one-sided jerk, like a pill. While I took a bit myself, and he looked me in the face for a second piece, I considered by what name I should call him. I thought Merrychance would be an expressive name, under the circumstances; and I was elated, I recollect by inventing such a good one, when Merrychance began to growl at me in a most ferocious manner.

I wondered he was not ashamed of himself, but he didn't care for that; on the contrary he growled a good deal more. With his mouth watering, and his eyes glistening, and his nose in a very damp state, and his head very much on one side, he sidled about on the pavement in a threatening manner and growled at me, until he suddenly made a snap at the small German, tore it out of my hand, and went off with it. He never came back to help me seek my fortune. From that hour to the present, when I am forty years of age, I have never seen my faithful Merrychance again.

I felt very lonely. Not so much for the loss of the small German, though it was delicious (I knew nothing about highly-peppered horse at that time), as on account of Merrychance's disappointing me so cruelly; for I had hoped he would

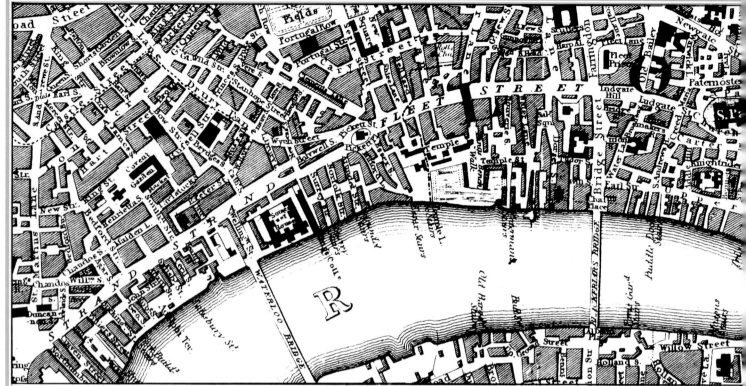

From Trafalgar Square to Wellclose Square,
the wanderings of a 9-year-old lost in London.

do every friendly thing but speak, and perhaps even come to that. I cried a little more, and began to wish that the object of my affections had been lost with me, for company's sake. But, then I remembered that *she* could not go into the army as a drummer; and I dried my eyes and ate my loaf. Coming out, I met a milk-woman, of whom I bought a pennyworth of milk; quite set up again by my repast, I began to roam about the City, and to seek my fortune in the Whittington direction. . . .

Thus I wandered about the City, like a child in a dream, staring at the British merchants, and inspired by a mighty faith in the marvellousness of everything. Up courts and down courts – in and out of yards and little squares – peeping into counting-house passages and running away – poorly feeding the echoes in the court of the South Sea House with my timid steps – roaming down into Austin Friars, and wondering how the Friars used to like it – ever staring at the British merchants, and never tired of the shops – I rambled on, all through the day. In such stories as I made, to account for the different places, I believed as devoutly as in the City itself. I particularly remember that when I found myself on 'Change, and saw the shabby people sitting under the placards about ships, I settled that they were Misers, who had embarked all their wealth to go and buy gold-dust or something of that sort, and were waiting for their respective captains to come and tell they were ready to set sail. I observed that they all munched dry biscuits, and I thought it was to keep off sea-sickness.

This was very delightful; but it still produced no result according to the Whittington precedent. There was a dinner preparing at the Mansion House, and when I peeped in at a grated kitchen window, and saw the men cooks at work in

36

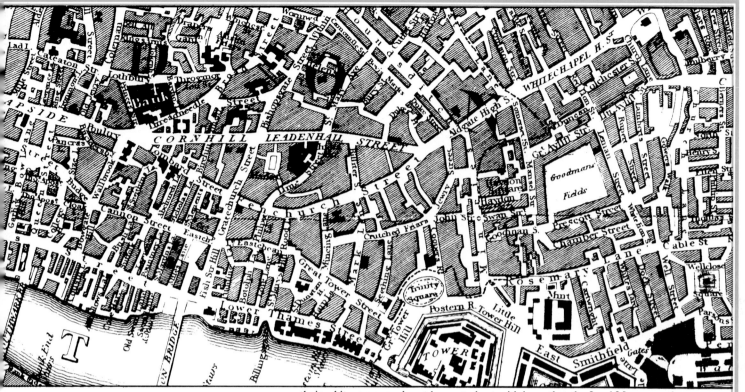

their white caps, my heart began to beat with hope that the Lord Mayor, or the Lady Mayoress, or one of the young Princesses their daughters, would look out of an upper apartment and direct me to be taken in. But, nothing of the kind occurred. It was not until I had been peeping in some time that one of the cooks called to me (the window was open) 'Cut away, you sir!' which frightened me so, on account of his black whiskers, that I instantly obeyed.

After that, I came to the India House, and asked a boy what it was, who made faces and pulled my hair before he told me, and behaved altogether in an ungenteel and discourteous manner. . . .

Thinking much about boys who went to India, and who immediately, without being sick, smoked pipes like curled up bell-ropes, terminating in a large cut-glass sugar basin upside down, I got among the outfitting shops. There, I read the lists of things that were necessary for an India-going boy, and when I came to 'one brace of pistols,' thought what happiness to be reserved for such a fate! Still no British merchant seemed at all disposed to take me into his house. The only exception was a chimney-sweep – he looked at me as if he thought me suitable to his business; but I ran away from him.

I suffered very much, all day, from boys; they chased me down turnings, brought me to bay in doorways, and treated me quite savagely, though I am sure I gave them no offence. One boy, who had a stump of black-lead pencil in his pocket, wrote his mother's name and address (as he said) on my white hat, outside the crown. Mrs Blores, Wooden Leg Walk, Tobacco-stopper Row, Wapping. And I couldn't rub it out.

I recollect resting in a little churchyard after this persecution, disposed to think

upon the whole, that if I and the object of my affections could be buried there together, at once, it would be comfortable. But, another nap, and a pump, and a bun, and above all a picture that I saw, brought me round again.

I must have strayed by that time, as I recall my course, into Goodman's Fields, or somewhere thereabouts. The picture represented a scene in a play then performing at a theatre in that neighbourhood which is no longer in existence. It stimulated me to go to that theatre and see that play. . . .

I found out the theatre – of its external appearance I only remember the loyal initials G. R. untidily painted in yellow ochre on the front – and waited, with a pretty large crowd, for the opening of the gallery doors. The greater part of the sailors and others composing the crowd, were of the lowest description, and their conversation was not improving; but I understood little or nothing of what was bad in it then, and it had no depraving influence on me. I have wondered since, how long it would take, by means of such association, to corrupt a child nurtured as I had been, and innocent as I was.

Whenever I saw that my appearance attracted attention, either outside the doors or afterwards within the theatre, I pretended to look out for somebody who was taking care of me, and from whom I was separated, and to exchange nods and smiles with that creature of my imagination. This answered very well. I had my sixpence clutched in my hand ready to pay; and when the doors opened, with a clattering of bolts, and some screaming from women in the crowd, I went on with the current like a straw. My sixpence was rapidly swallowed up in the

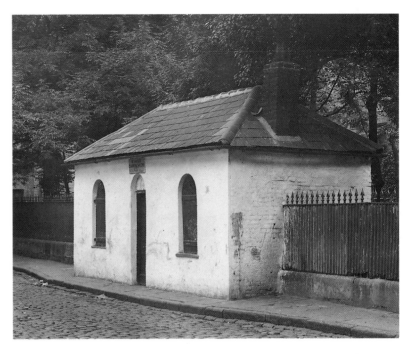

money-taker's pigeon-hole, which looked to me like a sort of mouth, and I got into the freer staircase above and ran on (as everybody else did) to get a good place. When I came to the back of the gallery, there were very few people in it, and the seats looked so horribly steep, and so like a diving arrangement to send me, headforemost, into the pit, that I held by one of them in a terrible fright. However, there was a good-natured baker with a young woman, who gave me his hand, and we all three scrambled over the seats together down into the corner of the first row. The baker was very fond of the young woman, and kissed her a good deal in the course of the evening.

I was no sooner comfortably settled, than a weight fell upon my mind, which tormented it most dreadfully, and which I must explain. It was a benefit night – the benefit of the comic actor – a little fat man with a very large face, and, as I thought then, the smallest and most diverting hat that ever was seen. This comedian, for the gratification of his friends and patrons, had undertaken to sing a comic song on a donkey's back, and afterwards to give away the donkey so distinguished, by lottery. In this lottery, every person admitted to the pit and gallery had a chance. On paying my sixpence, I had received the number, forty-seven; and I now thought, in a perspiration of terror, what should I ever do if that number was to come up the prize, and I was to win the donkey!

It made me tremble all over to think of the possibility of my good fortune. I knew I never could conceal the fact of my holding forty-seven, in case that number came up, because, not to speak of my confusion, which would

39

immediately condemn me. I had shown my number to the baker. Then, I pictured to myself the being called upon to come down to the stage and receive the donkey. I thought how all the people would shriek when they saw it had fallen to a little fellow like me. How should I lead him out – for of course he wouldn't go? If he began to bray, what should I do? If he kicked, what would become of me? . . .

These apprehensions took away all my pleasure in the first piece. When the ship came on – a real man-of-war she was called in the bills – and rolled prodigiously in a very heavy sea, I couldn't, even in the terrors of the storm, forget the donkey. It was awful to see the sailors pitching about, with telescopes and speaking trumpets (they looked very tall indeed aboard the man-of-war), and it was awful to suspect the pilot of treachery, though impossible to avoid it, for when he cried – 'We are lost! To the raft, to the raft! A thunderbolt has struck the mainmast!' – I myself saw him take the mainmast out of its socket and drop it overboard; but even these impressive circumstances paled before my dread of the donkey. Even, when the good sailor (and he was very good) came to good fortune, and the bad sailor (and he was very bad) threw himself into the ocean from the summit of a curious rock, presenting something of the appearance of a pair of steps, I saw the dreadful donkey through my tears.

At last the time came when the fiddler struck up the comic song, and the dreaded animal, with new shoes on, as I inferred from the noise they made, came clattering in with the comic actor on his back. He was dressed out with ribbons (I mean the donkey was) and as he persisted in turning his tail to the audience, the comedian got off him, turned about, and sitting with his face that way, sang the song three times, amid thunders of applause. All this time I was fearfully agitated; and when two pale people, a good deal splashed with the mud of the streets, were invited out of the pit to superintend the drawing of the lottery, and were received with a round of laughter from everybody else, I could have begged and prayed them to have mercy on me, and not draw number forty-seven.

But I was soon put out of my pain now, for a gentleman behind me, in a flannel jacket and a yellow neck-kerchief, who had eaten two fried soles and all his pockets-full of nuts before the storm began to rage, answered to the winning number, and went down to take possession of the prize. . . .

Calmed myself by the immense relief I had sustained, I enjoyed the rest of the performance very much indeed. I remember there were a good many dances, some in fetters and some in roses, and one by a most divine little creature, who made the object of my affections look but commonplace. In the concluding drama, she re-appeared as a boy (in arms, mostly), and was fought for, several times. I rather think a Baron wanted to drown her, and was on various occasions prevented by the comedian, a ghost, a Newfoundland dog, and a church bell. I only remember beyond this, that I wondered where the Baron expected to go to, and that he went there in a shower of sparks. The lights were turned out while the sparks died out, and it appeared to me as if the whole play – ship, donkey, men and women, divine little creature, and all – were a wonderful firework that had gone off, and left nothing but dust and darkness behind it.

It was late when I got out into the streets, and there was no moon, and there were no stars, and the rain fell heavily. When I emerged from the dispersing crowd, the ghost and the baron had an ugly look in my remembrance; I felt unspeakably forlorn; and now, for the first time, my little bed and the dear familiar

40

The Hungerford Suspension Bridge, an elegant footbridge designed by Brunel, it had a span of 676 feet. It crossed the Thames between Waterloo and Westminster bridges, its northern part abutting on Hungerford market. While feverishly covering pots of paste-blacking at Warren's, Dickens view would have been dominated by Waterloo Bridge, just visible here, since Hungerford Bridge was not completed until 1845 when this photograph was taken.

faces came before me, and touched my heart. By daylight, I had never thought of the grief at home. I had never thought of my mother. I had never thought of anything but adapting myself to the circumstances in which I found myself, and going to seek my fortune.

For a boy who could do nothing but cry, and run about, saying, "O I am lost!" to think of going into the army was, I felt sensible, out of the question. I abandoned the idea of asking my way to the barracks – or rather the idea abandoned me – and ran about, until I found a watchman in his box. It is amazing to me now, that he should have been sober; but I am inclined to think he was too feeble to get drunk.

This venerable man took me to the nearest watch-house; I say he took me, but

41

In David Copperfield, *Warren's became Murdstone and Grinby's: 'Murdstone and Grinby's warehouse was at the waterside. It was down in Blackfriars. Modern improvements have altered the place; but it was the last house at the bottom of a narrow street, curving down hill to the river, with some stairs at the end, where people took boat. It was a crazy old house with a wharf of its own, abutting on the water when the tide was in, and on the mud when the tide was out, and literally overrun with rats. Its panelled rooms, discoloured with the dirt and smoke of a hundred years, I dare say; its decaying floors and staircase; the squeaking and scuffling of the old grey rats down in the cellars; and the dirt and rottenness of the place; are things, not of many years ago, in my mind, but of the present instant. They are all before me, just as they were in the evil hour when I went among them for the first time, with my trembling hand in Mr Quinion's.*

'Murdstone and Grinby's trade was among a good many kinds of people, but an important branch of it was the supply of wines and spirits to certain packet ships. I forget now where they chiefly went, but I think there were some among them that made voyages both to the East and West Indies. I know that a great many empty bottles were one of the consequences of this traffic, and that certain men and boys were employed to examine them against the light, and reject those that were flawed, and to rinse and wash them. When the empty bottles ran short, there were labels to be pasted on full ones, or corks to be fitted to them, or seals to be put upon the corks, or finished bottles to be packed in casks. All this work was my work, and of the boys employed upon it I was one.'

in fact I took him, for when I think of us in the rain, I recollect that we must have made a composition, like a vignette of Infancy leading Age. He had a dreadful cough, and was obliged to lean against a wall whenever it came on. We got at last to the watchhouse, a warm and drowsy sort of place embellished with great-coats and rattles hanging up. When a paralytic messenger had been sent to make inquiries about me, I fell asleep by the fire, and awoke no more until my eyes opened on my father's face. This is literally and exactly how I went astray. They used to say I was an odd child, and I suppose I was. I am an odd man perhaps.

With John's creditors closing in, his wife opened a school in Gower Street North in a desperate bid for survival. Here the family also encamped. Charles, as David Copperfield, describes what happened:

Poor Mrs Micawber! She said she had tried to exert herself; and so, I have no doubt, she had. The centre of the street door was perfectly covered with a great brass-plate, on which was engraved 'Mrs Micawber's Boarding Establishment for Young Ladies': but I never found that any young lady had ever been to school there; or that any young lady ever came, or proposed to come; or that the least preparation was ever made to receive any young lady. The only visitors I ever saw, or heard of, were creditors. *They* used to come at all hours, and some of them were quite ferocious.

The general feeling of financial panic now led to a decision prompted by James Lamert, cousin to Charles by his aunt's marriage, who had lodged with the family in the crowded Bayham Street house, that Charles should go to work at Warren's blacking factory. In an autobiographical fragment Dickens explains the effect this decision had upon him:

This speculation was a rivalry of 'Warren's Blacking, 30, Strand,' at that time very famous. One Jonathan Warren (the famous one was Robert), living at 30, Hungerford Stairs, or Market, Strand (for I forget which it was called then), claimed to have been the original inventor or proprietor of the blacking recipe, and to have been deposed and ill-used by his renowned relation. At last he put himself in the way of selling his recipe, and his name, and his 30, Hungerford Stairs, Strand (30, Strand, very large, and the intermediate direction very small), for an annuity; and he set forth by his agents that a little capital would make a great business of it. The man of some property was found in George Lamert, the cousin and brother-in-law of James. He bought this right and title, and went into the blacking business and the blacking premises.
—In an evil hour for me, as I often bitterly thought. Its chief manager, James Lamert, the relative who had lived with us in Bayham Street, seeing how I was employed from day to day, and knowing what our domestic circumstances then were, proposed that I should go into the blacking warehouse, to be as useful as I could, at a salary, I think, of six shillings a week. I am not clear whether it was six or seven. I am inclined to believe, from my uncertainty on this head, that it was six at first, and seven afterwards. At any rate, the offer was accepted very willingly by my father and mother, and on a Monday morning I went down to the blacking warehouse to begin my business life.
It is wonderful to me how I could have been so easily cast away at such an age. It is wonderful to me that, even after my descent into the poor little drudge I had been since we came to London, no one had compassion enough on me – a child of

singular abilities: quick, eager, delicate, and soon hurt, bodily or mentally – to suggest that something might have been spared, as certainly it might have been, to place me at any common school. Our friends, I take it, were tired out. No one made any sign. My father and mother were quite satisfied. They could hardly have been more so, if I had been twenty years of age, distinguished at a grammar-school, and going to Cambridge.

The blacking warehouse was the last house on the left-hand side of the way, at old Hungerford Stairs. It was a crazy, tumbledown old house, abutting of course on the river, and literally overrun with rats. Its wainscotted rooms and its rotten floors and staircase, and the old grey rats swarming down in the cellars, and the sound of their squeaking and scuffling coming up the stairs at all times, and the

'I was often up at six o'clock, and my favourite lounging-place was old London Bridge, where I was wont to sit in one of the stone recesses, watching the people going by, or to look over the balustrades at the sun shining in the water, and lighting up the golden flame on the Monument.' David Copperfield

44

dirt and decay of the place, rise up visibly before me, as if I were there again. The counting-house was on the first floor, looking over the coal-barges and the river. There was a recess in it, in which I was to sit and work. My work was to cover the pots of paste-blacking: first with a piece of oil-paper, and then with a piece of blue paper; to tie them round with a string; and then to clip the paper close and neat all round, until it looked as smart as a pot of ointment from an apothecary's shop. When a certain number of grosses of pots had attained this pitch of perfection, I was to paste on each a printed label; and then go on again with more pots. Two or three other boys were kept at similar duty downstairs on similar wages. One of them came up, in a ragged apron and a paper cap, on the first Monday morning, to show me the trick of using the string and tying the knot. His name was Bob Fagin; and I took the liberty of using his name, long afterwards, in *Oliver Twist.*

Our relative had kindly arranged to teach me something in the dinner-hour; from twelve to one, I think it was; every day. But an arrangement so incompatible with counting-house business soon died away, from no fault of his or mine; and for the same reason, my small work-table, and my grosses of pots, my papers, string, scissors, paste-pot and labels, by little and little, vanished out of the recess in the counting-house, and kept company with the other small work-tables, grosses of pots, papers, string, scissors and paste-pots downstairs. It was not long before Bob Fagin and I, and another boy whose name was Paul Green, but who was currently believed to have been christened Poll (a belief which I transferred, long afterwards, again, to Mr. Sweedlepipe, in *Martin Chuzzlewit*), worked generally, side by side. Bob Fagin was an orphan, and lived with his brother-in-law, a waterman. Poll Green's father had the additional distinction of being a fireman, and was employed at Drury Lane theatre; where another relation of Poll's, I think his little sister, did imps in the pantomimes.

No words can express the secret agony of my soul as I sunk into this companionship; compared these everyday associates with those of my happier childhood; and felt my early hopes of growing up to be a learned and distinguished man crushed in my breast. The deep remembrance of the sense I had of being utterly neglected and hopeless; of the shame I felt in the position; of the misery it was to my young heart to believe that, day by day, what I had learned, and thought, and delighted in, and raised my fancy and my emulation up by, was passing away from me, never to be brought back any more; cannot be written. . . .

My whole nature was so penetrated with the grief and humiliation of such considerations, that even now, famous and carressed and happy, I often forget in my dreams that I have a dear wife and children; even that I am a man; and wander desolately back to that time of my life. . . .

We had half an hour, I think, for tea. When I had money enough, I used to go to a coffee-shop, and have half a pint of coffee, and a slice of bread and butter. When I had no money, I took a turn in Covent Garden Market, and stared at the pineapples. The coffee-shops to which I most resorted were, one in Maiden Lane; one in a court (non-existent now) close to Hungerford Market; and one in St Martin's Lane, of which I only recollect that it stood near the church, and that in the door there was an oval glass plate, with COFFEE-ROOM painted on it, addressed towards the street. If I ever find myself in a very different kind of

coffee-room now, but where there is such an inscription on glass, and read it backward on the wrong side MOOR-EEFFOC (as I often used to do then, in a dismal reverie), a shock goes through my blood.

I know I do not exaggerate, unconsciously and unintentionally, the scantiness of my resources and the difficulties of my life. I know that if a shilling or so were given me by anyone, I spent it in a dinner or a tea. I know that I worked, from morning to night, with common men and boys, a shabby child. I know that I tried but ineffectually, not to anticipate my money, and to make it last the week through by putting it away in a drawer I had in the counting-house, wrapped into six little parcels, each parcel containing the same amount, and labelled with a

'And even now, as he paced the streets and listlessly looked round on the gradually increasing bustle and preparation for the day, everything appeared to yield him some new occasion for despondency.' Nicholas Nickleby

46

Southwark Bridge, the 'iron bridge' of Little Dorrit, *pictured in 1864 and since replaced by another. Dickens recalls an occasion when he was to visit his father in the Marshalsea prison and his colleague Bob Fagin insisted on accompanying him from Warren's, following one of Dickens' quite frequent spasm attacks – 'I was too proud to let him know about the prison; and after making several efforts to get rid of him, to all of which Bob Fagin in his goodness was deaf, shook hands with him on the steps of a house near Southwark Bridge on the Surrey side, making believe that I lived there. As a finishing piece of reality in case of his looking back, I knocked at the door, I recollect, and asked, when the woman opened it, if that was Mr Robert Fagin's house.'*

different day. I know that I have lounged about the streets, insufficiently and unsatisfactorily fed. I know that, but for the mercy of God, I might easily have been, for any care that was taken of me, a little robber or a little vagabond.

But I had some station at the blacking warehouse too. Besides that my relative at the counting-house did what a man so occupied, and dealing with a thing so anomalous, could, to treat me as one upon a different footing from the rest, I never said, to man or boy, how it was that I came to be there, or gave the least indication of being sorry that I was there. That I suffered in secret, and that I suffered exquisitely, no one every knew but I. How much I suffered, it is, as I have said already, utterly beyond my power to tell. No man's imagination can overstep the reality. But I kept my own counsel, and I did my work. I knew from the first that, if could not do my work as well as any of the rest, I could not hold myself above a slight and contempt. I soon became at least as expeditious and as skilful with my hands as either of the other boys. Though perfectly familiar with them, my conduct and manners were different enough from theirs to place a space between us. They, and the men, always spoke of me as 'the young gentleman.' A certain man (a soldier once) named Thomas, who was the foreman, and another named Harry, who was the carman and wore a red jacket, used to call me 'Charles' sometimes, in speaking to me; but I think it was mostly when we were very confidential, and when I had made some efforts to entertain them over our work with the results of some of the old readings, which were fast perishing out of my mind. Poll Green uprose once, and rebelled against the 'young-gentleman' usage; but Bob Fagin settled him speedily.

47

Dickens' reaction to working with the lads in Warren's might reasonably be deemed extreme. The Dickens family had itself never been rich, indeed had always just scraped by. But one has to remember that the child was already sensitive to loss of prestige and position following the enforced cessation of his education. Moreover, early Victorians were highly susceptible to fine differences in class, especially those Victorians who had risen in social status. John's parents had both been in service.

The people young Charles was forced to work with – the boys in Warren's – would have been thought of as 'honest working class' (a class distinguished by Victorians from 'the urban poor'). But by 1822 the Dickens family was lower middle class or perhaps more characteristically 'shabby genteel', a class of people Dickens himself singled out for marvellously graphic and witty treatment in his *Sketches*:

We were once haunted by a shabby-genteel man; he was bodily present to our senses all day, and he was in our mind's eye all night. The man of whom Sir Walter Scott speaks in his Demonology did not suffer half the persecution from his imaginary gentleman-usher in black velvet, that we sustained from our friend in quandam black cloth. He first attracted our notice by sitting opposite to us in the reading-room at the British Museum; and what made the man more remarkable was, that he had always got before him a couple of shabby-genteel books – two old dog's-eared folios, in mouldy worm-eaten covers, which had once been smart. He was in his chair, every morning, just as the clock struck ten; he was always the last to leave the room in the afternoon; and, when he did, he quitted it with the air of a man who knew not where else to go for warmth and quiet. There he used to sit all day, as close to the table as possible, in order to conceal the lack of buttons on his coat: with his old hat carefully deposited at his feet, where he evidently flattered himself it escaped observation.

About two o'clock, you would see him munching a French roll or a penny loaf; not taking it boldly out of his pocket at once, like a man who knew he was only making a lunch; but breaking off little bits in his pocket and eating them by stealth. He knew too well it was his dinner.

When we first saw this poor object, we thought it quite impossible that his attire could ever become worse. We even went so far as to speculate on the possibility of his shortly appearing in a decent second-hand suit. We knew nothing about the matter; he grew more and more shabby-genteel every day. The buttons dropped off his waistcoat, one by one; then, he buttoned his coat; and, when one side of the coat was reduced to the same condition as the waistcoat, he buttoned it over on the other side. He looked somewhat better at the beginning of the week than at the conclusion, because the neckerchief, though yellow, was not quite so dingy; and, in the midst of all this wretchedness, he never appeared without gloves and straps. He remained in this state for a week or two. At length, one of the buttons on the back of the coat fell off, and then the man himself disappeared, and we thought he was dead.

We were sitting at the same table about a week after his disappearance, and, as our eyes rested on his vacant chair, we insensibly fell into a train of meditation on the subject of his retirement from public life. We were wondering whether he had

'My usual way home [to Lant Street] was over Blackfriars Bridge, and down that turning in the Blackfriars Road which has Rowland Hill's chapel on one side, and the likeness of a golden dog licking a golden pot over a shop door on the other.'

Left:
'When he thought how regularly things went on from day to day in the same unvarying round – how youth and beauty died and ugly griping age lived tottering on – how crafty avarice grew rich, and many honest hearts were poor and sad . . . when he thought all this, and selected from the mass one slight case on which his thoughts were bent, he felt indeed that there was little ground for hope, and little cause or reason why it should not form an atom in the huge aggregate of distress and sorrow, and add one small and unimportant unit to swell that great amount.' Nicholas Nickleby

hung himself, or thrown himself off a bridge – whether he really was dead, or had only been arrested – when our conjectures were suddenly set at rest by the entry of the very man himself. He had undergone some strange metamorphosis, and walked up the centre of the room with an air which showed he was fully conscious of the improvement in his appearance. It was very odd. His clothes were a fine, deep, glossy black; and yet they looked like the same suit; nay, there were the very darns with which old acquaintances had made us familiar. The hat, too – nobody could mistake the shape of the hat, with its high crown gradually increasing in circumference towards the top. Long service had imparted to it a reddish-brown tint; but, now, it was as black as the coat. The truth flashed suddenly upon us – they had been 'revived.' It is a deceitful liquid that black and

49

blue reviver; we have watched its effects on many a shabby-genteel man. It betrays its victims into a temporary assumption of importance; possibly into the purchase of a new pair of gloves, or a cheap stock, or some other trifling article of dress. It elevates their spirits for a week, only to depress them, if possible, below their original level. It was so in this case; the transit dignity of the unhappy man decreased, in exact proportion as the 'reviver' wore off. The knees of the unmentionables, and the elbows of the coat, and the seams generally, soon began to get alarmingly white. The hat was once more deposited under the table, and its owner crept into his seat as quietly as ever.

Just weeks after he began work at Warren's, his father's creditors closed in, and John was arrested and sent to the Marshalsea prison.

'Whosoever goes into Marshalsea Place turning out of Angel Court [now Angel Place], leading to Bermondsey, will find his feet on the very stones of the extinct Marshalsea Jail,' wrote Dickens in the Preface to

Little Dorrit. A description of the place where Little Dorrit herself was born to her debtor father William (another character inspired by his own father), is provided by Dickens in Chapter 6:

Thirty years ago there stood, a few doors short of the church of Saint George, in the borough of Southwark, on the left-hand side of the way going southward, the Marshalsea Prison. It had stood there many years before, and it remained there some years afterwards; but it is gone now, and the world is none the worse without it.

It was an oblong pile of barrack building, partitioned into squalid houses standing back to back, so that there were no back rooms; environed by a narrow paved yard, hemmed in by high walls duly spiked at top. Itself a close and confined prison for debtors, it contained within it a much closer and more confined jail for smugglers. Offenders against the revenue laws, and defaulters to excise or customs who had incurred fines which they were unable to pay, were supposed to be incarcerated behind an iron-plated door closing up a second prison, consisting of a strong cell or two, and a blind alley some yard and a half wide, which formed the mysterious termination of the very limited skittle-ground in which the Marshalsea debtors bowled down their troubles.

Supposed to be incarcerated there, because the time had rather outgrown the strong cells and the blind alley. In practice they had come to be considered a little too bad, though in theory they were quite as good as ever; which may be observed to be the case at the present day with other cells that are not at all strong, and with other blind alleys that are stone-blind. Hence the smugglers habitually consorted with the debtors (who received them with open arms), except at certain constitutional moments when somebody came from some Office, to go through some form of overlooking something which neither he nor anybody else knew anything about. On these truly British occasions, the smugglers, if any, made a feint of walking into the strong cells and the blind alley, while this somebody pretended to do his something: and made a reality of walking out again as soon as he hadn't done it – neatly epitomising the administration of most of the public affairs in our right little, tight little, island.

The Marshalsea Prison: 'It was an oblong piece of barrack building, partitioned into squalid houses standing back to back, so that there were no back rooms; environed by a narrow paved yard, hemmed in by high walls duly spiked at top.' Little Dorrit

'The last words said to him by his father, before he was finally carried to the Marshalsea,' relates Forster, 'were to the effect that the sun was set upon him for ever. "I really believed at the time," said Dickens to me, "that they had broken my heart." ' Soon afterwards the whole family moved from Gower Street North into the Marshalsea, except for Fanny, and Charles who moved to lodgings in Little College Street, Camden Town.

For a record of the boy's first visit to his father in prison we can again turn to *Copperfield*. The passage (with real names) was actually written two or three years before the novel had even entered his thoughts.

Mr Micawber was waiting for me within the gate, and we went up to his room

After Dickens' father was taken to the Marshalsea prison, the boy's imagination was put to good use in his lonely abode in Little College Street, shown here. 'The key of the house [Gower Street North] was sent back to the landlord, who was very glad to get it; and I (small Cain that I was, except that I had never done harm to anyone) was handed over as a lodger to a reduced old lady [Mrs Elizabeth Roylance], long known to our family, in Little College Street, Camden Town, who took children in to board, and had once done so at Brighton; and who, with a few alterations and embellishments, unconsciously began to sit for Mrs Pipchin in Dombey, *when she took in me.'*

(top story but one), and cried very much. He solemnly conjured me, I remember, to take warning by his fate; and to observe that if a man had twenty pounds a-year for his income, and spent nineteen pounds nineteen shillings and sixpence, he would be happy, but that if he spent twenty pounds one he would be miserable. After which he borrowed a shilling of me for porter, gave me a written order on Mrs Micawber for the amount, and put away his pocket-handkerchief, and cheered up.

We sat before a little fire, with two bricks put within the rusted grate, one on each side, to prevent its burning too many coals; until another debtor, who shared the room with Mr Micawber, came in from the bakehouse with the loin of mutton which was our joint-stock repast. Then I was sent up to 'Captain Hopkins' in the room overhead, with Mr Micawber's compliments, and I was his young friend, and would Captain Hopkins lend me a knife and fork.

Captain Hopkins lent me the knife and fork, with his compliments to Mr Micawber. There was a very dirty lady in his little room, and two wan girls, his daughters, with shock heads of hair. I thought it was better to borrow Captain Hopkins's knife and fork, than Captain Hopkins's comb. The Captain himself was in the last extremity of shabbiness, with large whiskers, and an old, old brown great-coat with no other coat below it. I saw his bed rolled up in a corner; and what plates and dishes and pots he had, on a shelf; and I divined (God knows how) that though the two girls with the shock heads of hair were Captain Hopkins's

Borough High Street, off which Lant Street is situated. Charles Dickens eventually moved there to be near his parents in prison.

children, the dirty lady was not married to Captain Hopkins. My timid station on his threshold was not occupied more than a couple of minutes at most; but I came down again with all this in my knowledge, as surely as the knife and fork were in my hand.

There was something gipsy-like and agreeable in the dinner, after all. I took back Captain Hopkins's knife and fork early in the afternoon, and went home to comfort Mrs Micawber with an account of my visit. She fainted when she saw me return, and made a little jug of egg-hot afterwards to console us while we talked it over.

I don't know how the household furniture came to be sold for the family benefit, or who sold it, except that *I* did not. Sold it was, however, and carried away in a van; except the bed, a few chairs, and the kitchen table. With these possessions we encamped, as it were, in the two parlours of the emptied house in Windsor Terrace; Mrs Micawber, the children, the Orfling, and myself; and lived in those rooms night and day. I have no idea for how long, though it seems to me for a long time. At last Mrs Micawber resolved to move into the prison, where Mr Micawber had now secured a room to himself. So I took the key of the house to the landlord, who was very glad to get it; and the beds were sent over to the King's Bench, except mine, for which a little room was hired outside the walls in the neighbourhood of that Institution, very much to my satisfaction, since the Micawbers and I had become too used to one another, in our troubles, to part.

53

The Orfling was likewise accommodated with an inexpensive lodging in the same neighbourhood. Mine was a quiet back-garret with a sloping roof, commanding a pleasant prospect of a timberyard; and when I took possession of it, with the reflection that Mr Micawber's troubles had come to a crisis at last, I thought it quite a paradise.

The Kings Bench and the Orfling were, respectively, the Marshalsea and a girl from Chatham Workhouse who lodged with the Dickens family. Dickens himself grew desperately unhappy, as here he describes:

My rescue from this kind of existence I considered quite hopeless, and abandoned as such, altogether; though I am solemnly convinced that I never, for one hour, was reconciled to it, or was otherwise than miserably unhappy. I felt keenly, however, the being so cut off from my parents, my brothers, and sisters; and, when my day's work was done, going home to such a miserable blank; and *that*, I thought, might be corrected. One Sunday night I remonstrated with my father on his head, so pathetically and with so many tears, that his kind nature gave way. He began to think that it was not quite right. I do believe he had never thought so before, or thought about it. It was the first remonstrance I had ever made about my lot, and perhaps it opened up a little more than I intended. A back-attic was found for me at the house of an insolvent court agent, who lived in Lant Street in the Borough, where Bob Sawyer lodged many years afterwards. A bed and bedding were sent over for me, and made up on the floor. The little window had a pleasant prospect of a timber-yard; and when I took possession of my new abode, I thought it was a Paradise.

Paradise it may have seemed, but Dickens' description of the place in his first novel, *The Pickwick Papers*, ironically lends more realism to it:

There is a repose about Lant Street, in the borough, which sheds a gentle melancholy upon the soul. There are always a good many houses to let in the street: it is a bye-street too, and its dulness is soothing. A house in Lant Street would not come within the denomination of a first-rate residence, in the strict acceptation of the term; but it is a most desirable spot nevertheless. If a man wished to abstract himself from the world – to remove himself from within the reach of temptation – to place himself beyond the possibility of any inducement to look out of the window – he should by all means go to Lant Street.

In this happy retreat are colonised a few clear-starchers, a sprinkling of journeymen bookbinders, one or two prison agents for the Insolvent Court, several small housekeepers who are employed in the Docks, a handful of mantua-makers, and a seasoning of jobbing tailors. The majority of the inhabitants either direct their energies to the letting of furnished apartments, or devote themselves to the healthful and invigorating pursuit of mangling. The chief features in the still life of the street are green shutters, lodging-bills, brass door-plates, and bell-handles; the principal specimens of animated nature, the pot-boy, the muffin youth, and the baked-potato man. The population is migratory, usually disappearing on the verge of quarter-day, and generally by

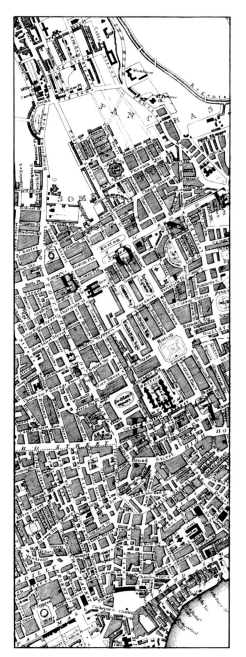

*'He was a very little and a very sickly boy. . . .
He was never a good little cricket-player; he
was never a first-rate hand at marbles, or peg-
top, or prisoner's base: but he had great
pleasure in watching the other boys . . . at
these games, reading while they played.'*

night. His Majesty's revenues are seldom collected in this happy valley; the rents
are dubious; and the water communication is very frequently cut off.

Alienation

Some time later, the young journalist Dickens was able to describe his
first-hand experience of alienation on the streets of London, and in so
doing formulate a theme which was to become so important in nineteenth
and twentieth-century literature.

'Tis strange with how little notice, good, bad, or indifferent, a man may live and
die in London. He awakens no sympathy in the breast of any single person; his
existence is a matter of interest to no one save himself; and he cannot be said to
be forgotten when he dies, for no one remembered him when he was alive. There
is a very numerous class of people in this great metropolis who seem not to
possess a single friend, and whom nobody appears to care for. Urged by
imperative necessity in the first instance, they have resorted to London in search

of employment and the means of subsistence. It is hard, we know, to break the ties which bind us to our homes and friends, and harder still to efface the thousand recollections of happy days and old times which have been slumbering in our bosoms for years, and only rush upon the mind to bring before it with startling reality associations connected with the friends we have left, the scenes we have beheld too probably for the last time, and the hopes we once cherished, but may entertain no more. These men, however, happily for themselves, have long since forgotten such thoughts. Old country friends have died or emigrated; former correspondents have become lost, like themselves, in the crowd and turmoil of some busy city; and they have gradually settled down into more passive creatures of habit and endurance.

But it seems that even prior to his abandonment by his parents, Charles had been something of an isolated figure. Forster recalls how he would watch rather than play with the other boys, a 'queer small boy . . . and a very sickly boy,' he says, 'Never a good little cricket-player . . . never a first-rate hand at marbles, or peg-top, or prisoner's base.' Perhaps too his unusual childhood brightness and a childhood sickness – regular attacks of violent spasms – helped set him apart from the rest of his little world at this very early age. One wonders how accurately his own remembrances of childhood are contained in the following piece from *A Christmas Carol* in which Scrooge is made to see himself as he really was, 'a solitary child':

They walked along the road; Scrooge recognising every gate, and post, and tree; until a little market-town appeared in the distance, with its bridge, its church, and winding river. Some shaggy ponies now were seen trotting towards them with boys upon their backs, who called to other boys in country gigs and carts, driven by farmers. All these boys were in great spirits, and shouted to each other, until the broad fields were so full of merry music, that the crisp air laughed to hear it.
  'These are but shadows of the things that have been,' said the Ghost. 'They have no consciousness of us.'
  The jocund travellers came on; and as they came, Scrooge knew and named them every one. Why was he rejoiced beyond all bounds to see them! Why did his cold eye glisten, and his heart leap up as they went past! Why was he filled with gladness when he heard them give each other Merry Christmas, as they parted at cross-roads and bye-ways, for their several homes! What was merry Christmas to Scrooge? Out upon merry Christmas! What good had it ever done to him?
  'The school is not quite deserted,' said the Ghost. 'A solitary child, neglected by his friends, is left there still.'
  Scrooge said he knew it. And he sobbed.
  They left the high-road, by a well remembered lane, and soon approached a mansion of dull red brick, with a little weathercock-surmounted cupola on the roof, and a bell hanging in it. It was a large house, but one of broken fortunes; for the spacious offices were little used, their walls were damp and mossy, their windows broken, and their gates decayed. Fowls clucked and strutted in the stables; and the coach-houses and sheds were over-run with grass. Nor was it

'I've got to be in London tonight; and I know a 'spectable old gentleman as lives there, wot'll give you lodgings for nothink, and never ask for the change – that is, if any gentleman he knows interduces you.' Oliver Twist

'No lad of spirit need want in London . . . there were ways of living in that vast city, which those who had been bred up in country parts had no idea of.' Oliver Twist

more retentive of its ancient state, within; for entering the dreary hall, and glancing through the open doors of many rooms, they found them poorly furnished, cold and vast. There was an earthy savour in the air, a chilly bareness in the place, which associated itself somehow with too much getting up by candle-light, and not too much to eat.

They went, the Ghost and Scrooge, across the hall, to a door at the back of the house. It opened before them, and disclosed a long, bare, melancholy room, made barer still by lines of plain deal forms and desks. At one of these a lonely boy was reading near a feeble fire; and Scrooge sat down upon a form, and wept to see his poor forgotten self as he had used to be.

Not a latent echo in the house, not a squeak and scuffle from the mice behind the panelling, not a drip from the half-thawed water-spout in the dull yard behind, not a sigh among the leafless boughs of one despondent poplar, not the idle swinging of an empty store-house door, no, not a clicking in the fire, but fell upon the heart of Scrooge with a softening influence, and gave a freer passage to his tears.

The Spirit touched him on the arm, and pointed to his younger self, intent upon his reading. Suddenly a man, in foreign garments: wonderfully real and distinct to look at: stood outside the window, with an axe stuck in his belt, and leading an ass laden with wood by the bridle.

'Why, it's Ali Baba!' Scrooge exclaimed in ecstasy. 'It's dear old honest Ali Baba! Yes, yes, I know! One Christmas time, when yonder solitary child was left here all alone, he *did* come, for the first time, just like that. Poor boy! And Valentine,' said Scrooge, 'and his wild brother, Orson; there they go! And what's his name, who was put down in his drawers, asleep, at the Gate of Damascus; don't you see him! And the Sultan's Groom turned upside-down by the Genii; there he is upon his head! Serve him right. I'm glad of it. What business had *he* to be married to the Princess!'

To hear Scrooge expending all the earnestness of his nature on such subjects, in a most extraordinary voice between laughing and crying; and to see his heightened and excited face; would have been a surprise to his business friends in the city, indeed.

'There's the Parrot!' cried Scrooge. Green body and yellow tail, with a thing like a lettuce growing out of the top of his head; there he is! Poor Robin Crusoe, he called him, when he came home again after sailing round the island. "Poor Robin Crusoe, where have you been, Robin Crusoe?" The man thought he was dreaming, but he wasn't. It was the Parrot, you know. There goes Friday, running for his life to the little creek! Halloa! Hoop! Halloo!'

Then, with a rapidity of transition very foreign to his usual character, he said, in pity for his former self, 'Poor boy!' and cried again.

'I wish,' Scrooge muttered, putting his hand in his pocket, and looking about him, after drying his eyes with his cuff: 'but it's too late now.'

'What is the matter?' asked the Spirit.

'Nothing,' said Scrooge. 'Nothing. There was a boy singing a Christmas Carol at my door last night. I should like to have given him something: that's all.'

To this hungry, lonely, unusually small and young-looking twelve-year-old, London must have seemed a desolate place. The feeling comes poignantly through a joyful exchange between Nicholas Nickleby and Cheeryble, as Nicholas studies the job vacancies through the window of The Register Office. Struck by the stranger's benevolent countenance he tells Cheeryble that he is desperate for a job, and then attempts to explain the outburst by saying:

'Merely that your kind face and manner – both so unlike any I have ever seen –

'"*What makes you take so much pains about one chalk-faced kid, when you know there are fifty boys snoozing about Common Garden every night, as you might pick and choose from?" "Because they're of no use to me, my dear," replied the Jew, with some confusion, "not worth the taking. Their looks convict 'em when they get into trouble, and I lose 'em all. With this boy, properly managed, my dear, I could do what I couldn't with twenty of them."*'
Bill Sikes and Fagin in* Oliver Twist

tempted me into an avowal, which, to any other stranger in this wilderness of London, I should not have dreamt of making,' returned Nicholas.

'Wilderness! Yes it is, it is. Good. It *is* a wilderness,' said the old man with such animation. 'It was a wilderness to me once. I came here barefoot – I have never forgotten it. Thank God!' and he raised his hat from his head, and looked very grave.

Alone in the wilderness of the metropolis, Charles identifies with the orphan poor, and his own early naivety is marvellously captured in Oliver's first entry to London after escaping the workhouse:

'Do you live in London?' inquired Oliver.

'Yes. I do, when I'm at home,' replied the boy. 'I suppose you want some place to sleep in tonight, don't you?'

'I do, indeed,' answered Oliver. 'I have not slept under a roof since I left the country.'

'Don't fret your eyelids on that score,' said the young gentleman. 'I've got to be in London tonight; and I know a 'spectable old gentleman as lives there, wot'll give you lodgings for nothink, and never ask for the change – that is, if any gentleman he knows interduces you. And don't he know me? Oh, no! Not in the least! By no means. Certainly not!'

The young gentleman smiled, as if to intimate that the latter fragments of discourse were playfully ironical; and finished the beer as he did so.

This unexpected offer of shelter was too tempting to be resisted; especially as it was immediately followed up, by the assurance that the old gentleman referred to, would doubtless provide Oliver with a comfortable place, without loss of time. This led to a more friendly and confidential dialogue; from which Oliver discovered that his friend's name was Jack Dawkins, and that he was a peculiar pet and *protégé* of the elderly gentleman before mentioned.

Mr Dawkins's appearance did not say a vast deal in favour of the comforts which his patron's interest obtained for those whom he took under his protection; but, as he had a rather flighty and dissolute mode of conversing, and furthermore avowed that among his intimate friends he was better known by the *sobriquet* of 'The artful Dodger', Oliver concluded that, being of a dissipated and careless turn, the moral precepts of his benefactor had hitherto been thrown away upon him. Under his impression, he secretly resolved to cultivate the good opinion of the old gentleman as quickly as possible; and, if he found the Dodger incorrigible, as he more than half suspected he should, to decline the honour of his further acquaintance.

As John Dawkins objected to their entering London before nightfall, it was nearly eleven o'clock when they reached the turnpike at Islington. They crossed from the Angel into St John's Road; struck down the small street which terminates at Sadler's Wells Theatre; through Exmouth Street and Coppice Row; down the little court by the side of the workhouse; across the classic ground which once bore the name of Hockley-in-the-Hole; thence into Little Saffron Hill; and so into Saffron Hill the Great, along which the Dodger scudded at a rapid pace, directing Oliver to follow close at his heels.

Although Oliver had enough to occupy his attention in keeping sight of his leader, he could not help bestowing a few hasty glances on either side of the way, as he passed along. A dirtier or more wretched place he had never seen. The street was very narrow and muddy, and the air was impregnated with filthy odours. There were a good many small shops; but the only stock in trade appeared to be heaps of children, who, even at that time of night, were crawling in and out at the doors, or screaming from the inside. The sole places that seemed to prosper amid the general blight of the place, were the public-houses; and in them, the lowest orders of Irish were wrangling with might and main. Covered ways and yards, which here and there diverged from the main street, disclosed little knots of houses, where drunken men and women were positively wallowing in filth; and from several of the door-ways, great ill-looking fellows were cautiously emerging, bound, to all appearance, on no very well-disposed or harmless errands.

Oliver was just considering whether he hadn't better run away, when they reached the bottom of the hill. His conductor, catching him by the arm, pushed open the door of a house near Field Lane; and, drawing him into the passage, closed it behind them.

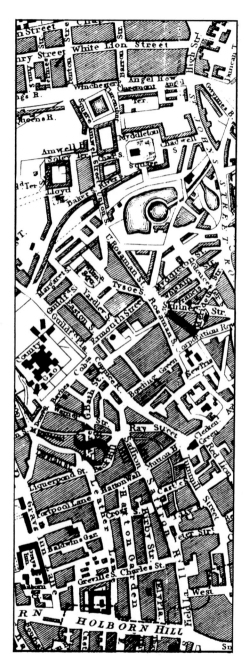

OLIVER TWIST

60

'It is night. Calm and unmoved amidst the scenes that darkness favours, the great Heart of London throbs in its Giant breast. Wealth and beggary, vice and virtue, guilt and innocence, repletion and direst hunger, all treading on each other and crowding together, are gathered around it . . . Does not this Heart of London, that nothing moves, nor stops, nor quickens, – that goes on the same, let what will be done, – does it not express the city's character well?' Reprinted Pieces

Left:
Oliver enters London. From the Angel, Islington to Fagin's den on Saffron Hill – London as it was in Dickens' day.

Dickens' own solitary introduction to the streets of London, beyond the immediate vicinity of Bayham Street, came in the form of a twice daily walk between Gower Street North, and later his lodgings in Camden Town, and the factory in the Strand.

It was a long way to go and return within the dinner-hour, and, usually, I either carried my dinner with me, or went and bought it at some neighbouring shop. In the latter case, it was commonly a saveloy and a penny loaf; sometimes, a fourpenny plate of beef from a cook's shop; sometimes, a plate of bread and cheese, and a glass of beer, from a miserable old public-house over the way; the Swan, if I remember right, or the Swan and something else that I have forgotten. Once, I remember tucking my own bread (which I had brought from home in the

Great Ormond Yard, one of a number of busy stable-yards in Holborn, and similar to the one where Mr Plornish resolves Tip Dorrit's problems.

In Bleak House, Mr Snagsby tells his apprentices that there was a time when 'a brook "as clear as crystal" ran down the middle of Holborn, when Turnstile really was a turnstile, leading slap way into meadows'. Great Turnstile is now a narrow passageway between Holborn and Lincoln's Inn.

Drury Lane: 'Once, I remember tucking my own bread (which I had brought from home in the morning) under my arm, wrapped up in a piece of paper like a book, and going into the best dining-room in Johnson's alamode beef-house in Clare Court, Drury Lane, and magnificently ordering a small plate of alamode beef to eat with it. What the waiter thought of such a strange little apparition, coming in all alone, I don't know; but I can see him now, staring at me as I ate my dinner and bringing up the other waiter to look. I gave him a halfpenny, and I wish, now, that he hadn't taken it.'

morning) under my arm wrapped up in a piece of paper like a book, and going into the best dining-room in Johnson's alamode beef-house in Clare Court, Drury Lane, and magnificently ordering a small plate of alamode beef to eat with it. What the waiter thought of such a strange little apparition, coming in all alone, I don't know; but I can see him now, staring at me as I ate my dinner, and bringing up the other waiter to look. I gave him a halfpenny, and I wish, now, that he hadn't taken it.

63

And later, on his way from Camden Town to the Strand:

I could not resist the stale pastry put out at half-price on trays at the confectioners' doors in Tottenham Court Road; and I often spent in that the money I should have kept for my dinner. Then I went without my dinner, or bought a roll, or a slice of pudding. There were two pudding shops between which I was divided, according to my finances. One was in a court close to St Martin's Church (at the back of the church), which is now removed altogether. The pudding at that shop was made with currants, and was rather a special pudding, but was dear: two penn'orth not being larger than a penn'orth of more ordinary pudding. A good shop for the latter was in the Strand, somewhere near where the Lowther Arcade is now. It was a stout, hale pudding, heavy and flabby; with great raisins in it, stuck in whole, at great distances apart. It came up hot, at about noon every day: and many and many a day did I dine off it.

Both passages are repeated practically verbatim in Chapter 11 of *David Copperfield*. Sometimes, as the chapter continues to show, he would stop and buy a beer to wash down his lunch.

I was such a child, and so little, that frequently when I went into the bar of a strange public-house for a glass of ale or porter, to moisten what I had had for dinner, they were afraid to give it me. I remember one hot evening I went into the bar of a public-house, and said to the landlord:
 'What is your best – your *very best* – ale a glass?' For it was a special occasion. I don't know what. It may have been my birthday.
 'Twopence-halfpenny,' says the landlord, 'is the price of the Genuine Stunning ale.'
 'Then,' says I, producing the money, 'just draw me a glass of the Genuine Stunning, if you please, with a good head to it.'
 The landlord looked at me in return over the bar, from head to foot, with a strange smile on his face; and instead of drawing the beer, looked round the screen and said something to his wife. She came out from behind it, with her work in her hand, and joined him in surveying me. Here we stand, all three, before me now. The landlord in his shirt-sleeves, leaning against the bar window-frame; his wife looking over the little half-door; and I, in some confusion, looking up at them from outside the partition. They asked me a good many questions; as, what my name was, how old I was, where I lived, how I was employed, and how I came there. To all of which, that I might commit nobody, I invented, I am afraid, appropriate answers. They served me with the ale, though I suspect it was not the Genuine Stunning; and the landlord's wife, opening the little half-door of the bar, and bending down, gave me my money back, and gave me a kiss that was half admiring and half compassionate, but all womanly and good, I am sure.

As Dickens became more adventurous he ventured into Soho; an uncle called Thomas Barrow had lodgings in Gerrard Street. A few minutes away lay Seven Dials – 'What wild visions of prodigies of wickedness,

'I was such a child, and so little, that frequently when I went into the bar of a strange public-house for a glass of ale or porter, to moisten what I had had for dinner, they were afraid to give it me. I remember one hot evening I went into the bar of a public-house and said to the landlord:
'What is your best – your very best – ale a glass?' For it was a special occasion. I don't know what. It may have been my birthday.
'Two pence-halfpenny,' says the landlord, 'is the price of the Genuine Stunning ale.'
'Then,' says I, producing the money, 'just draw me a glass of the Genuine Stunning, if you please, with a good head on it.' David Copperfield

Seven Dials, Covent Garden: 'What wild visions of prodigies of wickedness, want, and beggary, arose in my mind out of that place!'

want and beggary, arose in my mind out of that place,' he recalled of his times spent there. Covent Garden was an especially favourite resort. He would walk or just stand around, looking down dark alleys and courts, noting the strange characters that he saw. Of Monmouth Street, he recalled:

We have always entertained a particular attachment towards Monmouth Street, as the only true and real emporium for second-hand wearing apparel. Monmouth Street is venerable from its antiquity, and respectable from its usefulness. Holywell Street we despise; the red-headed and red-whiskered Jews who forcibly haul you into their squalid houses, and thrust you into a suit of clothes, whether you will or not, we detest.

The inhabitants of Monmouth Street are a distinct class; a peaceable and retiring race, who immure themselves, for the most part, in deep cellars or small back-parlours, and who seldom come forth into the world, except in the dusk and coolness of evening, when they may be seen seated in chairs on the pavement, smoking their pipes, or watching the gambols of their engaging children as they revel in the gutter, a happy troop of infantine scavengers. Their countenances bear a thoughtful and a dirty cast, certain indications of their love of traffic; and their habitations are distinguished by that disregard of outward appearance, and neglect of personal comfort, so common among people who are constantly

Charles would visit his uncle, Thomas Barrow, with whom his father had shared an office during his first period as a clerk in Somerset House in 1905, and through whom he had met his wife, Elizabeth. Thomas Barrow lived in lodgings in Gerrard Street, Soho, where years later, in Great Expectations, Pip was invited to dinner by Jaggers: 'He conducted us to Gerrard Street, Soho, to a house on the south side of that street. Rather a stately house of its kind, but dolefully in want of painting, and with dirty windows. He took out his key and opened the door, and we all went into a stone hall, bare, gloomy and little used. So, up a dark brown staircase into a series of three dark brown rooms on the first floor. There were carved garlands on the panelled walls, and as he stood among them giving us welcome, I know what kind of loops I thought they looked like.'

immersed in profound speculations, and deeply engaged in sedentary pursuits.

SKETCHES

Perhaps in Monmouth Street was sown the seed of the character of the street trader in *David Copperfield*, to whom the young destitute endeavours to sell his jacket:

Very stiff and sore of foot I was in the morning, and quite dazed by the beating of drums and marching of troops, which seemed to hem in on every side when I went down towards the long narrow street. Feeling that I could go but a very little way that day, if I were to reserve any strength for getting to my journey's end, I resolved to make the sale of my jacket its principal business. Accordingly, I took the jacket off, that I might learn to do without it; and carrying it under my arm, began a tour of inspection of the various slop-shops.

It was a likely place to sell a jacket in; for the dealers in second-hand clothes were numerous, and were, generally speaking, on the look-out for customers at their shop doors. But as most of them had, hanging up among their stock, an officer's coat or two, epaulettes and all, I was rendered timid by the costly nature of their dealings, and walked about for a long time without offering my merchandise to anyone.

66

This modesty of mine directed my attention to the marinestore shops, and such shops as Mr Dolloby's, in preference to the regular dealers. At last I found one that I thought looked promising, at the corner of a dirty lane, ending in an enclosure full of stinging-nettles, against the palings of which some second-hand sailors' clothes, that seemed to have overflowed the shop, were fluttering among some cots, and rusty guns, and oilskin hats, and certain trays full of so many old rusty keys of so many sizes that they seemed various enough to open all the doors in the world.

Into this shop, which was low and small, and which was darkened rather than lighted by a little window, overhung with clothes, and was descended into by some steps, I went with a palpitating heart; which was not relieved when an ugly old man, with the lower part of his face all covered with a stubbly grey beard, rushed out of a dirty den behind it, and seized me by the hair of my head. He was

67

a dreadful old man to look at, in a filthy flannel waistcoat, and smelling terribly of rum. His bedstead, covered with a tumbled and ragged piece of patchwork, was in the den he had come from, where another little window showed a prospect of more stinging-nettles, and a lame donkey.

'Oh, what do you want?' grinned this old man, in a fierce, monotonous whine. 'Oh, my eyes and limbs, what do you want? Oh, my lungs and liver, what do you want? Oh, goroo, goroo!'

I was so much dismayed by these words, and particularly by the repetition of the last unknown one, which was a kind of rattle in his throat, that I could make no answer; hereupon the old man, still holding me by the hair, repeated:

'Oh, what do you want?' Oh, my eyes and limbs, what do you want? Oh, my lungs and liver, what do you want? Oh, goroo! – which he screwed out of himself, with an energy that made his eyes start in his head.

'I wanted to know,' I said, trembling, 'if you would buy a jacket.'

'Oh, let's see the jacket!' cried the old man. 'Oh, my heart on fire, show the jacket to us! Oh, my eyes and limbs, bring the jacket out!'

With that he took his trembling hands, which were like the claws of a great bird, out of my hair; and put on a pair of spectacles, not at all ornamental to his inflamed eyes.

'Oh, how much for the jacket?' cried the old man, after examining it. 'Oh – goroo! – how much for the jacket?'

'Half-a-crown,' I answered, recovering myself.

'Oh, my lungs and liver,' cried the old man, 'no! Oh, my eyes, no! Oh, my limbs, no! Eighteenpence. Goroo!'

Every time he uttered this ejaculation, his eyes seemed to be in danger of starting out; and every sentence he spoke, he delivered in a sort of tune, always exactly the same, and more like a gust of wind, which begins low, mounts up high, and falls again, than any other comparison I can find for it.

'Well,' said I, glad to have closed the bargain, 'I'll take eighteenpence.'

'Oh, my liver!' cried the old man, throwing the jacket on a shelf. 'Get out of the shop! Oh, my lungs, get out of the shop! Oh, my eyes and limbs – goroo! – don't ask for money; make it an exchange.'

I never was so frightened in my life, before or since; but I told him humbly that I wanted money, and that nothing else was of any use to me, but that I would wait for it, as he desired, outside, and had no wish to hurry him. So I went outside, and sat down in the shade in a corner. And I sat there so many hours, that the shade became sunlight, and the sunlight became shade again, and still I sat there waiting for the money.

There never was such another drunken madman in that line of business, I hope. That he was well known in the neighbourhood, and enjoyed the reputation of having sold himself to the devil, I soon understood from the visits he received from the boys, who continually came skirmishing about the shop, shouting that legend, and calling to him to bring out his gold. 'You ain't poor, you know, Charley, as you pretend. Bring out your gold. Bring out some of the gold you sold yourself to the devil for. Come! It's in the lining of the mattress, Charley. Rip it open and let's have some!' This, and many offers to lend him a knife for the purpose, exasperated him to such a degree, that the whole day was a succession of rushes on his part, and flights on the part of the boys. Sometimes in his rage he would take me for one of them, and come at me, mouthing as if he were going to tear me in pieces; then, remembering me, just in time, would dive into the shop, and lie upon his bed, as I thought from the sound of his voice, yelling in a frantic way, to his own windy tune, the 'Death of Nelson'; with an Oh! before every line, and innumerable Goroos interspersed. As if this were not bad enough for me, the boys, connecting me with the establishments, on account of the patience and perseverance with which I sat outside, half-dressed, pelted me, and used me very ill all day.

He made many attempts to induce me to consent to an exchange; at one time coming out with a fishing-rod, at another with a fiddle, at another with a cocked hat, at another with a flute. But I resisted all these overtures, and sat there in desperation; each time asking him, with tears in my eyes, for my money or my jacket. At last he began to pay me in halfpence at a time; and was full two hours getting by easy stages to a shilling.

'Oh, my eyes and limbs!' he then cried, peeping hideously out of the shop, after a long pause, 'will you go for twopence more?'

'I can't,' I said; 'I shall be starved.'

'Oh, my lungs and liver, will you go for threepence?'

'I would go for nothing, if I could,' I said, 'but I want the money badly.'

'Oh, go – roo!' (it is really impossible to express how he twisted this ejaculation out of himself, as he peeped round the door-post at me, showing nothing but his crafty old head); 'will you go for fourpence?'

I was so faint and weary that I closed with this offer; and taking the money out of his claw, not without trembling, went away more hungry and thirsty than I had ever been, a little before sunset. But at an expense of threepence I soon refreshed myself completely; and, being in better spirits then, limped seven miles upon my road. . . .

At weekends he might make a visit to his godfather, Charles Huffam, his walk taking him down by the river to Limehouse. He would have had time to study the boatmen of the Thames, to whom Huffam supplied rigging and other naval artefacts – men like Rogue Riderhood in *Our Mutual Friend*:

Rogue Riderhood dwelt deep and dark in Limehouse Hole, among the riggers, and the mast, oar and block makers, and the boat-builders, and the sail-lofts, as in a kind of ship's hold stored full of waterside characters, some no better than himself, some very much better, and none much worse. The Hole, albeit in a general way not over nice in its choice of company, was rather shy in reference to the honour of cultivating the Rogue's acquaintance; more frequently giving him the cold shoulder than the warm hand, and seldom or never drinking with him unless at his own expense.

Another favourite walk was through the back streets of the Adelphi Theatre. The Adelphi Arches must have seemed a threatening, nightmarish place to this 'queer, small boy', a bit like one of those paintings by de Chirico where pillar follows pillar after pillar. But like a child who is attracted by a flame which he knows he mustn't touch (but

A view of the river at Limehouse.

does so all the same) Dickens was by now attracted to monstrous London 'in very repulsion': 'I was fond,' he recalls in *Copperfield*, 'of wandering about the Adelphi, because it was a mysterious place, with those dark arches. I see myself emerging one evening from some of these arches, on a little public-house close to the river, with an open space before it, where some coal-heavers were dancing, to look at whom I sat down upon a bench. I wonder what they thought of me!' And later David ponders on the old days 'when I used to roam about its subterranean arches, and on the happy changes which had brought me to the surface.'

The fierce fire in which the boy's vision of London was cast ensured that his 'child's eye view' would never be lost when boy became man. In *A Christmas Carol* the narrator confesses a desire 'to have had the licence of a child, and yet been man enough to know its value'. Dickens' talent provided the opportunity in his novels. The child was reborn in Oliver, David Copperfield, Smike in *Nicholas Nickleby*, even poor Jo in *Bleak House* – all innocents threatened with injustice, all teetering on the edge of disaster or corruption.

The dangers posed by criminals in London were real enough. There were 'no-go' areas in the rookeries and the slums, and in 1867 we are told that

Dickens would walk to Limehouse to visit his godfather, Christopher Huffam, and the area appeared in a number of his later writings. Pictured here is The Grapes Inn, Narrow Street, on which he based the Six Jolly Fellowship Porters Tavern in Our Mutual Friend: *'Externally, it was a narrow lopsided wooden jumble of corpulent windows heaped one upon another as you might heap as many toppling oranges, with a crazy wooden verandah impending over the water; indeed the whole house, inclusive of the complaining flag-staff on the roof, impended over the water, but seemed to have got into the condition of a faint-hearted diver who has paused so long on the brink that he will never go in at all.'*

there were 100,000 persons who lived by plunder. For a boy alone, one crime in particular would have threatened – child kidnapping (and stealing their clothes) was common at the time. In *Dombey and Son*, Florence Dombey (daughter of the proud industrialist) loses her guardian, as Dickens himself had done once before, and is swept up in the seemy side of London's underworld:

Surprises, like misfortunes, rarely come along. The astonished Susan Nipper and her two young charges were rescued by the bystanders from under the very

wheels of a passing carriage before they knew what had happened; and at that moment (it was market day) a thundering alarm of 'Mad Bull!' was raised.

With a wild confusion before her, of people running up and down, and shouting, and wheels running over them, and boys fighting, and mad bulls coming up, and the nurse in the midst of all these dangers being torn to pieces, Florence screamed and ran. She ran till she was exhausted, urging Susan to do the same; and then, stopping and wringing her hands as she remembered they had left the other nurse behind, found, with a sensation of terror not to be described, that she was quite alone.

'Susan! Susan!' cried Florence, clapping her hands in the very ecstasy of her alarm. 'Oh, where are they? where are they?'

'Where are they?' said an old woman, coming hobbling across as fast as she could from the opposite side of the way. 'Why did you run away from 'em?'

'I was frightened,' answered Florence. 'I didn't know what I did. I thought they were with me. Where are they?'

The old woman took her by the wrist, and said, 'I'll show you.'

She was a very ugly old woman, with red rims round her eyes, and a mouth that mumbled and chattered of itself when she was not speaking. She was miserably dressed, and carried some skins over her arm. She seemed to have followed Florence some little way at all events, for she had lost her breath; and this made her uglier still, as she stood trying to regain it: working her shrivelled yellow face and throat into all sorts of contortions.

72

'With a wild confusion before her, of people running up and down, and shouting, and wheels running over them, and boys fighting, and mad bulls coming up, the nurse in the midst of all these dangers being torn to pieces, Florence screamed and ran.' Dombey and Son

Florence was afraid of her, and looked, hesitating, up the street, of which she had almost reached the bottom. It was a solitary place – more a back road than a street – and there was no one in it but herself and the old woman.

'You needn't be frightened now,' said the old woman, still holding her tight. 'Come along with me.'

'I-I don't know you. What's your name?' asked Florence.

'Mrs Brown,' said the old woman. 'Good Mrs Brown.'

'Are they near here?' asked Florence, beginning to be led away.

'Susan ain't far off,' said Good Mrs Brown; 'and the others are close to her.'

'Is anybody hurt?' cried Florence.

'Not a bit of it,' said Good Mrs Brown.

The child shed tears of delight on hearing this, and accompanied the old woman willingly; though she could not help glancing at her face as they went along – particularly at that industrious mouth – and wondering whether Bad Mrs Brown, if there were such a person, was at all like her.

They had not gone far, but had gone by some very uncomfortable places, such as brick-fields and tile-yards, when the old woman turned down a dirty lane, where the mud lay in deep black ruts in the middle of the road. She stopped before a shabby little house, as closely shut up as a house that was full of cracks and crevices could be. Opening the door with a key she took out of her bonnet, she pushed the child before her into a back room, where there was a great heap of rags of different colours lying on the floor; a heap of bones, and a heap of sifted dust or cinders; but there was no furniture at all, and the walls and ceiling were quite black.

The child became so terrified that she was stricken speechless, and looked as though about to swoon.

'Now don't be a young mule,' said Good Mrs Brown, reviving her with a shake. 'I'm not a going to hurt you. Sit upon the rags.'

Florence obeyed her, holding out her folded hands, in mute supplication.

'I'm not a going to keep you, even, above an hour,' said Mrs Brown. 'D'ye understand what I say?'

The child answered with great difficulty, 'Yes.'

'Then,' said Good Mrs Brown, taking her own seat on the bones, 'don't vex me. If you don't, I tell you I won't hurt you. But if you do, I'll kill you. I could have you killed at any time – even if you was in your own bed at home. Now let's know who you are, and what you are, and all about it.'

The old woman's threats and promises; the dread of giving her offence; and the habit, unusual to a child, but almost natural to Florence now, of being quiet, and repressing what she felt, and feared, and hoped; enabled her to do this bidding, and to tell her little history, or what she knew of it. Mrs Brown listened attentively, until she had finished.

'So your name's Dombey, eh?' said Mrs Brown.

'Yes, Ma'am.'

'I want that pretty frock, Miss Dombey,' said Good Mrs Brown, 'and that little bonnet, and a petticoat or two, and anything else you can spare. Come! Take 'em off.'

Florence obeyed, as fast as her trembling hands would allow; keeping, all the while, a frightened eye on Mrs Brown. When she had divested herself of all the articles of apparel mentioned by that lady, Mrs B. examined them at leisure, and seemed tolerably well satisfied with their quality and value.

'Humph!' she said, running her eyes over the child's slight figure, 'I don't see anything else – except the shoes. I must have the shoes, Miss Dombey.'

Poor little Florence took them off with equal alacrity, only too glad to have any more means of conciliation about her. The old woman then produced some wretched substitutes from the bottom of the heap of rags, which she turned up for that purpose; together with a girl's cloak, quite worn out and very old; and the crushed remains of a bonnet that had probably been picked up from some ditch or dunghill. In this dainty raiment, she instructed Florence to dress herself; and as such preparation seemed a prelude to her release, the child complied with increased readiness, if possible.

In hurriedly putting on the bonnet, if that may be called a bonnet which was more like a pad to carry loads on, she caught it in her hair which grew luxuriantly, and could not immediately disentangle it. Good Mrs Brown whipped out a large pair of scissors, and fell into an unaccountable state of excitement.

'Why couldn't you let me be!' said Mrs Brown, 'when I was contented? You

74

little fool!'

'I beg your pardon. I don't know what I have done,' panted Florence. 'I couldn't help it.'

'Couldn't help it!' cried Mrs Brown. 'How do you expect I can help it? Why, Lord!' said the old woman, ruffling her curls with a furious pleasure, 'anybody but me would have had 'em off, first of all.'

Florence was so relieved to find that it was only her hair and not her head which Mrs Brown coveted, that she offered no resistance or entreaty, and merely raised her mild eyes towards the face of that good soul.

'If I hadn't once had a gal of my own – beyond seas now – that was proud of her hair,' said Mrs Brown, 'I'd have had every lock of it. She's far away, she's far away! Oho! Oho!'

Mrs Brown's was not a melodious cry, but, accompanied with a wild tossing up of her lean arms, it was full of passionate grief, and thrilled to the heart of Florence, whom it frightened more than ever. It had its part, perhaps, in saving her curls; for Mrs Brown, after hovering about her with the scissors for some moments, like a new kind of butterfly, bade her hide them under the bonnet and let no trace of them escape to tempt her. Having accomplished this victory over herself, Mrs Brown resumed her seat on the bones, and smoked a very short black pipe, mowing and mumbling all the time, as if she were eating the stem.

When the pipe was smoked out, she gave the child a rabbit-skin to carry, that she might appear the more like her ordinary companion, and told her that she was now going to lead her to a public street whence she could inquire her way to her friends. But she cautioned her, with threats of summary and deadly vengeance in case of disobedience, not to talk to strangers, nor to repair to her own home (which may have been too near for Mrs Brown's convenience), but to her father's office in the City; also to wait at the street corner where she would be left, until the clock struck three. These directions Mrs Brown enforced with assurances that there would be potent eyes and ears in her employment cognizant of all she did; and these directions Florence promised faithfully and earnestly to observe.

At length, Mrs Brown, issuing forth, conducted her changed and ragged little friend through a labyrinth of narrow streets and lanes and alleys, which emerged, after a long time, upon a stable yard, with a gateway at the end, whence the roar of a great thoroughfare made itself audible. Pointing out this gateway, and informing Florence that when the clocks struck three she was to go to the left, Mrs Brown, after making a parting grasp at her hair which seemed involuntary and quite beyond her own control, told her she knew what to do, and bade her go and do it: remembering that she was watched.

Streets, Courts and Theatres

John Dickens inherited £450 following the death of his mother in 1824, not enough to make him solvent but sufficient to satisfy his debtors temporarily and secure his release from prison.

The Dickens family moved to Somers Town, not far from Kings Cross, an even worse area than Camden Town's Bayham Street, where they had dwelt during the previous low point of their fortunes. John resumed his job with the Navy Pay Office, not at all sure whether the authorities would allow an insolvent to continue in a governmental position. He petitioned for early retirement on health grounds, and just nine months after he had left the Marshalsea he was granted a very basic pension of £145 p.a.

One can imagine that this created relief on both sides, but to his credit (and not at all characteristic of his fictional counterpart, Micawber), John Dickens determined to supplement his pension through journalism, and did indeed manage to become a parliamentary reporter in the House of Commons gallery.

Meanwhile Charles had remained at Warrens', though the factory had moved from Hungerford Stairs to Chandos Street, Covent Garden. Then, a month or so after his retirement, his father suddenly took the boy out of the blacking factory and delivered him to the Wellington House Academy (possibly the original of Mr Creakle's Salem House Academy in *David Copperfield*), situated on the corner of Granby Street and Hampstead Road. Charles threw himself into the whirl of schoolboy life, but any attempt to recapture his lost youth was short-lived. A mere two years after his enrolment he was taken out and once again sent to work – still only 15 – this time as a clerk at a law firm called Ellis and Blackmore in Gray's Inn, Holborn.

He worked there for a modest salary, aware that he was but one among many office lads 'in their first surtout', and with little hope of advancement or fulfilment. But he was out of the blacking factory forever, and determined never to go back.

Dickens' restless but unapplied mind found an outlet in walking the streets of London, a pursuit he undertook with customary commitment. 'I thought I knew something of the town,' recalled George Lear, a colleague of his at Ellis and Blackmore, 'but after a little talk with Dickens I found that I knew nothing. He knew it all from Bow to Brentford.' This knowledge of the city is apparent in his early writings, accompanied by a sense of claustrophobia: 'What involutions can compare with those of Seven Dials? Where is there such another maze of streets, courts, lanes and alleys?' wrote Dickens in *Sketches*. We no longer see the 'wild

Upon John Dickens' release from prison, the family took up residence at 29 Johnson Street, Somers Town.

visions' of a lonely, terrified, wide-eyed boy, as recalled from youth for his biographer John Forster, this is the London of the young clerk, burning with ambition yet uncertain of his way in the labyrinthine complexity of city life.

In the opening pages of *The Old Curiosity Shop*, the narrator's night-time wanderings (a habit Dickens developed at this time), are given direction by the determined hand of youth – little Nell:

Staple Inn, near where Dickens worked as a lawyer's clerk. 'Behind the most ancient part of Holborn, London, where certain gabled houses some centuries of age still stand looking on the public way, as if disconsolately looking for the old Bourne that has long run dry, is a little nook composed of two irregular quadrangles, called Staple Inn. Edwin Drood

'Covent Garden market, and avenues leading to it, are thronged with carts of all sorts, sizes and descriptions from the heavy lumbering waggon, with its four stout horses, to the jingling costermonger's cart, with its consumptive donkey.' Sketches

The Oxford Arms, Holborn, typical of the sort of place Dickens would have lodged while a solicitor's clerk.

Night is generally my time for walking. In the summer I often leave home early in the morning, and roam about fields and lanes all day, or even escape for days or weeks together, but saving in the country I seldom go out until after dark, though, Heaven be thanked, I love its light and feel the cheerfulness it sheds upon the earth, as much as any creature living.

I have fallen insensibly into this habit, both because it favours my infirmity and because it affords me greater opportunity of speculating on the characters and

occupations of those who fill the streets. The glare and hurry of broad noon are not adapted to idle pursuits like mine; a glimpse of passing faces caught by the light of a street lamp or a shop window is often better for my purpose than their full revelation in the daylight, and, if I must add the truth, night is kinder in this respect than day, which too often destroys an air-built castle at the moment of its completion, without the smallest ceremony or remorse.

That constant pacing to and fro, that never-ending restlessness, that incessant tread of feet wearing the rough stones smooth and glossy – is it not a wonder how

'Seven Dials! The region of song and poetry – first effusions and last dying speeches: hallowed by the names of Catnac and of Pitts – names that will entwine themselves with costermongers and barrel-organs, when penny magazines shall have superseded penny yards of song, and capital punishment be unknown!'
Sketches

The forbidding view that Dickens would have had from Lincoln's Inn when he worked for Charles Molloy.

the dwellers in narrow ways can bear to hear it! Think of a sick man in such a place as Saint Martin's Court, listening to the footsteps, and in the midst of pain and weariness obliged, despite himself (as though it were a task he must perform) to detect the child's step from the man's, the slipshod beggar from the booted exquisite, the lounging from the busy, the dull heel of the sauntering outcast from the quick tread of an expectant pleasure-seeker – think of the hum and noise being always present to his senses, and of the stream of life that will not stop, pouring on, on, on, through all his restless dreams, as if he were condemned to lie dead but conscious, in a noisy churchyard, and had no hope of rest for centuries to come.

Then the crowds for ever passing and repassing on the bridges (on those which are free of toll at least) where many stop on fine evenings looking listlessly down upon the water with some vague idea that by-and-by it runs between green banks which grow wider and wider until at last it joins the broad vast sea – where some halt to rest from heavy loads and think as they look over the parapet that to smoke and lounge away one's life, and lie sleeping in the sun upon a hot tarpaulin, in a dull slow sluggish barge, must be happiness unalloyed – and where some, and a very different class, pause with heavier loads than they, remembering to have heard or read in some old time that drowning was not a hard death, but of all means of suicide the easiest and best.

Covent Garden Market at sunrise too, in the spring or summer, when the fragrance of sweet flowers is in the air, overpowering even the unwholesome steams of last night's debauchery, and driving the dusky thrush, whose cage has hung outside a garret window all night long, half mad with joy! Poor bird! the only neighbouring thing at all akin to the other little captives, some of whom, shrinking from the hot hands of drunken purchasers, lie drooping on the path already, while others, soddened by close contact, await the time when they shall be watered and freshened up to please more sober company, and make old clerks who pass them on their road to business, wonder what has filled their breasts with visions of the country.

But my present purpose is not to expatiate upon my walks. An adventure which I am about to relate, and to which I shall recur at intervals, arose out of one of these rambles, and thus I have been led to speak of them by way of preface.

One night I had roamed into the city, and was walking slowly on in my usual way, musing upon a great many things, when I was arrested by an inquiry, the purport of which did not reach me, but which seemed to be addressed to myself, and was preferred in a soft sweet voice that struck me very pleasantly. I turned hastily round and found at my elbow a pretty little girl, who begged to be directed to a certain street at a considerable distance, and indeed in quite another quarter of the town.

'It is a very long way from here,' said I, 'my child.'

'I know that, sir,' she replied timidly. 'I am afraid it is a very long way, for I came from there to-night.'

'Alone?' said I, in some surprise.

'Oh yes, I don't mind that, but I am a little frightened now, for I have lost my road.'

'And what made you ask it of me? Suppose I should tell you wrong.'

'I am sure you will not do that,' said the little creature, 'you are such a very old

New Square, Lincoln's Inn, near where Dickens worked as a solicitor's clerk.

Bell Yard, Carter Lane where later he rented an office while a reporter in the Doctors' Commons.

82

Johnson Court, where Dickens dropped off what became his first published piece – 'A Dinner at Poplar Walk' – 'stealthily one evening at twilight, with fear and trembling, into a dark letter-box in a dark office up a dark corner in Fleet Street.' And when it appeared in Monthly *magazine, 'I walked down to Westminster Hall, and turned into it for half an hour, because my eyes were so dimmed with joy and pride that they could not bear the street, and were not fit to be seen there.'*

gentleman, and walk so slow yourself.'

I cannot describe how much I was impressed by this appeal and the energy with which it was made, which brought a tear into the child's clear eye, and made her slight figure tremble as she looked up into my face.

'Come,' said I, 'I'll take you there.'

She put her hand in mine as confidingly as if she had known me from her cradle, and we trudged away together: the little creature accommodating her pace to mine, and rather seeming to lead and take care of me than I to be protecting her. I observed that every now and then she stole a curious look at my face as if to make quite sure that I was not deceiving her, and that these glances (very sharp and keen they were too) seemed to increase her confidence at every repetition.

For my part, my curiosity and interest were at least equal to the child's, for

child she certainly was, although I thought it probable from what I could make out, that her very small and delicate frame imparted a peculiar youthfulness to her appearance. Though more scantily attired than she might have been she was dressed with perfect neatness, and betrayed no marks of poverty or neglect.

'Who has sent you so far by yourself?' said I.

'Somebody who is very kind to me, sir.'

'And what have you been doing?'

'That, I must not tell,' said the child firmly.

There was something in the manner of this reply which caused me to look at

From his days in the parliamentary corps, Dickens did not derive a great deal of respect for the parliamentary process, but he very quickly shone as 'a first class reporter' in conditions which appalled him: 'I have worn my knees by writing on them in the old Gallery of the Old House of Commons; and I have worn my feet by standing to write in a preposterous pen in the Old House of Lords.'

The offices of the Morning Chronicle where Dickens was a reporter. 'Night after night, I record predictions that never come to pass, professions that are never fulfilled, explanations that are only meant to mystify. I wallow in words. Britannia, that unfortunate female, is always before me, like a trussed fowl: skewered through and through with office-pens, and bound hand and foot with red tape. David Copperfield

the little creature with an involuntary expression of surprise; for I wondered what kind of errand it might be that occasioned her to be prepared for questioning. Her quick eye seemed to read my thoughts, for as it met mine she added that there was no harm in what she had been doing, but it was a great secret – a secret which she did not even know herself.

This was said with no appearance of cunning or deceit, but with an unsuspicious frankness that bore the impress of truth. She walked on as before, growing more familiar with me as we proceeded and talking cheerfully by the way, but she said no more about her home, beyond remarking that we were going quite a new road

and asking if it were a short one.

While we were thus engaged, I revolved in my mind a hundred different explanations of the riddle and rejected them every one. I really felt ashamed to take advantage of the ingenuousness or grateful feeling of the child for the purpose of gratifying my curiosity. I love these little people; and it is not a slight thing when they, who are so fresh from God, love us. As I had felt pleased at first by her confidence I determined to deserve it, and to do credit to the nature which had prompted her to repose it in me.

There was no reason, however, why I should refrain from seeing the person who had inconsiderately sent her to so great a distance by night and alone, and as it was not improbable that if she found herself near home she might take farewell of me and deprive me of the opportunity, I avoided the most frequented ways and took the most intricate, and thus it was not until we arrived in the street itself that she knew where we were. Clapping her hands with pleasure and running on before me for a short distance, my little acquaintance stopped at a door, and remaining on the step till I came up knocked at it when I joined her.

In 1828 Dickens left Blackmore's, and took up a position with the solicitor Charles Molloy. Predictably, this also failed to satisfy his restless

Later Dickens was to recall the hopelessness of trying to write apart from the city that was his inspiration. While trying to write in Genoa, he complained in a letter to John Forster, 'Never did I stagger so upon a threshold before. I seem as if I have plucked myself out of my proper soil. . . and could take root no more until I return to it.'

ambitions. Perhaps influenced by his father's example, or by the money he could earn (fifteen guineas a week), or by the thought that other great men had begun their life in the parliamentary corps, Dickens decided to become a journalist. As yet too young for the reporters' gallery, he became a reporter at the Court of Doctor's Commons – 'a lazy old nook near Saint Paul's Churchyard . . . that has an ancient monopoly in suits

87

about people's wills and people's marriages.' (Steerforth in *David Copperfield*)

Immediately he had resolved upon this course, he set about mastering shorthand; his description of which – 'about equal in difficulty to the mastery of six languages' – characterises once more the persistence with which he pursued everything: 'The changes that were rung upon dots, which in such a position meant such a thing, and in such another position something else entirely different; the wonderful vagaries that were played by circles; the unaccountable consequences that resulted from marks like flies' legs; the tremendous effects of a curve in the wrong place, not only troubled my waking hours, but reappeared before me in my sleep. When I had groped my way, blindly, through these difficulties, and had mastered the alphabet, there then appeared a procession of new horrors, called arbitrary characters; the most despotic characters I have ever known; who insisted, for instance, that a thing like the beginning of a cobweb meant "expectation", and that a pen-and-ink sky-rocket stood for "disadvantageous". When I had fixed these wretches in my mind, I found that they had driven everything else out of it; then, beginning again, I forgot them; while I was picking them up, I dropped the other fragments of the system; in short, it was almost heart-breaking.'

The door knocker at No 16 Bayham Street.

It was two years after his decision to become a journalist that he actually became a parliamentary reporter, and a further three before he was taken on by a proper daily newspaper – the *Morning Chronicle* – where he exercised his skills to the disadvantage of the rival *Times*. He later claimed that 'to the wholesome training of severe newspaper work, when I was a very young man, I constantly refer my first successes.' The requirements of strict accuracy of detail and strict deadlines gave form to his teeming imagination, the first being characteristic of so much of his work and particularly of *Sketches* by Boz. See how his mind worked on the doors that remained closed to him during his London walks:

We are very fond of speculating, as we walk through a street, on the character and pursuits of the people who inhabit it; and nothing so materially assists us in these speculations as the appearance of the house-doors. The various expressions of the human countenance afford a beautiful and interesting study; but there is something in the physiognomy of street-door knockers almost as characteristic, and nearly as infallible. Whenever we visit a man for the first time, we contemplate the features of his knocker with the greatest curiosity, for we well know that, between the man and his knocker, there will inevitably be a greater or less degree of resemblance and sympathy.

For instance, there is one description of knocker that used to be common enough, but which is fast passing away – a large round one, with the jolly face of a convivial lion smiling blandly at you, as you twist the sides of your hair into a curl, or pull up your shirt collar while you are waiting for the door to be opened; we

'Such strange churchyards hide in the City of London; churchyards sometimes so entirely detached from churches, always so pressed upon by houses; so small, so rank, so silent, so forgotten, except by the few people who ever look down into them from their smoky windows. As I stand peeping in through the iron gates and rails I can peel the rusty metal off, like bark from an old tree. . . .' The Uncommercial Traveller

never saw that knocker on the door of a churchish man – so far as our experience is concerned, it invariably bespoke hospitality and another bottle.

No man ever saw this knocker on the door of a small attorney or bill broker; they always patronise the other lion; a heavy ferocious-looking fellow, with a countenance expressive of savage stupidity – a sort of grand master among the knockers, and a great favourite with the selfish and brutal.

89

Then there is a little pert Egyptian knocker, with a long thin face, a pinched-up nose, and a very sharp chin; he is most in vogue with your government-office people, in light drabs and starched cravats: little spare priggish men, who are perfectly satisfied with their own opinions, and consider themselves of paramount importance.

We were greatly troubled, a few years ago, by the innovation of a new kind of knocker, without any face at all, composed of a wreath, depending from a hand or small truncheon. A little trouble and attention, however, enabled us to overcome this difficulty, and to reconcile the new system to our favourite theory. You will invariably find this knocker on the doors of cold and formal people, who always ask you why you *don't* come, and never say *do*...

Some phrenologists affirm that the agitation of a man's brain by different

'She [Nell] walked out into the churchyard, brushing the dew from the long grass with her feet. . . . She felt a curious kind of pleasure in lingering among these houses of the dead, and read the inscriptions on the tombs of the good people. . . , passing on from one to another with increasing interest.' The Old Curiosity Shop

passions produces corresponding developments in the form of his skull. Do not let us be understood as pushing our theory to the length of asserting, that any alteration in a man's disposition would produce a visible effect on the feature of his knocker. Our position merely is, that in such a case, the magnetism which must exist between a man and his knocker would induce the man to remove, and seek some knocker more congenial to his altered feelings. If you ever find a man changing his habitation without any reasonable pretext, depend upon it that, although he may not be aware of the fact himself, it is because he and his knocker are at variance. This is a new theory, but we venture to launch it, nevertheless, as being quite as ingenious and infallible as many thousand of the learned speculations which are daily broached for public good and private fortune-making.

Entertaining these feelings on the subject of knockers, it will be readily imagined with what consternation we viewed the entire removal of the knocker from the door of the next house to the one we lived in, some time ago, and the substitution of a bell. This was a calamity we had never anticipated. The bare idea of anybody being able to exist without a knocker appeared so wild and visionary, that it had never for one instant entered our imagination.

'I am always wandering here and there from my rooms in Covent-garden, London,' Dickens wrote in *The Uncommercial Traveller*. Yet there were moments of rest, when he withdrew into the city churches, sanctuaries against the teeming life of London's streets:

Among the Uncommercial travels in which I have engaged, this year of Sunday travel occupies its own place, apart from all the rest. Whether I think of the church where the sails of the oyster-boats in the river almost flapped against the windows, or of the church where the railroad made the bells hum as the train rushed by above the roof, I recall a curious experience. On summer Sundays, in the gentle rain or the bright sunshine – either, deepening the idleness of the idle City – I have sat, in that singular silence which belongs to resting-places usually astir, in scores of buildings at the heart of the world's metropolis, unknown to far greater numbers of people speaking the English tongue, than the ancient edifices of the Eternal City, or the Pyramids of Egypt. The dark vestries and registries into which I have peeped, and the little hemmed-in churchyards that have echoed to my feet, have left impressions on my memory as distinct and quaint as any it has in that way received. In all those dusty registers that the worms are eating, there is not a line but made some hearts leap, or some tears flow, in their day. Still and dry now, still and dry! and the old tree at the window with no room for its branches, has seen them all out. So with the tomb of the old Master of the old Company, on which it drips. His son restored it and died, his daughter restored it and died, and then he had been remembered long enough, and the tree took possession of him, and his name cracked out.

There are few more striking indications of the changes of manners and customs that two or three hundred years have brought about, than these deserted churches. Many of them are handsome and costly structures, several of them were designed by Wren, many of them arose from the ashes of the great fire, others of them outlived the plague and the fire too, to die a slow death in these later days. No one can be sure of the coming time; but it is not too much to say of it that it has no sign in its outsetting tides, of the reflux to these churches of their congregations and uses. They remain like the tombs of the old citizens who lie beneath them and around them, Monuments of another age. They are worth a Sunday exploration, now and then, for they yet echo, not unharmoniously, to the time when the City of London really was London; when the Prentices and Trained Bands were of mark in the state; when even the Lord Mayor himself was a Reality – not a Fiction conventionally be-puffed on one day in the year by illustrious friends, who no less conventionally laugh at him on the remaining three hundred and sixty-four days.

Theatrical London

It was during his time at Doctor's Commons – a period that also convinced him of the hopeless inadequacy and burdensome operation of the Law – that Dickens' love of the theatre grew into an urge to become an actor. He went to the theatre practically every evening, often entering after nine o'clock when admission was cheaper but a large part of the show was still to come. Energetic, increasingly self-confident, and at the same time disillusioned with the mundane work and monotony of the legal profession (both as clerk and journalist), Dickens came to the conclusion that the theatre might offer speedier success. He had already acted successfully in private theatricals, and now with typical energy he threw himself into an actor's routine, practising 'often four, five, six hours a day; shut up in my own room, or walking about in fields. I prescribed to myself, too, a sort of Hamiltonian system for learning parts; and learnt a great number.' When his progress satisfied him, he offered himself to Covent Garden, describing himself as having 'a strong perception of character and oddity, and a natural power of reproducing . . .' – a description applicable to actor, journalist or novelist.

Fortunately, on the day of the crucial audition he had 'a terrible bad cold and an inflammation of the face' and was unable to attend, and a simultaneous offer of a position as a gallery reporter on his uncle's paper, *The Mirror of Parliament*, saved him from 'another sort of life'. At this time, Dickens was nineteen years of age.

In all his descriptions of the theatre in the novels, we are offered a brief escape, a sense of holiday spirits, when for a time the grinding horrors of poverty and daily care are temporarily suspended. But it is noticeable how, in the passage about Astley's (Westminster Road, now demolished), Dickens' attention is divided between stage and audience, as he finds entertainment in the clumsiness and peculiarities of assembled humanity:

. . . It was high time now to be thinking of the play; for which great preparation was required in the way of shawls and bonnets, not to mention one handkerchief full of oranges and another of apples, which took some time tying up, in consequence of the fruit having a tendency to roll out at the corners. At length

Dickens realised the power of theatre in involving his mass audience because he had witnessed, time and again, the impact of theatre upon the least educated audience. In an article entitled 'The Amusements of the People' he describes a trip to Victoria Theatre with Joe Whelks, of the New Cut, Lambeth, who 'is not much of a reader, has no great store of books, no very commodious room to read in, no very decided inclination to read. . .'. Much is said of the absurdity of the melodrama, but an abundant audience watches with rapt attention.

everything was ready and they went off very fast; Kit's mother carrying the baby, who was dreadfully wide awake, and Kit holding little Jacob in one hand, and escorting Barbara with the other – a state of things which occasioned the two mothers, who walked behind, to declare that they looked quite family folks, and caused Barbara to blush and say, 'Now don't, mother.' But Kit said she had no call to mind what they said; and indeed she need not have had, if she had known how very far from Kit's thoughts any love-making was. Poor Barbara!

At last they got to the theatre, which was Astley's; and in some two minutes after they had reached the yet unopened door, little Jacob was squeezed flat, and the baby had received divers concussions, and Barbara's mother's umbrella had been carried several yards off and passed back to her over the shoulders of the people, and Kit had hit a man on the head with the handkerchief of apples for 'scrowdging' his parent with unnecessary violence, and there was a great uproar. But when they were once past the pay-place and tearing away for very life with their checks in their hands; and above all, when they were fairly in the theatre, and seated in such places that they couldn't have had better if they had picked them out and taken them beforehand; all this was looked upon as quite a capital joke, and an essential part of the entertainment.

Dear, dear, what a place it looked, that Astley's! with all the paint, gilding, and looking-glass; the vague smell of horses suggestive of coming wonders; the curtain that hid such gorgeous mysteries; the clean white sawdust down in the

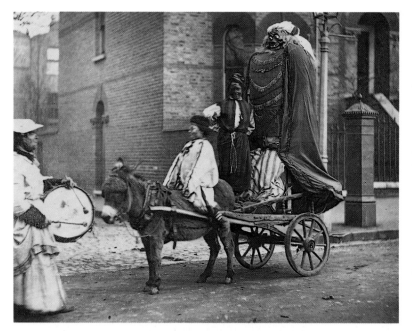

An example of street entertainers that toured England in Dickens' day. 'When they came to any town or village, or even to a detached house of good appearance, Short blew a blast upon the brazen trumpet and carolled a fragment of song in that hilarious tone common to Punches and their consorts. If people hurried to their windows, Mr Codlin pitched the temple, and hastily unfurling the drapery and concealing Short therewith, flourished hysterically on the Pipes and performed an air. Then the entertainment began as soon as might be; Mr Codlin having the responsibility of deciding on its length and of protracting or expediting the time for the hero's final triumph over the enemy of mankind, according as he judged whether the after-crop of halfpence would be plentiful or scant. When it had been gathered in to the last farthing, he resumed his load and on they went again.' The Old Curiosity Shop

circus; the company coming in and taking their places; the fiddlers looking carelessly up at them while they tuned their instruments, as if they didn't want the play to begin, and knew it all beforehand! What a glow was that which burst upon them all, when that long, clear, brilliant row of lights came slowly up; and what the feverish excitement when the little bell rang and the music began in good earnest, with strong parts for the drums, and sweet effects for the triangles! Well might Barbara's mother say to Kit's mother that the gallery was the place to see from, and wonder it wasn't much dearer than the boxes; and well might Barbara feel doubtful whether to laugh or cry, in her flutter of delight.

Then the play itself! the horses which little Jacob believed from the first to be alive, and the ladies and gentlemen of whose reality he could be by no means persuaded, having never seen or heard anything at all like them – the firing, which made Barbara wink – the forlorn lady, who made her cry – the tyrant, who made her tremble – the man who sung the song with the lady's-maid and danced the chorus, who made her laugh – the pony who reared up on his hind legs when he saw the murderer, and wouldn't hear of walking on all fours again until he was taken into custody – the clown who ventured on such familiarities with the military man in boots – the lady who jumped over the nine-and-twenty ribbons and came down safe upon the horse's back – everything was delightful, splendid, and surprising. Little Jacob applauded till his hands were sore; Kit cried 'an-kor' at the end of everything, the three-act piece included; and Barbara's mother beat her umbrella on the floor, in her ecstacies, until it was nearly worn down to the gingham.

THE OLD CURIOSITY SHOP

Dickens lamented the demise of the playhouse as an institution, 'those wonderful houses about Drury Lane Theatre, which in the palmy days of theatres were prosperous and long settled places of business, and which now change hands every week.' However, minor theatres continued to thrive as did street theatre, shown here.

A friend once noted that Dickens found in ordinary people material for entertainment equal to that of any play, and took them as his parts: 'He could imitate, in a manner that I have never heard equalled the low population of the streets of London in all their varieties, whether mere loafers or sellers of fruit, vegetables, or anything else.' In some of his novels there are very theatrical characters – Micawber is the obvious example, and in the same novel the eccentric, florid Mr Dick; there are also the theatrical types like Sam Weller or the hackney cabman in Pickwick Papers. But so many of his physical descriptions of people are marked by a sense of theatre – they do not simply describe as evoke the

95

vivid sense in which they are held in the writer's mind – Uriah Heap comes instantly to mind, writhing and wringing his hands in practised humility. The visual effect is that of theatre, and quite inescapable.

Dickens' theatrical vision is a powerful weapon too in his exposure of the thin veneer of New Victorian Society:

Mr and Mrs Veneering were bran-new people in a bran-new house in a bran-new quarter of London. Everything about the Veneerings was spick and span new. All their furniture was new, all their friends were new, all their servants were new,

Left:

'It was Covent Garden Theatre that I chose; and there, from the back of a centre box, saw Julius Caesar and the new Pantomime. . . . But the mingled reality and mystery of the show, the influence upon me of the poetry, the lights, the music, the company, the smooth stupendous changes of glittering and brilliant scenery, were so dazzling, and opened up such illimitable regions of delight, that when I came out into the rainy street, at twelve o'clock at night, I felt as if I had come out of the clouds, where I had been leading a romantic life for ages, to a bawling, splashing, link-lighted, umbrella-struggling, hackney-coach-jostling, patten-clinking, muddy, miserable world.'
David Copperfield

their plate was new, their carriage was new, their harness was new, their horses were new, their pictures were new, they themselves were new, they were as newly married as was lawfully compatible with their having a bran-new baby, and if they had set up a great-grandfather, he would have come home in matting from the Pantechnicon, without a scratch upon him, French polished to the crown of his head.

For, in the Veneering establishment, from the hall-chairs with the new coat of arms, to the grand pianoforte with the new action, and upstairs again to the new fire-escape, all things were in a state of high varnish and polish. And what was observable in the furniture, was observable in the Veneerings – the surface smelt a little too much of the workshop and was a trifle stickey. . . .

The great looking-glass above the sideboard, reflects the table and the company. Reflects the new Veneering crest, in gold and eke in silver, frosted and also thawed, a camel of all work. The Heralds' College found out a Crusading ancestor for Veneering who bore a camel on his shield (or might have done it if he had thought of it), and a caravan of camels take charge of the fruits and flowers and candles, and kneel down to be loaded with the salt. Reflects Veneering; forty, wavy-haired, dark, tending to corpulence, sly, mysterious, filmy – a kind of sufficiently well-looking veiled-prophet, not prophesying. Reflects Mrs Veneering; fair, aquiline-nosed and fingered, not so much light hair as she might have, gorgeous in raiment and jewels, enthusiastic, propitiatory, conscious that a corner of her husband's veil is over herself. Reflects Podsnap; prosperously feeding, two little light-coloured wiry wings, one on either side of his else bald head, looking as like his hairbrushes as his hair, dissolving view of red beads on his forehead, large allowance of crumpled shirt-collar up behind. Reflects Mrs Podsnap; fine woman for Professor Owen, quantity of bone, neck and nostrils like a rocking-horse, hard features, majestic head-dress in which Podsnap has hung golden offerings. Reflects Twemlow; grey, dry, polite, susceptible to east wind, First-Gentleman-in-Europe collar and cravat, cheeks drawn in as if he had made a great effort to retire into himself some years ago, and had got so far and had never got any farther. Reflects mature young lady; raven locks, and complexion that lights up well when well powdered – as it is – carrying on considerably in the captivation of mature young gentleman; with too much nose in his face, too much ginger in his whiskers, too much torso in his waistcoat, too much sparkle in his studs, his eyes, his buttons, his talk, and his teeth. Reflects charming old Lady Tippins on Veneering's right; with an immense obtuse drab oblong face, like a face in a tablespoon, and a dyed Long Walk up the top of her head, as a convenient public approach to the bunch of false hair behind, pleased to patronize Mrs Veneering opposite, who is pleased to be patronized. Reflects a certain 'Mortimer', another of Veneering's oldest friends; who never was in the house before, and appears not to want to come again, who sits disconsolate on Mrs Veneering's left, and who was inveigled by Lady Tippins (a friend of his boyhood) to come to these people's and talk, and who won't talk. Reflects Eugene, friend of Mortimer; buried alive in the back of his chair, behind a shoulder – with a powder-epaulette on it – of the mature young lady, and gloomily resorting to the champagne chalice whenever proffered by the Analytical Chemist. Lastly, the looking-glass reflects Boots and Brewer, and two other stuffed Buffers interposed between the rest of the company and possible accidents.

OUR MUTUAL FRIEND

As today, whole areas of London came in and went out of fashion. In Nicholas Nickleby, *the uncertainty concerning Ralph Nickleby's work and social position is reflected in his house in Golden Square: 'Although a few members of the graver professions live about Golden Square, it is not exactly in anybody's way to or from anywhere. It is one of the squares that have been; a quarter of the town that has gone down in the world, and taken to letting lodgings. Many of the first and second floors are let furnished to single gentlemen, and it takes boarders besides. It is a great resort of foreigners.' Not at all the sort of place one might visit the Veneerings.*

It has been said that Dickens' theatrical vision of London was his way of displacing the horror and hopelessness with which he held the place as a lonely child; everything could become a joke, as it were. Perhaps his theatricality had that effect, but his singing and acting skills had showed themselves from a very early age and made him the centre of attention at home. The vision also reached back into Dickens' memories of being taken to Christmas pantomimes in London, or seeing the famous Edmund Kean and the clown Joe Grimaldi. He also wrote plays, the earliest in his childhood circle in Chatham, a tragedy called *Misnor, the Sultan of India*. So, Dickens' love of the theatre arose in the mind of the child – a time when the division between the real and imagined is never quite certain; when the inanimate seems to have a life of its own; when the little world and the big world found in fairy tales and contemporary animated cartoons can exchange places. It was a time that Dickens could never

*The extraordinary thing about Dickens'
London was that within the city, extremes of
the human condition lived side-by-side –
minutes away from Dickens' home in Doughty
Street (where he lived as a successful young
writer), lay Fagin's manor, Saffron Hill – and
yet 'genteel respectability' remained largely
unaware of the appalling conditions in which
the poorest classes lived. 'There are two houses
separated by but an inch or two of wall. In one,
there are quiet minds at rest; in the other, a
waking conscience that one might think would
trouble the very air. . . . In the handsome
street, there are folks asleep who have dwelt
there all their lives, and have no more
knowledge of these things than if they had never
been.'* Master Humphrey's Clock

forget, returning to it in his novels, as in *Our Mutual Friend*. Let
Cinderella – the dwarf doll-maker Jenny Wren, with whose method
Dickens had more than a little in common – and her fairy godmother, the
good Jew Riah re-create the pantomime scene on London's streets:

In the evening of this same foggy day when the yellow window-blind of Pubsey
and Co. was drawn down upon the day's work, Riah the Jew once more came
forth into Saint Mary Axe. But this time he carried no bag, and was not bound on
his master's affairs. He passed over London Bridge, and returned to the
Middlesex shore by that of Westminster, and so, ever wading through the fog,
waded to the doorstep of the dolls' dressmaker.

Miss Wren expected him. He could see her through the window by the light of
her low fire – carefully banked up with damp cinders that it might last the longer
and waste the less when she was out – sitting waiting for him in her bonnet. His
tap at the glass roused her from the musing solitude in which she sat, and she
came to the door to open it; aiding her steps with a little crutch-stick.

'Good evening, godmother!' said Miss Jenny Wren.

The old man laughed, and gave her his arm to lean on.

'Won't you come in and warm yourself, godmother?' asked Miss Jenny Wren.

99

It is noticeable in some Victorian photographs that subjects pose in a 'staged' way. Duration of exposure in the early days of photography required this, but the theatricality of some shots also demonstrates the Victorian love of representative vignette. Putting the theatrical shots next to the harsh documentary photographs of street life as it really was, provides an interesting indication of the way in which Dickens' own imagination sometimes worked.

'Not if you are ready, Cinderella, my dear.'

'Well!' exclaimed Miss Wren, delighted. 'Now you *are* a clever old boy! If we gave prizes at this establishment (but we only keep blanks), you should have the first silver medal, for taking me up so quick.' As she spoke thus, Miss Wren removed the key of the house-door from the keyhole and put it in her pocket, and then bustlingly closed the door, and tried it as they both stood on the step. Satisfied that her dwelling was safe, she drew one hand through the old man's arm and prepared to ply her crutch-stick with the other. But the key was an instrument of such gigantic proportions, that before they started Riah proposed to carry it.

'No, no, no! I'll carry it myself,' returned Miss Wren. 'I'm awfully lopsided, you know, and stowed down in my pocket it'll trim the ship. To let you into a secret, godmother, I wear my pocket on my high side, o' purpose.'

With that they began their plodding through the fog.

100

'Yes, it was truly sharp of you, godmother,' resumed Miss Wren with great approbation, 'to understand me. But, you see, you *are* so like the fairy godmother in the bright little books! You look so unlike the rest of people, and so much as if you had changed yourself into that shape, just this moment, with some benevolent object. Boh!' cried Miss Jenny, putting her face close to the old man's. 'I can see your features, godmother, behind the beard.'

'Does the fancy go to my changing other objects too, Jenny?'

'Ah! That it does! If you'd only borrow my stick and tap this piece of pavement – this dirty stone that my foot taps – it would start up a coach and six. I say! Let's believe so!' . . .

Thus conversing, and having crossed Westminster Bridge, they traversed the ground that Riah had lately traversed, and new ground likewise; for, when they had recrossed the Thames by way of London Bridge, they struck down by the river and held their still foggier course that way.

But previously, as they were going along, Jenny twisted her venerable friend aside to a brilliantly-lighted toy-shop window, and said: 'Now look at 'em! All my work!'

This referred to a dazzling semicircle of dolls in all the colours of the rainbow, who were dressed for presentation at court, for going to balls, for going out driving, for going out on horseback, for going out walking, for going to get married, for going to help other dolls to get married, for all the gay events of life.'

'Pretty, pretty, pretty!' said the old man with a clap of his hands. 'Most elegant taste!'

'Glad you like 'em,' returned Miss Wren, loftily. 'But the fun is, godmother, how I make the great ladies try my dresses on. Though it's the hardest part of my business, and would be, even if my back were not bad and my legs queer.'

He looked at her as not understanding what she said.

'Bless you, godmother,' said Miss Wren, 'I have to scud about town at all hours. If it was only sitting at my bench, cutting out and sewing, it would be comparatively easy work; but it's the trying-on by the great ladies that takes it out of me.'

'How, the trying-on?' asked Riah.

'What a mooney godmother you are, after all!' returned Miss Wren. 'Look here. There's a Drawing Room, or a grand day in the Park, or a Show, or a Fête, or what you like. Very well. I squeeze among the crowd, and I look about me. When I see a great lady very suitable for my business, I say, "You'll do, my dear!" and I take particular notice of her, and run home and cut her out and baste her. Then another day, I come scudding back again to try on, and then I take particular notice of her again. Sometimes she plainly seems to say, "How that little creature is staring!" and sometimes likes it and sometimes don't, but much more often yes than no. All the time I am only saying to myself, "I must hollow out a bit here; I must slope away there;" and I am making a perfect slave of her, with making her try on my doll's dress. Evening parties are severer work for me, because there's only a doorway for a full view, and what with hobbling among the wheels of the carriages and the legs of the horses, I fully expect to be run over some night. However, there I have 'em, just the same. When they go bobbing into the hall from the carriage, and catch a glimpse of my little physiognomy poked out from behind a policeman's cape in the rain, I dare say they think I am wondering and admiring with all my eyes and heart, but they little think they're only working for my dolls! There was Lady Belinda Whitrose. I made her do double duty in one night. I said when she came out of the carriage, "*You*'ll do, my dear!" and I ran straight home and cut her out and basted her. Back I came again, and waited behind the men that called the carriages. Very bad night too. At last, "Lady Belinda Whitrose's carriage! Lady Belinda Whitrose coming down!" And I made her try on – oh! and take pains about it too – before she got seated. That's Lady Belinda hanging up by the waist, much too near the gaslight for a wax one, with her toes turned in.'

Alive in Dickens' London

Dickens was the first great novelist of the city and he lived in an era when the city itself became the image of a modern civilisation.

During the first half of the nineteenth century Britain as a whole became an urbanised society; hitherto more than half its population had lived in the countryside. What caused the exodus was hardship and the promise of work (life was especially bad for the rural unemployed), and the certainty of a roof – or at least a bridge – over one's head. But what particularly enticed people to London was a sense that something was going on: theatres, music halls, brightly lit streets, huge crowds, hubbub in the streets. 'Who could wonder,' wrote H. Llewellyn Smith in 1892, 'that men are drawn into such a vortex, even were the penalty heavier than this.'

The penalty was heavy indeed. By 1851 2,362,000 people were domiciled in London (a far smaller city than today); many of them in the most hideously overcrowded conditions. 'Suitable housing did not exist,' records the social historian, Kitson Clark, 'and the additional numbers were crammed into every nook and cranny from attic to cellar of old decaying property . . . with little or no access to light and air.' London's infrastructure – what there was of it – groaned under the weight of a massive immigration: inadequate domestic sanitation and public sewerage led to contamination and disease; overcrowding led to infection on a desperate scale; lack of information and scientific knowledge about the sources and nature of infection compounded the problems; and while medical men and bureaucrats, lawyers and politicians groped frantically for a solution, the great Industrial Revolution got under way.

Vision of Death

The coming of the steam railway, that great Victorian symbol of change and prosperity, conjured up unprecedented and powerful images. Today we are more accustomed to giving up great swathes of countryside to new roads, motorways, airports and even unsightly power stations, but these novel, mechanical monsters, demanding the public's attention with their noise, their plumes of smoke and ringing bells, must have made an awesome sight.

But if the railway fulfilled its promise in terms of trade and industry, it also actively contributed to the housing problem. Railways in Britain were constructed by private companies, and initially there were few limitations about how they went on. Huge areas of slum-land were cleared away – but without a thought for the uprooted families. In London 76,000 people were re-moved by the railway, inhabitants of demolished slums going in search for accommodation in some other back alley or

103

court – swelling yet more disastrously the problems of overcrowding and disease.

Not until 1853 was anything done to stem the tide, and then it was only to have the companies inform the government of the number of homes being demolished and what steps they planned, to meet the consequent 'inconvenience'.

Dickens knew from personal experience the damage wrought by the railway. The London to Birmingham line ripped through his old school, the Wellington House Academy, in the Hampstead Road.

In 1851 he wrote: 'A great trunk-line had swallowed the play-ground, sliced away the school-room, and pared off the corner of the house; which, thus curtailed of its proportions, presented itself, in a green stage of stucco, profilewise towards the road, like a forlorn flat-iron without a handle, standing on end.'

Seated behind the carriage windows people were given what was often a first opportunity to see the slums, and in *Dombey and Son*, shortly after

Rush hour across London Bridge: 'The set of humanity outward from the City is as a set of prisoners departing from gaol, and dismal Newgate seems quite as fit a stronghold for the mighty Lord Mayor as his own state-dwelling.' Our Mutual Friend

104

the death of his favourite child, Paul, Dombey takes a train ride through the slums of Camden Town where Dickens himself had lived. The image of death derives from Dombey's feelings about Paul's death, but transfers to the railway itself.

The very speed at which the train was whirled along, mocked the swift course of the young life that had been borne away so steadily and so inexorably to its foredoomed end. The power that forced itself upon its iron way – its own – defiant of all paths and roads, piercing through the heart of every obstacle, and dragging living creatures of all classes, ages, and degrees behind it, was a type of the triumphant monster, Death.

Away, with a shriek, and a roar, and a rattle, from the town, burrowing among the dwellings of men making the streets hum, flashing out into the meadows for a moment, mining in through the damp earth, booming on in darkness and heavy air, bursting out again into the sunny day so bright and wide; away, with a shriek, and a roar, and a rattle, through the fields, through the woods, through the corn, through the hay, through the chalk, through the mould, through the clay, through the rock, among objects close at hand and almost in the grasp, ever flying from the traveller, and a deceitful distance ever moving slowly within him: like as in the track of the remorseless monster, Death!

Through the hollow, on the height, by the heath, by the orchard, by the park, by the garden, over the canal, across the river, where the sheep are feeding, where the mill is going, where the barge is floating, where the dead are lying, where the factory is smoking, where the stream is running, where the village clusters, where the great cathedral rises, where the bleak moor lies, and the wild breeze smooths or ruffles it at its inconstant will; away, with a shriek, and a roar, and a rattle, and no trace to leave behind but dust and vapour: like as in the track of the remorseless monster, Death!

Breasting the wind and light, the shower and sunshine, away, and still away, it roll and roars, fierce and rapid, smooth and certain, and great works and massive bridges crossing up above, fall like a beam of shadow an inch broad, upon the eye, and then are lost. Away, and still away, onward and onward ever: glimpses of cottage-homes, of houses, mansions, rich estates, of husbandry and handicraft, of people, of old roads and paths that look deserted, small, and insignificant as they are left behind: and so they do and what else is there but such glimpses, in the track of the indomitable monster, Death!

Away, with a shriek, and a roar, and a rattle, plunging down into the earth again, and working on in such a storm of energy and perseverance, that amidst the darkness and whirlwind the motion seems reversed, and to tend furiously backward, until a ray of light upon the wet wall shows its surface flying past like a fierce stream. Away once more into the day, and through the day, with a shrill yell of exultation, roaring, rattling, tearing on, spurning everything with its dark breath, sometimes pausing for a minute where a crowd of faces are, that in a minute more are not; sometimes lapping water greedily, and before the spout at which it drinks has ceased to drip upon the ground, shrieking, roaring, rattling through the purple distance!

Louder and louder yet, it shrieks and cries as it comes tearing on resistless to the goal: and now its way, still like the way of Death, is strewn with ashes thickly.

Farringdon Street, running beneath the recently opened Holborn Viaduct. The first stone had been laid in 1867 and it was completed in 1869.

Everything around is blackened. There are dark pools of water, muddy lanes, and miserable habitations far below. There are jagged walls and falling houses close at hand, and through the battered roofs and broken windows, wretched rooms are seen, where want and fever hide themselves in many wretched shapes, while smoke and crowded gables, and distorted chimneys, and deformity of brick and mortar penning up deformity of mind and body, choke the murky distance. As Mr Dombey looks out of his carriage window, it is never in his thoughts that the monster who has brought him there has let the light of day in on these things: not made or caused them. It was the journey's fitting end, and might have been the end of everything; it was so ruinous and dreary.

The railway entirely changed the face of London. Again in *Dombey*, Dickens describes what happened to one particular area. In the first

106

The railway was the most visible element of change; it changed the landscape dramatically. But it also allowed people to see from their carriage windows – often for the first time – what terrible conditions poor people lived in.

excerpt, the nurse Polly, or 'Richards' as Dombey insisted on naming her, takes Paul and his sister Florence to the area where her family lives:

This euphonious locality was situated in a suburb, known by the inhabitants of Staggs's Gardens by the name of Camberling Town; a designation which the Strangers' Map of London, is printed (with a view to pleasant and commodious reference) on pocket-handkerchiefs, condenses, with some show of reason, into Camden Town. Hither the two nurses bent their steps, accompanied by their charges; Richards carrying Paul, of course, and Susan leading little Florence by the hand, and giving her such jerks and pokes from time to time, as she considered it wholesome to administer.

The first shock of a great earthquake had, just at that period, rent the whole neighbourhood into its centre. Traces of its course were visible on every side. Houses were knocked down; streets broken through and stopped; deep pits and trenches dug in the ground; enormous heaps of earth and clay thrown up; buildings that were undermined and shaking, propped by great beams of wood. Here, a chaos of carts, overthrown and jumbled together, lay topsy-turvy at the

The Victorian Embankment under construction in the 1860s. The great bulk of Charing Cross Station can be seen, just completed, on the right-hand side of the photograph. The first street nearer the camera, running parallel to the station, is Craven Street, down which Warren's would have been reached.

bottom of a steep unnatural hill; there, confused treasures of iron soaked and rusted in something that had accidentally become a pond. Everywhere were bridges that led nowhere; thoroughfares that were wholly impassable; Babel towers of chimneys, wanting half their height; temporary wooden houses and enclosures, in the most unlikely situations; carcases of ragged tenements, and fragments of unfinished walls and arches, and piles of scaffolding, and wildernesses of bricks, and giant forms of cranes, and tripods straddling above nothing. There were a hundred thousand shapes and substances of incompleteness, wildly mingled out of their places, upside down, burrowing in the earth, aspiring in the air, mouldering in the water, and unintelligible as any dream. Hot springs and fiery eruptions, the usual attendants upon earthquakes, lent their contributions of confusion to the scene. Boiling water hissed and heaved within dilapidated walls; whence, also, the glare and roar of flames came issuing forth; and mounds of ashes blocked up rights of way, and wholly changed the law and custom of the neighbourhood.

In short, the yet unfinished and unopened Railroad was in progress; and, from

The demolition of Hungerford market (1862) to make way for Charing Cross Station. The market – a magnificent place, and similar to Covent Garden in its Tuscan granite columns – had only been built in 1831.

the very core of all this dire disorder, trailed smoothly away, upon its mighty course of civilisation and improvement.

But as yet, the neighbourhood was shy to own the Railroad. One or two bold speculators had projected streets; and one had built a little, but had stopped among the mud and ashes to consider further of it. A bran-new Tavern, redolent of fresh mortar and size, and fronting nothing at all, had taken for its sign The

Railway Arms; but that might be rash enterprise – and then it hoped to sell drink to the workmen. So, the Excavators' House of Call had sprung up from a beer-shop; and the old-established Ham and Beef Shop had become the Railway Eating house, with a roast leg of pork daily, through interested motives of a similar immediate and popular description. Lodging-house keepers were favourable in like manner; and for the like reasons were not to be trusted. The general belief was very slow. There were frowzy fields, and cow-houses, and dunghills, and dustheaps, and ditches, and gardens, and summer-houses, and carpet-beating grounds, at the very door of the Railway. Little tumuli of oyster shells in the oyster season, and of lobster shells in the lobster season, encroached upon its high places. Posts, and rails, and old cautions to trespassers, and of broken crockery and faded cabbage leaves in all seasons, and backs of mean houses, and patches of wretched vegetation, stared it out of countenance. Nothing was the better for it, or thought of being so. If the miserable waste ground lying near it could have laughed, it would have laughed it to scorn, like many of the miserable neighbours.

Staggs's Gardens was uncommonly incredulous. It was a little row of houses, with little squalid patches of ground before them, fenced off with old doors, barrel staves, scraps of tarpaulin, and dead bushes; with bottomless tin kettles and exhausted iron fenders, thrust into the gaps. Here, the Staggs's Gardeners trained scarlet beans, kept fowls and rabbits, erected summer-houses (one was

The shore-line of the Thames at Lambeth before the embankment was constructed in 1865.

an old boat), dried clothes, and smoked pipes. Some were of opinion that Staggs's Gardens derived its name from a deceased capitalist, one Mr Stagg's, who had built it for his delectation. Others, who had a natural taste of the country, held that it dated from those rural times when the antlered herd, under the familiar denomination of Staggses, had resorted to its shady precincts. Be this as it may, Staggs's Gardens was regarded by its population as a sacred grove not to be withered by Railroads; and so confident were they generally of its long outliving any such ridiculous inventions, that the master chimney-sweeper at the corner, who was understood to take the lead in the local politics of the Gardens, had publicly declared that on the occasion of the Railroad opening, if ever it did open, two of his boys should ascend the flues of his dwelling, with instructions to hail the failure with derisive cheers from the chimney-pots.

On a later occasion, Walter Gay re-visits Staggs's Gardens in order to bring Polly to Paul in the hour of his death:

There was no such place as Staggs's Gardens. It had vanished from the earth. Where the old rotten summer-houses once had stood, palaces now reared their heads, and granite columns of gigantic girth opened a vista to the railway world beyond. The miserable waste ground, where the refuse-matter had been heaped of yore, was swallowed up and gone; and in it frowsy stead were tiers of warehouses, crammed with rich goods and costly merchandise. The old by-streets now swarmed with passengers and vehicles of every kind: the new streets that had stopped disheartened in the mud and waggon-ruts, formed towns within themselves, originating wholesome comforts and conveniences belonging to themselves, and never tried nor thought of until they sprung into existence. Bridges that had led to nothing, led to villas, gardens, churches, healthy public walks. The carcasses of houses, and beginnings of new thoroughfares, had started off upon the line at steam's own speed, and shot away into the country in a monster train.

As to the neighbourhood which had hesitated to acknowledge the railroad in its straggling days, that had grown wise and penitent, as any Christian might in such a case, and now boasted of its powerful and prosperous relation. There were railway patterns in its drapers' shops, and railway journals in the windows of its newsmen. There were railway hotels, office-houses, lodging-houses, boarding-houses; railway plans, maps, views, wrappers, bottles, sandwich-boxes, and time-tables; railway hackney-coach and cab-stands; railway omnibuses, railway

The Steam Boilers installed in the Western Annexe of the International Exhibition, 1862. Dickens' imagination was caught by the immensity of scale and noise, the unreal, fantastic elements of the new engineering: 'In a large and lofty building, supported by pillars of iron, with great black apertures in the upper walls, open to the external air; echoing to the roof with the beating of hammers and the roar of furnaces, mingled with the hissing of red-hot metal plunged in water, and a hundred strange unearthly noises never heard elsewhere; in this gloomy place, moving like demons among the flame and smoke, dimly and fitfully seen, flushed and tormented by the burning fires, and wielding great weapons, a faulty blow from any one of which must have crushed some workman's skull, a number of men laboured like giants.' The Old Curiosity Shop

streets and buildings, railway hangers-on and parasites, and flatterers out of all calculation. There was even railway time observed in clocks, as if the sun itself had given in. Among the vanquished was the master chimney-sweeper, whilom incredulous at Stagg's Gardens, who now lived in a stuccoed house three stories high, and gave himself out, with golden flourishes upon a varnished board, as contractor for the cleansing of railway chimneys by machinery.

To and from the heart of this great change, all day and night, throbbing currents rushed and returned incessantly like its life's blood. Crowds of people and mountains of goods, departing and arriving scores upon scores of times in every four-and-twenty hours, produced a fermentation in the place that was always in action. The very houses seemed disposed to pack up and take trips. Wonderful Members of Parliament, who, little more than twenty years before, had made themselves merry with the wild railroad theories of engineers, and given them the liveliest rubs in cross-examination, went down into the north with their watches in their hands, and sent on messages before by the electric telegraph, to say that they were coming. Night and day the conquering engines rumbled at their distant work, or, advancing smoothly to their journey's end, and gliding like tame dragons into the allotted corners grooved out to the inch for their reception, stood bubbling and trembling there, making the walls quake, as if they were dilating with the secret knowledge of great powers yet unsuspected in them, and strong purposes not yet achieved.

But Staggs's Gardens had been cut up root and branch. Oh woe the day when 'not a rood of English ground' – laid out in Staggs's Gardens – is secure!

A view along Holborn towards the Viaduct, a marvellous construction, the completion of which greatly eased the traffic, by replacing the notoriously impassable Holborn hill.

Later, Dickens wrote: 'It has ever since been unable to settle down to any one thing, and will never settle down again. The Railroad has done it all.' But although Dickens disliked many aspects of the commercial and industrial world, he never condemned it as a false path for civilisation to take. He was not anti-industrialist or anti-commercial.

In *Hard Times*, a novel set in Coketown – a northern city based on Preston, he certainly satirises Thomas Gradgrind, but it is the industrialist's mistaken philosophy (his suppression of 'imagination') that is the target. On the whole in his fiction, Dickens is much more inclined to favour industrialists than he is to condemn them. What worried him was what motivated some of them; he wanted change provided it was motivated by humanitarian concerns, not by money.

114

Holborn before the Viaduct. The difficulty experienced by both traffic and pedestrians ascending old Holborn Hill is described in The Pickwick Papers *when Job Trotter goes to visit the lawyer Mr Perker with some important news from Pickwick: '[He] ran up Holborn, sometimes in the middle of the road, sometimes on the pavement, and sometimes in the gutter, as the chances of getting along varies with the press of men, women, children and coaches, in each division of the thoroughfair. . .'*

London, City of Fever

It was in this seething bed of change that the roots of Dickens' ideas took hold. In his writings he worked tirelessly to bring both the deteriorating values and living conditions before the notice of his public.

It was a Sunday evening in London, gloomy, close, and stale. Maddening church bells of all degrees of dissonance, sharp and flat, cracked and clear, fast and slow, made the brick-and-mortar echoes hideous. Melancholy streets, in a penitential garb of soot, steeped the souls of the people who were condemned to look at them out of windows, in dire despondency. In every thoroughfare, up almost every alley, and down almost every turning, some doleful bell was throbbing, jerking, tolling, as if the Plague were in the city and the dead-carts were going round. Everything was bolted and barred that could by possibility furnish relief to

115

an overworked people. No pictures, no unfamiliar animals, no rare plants or flowers, no natural or artificial wonders of the ancient world – all *taboo* with that enlightened strictness, that the ugly South Sea gods in the British Museum might have supposed themselves at home again. Nothing to see but streets, streets, streets. Nothing to breathe but streets, streets, streets. Nothing to change the brooding mind, or raise it up. Nothing for the spent toiler to do, but to compare the monotony of his seventh day with the monotony of his six days, think what a weary life he led, and make the best of it – or the worst, according to the probabilities.

   At such a happy time, so propitious to the interests of religion and morality, Mr Arthur Clennam, newly arrived from Marseilles by way of Dover, and by Dover coach the Blue-eyed Maid, sat in the window of a coffee-house on Ludgate Hill. Ten thousand responsible houses surrounded him, frowning as heavily on the streets they composed, as if they were every one inhabited by the ten young men of the Calender's story, who blackened their faces and bemoaned their miseries every night. Fifty thousand lairs surrounded him where people lived so unwholesomely that fair water put into their crowded rooms on Saturday night,

'"The man," Mortimer goes on, addressing Eugene, "whose name is Harmon, was only son of a tremendous old rascal who made his money by Dust."' Our Mutual Friend. *Dust mounds were fairly common sights in Dickens' day, and very good business, fetching anything between £10,000 and £40,000 each. Domestic refuse would be collected by contractors and dumped in private yards. Then the sifting and sorting could begin.*

In Our Mutual Friend, *a novel erected upon the dust mounds that marked suburban London, Silas Wegg is corrupted by greed and meets an appropriate end: 'Mr Sloppy's instructions had been to deposit his burden in the road; but a scavenger's cart happening to stand unattended at the corner, with its little ladder planted against the wheel, Mr Sloppy found it impossible to resist the temptation of shooting Mr Silas Wegg into the cart's contents. A somewhat difficult feat, achieved with great dexterity, and with a prodigious splash.'*

would be corrupt on Sunday morning; albeit my lord, their county member, was amazed that they failed to sleep in company with their butcher's meat. Miles of close wells and pits of houses, where the inhabitants gasped for air, stretched far away towards every point of the compass. Through the heart of the town a deadly sewer ebbed and flowed, in the place of a fine fresh river. What secular want could the million or so of human beings whose daily labour, six days in the week, lay among these Arcadian objects, from the sweet sameness of which they had no escape between the cradle and the grave – what secular want could they possibly have upon their seventh day? Clearly they could want nothing but a stringent policeman.

Mr Arthur Clennam sat in the window of the coffee-house on Ludgate Hill, counting one of the neighbouring bells, making sentences and burdens of songs out of it in spite of himself, and wondering how many sick people it might be the death of in the course of the year.   LITTLE DORRIT

According to a journalist colleague, 'Mr Dickens was a man who lived a lot by his nose. He always seemed to be smelling things. When we walked down by the Thames he would sniff and sniff – "I love the very smell of this," he used to say.' At times Dickens' love affair with the city sounds almost perverse, but perhaps the 'vortex' of London has never attracted its devotees solely for what might be adjudged its pleasanter aspects. Beneath the 'slime and ooze' of the polluted Thames, Dickens' imagination discovers a mystery and an atmosphere which imbues the novel, *Our Mutual Friend*:

117

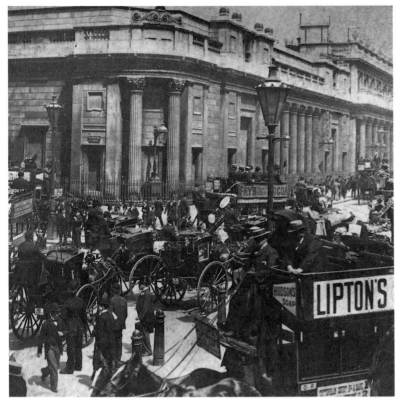

Bank, the City, 1860. 'As is well known to the wise in their generation, traffic in Shares is the one thing to have to do with in this world. Have no antecedents, no established character, no cultivation, no ideas, no manners; have Shares. . . . O mighty Shares! To set those blaring images so high, and to cause us smaller vermin, as under the influence of henbane or opium, to cry out, night and day, "Relieve us of our money, scatter it for us, buy us and sell us, ruin us, only we beseech ye take rank among the powers of the earth, and fatten on us!"' Our Mutual Friend

In these times of ours, though concerning the exact year there is no need to be precise, a boat of dirty and disreputable appearance, with two figures in it, floated on the Thames, between Southwark Bridge which is of iron, and London Bridge which is of stone, as an autumn evening was closing in.

The figures in this boat were those of a strong man with ragged grizzled hair and a sun-browned face, and a dark girl of nineteen or twenty, sufficiently like him to be recognizable as his daughter. The girl rowed, pulling a pair of sculls very easily; the man, with the rudder-lines slack in his hands, and his hands loose in his waistband, kept an eager look out. He had no net, hook, or line, and he could not be a fisherman; his boat had no cushion for a sitter, no paint, no inscription, no appliance beyond a rusty boathook and a coil of rope, and he could not be a waterman; his boat was too cazy and too small to take in cargo for delivery, and he could not be a lighterman or river-carrier; there was no clue to what he looked for, but he looked for something, with a most intent and searching gaze. The tide, which had turned an hour before, was running down, and his eyes watched every little race and eddy in its broad sweep, as the boat made slight head-way against it, or drove stern foremost before it, according as he directed his daughter by a

118

The London Coffee House, Ludgate Hill. 'Mr Arthur Clennam sat in the window of the coffee-house on Ludgate Hill, counting one of the neighbouring bells, making sentences and burdens of songs out of it in spite of himself, and wondering how many sick people it might be the death of in the course of the year.' Little Dorrit

movement of his head. She watched his face as earnestly as he watched the driver. But, in the intensity of her look there was a touch of dread or horror.

Allied to the bottom of the river rather than the surface, by reason of the slime and ooze with which it was covered, and its sodden state, this boat and the two figures in it obviously were doing something that they often did, and were seeking what they often sought. Half savage as the man showed, with no covering on his matted head, with his brown arms bare to between the elbow and the shoulder, with the loose knot of a looser kerchief lying low on his bare breast in a wilderness of beard and whisker, with such dress as he wore seeming to be made out of the mud that begrimed his boat, still there was business-like usage in his steady gaze. So with every lithe action of the girl, with every turn of her wrist, perhaps most of all with her look of dread or horror; they were things of usage.

'Keep her out, Lizzie. Tide runs strong here. Keep her well afore the sweep of it.'

Trusting to the girl's skill and making no use of the rudder, he eyed the coming tide with an absorbed attention. So the girl eyed him. But, it happened now, that a slant of light from the setting sun glanced into the bottom of the boat, and,

119

'Mr Dickens was a man who lived a lot by his nose,' wrote a journalist colleague. Here Dickens records his wanderings past the City of London Churches: 'Behind the monument the service had a flavour of damaged oranges, which, a little further down towards the river, tempered into herrings, and gradually turned into a cosmopolitan blast of fish.' The Uncommercial Traveller

touching a rotten stain there which bore some resemblance to the outline of a muffled human form, coloured it as though with diluted blood. This caught the girl's eye, and she shivered.

'What ails you?' said the man, immediately aware of it, though so intent on the advancing waters; 'I see nothing afloat.'

The red light was gone, the shudder was gone, and his gaze, which had come back to the boat for a moment, travelled away again. Wheresoever the strong tide met with an impediment, his gaze paused for an instant. At every mooring-chain and rope, at every stationary boat or barge that split the current into a broad-arrowhead, at the offsets from the piers of Southwark Bridge, at the paddles of the river steamboats as they beat the filthy water, at the floating logs of timber lashed together lying off certain wharves, his shining eyes darted a hungry look. After a darkening hour or so, suddenly the rudder-lines tightened in his hold, and he steered hard towards the Surrey shore.

Always watching his face, the girl instantly answered to the action in her sculling; presently the boat swung round, quivered as from a sudden jerk, and the upper half of the man was stretched out over the stern.

The girl pulled the hood of a cloak she wore, over her head and over her face, and, looking backward so that the front folds of this hood were turned down the river, kept the boat in that direction going before the tide. Until now, the boat had barely held her own, and had hovered about one spot; but now, the banks changed swiftly, and the deepening shadows and the kindling lights of London Bridge were passed, and the tiers of shipping lay on either hand.

Above left:
The Bull Inn, Holborn, where the disreputable Mrs Gamp and Betsey Prig nursed Mr Lewsome 'turn and turn about' (in an alternate day/night rota) in Martin Chuzzlewit.

120

Among the lowest of the low who scraped a living from the Thames were the 'river-finders' or dredgers', like Lizzie Hexham's father, Gaffer Hexham, in Our Mutual Friend. 'Dredgers,' wrote Henry Mayhew, social historian and contemporary of Dickens, 'are the men who found almost all the bodies of persons drowned. If there be a reward offered for the recovery of a body, numbers of dredgers will at once endeavour to obtain it . . . no body recovered by a dredgerman ever happens to have any money about it, when brought to shore.'

It was not until now that the upper half of the man came back into the boat. His arms were wet and dirty, and he washed them over the side. In his right hand he held something, and he washed that in the river too. It was money. He chinked it once, and he blew upon it once, and he spat upon it once, – 'for luck,' he hoarsely said – before he put it in his pocket.

'Lizzie!'

The girl turned her face towards him with a start, and rowed in silence. Her face was very pale. He was a hook-nosed man, and with that and his bright eyes and his ruffled head, bore a certain likeness to a roused bird of prey.

'Take that thing off your face.'

She put it back.

'Here! and give me hold of the sculls. I'll take the rest of the spell.'

'No, no, father! No! I can't indeed. Father! – I cannot sit so near it!'

He was moving towards her to change places, but her terrified expostulation

121

stopped him and he resumed his seat.

'What hurt can it do you?'

'None, none. But I cannot bear it.'

'It's my belief you hate the sight of the very river.'

'I – I do not like it, father.'

'As if it wasn't your living! As if it wasn't meat and drink to you!'

At these latter words the girl shivered again, and for a moment paused in her rowing, seeming to turn deadly faint. It escaped his attention, for he was glancing over the stern at something the boat had in tow.

'How can you be so thankless to your best friend, Lizzie? The very fire that warmed you when you were a babby, was picked out of the river alongside the coal barges. The very basket that you slept in, the tide washed ashore. The very rockers that I put it upon to make a cradle of it, I cut out of a piece of wood that drifted from some ship or another.'

Lizzie took her right hand from the scull it held, and touched her lips with it and for a moment held it out lovingly towards him: then, without speaking, she resumed her rowing, as another boat of similar appearance, though in rather better trim, came out from a dark place and dropped softly alongside.

'Lizzie's father, composing himself . . . slowly lighted a pipe, and smoked, and took a survey of what he had in tow. What he had in tow, lunged itself at him sometimes in an awful manner when the boat was checked, and sometimes seemed to try to wrench itself away, though for the most part it followed submissively. A neophyte might have fancied that the ripples passing over it were dreadfully like faint changes of expression on a sightless face; but Gaffer was no neophyte and had no such fancies.'

Right:
Saint Magnus the Martyr (with Saint Saviours), 'the giant-wardens of the ancient [London] bridge.' Oliver Twist

'In luck again, Gaffer?' said a man with a squinting leer, who sculled her and who was alone, 'I know'd you was in luck again, by your wake as you come down.'

'Ah!' replied the other, drily. 'So you're out, are you?'

'Yes, pardner.'

There was now a tender yellow moonlight on the river, and the new comer, keeping half his boat's length astern of the other boat looked hard at its track.

'I says to myself,' he went on, 'directly you hove in view, Yonder's Gaffer, and in luck again by George if he ain't! Scull it is, pardner – don't fret yourself – I didn't touch him.' This was in answer to a quick impatient movement on the part of Gaffer: the speaker at the same time unshipping his scull on that side, and laying his hand on the gunwale of Gaffer's boat and holding to it.

'He's had touches enough not to want no more, as well as I make him out, Gaffer! Been a knocking about with a pretty many tides, ain't he pardner? Such is my out-of-luck ways, you see! He must have passed me when he went up last time, for I was on the lookout below bridge here. I a'most think you're like the wulturs, pardner, and scent 'em out.'

He spoke in a dropped voice, and with more than one glance at Lizzie who had pulled on her hood again. Both men then looked with a weird unholy interest at the wake of Gaffer's boat.

'Easy does it, betwixt us. Shall I take him aboard, pardner?'

'No,' said the other. In so surly a tone that the man, after a blank stare, acknowledged it with the retort:

'– Arn't been eating nothing as has disagreed with you, have you, pardner?'

'Why, yes I have,' said Gaffer. 'I have been swallowing too much of that word, Pardner. I am no pardner of yours.'

'Since when was you no pardner of mine, Gaffer Hexam Esquire?'

'Since you was accused of robbing a man. Accused of robbing a live man!' said Gaffer, with great indignation.

'And what if I had been accused of robbing a dead man, Gaffer?'

'You COULDN'T do it.'

'Couldn't you, Gaffer?'

'No, Has a dead man any use for money? Is it possible for a dead man to have money? What world does a dead man belong to? 'Tother world. What world does money belong to? This world. How can money be a corpse's? Can a corpse own it, want it, spend it, claim it, miss it? Don't try to go confounding the rights and wrongs of things in that way. But it's worthy of the sneaking spirit that robs a live man.'

'I'll tell you what it is –.'

'No you won't *I*'ll tell you what it is. You've got off with a short time of it for putting your hand in the pocket of a sailor, a live sailor. Make the most of it and think yourself lucky, but don't think after that to come over *me* with your pardners. We have worked together in time past, but we work together no more in time present nor yet future. Let go, Cast off!'

'Gaffer! If you think to get rid of me this way –.'

'If I don't get rid of you this way, I'll try another, and chop you over the fingers with the stretcher, or take a pick at your head with the boat-hook. Cast off! Pull you, Lizzie. Pull home, since you won't let your father pull.'

Lizzie shot ahead, and the other boat fell astern. Lizzie's father, composing

himself into the easy attitude of one who had asserted the high moralities and taken an unassailable position, slowly lighted a pipe, and smoked, and took a survey of what he had in tow. What he had in tow, lunged itself at him sometimes in an awful manner when the boat was checked, and sometimes seemed to try to wrench itself away, though for the most part it followed submissively. A neophyte might have fancied that the ripples passing over it were dreadfully like faint changes of expression on a sightless face; but Gaffer was no neophyte and had no fancies.

The 1830s to the 1860s saw a period of frightening epidemics. In addition to typhus, typhoid, dysentry, TB, diphtheria, scarlet fever, small pox, and venereal disease, there were four major outbreaks of cholera. The first occurred between 1831 and 1832, and emanated from Jacob's Island, long famous as one of the vilest slums of London. Situated on the south bank of the Thames near Saviours Dock, the area became a reference point of squalor and degradation in Dickens' novels and other writings.

There are moments in his novels when the world stands still and he 'draws' a picture that seems to sum up the forces at work. In a letter to the philanthrope Miss Burdett-Coutts in 1853, he describes Jacob's Island in just such a way. The moment is a striking summation of the hopelessness of an impoverished outcast and his squalid slum dwelling,

'The river had an awful look, the buildings on the banks were muffled in black shrouds, and the reflected lights seemed to originate deep in the water, as if the spectres of suicides were holding them to show where they went down. The wild moon and clouds were as restless as an evil conscience in a tumbled bed, and the very shadow of the immensity of London seemed to lie oppressively upon the river.' The Uncommercial Traveller

124

'Fog everywhere. Fog up the river, where it flows among green aits and meadows; fog down the river, where it rolls defiled among the tiers of shipping, and the waterside pollutions of a great and dirty city.' Bleak House

the writer's words a mixture of sympathetic identification and true vision.

'There is a public house in it, with the odd sign of The Ship Aground, but it is wonderfully appropriate, for everything seems to have got aground there – never to be got off anymore until the whole globe is stopped in its rolling and shivered. No more mud there than in an American swamp – odious sheds for horses, and donkeys, and vagrants, and rubbish in front of the parlour windows – wooden houses like horrible old packing cases full of fever for a countless number of years. In a broken down gallery at the back of a row of these, there was a wan child looking over at a starved old white horse who was making a meal of oyster shells. The sun was going down and flaring out like an angry fire at the child – and

'Not a ship's hull, with its rusty links of cable run out of hawse-holes long discoloured with the iron's rusty tears, but seemed to be there with fell intention . . . everything so vaunted the spoiling influences of water – discoloured copper, rotten wood, honey-combed stone, green dank deposit.' Our Mutual Friend

the child and I, and the pale horse, stared at one another in silence for some five minutes as if we were so many figures in a dismal allegory. I went round to look at the front of the house, but the windows were all broken and the door was shut up as tight as anything so dismantled could be. Lord knows when anybody will go in to the child, but I suppose it's looking over still – with a little wiry head of hair, as pale as the horse, all sticking up on its head – and an old weazen face – and two bony hands holding on the rail of the gallery, with little fingers like convulsed skewers.'

In 1849, 53,293 people died of cholera. The disease reappeared in August 1853 and there was a fourth epidemic in 1865. But for every death from major disease, there were many more cases of sickness. Because of the appalling living conditions – sewerage in the drinking water and so on, most people felt sick virtually all the time they were in London.

Nor were there any ready solutions. Knowledge about how disease spread was minimal – nothing was known about the role of microbes in infection, so overcrowded living conditions, which were really at the root of infection, attracted none of the authorities' attention. Indeed, until

Right:
The raw material for the hideous dwarf Quilp's wharf in The Old Curiosity Shop*: 'On the Surrey side of the river was a small rat-infested dreary yard called "Quilp's Wharf," in which were a little wooden counting-house burrowing all awry in the dust as if it had fallen from the clouds and ploughed into the ground; a few fragments of rusty anchors; several large iron rings; some piles of rotten wood; and two or three heaps of old sheet copper, crumpled, cracked, and battered.'*

126

1847 there were no medical officers of health at all, and some time after that before they could enter a property for inspection.

In 1858 the Second Annual Report of the medical officer to the Strand clearly states the need for a reappraisal of the direction of preventive measures: 'Let me urge the dismissal from your minds of the idea, long entertained by many that sanitary improvements consist exclusively in

A water cart. Half the population relied upon water which was piped directly from the Thames, a river into which 200 open sewers flowed – 'a deadly sewer . . . in the place of a fine fresh river.' Little Dorrit

works of drainage and of water supply. Overcrowding is without doubt the most important, and at the same time the most difficult problem with which you are called upon to deal; and sooner or later it must be dealt with. Houses and streets may be drained most perfectly, the district may be paved and lighted in such a manner as to excite the jealous envy of other Local Authorities; new thoroughfares may be constructed and every house in the District furnished with a constant supply of pure water; the Thames may be embanked, and all entrance of sewerage into that river intercepted; but so long as twenty, thirty, or even forty individuals are permitted – it might almost be said compelled – to reside in houses originally built for the accommodation of a single family or at most two families, so long will the evils pointed out in regard of health . . . continue to exist almost unchecked.'

The problems of slum dwellings and the ignorant poor - living, as it were, apart in a society that didn't care – are described by Dickens in *Bleak House*. Tom-All-Alone's is a slum beneath the shadow of Southwark Cathedral; Jo is the poor crossing-sweeper:

Jo sweeps his crossing all day long...he sums up his mental condition, when asked a question, by replying that he 'don't know nothink.' He knows that it's hard to keep the mud off the crossing in dirty weather, and harder still to live by doing it. Nobody taught him, even that much; he found it out.

128

Of all improvements that were so desperately needed in Dickens' London sanitation was the priority in his journalistic battles. The century saw the most incredible constructions in this area, many still relied upon today. Here the Crossness Pumping Station – a new sewerage outflow into the Thames – is seen under construction. In the foreground are the filtration beds, behind which are being built the pumping station and chimney.

Jo lives – that is to say, Jo has not yet died – in a ruinous place, known to the like of him by the name of Tom-all-Alone's. It is a black, dilapidated street, avoided by all decent people; where the crazy houses were seized upon, when their decay was far advanced, by some bold vagrants, who, after establishing their own possession, took to letting them out in lodgings. Now, these tumbling tenements contain, by night, a swarm of misery. As on the ruined human wretch, vermin parasites appear, so, these ruined shelters have bred a crowd of foul existence that crawls in and out of gaps in walls and boards; and coils itself to sleep, in maggot numbers, where the rain drips in; and comes and goes, fetching and carrying fever, and sowing more evil in its every footprint than Lord Coodle and Sir Thomas Doodle, and the Duke of Foodle, and all the fine gentlemen in office, down to Zoodle, shall set right in five hundred years – though born expressly to do it.

Twice, lately, there has been a crash and a cloud of dust, like the springing of a mine, in Tom-all-Alone's; and, each time, a house has fallen. These accidents have made a paragraph in the newspapers, and have filled a bed or two in the nearest hospital. The gaps remain, and there are not unpopular lodgings among the rubbish. As several more houses are nearly ready to go, the next crash in Tom-all-Alone's may be expected to be a good one.

This desirable property is in Chancery, of course. It would be an insult to the discernment of any man with half an eye, to tell him so. Whether 'Tom' is the popular representative of the original plaintiff or defendant in Jarndyce and Jarndyce; or, whether Tom lived here when the suit had laid the street waste, all alone, until other settlers came to join him; or, whether the traditional title is a

comprehensive name for a retreat cut off from honest company and put out of the pale of hope; perhaps nobody knows. Certainly, Jo don't know.

'For *I* don't,' says Jo, '*I* don't know nothink.'

It must be a strange state to be like Jo! To shuffle through the streets, unfamiliar with the shapes and in utter darkness as to the meaning, of those mysterious symbols, so abundant over the shops, and the corner of streets, and on the doors, and in the windows! To see people read, and to see people write, and to see the postman deliver letters, and not to have the least idea of all that language – to be, to every scrap of it, stone blind and dumb! It must be very puzzling to see the good company going to the churches on Sundays, with their books in their hands and to think (for perhaps Jo *does* think, at odd times) what does it all mean, and if it means anything to anybody, how comes it that it means nothing to me? To be hustled, and jostled, and moved on; and really to feel that it would appear to be perfectly true that I have no business here, or there, or anywhere; and yet to be perplexed by the consideration that I *am* here somehow, too, and everybody overlooked me until I became the creature that I am! It must be a strange state, not merely to be told that I am scarcely human (as in the case of my offering myself for a witness), but to feel it of my own knowledge all my life! To see the horses, dogs, and cattle, go by me, and to know that in ignorance I belong to them, and not to the superior beings in my shape, whose delicacy I offend! Jo's ideas of a Criminal Trial, or a Judge, or a Bishop, or a Government, or that inestimable jewel to him (if he only knew it) the Constitution, should be

130

strange! His whole material and immaterial life is wonderfully strange: his death, the strangest thing of all.

Jo comes out of Tom-all-Alone's, meeting the tardy morning which is always late in getting down there, and munches his dirty bit of bread as he comes along. His way lying through many streets, and the houses not yet being open, he sits down to breakfast on the door-step of the Society for the Propagation of the Gospel in Foreign Parts, and gives it a brush when he has finished, as an acknowledgment of the accommodation. He admires the size of the edifice, and wonders what it's all about. He has no idea, poor wretch, of the spiritual destitution of a coral reef in the Pacific, or what it costs to look up the precious souls among the cocoanuts and bread-fruit.

He goes to his crossing, and begins to lay it out for the day. The town awakes; the great tee-totum is set up for its daily spin and whirl; all that unaccountable reading and writing, which has been suspended for a few hours, recommences. Jo, and the other lower animals, get on in the unintelligible mess as they can. It is market-day. The blinded oxen, over-goaded, over-driven, never guided, run into wrong places and are beaten out; and plunge, red-eyed and foaming, at stone walls; and often sorely hurt the innocent, and often sorely hurt themselves. Very like Jo and his order; very, very like!

A band of music comes and plays. Jo listens to it. So does a dog – a drover's dog, waiting for his master outside a butcher's shop, and evidently thinking about those sheep he has had upon his mind for some hours, and is happily rid of. He seems perplexed respecting three or four; can't remember where he left them; looks up and down the street, as half expecting to see them astray; suddenly pricks up his ears and remembers all about it. A thoroughly vagabond dog, accustomed to low company and public-houses; a terrific dog to sheep; ready at a whistle to scamper over their backs, and tear out mouthfuls of their wool; but an educated, improved, developed dog, who has been taught his duties and knows how to discharge them. He and Jo listen to the music, probably with much the same amount of animal satisfaction; likewise as to awakened association, aspiration or regret, melancholy or joyful reference to things beyond the senses, they are probably upon a par. But, otherwise, how far above the human listener is the brute!

Turn that dog's descendants wild, like Jo, and in a very few years they will so degenerate that they will lose even their bark – but not their bite.

The day changes as it wears itself away, and becomes dark and drizzly. Jo fights it out, at his crossing, among the mud and wheels, the horses whips, and umbrellas, and gets but a scantly sum to pay for the unsavoury shelter of Tom-all-Alone's. Twilight comes on; gas begins to start up in the shops; the lamplighter, with his ladder, runs along the margin of the pavement. A wretched evening is beginning to close in.

Later in the novel, Mr Bucket, the first detective in English fiction, goes looking for Jo:

When they come at last to Tom-all-Alone's, Mr Bucket stops for a moment at the corner, and takes a lighted bull's-eye from the constable on duty there, who then accompanies him with his own particular bull's-eye at his waist. Between his two conductors, Mr Snagsby passes along the middle of a villainous street, undrained, unventilated, deep in black mud and corrupt water – though the roads are dry elsewhere – and reeking with such smells and sights that he, who has lived in London all his life, can scarce believe his senses. Branching from this street and its heaps of ruins, are other streets and courts so infamous that Mr Snagsby sickens in body and mind, and feels as if he were going, every moment deeper down, into the infernal gulf.

'Draw off a bit here, Mr Snagsby,' says Bucket, as a kind of shabby palanquin is borne towards them, surrounded by a noisy crowd. 'Here's the fever coming up the street!'

As the unseen wretch goes by, the crowd, leaving that object of attraction, hovers round the three visitors like a dream of horrible faces, and fades away up alleys and into ruins, and behind walls; and with occasional cries and shrill whistles of warning, thenceforth flits about them until they leave the place.

'Are those the fever-houses, Darby?' Mr Bucket coolly asks, as he turns his bull's-eye on a line of stinking ruins.

Darby replies that 'all them are,' and further that in all, for months and months, the people 'have been down by dozens,' and have been carried out, dead and dying 'like sheep with the rot.' Bucket observing to Mr Snagsby as they go on again, that he looks a little poorly, Mr Snagsby answers that he feels as if he couldn't breathe the dreadful air.

There is inquiry made, at various houses, for a boy named Jo. As few people are known in Tom-all-Alone's by any Christian sign, there is much reference to Mr Snagsby whether he means Carrots, or the Colonel, or Gallows, or Young Chisel, or Terrier Tip, or Lanky, or the Brick. Mr Snagsby describes over and over again. There are conflicting opinions respecting the original of his picture. Some think it must be Carrots; some say the Brick. The Colonel is produced, but is not at all near the thing. Whenever Mr Snagsby and his conductors are stationary, the crowd flows round, and from its squalid depths obsequious advice heaves up to Mr Bucket. Whenever they move, and the angry bull's-eyes glare, it fades away, and flits about them up the alleys, and in the ruins, and behind the walls, as before.

At last is a lair found out where Toughy, or the Tough Subject, lays him down at night; and it is thought that the Tough Subject may be Jo. Comparison of notes between Mr Snagsby and the proprietress of the house – a drunken face tied up in a black bundle, and flaring out of a heap of rags on the floor of a hutch which is her private apartment – leads to the establishment of this conclusion. Toughy has gone to the Doctor's to get a bottle of stuff for a sick woman, but will be here anon.

'And who have we got here tonight?' says Mr Bucket, opening another door and glaring in with his bull's-eye. 'Two drunken men, eh? And two women? The men are sound enough,' turning back each sleeper's arm from his face to look at him. 'Are these your good men, my dears?'

'Yes, sir,' returns one of the women. 'They are our husbands.'

'Brickmakers, eh?'

'Yes, Sir.'

'What are you doing here? You don't belong to London.'

'No, sir. We belong to Hertfordshire.'

132

'How many people may there be in London, who, if we had brought them deviously and blindfold, to this street, fifty paces from the Station House, and within call of Saint Giles's church, would know it for a not remote part of the city in which their lives are passed? How many, who, amidst this compound of sickening smells, these heaps of filth, these tumbling houses, with all their vile contents, animate and inanimate, slimily overflowing into the black road, would believe that they breathe this air?' Reprinted Pieces

'Whereabouts in Hertfordshire?'

'Saint Albans.'

'Come up on the tramp?'

'We walked up yesterday. There's no work down with us at present, but we have done no good by coming here, and shall do none, I expect.'

'That's not the way to do much good,' says Mr Bucket, turning his head in the direction of the unconscious figures on the ground.

'It an't indeed,' replies the women with a sigh. 'Jenny and me knows it full well.'

The room, though two and three feet higher than the door, is so low that the head of the tallest visitors would touch the blackened ceiling if he stood upright. It is offensive to every sense; even the gross candle burns pale and sickly in the polluted air. There are a couple of benches, and a higher bench by way of table. The men lie asleep where they stumbled down, but the women sit by the candle. Lying in the arms of the woman who has spoken, is a very young child.

'Why, what age do you call that little creature?' says Bucket. 'It looks as if it was born yesterday.' He is not at all rough about it; and as he turns light gently on the infant, Mr Snagsby is strangely reminded of another infant, encircled with light, that he has seen in pictures.

'He is not three weeks old yet, sir,' says the woman.

'Is he your child?'

'Mine.'

The other woman, who was bending over it when they came in, stoops down again, and kisses it as it lies asleep.

'You seem as fond of it as if you were the mother yourself,' says Mr Bucket.

'I was the mother of one like it, master, and it died.'

'Ah Jenny, Jenny! says the other woman to her; 'better so. Much better to think of dead than alive, Jenny! Much better!'

'Why, you an't such an unnatural woman, I hope,' returns Bucket, sternly, 'as to wish your own child dead?'

'God knows you are right, master,' she returns. 'I am not. I'd stand between it and death, with my own life if I could, as true as any pretty lady.'

'Then don't talk in that wrong manner,' says Mr Bucket, mollified again. 'Why do you do it?'

'It's brought into my head, master,' returns the woman, her eyes filling with tears, 'when I look down at the child lying so. If it was never to wake no more, you'd think me mad, I should take on so, I know that very well. I was with Jenny when she lost hers – warn't I, Jenny? – and I know how she grieved. But look around you, at this place. Look at them;' glancing at the sleepers on the ground. 'Look at the boy you're waiting for, who's gone out to do me a good turn. Think of the children that your business lays with often and often, and that *you* see grow up!'

'Well, well,' says Mr Bucket, 'you train him respectable, and he'll be a comfort to you, and look after you in your old age, you know.'

'I mean to try hard,' she answers, wiping her eyes. 'But I have been a-thinking, being over-tired to-night, and not well with the ague, of all the many things that'll come in his way. My master will be against it, and he'll be beat, and see me beat, and made to fear his home, and perhaps to stray wild. If I work for him ever so much, and ever so hard, there's no one to help me; and if he should be turned bad, 'spite of all I could do, and the time should come when I should sit by him in his sleep, made hard and changed, an't it likely I should think of him as he lies in my lap now, and wish he had died as Jenny's child died!'

'There, there!' says Jenny. 'Liz, you're tired and ill. Let me take him.'

In doing so, she displaces the mother's dress but quickly readjusts it over the wounded and bruised bosom where the baby has been lying.

'It's my dead child,' says Jenny, walking up and down as she nurses, 'that makes me love this child so dear, and it's my dead child that makes her love it so dear too, as even to think of its being taken away from her now. While she thinks that, *I* think what fortune would I give to have my darling back. But we mean the same thing, if we know how to say it, us two mothers does in our poor hearts!'

As Mr Snagsby blows his nose, and coughs his cough of sympathy, a step is heard without. Mr Bucket throws his light into the doorway, and says to Mr Snagsby, 'Now, what do you say to Toughy? Will *he* do?'

'That's Jo,' says Mr Snagsby.

Jo stands amazed on the disc of light, like a ragged figure in a magic-lantern, trembling to think that he has offended against the law in not having moved on far enough. Mr Snagsby, however, giving him the consolatory assurance, 'It's only a job you will be paid for, Jo,' he recovers; and, on being taken outside by Mr Bucket for a little private confabulation, tells his tale satisfactorily, though out of breath.

In the final excerpt, Dickens reflects upon the impediments to slum reform, and on disease, sickness and death as vengeance upon a

'The wretched woman with the infant in her arms, round whose meagre form the remnant of her own scanty shawl is carefully wrapped, had been attempting to sing some popular ballad, in the hope of wringing a few pence from the compassionate passer-by. A brutal laugh at her weak voice is all she has gained.' Sketches

government notable for its speech-making, theory and lack of practical action:

Darkness rests upon Tom-all-Alone's. Dilating and dilating since the sun went down last night, it has gradually swelled until it fills every void in the place. For a time there were some dungeon lights burning as the lamp of Life burns in Tom-all-Alone's, heavily, heavily, in the nauseous air, and winking – as that lamp, too, winks in Tom-all-Alone's – at many horrible things. But they are blotted out. The moon has eyed Tom with a dull cold stare, as admitting some puny emulation of herself in his desert region unfit for life and blasted by volcanic fires; but she has passed on, and is gone. The blackest nightmare in the infernal stables grazes on Tom-all-Alone's, and Tom is fast asleep.

Much mighty speech-making there has been, both in and out of Parliament, concerning Tom, and much wrathful disputation how Tom shall be got right. Whether he shall be put into the main road by constables, or by beadles, or by bellringing, or by force of figures, or by correct principles of taste, or by high church, or by low church, or by no church; whether he shall be set to splitting trusses of polemical straws with the crooked knife of his mind, or whether he shall be put to stone-breaking instead. In the midst of which dust and noise, there is but one thing perfectly clear, to wit, that Tom only may and can, or shall and will, be reclaimed according to somebody's theory but nobody's practice. And in the hopeful meantime, Tom goes to perdition head foremost in his old determined spirit.

But he has his revenge. Even the winds are his messengers, and they serve him in these hours of darkness. There is not a drop of Tom's corrupted blood but propagates infection and contagion somewhere. It shall pollute, this very night, the choice stream (in which chemists on analysis would find the genuine nobility) of a Norman house, and his Grace shall not be able to say Nay to the infamous alliance. There is not an atom of Tom's slime, not a cubic inch of any pestillential gas in which he lives, not one obscenity or degradation about him, not an ignorance, not a wickedness, not a brutality of his committing, but shall work its retribution, through every order of society, up to the proudest of the proud, and to the highest of the high. Verily, what with tainting, plundering, and spoiling, Tom has his revenge.

It is a moot point whether Tom-all-Alone's be uglier by day or by night; but on the argument that the more that is seen of it the more shocking it must be, and that no part of it left to the imagination is at all likely to be made so bad as the reality, day carries it. The day begins to break now; and in truth it might be better for the national glory even that the sun should sometimes set upon the British dominions, than that it should ever rise upon so vile a wonder as Tom.

A brown sunburnt gentleman, who appears in some inaptitude for sleep to be wandering abroad rather than counting the hours on a restless pillow, strolls hitherward at this quiet time. Attracted by curiosity, he often pauses and looks about him, up and down the miserable by-ways. Nor is he merely curious, for in his bright dark eye there is compassionate interest; and as he looks here and there, he seems to understand such wretchedness, and to have studied it before.

On the banks of the stagnant channel of mud which is the main street of Tom-all-Alone's, nothing is to be seen but the crazy houses, shut up and silent.

'He is not softened by distance and unfamiliarity; he is not a genuine foreign-grown savage; he is the ordinary home-made article. Dirty, ugly, disagreeable to all the senses, in body a common creature of the common streets, only in soul a heathen.' Bleak House

135

No waking creature save himself appears, except in one direction, where he sees the solitary figure of a woman sitting on a door-step. He walks that way. Approaching, he observes that she has journeyed a long distance, and is footsore and travel-stained. She sits on the door-step in the manner of one who is waiting, with her elbow on her knee and her head upon her hand. Beside her is a canvas bag, or bundle, she has carried. She is dozing probably, for she gives no heed for his steps as he comes toward her.

The broken footway is so narrow, that when Allan Woodcourt comes to where the woman sits, he has to turn into the road to pass her. Looking down at her face, his eye meets hers, and he stops.

'What is the matter?'

'Nothing, sir.'

'Can't you make them hear? Do you want to be let in?'

'I'm waiting till they get up at another house – a lodging house – not here,' the woman patiently returns. 'I'm waiting here because there will be sun here presently to warm me.

'I am afraid you are tired. I am sorry to see you sitting in the street.'

'Thank you sir. I don't matter.'

A habit in him of speaking to the poor, and of avoiding patronage or condescension, or childishness (which is the favourite device, many people deeming it quite a subtlety to talk to them like little spelling books), has put him on good terms with the woman easily.

Disease and death spread unchecked wherever conditions welcomed them. It is impossible to measure the fear that ignorance engendered, or the effect upon a family of the heartlessness with which the dead were cleared away:

They walked on, for some time, through the most crowded and densely inhabited part of the town; and then, striking down a narrow street more dirty and miserable than any they had yet passed through, paused to look for the house which was the object of their search. The houses on either side were high and large, but very old, and tenanted by people of the poorest class: as their neglected appearance would have sufficiently denoted, without the concurrent testimony afforded by the squalid looks of the few men and women who, with folded arms and bodies half doubled, occasionally skulked along. A great many of the tenements had shop-fronts; but they were fast closed, and mouldering away; only the upper rooms being inhabited. Some houses which had become insecure from age and decay, were prevented from falling into the street, by huge beams of wood reared against the walls, and firmly planted in the road; but even these crazy dens seemed to have been selected as the nightly haunts of some houseless wretches, for many of the rough boards which supplied the place of door and window, were wrenched from their positions, to afford an aperture wide enough for the passage of a human body. The kennel was stagnant and filthy. The very rats, which here and there lay putrefying in its rottenness, were hideous with famine.

There was neither knocker nor bell-handle at the open door where Oliver and his master stopped; so, groping his way cautiously through the dark passage, and bidding Oliver keep close to him and not be afraid, the undertaker mounted to the top of the first flight of stairs. Stumbling against a door on the landing, he rapped at it with his knuckles.

It was opened by a young girl of thirteen or fourteen. The undertaker at once saw enough of what the room contained, to know it was the apartment to which he had been directed. He stepped in; Oliver followed him.

There was no fire in the room; but a man was crouching mechanically over the empty stove. An old woman, too, had drawn a low stool to the cold hearth, and was sitting beside him. There were some ragged children in another corner; and in a small recess, opposite the door, there lay upon the ground, something covered with an old blanket. Oliver shuddered as he cast his eyes towards the place, and crept involuntarily closer to his master; for though it was covered up, the boy felt that it was a corpse.

The man's face was thin and very pale; his hair and beard were grizzly; his eyes were bloodshot. The old woman's face was wrinkled; her two remaining teeth protruded over her underlip; and her eyes were bright and piercing. Oliver was afraid to look at either her or the man. They seemed so like the rats he had seen outside.

'Nobody shall go near her,' said the man, starting fiercely up, as the undertaker approached the recess, 'Keep back! Damn you, keep back if you've a life to lose!'

'Nonsense, my good man,' said the undertaker, who was pretty well used to misery in all its shapes. 'Nonsense!'

'I tell you,' said the man: clenching his hands, and stamping furiously on the floor, – 'I tell you I won't have her put into the ground. She couldn't rest there. The worms would worry her – not eat her – she is so worn away.'

The undertaker offered no reply to this raving; but producing a tape from his pocket, knelt down for a moment by the side of the body.

'Ah!' said the man, bursting into tears, and sinking on his knees at the feet of the dead woman;' 'kneel down, kneel down – kneel round her, every one of you, and mark my words! I say she was starved to death. I never knew how bad she was, till the fever came upon her; and then her bones were starting through the skin. There was neither fire nor candle; she died in the dark – in the dark! She couldn't see her children's faces, though we heard her gasping out their names. I begged for her in the streets: and they sent me to prison. When I came back, she was dying; and all the blood in my heart has dried up, for they starved her to death. I swear it before the God that saw it! They starved her!' He twined his hands in his hair; and, with a loud scream, rolled grovelling upon the floor, his eyes fixed, and the foam covering his lips.

The terrified children cried bitterly; but the old woman, who had hitherto remained as quiet as if she had been wholly deaf to all that passed, managed them into silence. Having unloosed the cravat of the man who still remained extended on the ground, she tottered towards the undertaker.

'She was my daughter,' said the old woman, nodding her head in the direction of the corpse; and speaking with an idiotic leer, more ghastly than even the presence of death in such a place. 'Lord, Lord! Well it *is* strange that I who gave birth to her, and was a woman then should be alive and merry now, and she lying there so cold and stiff! Lord, Lord! – to think of it; it's as good as a play – as good as a play!'

As the wretched creature mumbled and chuckled in her hideous merriment, the undertaker turned to go away.

'Stop, stop!' said the old woman in a loud whisper. 'Will she be buried tomorrow, or next day, or tonight? I laid her out; and I must walk, you know. Send me a large cloak: a good warm one: for it is bitter cold. We should have cake and wine, too, before we go! Never mind: send some bread – only a loaf of bread and a cup of water. Shall we have some bread dear?' she said eagerly: catching at the undertaker's coat, as he once more moved towards the door.

'Yes, yes,' said the undertaker, 'of course. Anything you like!' He disengaged himself from the old woman's grasp; and, drawing Oliver after him, hurried away.

OLIVER TWIST

Rooms, suddenly vacant, attracted justifiable suspicion in would-be tenants, as here in *David Copperfield* when David accompanies his aunt, Betsey Trotwood, to look over his new abode near the Adelphi.

Away we went. The advertisement directed us to apply to Mrs Crupp on the premises, and we rung the area bell, which we supposed to communicate with Mrs Crupp. It was not until we had rung three or four times that we could prevail on Mrs Crupp to communicate with us, but at last she appeared, being a stout lady with a flounce of flannel petticoat below a nankeen gown.

'Let us see these chambers of yours, if you please, ma'am,' said my aunt.

'For this gentleman?' said Mrs Crupp, feeling in her pocket for her keys.

'Yes, for my nephew,' said my aunt.

'And a sweet set they is for sich!' said Mrs Crupp.

So we went upstairs.

They were on the top of the house – a great point with my aunt, being near the fire-escape – and consisted of a little half-blind entry where you could see hardly anything, a little stone-blind pantry where you could see nothing at all, a sitting-room, and a bedroom. The furniture was rather faded, but quite good enough for me; and, sure enough, the river was outside the windows.

As I was delighted with the place, my aunt and Mrs Crupp withdrew into the pantry to discuss terms, while I remained on the sitting-room sofa, hardly daring to think it possible that I could be destined to live in such a noble residence. After a single combat of some duration they returned, and I saw, to my joy, both in Mrs Crupp's countenance and in my aunt's, that the deed was done.

'Is it the last occupant's furniture?' inquired my aunt.

'Yes, it is, ma'am,' said Mrs Crupp.

'What's become of him?' asked my aunt.

Mrs Crupp was taken with a troublesome cough, in the midst of which she articulated with much difficulty. 'He was took ill here, ma'am, and – ugh! ugh! ugh! dear me! – and he died!'

'Hey! What did he die of?' asked my aunt.

'Well, ma'am, he died of drink,' said Mrs Crupp, in confidence. 'And smoke.'

'Smoke? You don't mean chimneys?' said my aunt.

'No, ma'am,' returned Mrs Crupp. 'Cigars and pipes.'

'*That's* not catching, Trot, at any rate,' remarked my aunt, turning to me.

'No, indeed,' said I.

138

Disinfectors. According to Edwin Chadwick, the sanitary reformer, 'all smell is disease'. As a result large parts of London were seen to be nothing other than a source of pestilence, a breeding ground of diseases which then permeated the entire capital.

It was 1855 before medical officers were empowered to enter a house for inspection purposes, and even then only on the order of a J.P. Not until 1868, after the worst crises of infection were over, did the Torrens Act enable inspection on an officer's own initiative.

Infant Death

In 1839 almost half the funerals in London were children under ten years of age. Most occurred among the poor and especially among children of working women, whose day-time minders would often drug their charges with opiates or gin. Dickens actively appealed for funds for the extension of the Great Ormond Street Hospital for sick children, founded in 1852, where Johnny of *Our Mutual Friend* finally dies.

In a speech on February 9th, 1858, Dickens acknowledged the hopelessness of caring for the infant poor in their own homes – 'Many a poor sick child have I seen most affectionately and kindly tended by poor people in an unwholesome house and under untoward circumstances, wherein its recovery was quite impossible.' But even when hospital facilities became available, the poor were characteristically reticent about making use of them. Mrs Boffin, who it has been agreed will shortly adopt Johnny, arrives at the impoverished home of his minder, Betty Higden, to see the boy –

. . . On the way down, they had stopped at a toy-shop, and had bought that noble charger, a description of whose points and trappings had on the last occasion conciliated the then worldly-minded orphan, and also a Noah's ark, and also a yellow bird with an artificial voice in him, and also a military doll so well dressed that if he had only been of life-size his brother-officers in the Guards might never have found him out. Bearing these gifts, they raised the latch of Betty Higden's door, and saw her sitting in the dimmest and furthest corner with poor Johnny in her lap.

'And how's my boy, Betty?' asked Mrs Boffin, sitting down beside her.

'He's bad! He's bad!' said Betty. 'I begin to be afeerd he'll not be yours any more than mine. All others belonging to him have gone to the Power of the Glory, and I have a mind that they're drawing him to them – leading him away.'

'No, no, no,' said Mrs Boffin.

'I don't know why else he clenches his little hand as if it had hold of a finger that I can't see. Look at it,' said Betty, opening the wrappers in which the flushed child lay, and showing his small right hand lying closed upon his breast. 'It's always so. It don't mind me.'

'Is he asleep?'.

'No, I think not. You're not asleep, my Johnny?'

'No,' said Johnny, with a quiet air of pity for himself, and without opening his eyes.

'Here's the lady, Johnny. And the horse.'

Johnny could bear the lady, with complete indifference, but not the horse. Opening his heavy eyes, he slowly broke into a smile on beholding that splendid

'She produced from her pocket an advertisement, carefully cut out of a newspaper, setting forth that in Buckingham Street in the Adelphi there was to be let furnished, with a view of the river, a singularly desirable, and compact set of chambers. . . .'
David Copperfield

phenomenon, and wanted to take it in his arms. As it was much too big, it was put upon a chair where he could hold it by the mane and contemplate it. Which he soon forgot to do.

But, Johnny murmuring something with his eyes closed, and Mrs Boffin not knowing what, old Betty bent her ear to listen and took pains to understand. Being asked by her to repeat what he had said, he did so two or three times, and then it came out that he must have seen more than they supposed when he looked up to see the horse, for the murmur was, 'Who is the boofer lady?' Now, the boofer, or beautiful, lady was Bella; and whereas this notice from the poor baby would have touched her of itself, it was rendered more pathetic by the late melting of her heart to her poor little father, and their joke about the lovely woman. So, Bella's behaviour was very tender and very natural when she kneeled on the brick floor to clasp the child, and when the child, with a child's

'But, on the way down, they had stopped at a toy-shop, and had bought that noble charger, a description of whose points and trappings had on the last occasion conciliated the then worldly-minded orphan, and also a Noah's ark, and also a yellow bird with an artificial voice in him, and also a military doll so well dressed that if he had only been of life-size his brother-officers in the Guards might never have found him out.' Our Mutual Friend

140

admiration of what is young and pretty, fondled the boofer lady.

'Now, my good dear Betty,' said Mrs Boffin, hoping that she saw her opportunity, and laying her hand persuasively on her arm; 'we have come to remove Johnny from this cottage to where he can be taken better care of.'

Instantly, and before another word could be spoken, the old woman started up with blazing eyes, and rushed at the door with the sick child.

'Stand away from me every one of ye!' she cried out wildly. 'I see what ye mean now. Let me go my way, all of ye. I'd sooner kill the Pretty, and kill myself!'

'Stay, stay!' said Rokesmith, soothing her. 'You don't understand.'

'I understand too well, I know too much about it, sir. I've run from it too many a year. No! Never for me, nor for the child, while there's water enough in England to cover us!'

The terror, the shame, the passion of horror and repugnance, firing the worn face and perfectly maddening it, would have been a quite terrible sight, if embodied in one old fellow-creature alone. Yet it 'crops up' – as our slang goes – my lords and gentlemen and honourable boards, in other fellow-creatures, rather frequently!

'It's been chasing me all my life, but it shall never take me nor mine alive!' cried old Betty. 'I've done with ye. I'd have fastened door and window and starved out, afore I'd ever have let ye in, if I had known what ye came for!'

But, catching sight of Mrs Boffin's wholesome face, she relented, and crouching down by the door and bending over her burden to hush it, said humbly: 'Maybe my fears has put me wrong. If they have so, tell me, and the good Lord forgive me! I'm quick to take this fright, I know, and my head is summ'at light within wearying and watching.'

'There, there, there!' returned Mrs Boffin. 'Come, come! Say no more of it, Betty. It was a mistake, a mistake. Any one of us might have made it in your place, and felt just as you do.'

'The Lord bless ye!' said the old woman, stretching out her hand.

'Now, see, Betty,' pursued the sweet compassionate soul, holding the hand kindly, 'what I really did mean, and what I should have begun by saying out, if I had only been a little wiser and handier. We want to move Johnny up to a place where there are none but children; a place set up on purpose for sick children; where the good doctors and nurses pass their lives with children, talk to none but children, touch none but children, comfort and cure none but children.'

'Is there really such a place?' asked the old woman, with a gaze of wonder.

'Yes, Betty, on my word, and you shall see it. If my home was a better place for the dear boy, I'd take him to it; but indeed indeed it's not.'

'You shall take him,' returned Betty, fervently kissing the comforting hand, 'where you will, my deary. I am not so hard, but that I believe your face and voice, and I will, as long as I can see and hear.'

This victory gained, Rokesmith made haste to profit by it, for he saw how wofully time had been lost. He despatched Sloppy to bring the carriage to the door; caused the child to be carefully wrapped up; bade old Betty get her bonnet on; collected the toys, enabling the little fellow to comprehend that his treasures were to be transported with him; and had all things prepared so easily that they were ready for the carriage as soon as it appeared, and in a minute afterwards were on their way. Sloppy they left behind, relieving his overcharged breast with

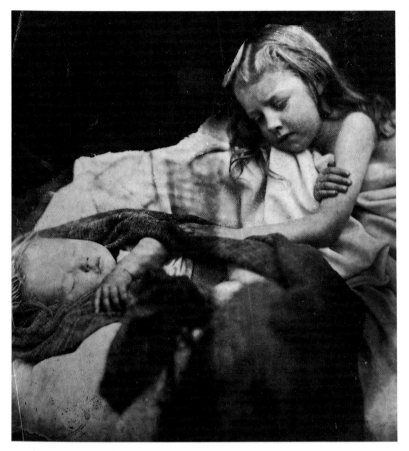

a paroxysm of mangling.

At the Children's Hospital, the gallant steed, the Noah's ark, yellow bird, and the officer of the Guards, were made as welcome as their child-owner. But the doctor said aside to Rokesmith, 'This should have been days ago. Too late!'

However, they were all carried up into a fresh airy room, and there Johnny came to himself, out of a sleep or a swoon or whatever it was, to find himself lying in a little quiet bed, with a little platform over his breast, on which were already arranged, to give him heart and urge him to cheer up, the Noah's ark, the noble steed, and the yellow bird; with the officer in the Guards doing duty over the whole, quite as much to the satisfaction of his country as if he had been upon Parade. And at the bed's head was a coloured picture beautiful to see, representing as it were another Johnny seated on the knee of some Angel surely who loved little children. And, marvellous fact, to lie and stare at: Johnny had become one of a little family, all in little quiet beds (except two playing dominoes in little arm-chairs at a little table on the hearth): and on all the little beds were little platforms whereon were to be seen dolls' houses, woolly dogs with mechanical barks in them not very dissimilar from the artificial voice pervading the bowels of the yellow bird, tin armies, Moorish tumblers, wooden tea things, and the riches of the earth.

As Johnny murmured something in his placid admiration, the ministering women at his bed's head asked him what he said. It seemed that he wanted to know whether all these were brothers and sisters of his? So they told him yes. It seemed then, that he wanted to know whether God had brought them all together there? So they told him yes again. They made out then, that he wanted to know whether they would all get out of pain? So they answered yes to that question likewise, and made him understand that the reply included himself.

Johnny's powers of sustaining conversation were as yet so very imperfectly developed, even in a state of health, that in sickness they were little more than monosyllabic. But, he had to be washed and tended, and remedies were applied, and though those offices were far, far more skilfully and lightly done than ever anything had been done for him in his little life, so rough and short, they would have hurt and tired him but for an amazing circumstance which laid hold of his attention. This was no less than the appearance on his own little platform in pairs, of All Creation, on its way into his own particular ark; the elephant leading, and the fly, with a diffident sense of his size, politely bringing up the rear. A very little brother lying in the next bed with a broken leg, was so enchanted by this spectacle that his delight exalted its enthralling interest; and so came rest and sleep.

'I see you are not afraid to leave the dear child here, Betty,' whispered Mrs Boffin.

'No, ma'am. Most willingly, most thankfully, with all my heart and soul.'

So, they kissed him, and left him there, and old Betty was to come back early in the morning, and nobody but Rokesmith knew for certain how that the doctor had said, 'This should have been days ago. Too late!'

But, Rokesmith knowing it, and knowing that his bearing it in mind would be acceptable thereafter to that good woman who had been the only light in the childhood of desolate John Harmon dead and gone, resolved that late at night he would go back to the bedside of John Harmon's namesake, and see how it fared with him.

The family whom God had brought together were not all asleep, but were all quiet. From bed to bed, a light womanly tread and a pleasant fresh face passed in the silence of the night. A little head would lift itself up into the softened light here and there, to be kissed as the face went by – for these little patients are very loving – and would then submit itself to be composed to rest again. The mite with the broken leg was restless, and moaned; but after a while turned his face toward's Johnny's bed, to fortify himself with a view of the ark, and fell asleep. Over most of the beds, the toys were yet grouped as the children had left them when they last laid themselves down, and, in their innocent grotesqueness and incongruity, they might have stood for the children's dreams.

The doctor came in too, to see how it fared with Johnny. And he and Rokesmith stood together, looking down with compassion on him.

'What is it, Johnny?' Rokesmith was the questioner, and put an arm round the poor baby as he made a struggle.

'Him!' said the little fellow. 'Those!'

The doctor was quick to understand children, and, taking the horse, the ark, the yellow bird, and the man in the Guards, from Johnny's bed, softly placed them on that of his next neighbour, the mite with the broken leg.

With a weary and yet a pleased smile, and with an action as if he stretched his little finger out to rest, the child heaved his body on the sustaining arm, and seeking Rokesmith's face with his lips, said:

'A kiss for the boofer lady.'

Having now bequeathed all he had to dispose of, and arranged his affairs in this world, Johnny, thus speaking, left it.

Dickens' Vision of the Poor

The popular picture of Victorian London and its poor comes to us, perhaps more than we would like to admit, on the wings of Dickens' imagination. Certainly, Dickens' novels are topical – almost every reference is a topical reference and the issues he takes on were popular talking points at the time. For an audience reading one of his novels upon first publication, it would have been a bit like reading a newspaper in terms of its topicality.

In practical terms, the novels did succeed in warning his audience of the evils of the new Victorian society: Dotheboys Hall not only laid low the Academy on which it was based, but eventually all the notorious Yorkshire schools which had preyed upon large numbers of illegitimate or unwanted children by offering their parents or guardians cheap terms and no holidays, and their pupils brutality and neglect. Similarly the tradition of night nurses satirised in the disreputable old nurse Sairey Gamp came to an end after publication of Martin Chuzzlewit. And *Oliver Twist*, which was published at the height of a two-year campaign by the *Times* against the Poor Law Amendment Act, must have been political dynamite.

Poor houses, or 'workhouses' as their more popular name suggests, had been built to provide work for the unemployed. In addition, the Speenhamland policy provided allowances – top-up wages – for workers whose earnings fell below a certain level.

However, it was claimed by the authorities that the Speenhamland policy encouraged employers to provide artificially low wages in the knowledge that their labourers could call upon relief from the State, and the Poor Law Amendment Act of 1834 sought to close this loophole – henceforth no 'outdoor' relief would be paid to low-paid or unemployed labourers. Relief would in future only be given within the confines of the workhouse, and in order to claim it you had to pass the 'workhouse test'; in effect you had to prove yourself a pauper.

This was the demeaning aspect of the law that caused such a furore, along with the awful workhouse conditions themselves. But from the government's point of view the law would reduce unemployment –

144

The Blue Boar at which David Copperfield stops on his way to school at Salem House for the first time. There he is met by a master:
'"You're the new boy?" he said.
"Yes, sir," I said.
I supposed I was. I didn't know.'

able-bodied men, hitherto unemployed, would have to get a job or starve; it would encourage all employers to pay at least a subsistence wage; it would lower the Poor Rate from which the wage-supplement had been paid; and it would prevent the pauper from breeding in idleness because once in the workhouse he would be separated from his wife.

The orphan Oliver Twist is sent first to a baby farm and then, as the second (and especially well known) of the following extracts describes, on his ninth birthday he is taken by the Beadle, Mr Bumble, before the local board of governors entrusted by the Poor Law Commission (pursuant to the Act of 1834) to run the workhouse:

The parish authorities inquired with dignity of the workhouse authorities, whether there was no female then domiciled in 'the house' who was in a situation to impart to Oliver Twist the consolation and nourishment of which he stood in need. The workhouse authorities replied with humility that there was not. Upon this, the parish authorities magnanimously and humanely resolved, that Oliver should be 'farmed', or, in other words, that he should be dispatched to a branch-workhouse some three miles off, where twenty or thirty other juvenile offenders against the poor-laws rolled about the floor all day, without the inconvenience of too much food or too much clothing, under the parental superintendence of an elderly female who received the culprits at and for the consideration of sevenpence-halfpenny per small head per week. Sevenpence-halfpenny's worth per week is a good round diet for a child; a great deal may be got for sevenpence-halfpenny – quite enough to overload its stomach, and make it uncomfortable. The elderly female was a woman of wisdom and experience; she knew what was good for children, and she had a very accurate perception of what was good for herself. So, she appropriated the greater part of the weekly stipend to her own use, and consigned the rising parochial generation to even a shorter allowance than was originally provided for them; thereby finding in the lowest depth a deeper still, and proving herself a very great experimental philosopher.

Everybody knows the story of another experimental philosopher, who had a great theory about a horse being able to live without eating, and who demonstrated it so well, that he got his own horse down to a straw a day, and would unquestionably have rendered him a very spirited and rampacious animal on nothing at all, if he had not died, just four-and-twenty hours before he was to have had his first comfortable bait of air. Unfortunately for the experimental philosophy of the female to whose protecting care Oliver Twist was delivered over, a similar result usually attended the operation of *her* system; for at the very moment when a child had contrived to exist upon the smallest possible portion of the weakest possible food, it did perversely happen in eight and a half cases out of ten, either that it sickened from want and cold, or fell into the fire from neglect, or got half smothered by accident; in any one of which cases, the miserable little being was usually summoned into another world, and there gathered to the fathers it had never known in this.

Occasionally, when there was some more than usually interesting inquest upon a parish child who had been overlooked in turning up a bedstead, or inadvertently scalded to death when there happened to be a washing, though the latter accident

was very scarce, – anything approaching to a washing being of rare occurrence in the farm, – the jury would take it into their heads to ask troublesome questions, or the parishioners would rebelliously affix their signatures to a remonstrance: but these impertinences were speedily checked by the evidence of the surgeon, and the testimony of the beadle; the former of whom had always opened the body and found nothing inside (which was very probable indeed), and the latter of whom invariably swore whatever the parish wanted, which was very self-devotional. Besides, the board made periodical pilgrimages to the farm, and always sent the beadle the day before, to say they were going. The children were neat and clean to behold, when *they* went; and what more would people have?

It cannot be expected that this system of farming would produce any very extraordinary or luxuriant crop. Oliver Twist's ninth birthday found him a pale thin child, somewhat diminutive in stature, and decidedly small in circumference.

146

A woman marks the entrance to the workhouse in Little Saffron Hill – 'A dirtier or more wretched place he had never seen.' (Oliver Twist). This is the street in which Fagin had his notorious den; it is also the locale of the Ragged School, which Dickens visited.

But nature or inheritance had implanted a good sturdy spirit in Oliver's breast: it had had plenty of room to expand, thanks to the spare diet of the establishment; and perhaps to this circumstance may be attributed his having any ninth birthday at all. Be this as it may, however, it *was* his ninth birthday; and he was keeping it in the coal-cellar with a select party of two other young gentlemen, who, after participating with him in a sound thrashing, had been locked up therein for atrociously presuming to be hungry, when Mrs Mann, the good lady of the house, was unexpectedly startled by the apparition of Mr Bumble the beadle striving to undo the wicket of the garden-gate.

'Goodness gracious! Is that you, Mr Bumble, sir?' said Mrs Mann, thrusting her head out of the window in well-affected ecstasies of joy. '(Susan, take Oliver and them two brats up stairs, and wash 'em directly.) My heart alive! Mr Bumble, how glad I am to see you, sure-ly!'

The ironic tone which Dickens adopts may suggest that he greatly exaggerates the sparseness of the workhouse diet described below. But in fact one such diet of 1836 amounted to 1½ pints of gruel per day, and

147

on Fridays, apart from the gruel, 12 ozs of bread, 14 ozs of suet or rice pudding and 2 ozs of cheese. Mr Bumble speaks:

'Oliver being now too old to remain here, the board have determined to have him back into the house, and I have come out myself to take him there, – so let me see him at once.'

'I'll fetch him directly,' said Mrs Mann, leaving the room for that purpose. And Oliver, having had by this time as much of the outer coat of dirt, which encrusted his face and hands, removed, as could be scrubbed off in one washing, was led into the room by his benevolent protectress.

'Make a bow to the gentleman, Oliver,' said Mrs Mann.

Oliver made a bow, which was divided between the beadle on the chair and the cocked hat on the table.

'Will you go along with me, Oliver?' said Mr Bumble in a majestic voice.

Oliver was about to say that he would go along with anybody with great readiness, when, glancing upward, he caught sight of Mrs Mann, who had got behind the beadle's chair, and was shaking her fist at him with a furious countenance. He took the hint at once, for the fist had too often impressed upon his body not to be deeply impressed upon his recollection.

'Will *she* go with me?' inquired poor Oliver.

'No, she can't,' replied Mr Bumble. 'But she'll come and see you sometimes.'

This was no very great consolation to the child; but, young as he was he had sense enough to make a feint of feeling great regret at going away. It was no very difficult matter for the boy to call tears into his eyes. Hunger and recent ill-usage are great assistants if you want to cry; and Oliver cried very naturally indeed. Mrs Mann gave him a thousand embraces, and, what Oliver wanted a great deal more, a piece of bread and butter, lest he should seem too hungry when he got to the workhouse. With the slice of bread in his hand, and the little brown-cloth parish cap on his head, Oliver was then led away by Mr Bumble from the wretched home where one kind word or look had never lighted the gloom of his infant years. And yet he burst into an agony of childish grief as the cottage-gate closed after him. Wretched as were the little companions in misery he was leaving behind, they were the only friends he had ever known; and a sense of his loneliness in the great wide world sank into the child's heart for the first time.

Mr Bumble walked on with long strides, and little Oliver, firmly grasping his gold-laced cuff, trotted beside him, inquiring at the end of every quarter of a mile whether they were 'nearly there'. To these interrogations Mr Bumble returned very brief and snappish replies; for the temporary blandness which gin-and-water awakens in some bosoms had by this time evaporated, and he was once again a beadle.

Oliver had not been within the walls of the workhouse a quarter of an hour, and had scarcely completed the demolition of a second slice of bread, when Mr Bumble, who had handed him over to the care of an old woman, returned, and, telling him it was a board night, informed him that the board had said he was to appear before it forthwith.

Not having a very clearly defined notion of what a live board was, Oliver was rather astounded by this intelligence, and was not quite certain whether he ought

An alternative to the workhouse was employment as a chimney-sweep's boy, many of whom were kept small and underfed not only to shin up chimneys, but also to squeeze through windows as accomplices in burglaries. In Oliver Twist, *Mr Gamfield offers to hire Oliver:*

'"Young boys have been smothered in chinneys before now," said another gentleman.

"That's acause they damped the straw afore they lit it in the chimbley to make 'em come down agin," said Gamfield. . . . "Boys is wery obstinit, and wery lazy, gen'lmen, and there's nothink like a good hot blaze to make 'em come down vith a run. It's humane too, gen'lmen, acause, even if they've stuck in the chimbley, roasting their feet makes 'em struggle to hextricate theirselves."'

to laugh or cry. He had no time to think about the matter, however; for Mr Bumble gave him a tap on the head with his cane to wake him up, and another on the back to make him lively, and bidding him follow, conducted him into a large whitewashed room where eight or ten fat gentlemen were sitting round a table, at the top of which, seated in an arm-chair rather higher than the rest, was a particularly fat gentleman with a very round, red face.

'Bow to the board,' said Bumble. Oliver brushed away two or three tears that were lingering in his eyes, and seeing no board but the table, fortunately bowed to that.

'What's your name, boy?' said the gentleman in the high chair.

Oliver was frightened at the sight of so many gentlemen which made him tremble; and the beadle gave him another tap behind, which made him cry; and these two causes made him answer in a very low and hesitating voice; whereupon a gentleman in a white waistcoat said he was a fool. Which was a capital way of raising his spirits, and putting him quite at his ease.

'Boy,' said the gentleman in the high chair, 'listen to me. You know you're an orphan, I suppose?'

'What's that, sir?' inquired poor Oliver.

'The boy *is* a fool – I thought he was,' said the gentleman in the white waistcoat, in a very decided tone. If one member of a class be blessed with an intuitive perception of others of the same race, the gentleman in the white waistcoat was unquestionably well qualified to pronounce an opinion on the matter.

'Hush!' said the gentleman who had spoken first. 'You know you've got no father or mother, and that you were brought up by the parish, don't you?'

'Yes, sir,' replied Oliver, weeping bitterly.

'What are you crying for?' inquired the gentleman in the white waistcoat. And to be sure it was very extraordinary. What *could* the boy be crying for?

'I hope you say your prayers every night,' said another gentleman in a gruff voice, 'and pray for the people who feed you, and take care of you, like a Christian.'

'Yes, sir,' stammered the boy. The gentleman who spoke last was unconsciously right. It would have been *very* like a Christian, and a marvellously good Christian, too, if Oliver had prayed for the people who fed and took care of *him*. But he hadn't, because nobody had taught him.

'Well! You have come here to be educated, and taught a useful trade,' said the red-faced gentleman in the high chair.

'So you'll begin to pick oakum tomorrow morning at six o'clock,' added the surly one in the white waistcoat.

For the combination of both these blessings in the one simple process of picking oakum, Oliver bowed low by the direction of the beadle, and was then hurried away to a large ward, where, on a rough, hard bed he sobbed himself to sleep. What a noble illustration of the tender laws of this favoured country! They let the paupers go to sleep!

Poor Oliver! He little thought, as he lay sleeping in happy unconsciousness of all around him, that the board had that very day arrived at a decision which would exercise the most material influence over all his future fortunes. But they had. And this was it:

The members of this board were very sage, deep, philosophical men, and when they came to turn their attention to the workhouse, they found out at once, what ordinary folks would never have discovered – the poor people liked it! It was a regular place of public entertainment for the poorer classes; a tavern where there was nothing to pay; a public breakfast, dinner, tea, and supper all the year

150

'So they established the rule, that all poor people should have the alternative (for they would compel nobody, not they), of being starved by a gradual process in the house, or by a quick one out of it.' Oliver Twist

round; a brick and mortar elysium, where it was all play and no work. 'Oho!' said the board, looking very knowing; 'we are the fellows to set this to rights; we'll stop it all, in no time.' So, they established the rule, that all poor people should have the alternative (for they would compel nobody, not they), of being starved by a gradual process in the house, or by a quick one out of it. With this view, they contracted with the water-works to lay on an unlimited supply of water; and with a corn-factor to supply periodically small quantities of oatmeal; and issued three meals of thin gruel a day, with an onion twice a week, and half a roll on Sundays. They made a great many other wise and humane regulations having reference to the ladies, which it is not necessary to repeat; kindly undertook to divorce poor married people, in consequence of the great expense of a suit in Doctors' Commons; and, instead of compelling a man to support his family, as they had theretofore done, took his family away from him, and made him a bachelor! There is no saying how many applicants for relief, under these last two heads, might have started up in all classes of society, if it had not been coupled with the workhouse; but the board were long-headed men, and had provided for this difficulty. The relief was inseparable from the workhouse and the gruel; and that frightened people.

For the first six months after Oliver Twist was removed, the system was in full operation. It was rather expensive at first, in consequence of the increase in the undertaker's bill, and the necessity of taking in the clothes of all the paupers, which fluttered loosely on their wasted, shrunken forms, after a week or two's gruel. But the number of workhouse inmates got thin as well as the paupers; and the board were in ecstasies.

The room in which the boys were fed was a large stone hall, with a copper at one end, out of which the master, dressed in an apron for the purpose, and assisted by one or two women, ladled the gruel at meal-times; of which composition each boy had one porringer, and no more – except on festive occasions, and then he had two ounces and a quarter of bread besides. The bowls never wanted washing. The boys polished them with their spoons till they shone again; and when they had performed this operation (which never took very long, the spoons being nearly as large as the bowls), they would sit staring at the copper with such eager eyes as if they could have devoured the very bricks of which it was composed; employing themselves, meanwhile, in sucking their fingers most assiduously, with the view of catching up any stray splashes of gruel that might have been cast thereon. Boys have generally excellent appetites. Oliver Twist and his companions suffered the tortures of slow starvation for three months: at last they got so voracious and wild with hunger, that one boy, who was tall for his age, and hadn't been used to that sort of thing (for his father had kept a small cookshop), hinted darkly to his companions, that unless he had another basin of gruel *per diem,* he was afraid he might some night happen to eat the boy who slept next to him, who happened to be a weakly youth of tender age. He had a wild, hungry eye; and they implicitly believed him. A council was held; lots were cast who should walk up to the master after supper that evening, and ask for more; and it fell to Oliver Twist.

The evening arrived; the boys took their places. The master, in his cook's uniform, stationed himself at the copper; his pauper assistants ranged themselves behind him; the gruel was served out; and a long grace was said over the short commons. The gruel disappeared; the boys whispered to each other, and winked at Oliver, while his next neighbours nudged him. Child as he was, he was desperate with hunger, and reckless with misery. He rose from the table, and advancing to the master, basin and spoon in hand, said: somewhat alarmed at his own temerity:

'Please, sir, I want some more.'

The master was a fat, healthy man; but he turned very pale. He gazed in stupefied astonishment on the small rebel for some seconds, and then clung for support to the copper. The assistants were paralysed with wonder; the boys with fear.

'What!' said the master at length, in a faint voice.

Dickens cared deeply about the plight of the underprivileged, but despite the topicality of his novels and the subsequent reform, it would be a mistake to see them as research material for the student of social history. Jo in *Bleak House* and Johnny in *Our Mutual Friend* are metaphors for the homeless poor and the infant sick respectively. They exist only in the theatre of imagination that he was creating in the streets of London. Dickens' contemporary, Henry Mayhew, on the other hand, was busy reporting on specific individuals; he was interested in the detail, in reporting the poor as they really were. But his division of the poor (in *London Labour and the London Poor*) into categories of those who will work, those who can't, and those who won't, hardly served Dickens' interests in the novels. In his journalism, Dickens is much more cool-headed and far-sighted, but his fiction comes from a different part of his brain; in the novels he is swamped by associations and memories of

'They made a great many other wise and humane regulations. . . [and] kindly undertook to divorce poor married people, in consequence of the great expense of a suit in Doctors' Commons; and instead of compelling a man to support his family, as they had theretofore done, took his family away from him, and made him a bachelor.' Oliver Twist

his own past.

In practical terms the novels provided an 'awakening of interest' and perhaps the best way of tackling the more intangible themes – the underside of the new Victorian system – monetary greed, inhumanity, authoritarianism, bureaucracy, ill-advised philanthropy, and the system's patronising attitude towards the poor:

Sales of *The Pickwick Papers*, Dickens' first novel and published like those that followed, in episodic form, were disappointing – until the introduction in the fourth number of his archetypal low-life figure, Sam Weller, who became Pickwick's servant:

There are in London several old inns, once the head-quarters of celebrated coaches in the days when coaches performed their journeys in a graver and more solemn manner than they do in these times; but which have now degenerated into little more than the abiding and booking places of country waggons. . . .

It was in the yard of one of these inns – of no less celebrated a one than the White Hart – that a man was busily employed in brushing the dirt off a pair of boots, early on the morning succeeding the events narrated in the last chapter. He was habited in a coarse-striped waistcoat, with black calico sleeves, and blue glass buttons; drab breeches and leggings. A bright red handkerchief was wound in a very loose and unstudied style round his neck, and an old white hat was carelessly thrown on one side of his head. There were two rows of boots before him, one cleaned and the other dirty, and at every addition he made to the clean row, he paused from his work, and contemplated its results with evident satisfaction.

Once Sam has engaged the interest of his audience, Dickens uses him to develop a favourite theme: 'why waste time and money on philanthropy abroad when so much needs to be done at home'. Sam performs better than any political broadsheet could. He goes to meet his new step-mother, whom he calls his mother-in-law, and finds her having tea with the greedy drunkard Stiggins, deputy Shepherd in the Ebenezer Temperance Association:

Sam looked round in the direction whence the voice proceeded. It came from a rather stout lady of comfortable appearance, who was seated beside the fire-place in the bar, blowing the fire to make the kettle boil for tea. She was not alone; for on the other side of the fire-place, sitting bolt upright in a high-backed chair, was a man in thread-bare black clothes, with a back almost as long and stiff as that of the chair itself, who caught Sam's most particular and special attention at once.

He was a prim-faced, red-nosed man, with a long, thin countenance, and a semi-rattlesnake sort of eye – rather sharp, but decidedly bad. He wore very short trousers, and black-cotton stockings, which, like the rest of his apparel, were particularly rusty. His looks were starched, but his white neckerchief was not, and its long limp ends straggled over his closely-buttoned waistcoat in a very uncouth and unpicturesque fashion. A pair of old, worn beaver gloves, a

'Picking' oakum – hemp or jute fibre used for such as caulking seams in ships. In The Uncommercial Traveller *Dickens visited the Refractories in Wapping Workhouse, remarking on their volubility:*

'Five pounds indeed! I hain't a going far to pick five pound,' said the Chief of the Refractories, keeping time to herself with her head and chin. 'More than enough to pick what we picks now, in such a place as this, and on wot we gets here!'

broad-brimmed hat, and a faded green umbrella, with plenty of whalebone sticking through the bottom, as if to counterbalance the want of a handle at the top, lay on a chair beside him, and, being disposed in a very tidy and careful manner, seemed to imply that the red-nosed man, whoever he was, had no intention of going away in a hurry.

The appearance of the red-nosed man had induced Sam, at first sight, to more than half suspect that he was the deputy shepherd of whom his estimable parent had spoken. The moment he saw him eat, all doubt on the subject was removed, and he perceived at once that if he purposed to take up his temporary quarters where he was, he must make his footing good without delay. He therefore commenced proceedings by putting his arm over the half-door of the bar, coolly unbolting it, and leisurely walking in.

'Mother-in-law,' said Sam, 'how are you?'

'Why I do believe he is a Weller!' said Mrs W., raising her eyes to Sam's face, with no very gratified expression of countenance.

'I rayther think he is,' said the imperturbable Sam; 'and I hope this here reverend gen'lm'n 'll excuse me saying that I wish I was *the* Weller as owns you, mother-in-law.'

This was a double-barrelled compliment. It implied that Mrs Weller was a most agreeable female, and also that Mr Stiggins had a clerical appearance. It made a visible impression at once; and Sam followed up his advantage by kissing his mother-in-law.

The White Hart Inn, Borough High Street, where Pickwick encounters Sam Weller: 'A double tier of bed-room galleries, with old clumsy balustrades, ran round two sides of the straggling area, and a double row of bells to correspond , sheltered from the weather by a little sloping roof, hung over the door leading to the bar and coffee-room. Two or three gigs and chaise-carts were wheeled up under different little sheds and pent-houses; and the occasional heavy tread of a carthorse, or rattling of a chain at the further end of the yard, announced to anybody who cared about the matter, that the stable lay in that direction.'

'Get along with you!' said Mrs Weller, pushing him away.

'For shame, young man!' said the gentleman with the red nose.

'No offence, sir, no offence,' replied Sam; 'you're wery right, though; it ain't the right sort o' thing, wen mothers-in-law is young and good looking, is it, sir?'

'It's all vanity,' said Mr Stiggins.

'Ah, so it is,' said Mrs Weller, setting her cap to rights.

Sam thought it was, too, but he held his peace.

The deputy shepherd seemed by no means best pleased with Sam's arrival; and when the first effervescence of the compliment had subsided, even Mrs Weller looked as if she could have spared him without the smallest inconvenience. However, there he was; and as he couldn't be decently turned out, they all three sat down to tea.

'And how's father?' said Sam.

At this inquiry, Mrs Weller raised her hands, and turned up her eyes, as if the subject were too painful to be alluded to.

Mr Stiggins groaned.

'What's the matter with that 'ere gen'lm'n?' inquired Sam.

'He's shocked at the way your father goes on in,' replied Mrs Weller.

'Oh, he is, is he?' said Sam.

'And with too good reason,' added Mrs Weller, gravely.

Mr Stiggins took up a fresh piece of toast, and groaned heavily.

'He is a dreadful reprobate,' said Mrs Weller.

'A man of wrath!' exclaimed Mr Stiggins. He took a large semi-circular bite out of the toast, and groaned again.

Sam felt very strongly disposed to give the reverend Mr Stiggins something to groan for, but he repressed his inclination, and merely asked. 'What's the old 'un up to, now?'

'Up to, indeed!' said Mrs Weller. 'Oh, he has a hard heart. Night after night does this excellent man – don't frown, Mr Stiggins: I *will* say you *are* an excellent man – come and sit here, for hours together, and it has not the least effect upon him.'

'Well, that is odd,' said Sam; 'it 'ud have a wery considerable effect upon me, if I wos in his place; I know that.'

'The fact is, my young friend,' said Mr Stiggins, solemnly, 'he has an obderrate bosom. Oh, my young friend, who else could have resisted the pleading of sixteen of our fairest sisters, and withstood their exhortations to subscribe to our noble society for providing the infant negroes in the West Indies with flannel waistcoats and moral pocket handkerchiefs?'

'What's a moral pocket ankercher?' said Sam; 'I never see one o' them articles o' furniter.'

'Those which combine amusement with instruction, my young friend,' replied Mr Stiggins: 'blending select tales with wood-cuts.'

'Oh, I know,' said Sam; 'them as hangs up in the linen-drapers' shops, with beggars' petitions and all that 'ere upon 'em?'

Mr Stiggins began a third round of toast, and nodded assent.

'And he wouldn't be persuaded by the ladies, wouldn't he?' said Sam.

'Sat and smoked his pipe, and said the infant negroes were – what did he say the infant negroes were?' said Mrs Weller.

'Little humbugs,' replied Mr Stiggins, deeply affected.

'Said the infant negroes were little humbugs,' repeated Mrs Weller. And they both groaned at the atrocious conduct of the old gentleman.

A great many more iniquities of a similar nature might have been disclosed, only the toast being all eaten, the tea having got very weak, and Sam holding out no indications of meaning to go, Mr Stiggins suddenly recollected that he had a most pressing appointment with the shepherd, and took himself off accordingly.

The tea-things had been scarcely put away, and the hearth swept up, when the London coach deposited Mr Weller senior at the door; his legs deposited him in the bar; and his eyes showed him his son.

'What, Sammy!' exclaimed the father.

'What, old Nobs!' ejaculated the son. And they shook hands heartily.

'Werry glad to see you, Sammy,' said the elder Mr Weller, 'though how you've managed to get over your mother-in-law, is a mystery to me. I only vish you'd

156

'"No, no; reg'lar rotation, as Jack Ketch said, wen he tied the men up. Sorry to keep you a waitin', sir, but I'll attend to you directly."'
Sam Weller, shoe-shine, in The Pickwick
Papers

write me out the receipt, that's all.'

'Hush!' said Sam, 'she's at home, old feller.'

'She ain't vithin hearin',' replied Mr Weller; 'she always goes and blows up, down stairs, for a couple of hours after tea; so we'll just give ourselves a damp, Sammy.'

'Saying this, Mr Weller mixed two glasses of spirits and water, and produced a couple of pipes. The father and son sitting down opposite each other: Sam on one side of the fire, in the high-backed chair, and Mr Weller senior on the other, in an

157

easy ditto: they proceeded to enjoy themselves with all due gravity.

'Anybody been here, Sammy?' asked Mr Weller senior, drily, after a long silence.

Sam nodded an expressive assent.

'Red-nosed chap?' inquired Mr Weller.

Sam nodded again.

'Amiable man that 'ere, Sammy,' said Mr Weller, smoking violently.

'Seems so,' observed Sam.

'Good hand at accounts,' said Mr Weller.

'Is he?' said Sam.

'Borrows eighteenpence on Monday, and comes on Tuesday for a shillin' to make it up half a crown; calls again on Vensday for another half crown to make it five shillin's; and goes on, doubling, till he gets it up to a five pund note in no time, like them sums in the 'rithmetic book 'bout the nails in the horse's shoes, Sammy.'

Sam intimated by a nod that he recollected the problem alluded to by his parent.

'So you vouldn't subscribe to the flannel veskits?' said Sam, after another interval of smoking.

'Cert'nly not,' replied Mr Weller; 'what's the good o' flannel veskits to the young nigglers abroad? But I'll tell you what it is, Sammy,' said Mr Weller, lowering his voice, and bending across the fire-place; 'I'd come down wery handsome towards strait veskits for some people at home.'

As Mr Weller said this, he slowly recovered his former position, and winked at his first-born, in a profound manner.

'It cert'nly seems a queer start to send out pocket ankerchers to people as don't know the use on 'em,' observed Sam.

'They're alvays a doin' some gammon of that sort, Sammy,' replied his father. 'T'other Sunday I wos walkin' up the road, wen who should I see, a standin' at a chapel-door, with a blue soup-plate in her hand, but your mother-in-law! I werily believe there was change for a couple o' suv'rins in it, then, Sammy, all in ha'pence; and as the people come out, they rattled the pennies in it, till you'd ha' thought that no mortal plate as ever was baked, could ha' stood the wear and tear. What d'ye think it was all for?'

'For another tea-drinkin', perhaps,' said Sam.

'Not a bit on it,' replied the father; 'for the shepherd's water-rate, Sammy.'

'The shepherd's water-rate!' said Sam.

'Ay,' replied Mr Weller, 'there was three quarters owin', and the shepherd hadn't paid a farden, not he – perhaps it might be on account that the water warn't o' much use to him, for it's wery little o' that tap he drinks, Sammy, wery; he knows a trick worth a good half dozen of that, he does. Hows'ever it warn't paid, and so they cuts the water off. Down goes the shepherd to chapel, gives out as he's a persecuted saint, and says he hopes the heart of the turncock as cut the water off, 'll be softened, and turned in the right vay: but he rayther thinks he's booked for somethin' uncomfortable. Upon this, the women calls a meetin', sings a hymn, wotes your mother-in-law into the chair, wolunteers a col-lection next Sunday, and hands it all over to the shepherd. And if he ain't got enough out on 'em, Sammy, to make him free of the water company for life,' said Mr Weller, in conclusion, 'I'm one Dutchman, and you're another, and that's all about it.'

Mr Weller smoked for some minutes in silence, and then resumed:

'The worst o' these here shepherds is, my boy, that they reg'larly turns the heads of all the young ladies, about here. Lord bless their little hearts, they thinks it's all right, and don't know no better; but they're the wictims o' gammon, Samivel, they're the wictims o' gammon.'

'I s'pose they are,' said Sam.

'Nothin' else,' said Mr Weller, shaking his head gravely; 'and wot aggrawates me, Samivel, is to see 'em a wastin' all their time and labour in making clothes for copper-coloured people as don't want 'em, and taking no notice of flesh-coloured Christians as do. If I'd my vay, Samivel, I'd just stick some o' these here lazy shepherds behind a heavy wheelbarrow, and run 'em up and down a fourteen-inch-wide plank all day. That 'ud shake the nonsense out of 'em, if anythin' vould.'

Mr Weller having delivered his gentle recipe with strong emphasis, eked out by a variety of nods and contortions of the eye, emptied his glass at a draught, and knocked the ashes out of his pipe, with native dignity.

The mosaic of change which occurred in the first half of the nineteenth century called into being the most elaborate bureaucratic apparatus the world had ever seen. Dickens satirises the paper pushers in many forms in his novels, not least in the person (it is as life-like in its full description as any of his characters) of the Circumlocution Office in *Little Dorrit*.

The Circumlocution Office was (as everybody knows without being told) the most important Department under Government. No public business of any kind could possibly be done at any time without the acquiescence of the Circumlocution Office. Its finger was in the largest public pie, and in the smallest public tart. It was equally impossible to do the plainest right and to undo the plainest wrong without the express authority of the Circumlocution Office. If another Gunpowder Plot had been discovered half an hour before the lighting of the match, nobody would have been justified in saving the parliament until there had been half a score of boards, half a bushel of minutes, several sacks of official memoranda, and a family-vault full of ungrammatical correspondence, on the part of the Circumlocution Office.

The glorious establishment had been early in the field, when the one sublime principle involving the difficult art of governing a country, was first distinctly revealed to statesmen. It had been foremost to study that bright revelation and to carry its shining influence through the whole of the official proceedings. Whatever was required to be done, the Circumlocution Office was beforehand with all the public departments in the art of perceiving – HOW NOT TO DO IT.

The bureaucrats who run the Circumlocution Office go under the name of Barnacle. Arthur Clennam intends to enquire of the nature of Mr Dorrit's debt, which has landed him in the Marshalsea prison:

The Barnacle family had for some time helped to administer the Circumlocution Office. The Tite Barnacle Branch, indeed, considered themselves in a general way as having vested rights in that direction, and took it ill if any other family had much to say to it. The Barnacles were a very high family, and a very large family. They were dispersed all over the public offices, and held all sorts of public places. Either the nation was under a load of obligations to the Barnacles, or the Barnacles were under a load of obligation to the nation. It was not quite unanimously settled which; the Barnacles having their opinion, the nation theirs....

Mr Barnacle dated from a better time, when the country was not so parisimonious and the Circumlocution Office was not so badgered. He wound and wound folds of white cravat round his neck, as he wound and wound folds of tape and paper round the neck of the country. His wristbands and collar were oppressive; his voice and manner were oppressive. He had a large watch-chain and bunch of seals, a coat buttoned up to inconvenience, a waistcoat buttoned up to inconvenience, an unwrinkled pair of trousers, a stiff pair of boots. He was altogether splendid, massive, overpowering, and impracticable. He seemed to have been sitting for his portrait to Sir Thomas Lawrence all the days of his life. 'Mr Clennam?' said Mr Barnacle. 'Be seated.'

Mr Clennam became seated.

'You have called on me, I believe,' said Mr Barnacle, 'at the Circumlocution –' giving it the air of a word of about five-and-twenty syllables – 'Office'.

'I have taken that liberty.'

Mr Barnacle solemnly bent his head as who should say, 'I do not deny that it is a liberty; proceed to take another liberty, and let me know your business.'

'Allow me to observe that I have been for some years in China, am quite a stranger at home, and have no personal motive or interest in the inquiry I am about to make.'

Mr Barnacle tapped his fingers on the table, and, as if he were now sitting for his portrait to a new strange artist, appeared to say to his visitor, 'If you will be good enough to take me with my present lofty expression, I shall feel obliged.'

I have found a debtor in the Marshalsea Prison of the name of Dorrit, who has been there many years. I wish to investigate his confused affairs so far as to ascertain whether it may not be possible, after this lapse of time, to ameliorate his unhappy condition. The name of Mr Tite Barnacle has been mentioned to me as representing some highly influential interest among his creditors. Am I correctly informed?'

It being one of the principles of the Circumlocution Office never, on any account whatever, to give a straightforward answer, Mr Barnacle said, 'Possibly.'

'On behalf of the Crown, may I ask, or as private individual?'

'The Circumlocution Department, sir,' Mr Barnacle replied, 'may have possibly recommended – possibly – I cannot say – that some public claim against the insolvent estate of a firm or co-partnership to which this person may have belonged, should be enforced. The question may have been, in the course of official business, referred to the Circumlocution Department for its consideration. The Department may have either originated, or confirmed, a Minute making that recommendation.'

160

'The monthly meetings of the Brick Lane Branch of the United Grand Junction Ebenezer Temperance Association, were held in a large room, pleasantly and airily situated at the top of a safe and commodious ladder.' The Pickwick Papers. *Here Brother Stiggins from the Dorking branch gets his just deserts at the hands of Sam Weller's father.*

'I assume this to be the case, then.'

'The Circumlocution Department,' said Mr Barnacle, 'is not responsible for any gentleman's assumptions.'

'May I inquire how I can obtain official information as to the real state of the case?'

'It is competent,' said Barnacle, 'to any member of the – Public,' mentioning that obscure body with reluctance, as his natural enemy, 'to memorialise the Circumlocution Department. Such formalities as are required to be observed in so doing, may be known on application to the proper branch of that Department.'

'Which is the proper branch?'

'I must refer you,' returned Mr Barnacle, ringing the bell, 'to the Department itself for a formal answer to that inquiry.'

'Excuse my mentioning –'

'The Department is accessible to the – Public,' Mr Barnacle was always checked a little by that word of impertinent signification, 'if the – Public approaches it according to the official forms; if the – Public does not approach it according to the official forms, the – Public has itself to blame.'

Mr Barnacle made him a severe bow, as a wounded man of family, a wounded man of place, and a wounded man of gentlemanly residence, all rolled into one; and he made Mr Barnacle a bow, and was shut out into Mews Street by the flabby footman.

Having got to this pass, he resolved as an exercise in perseverance, to betake himself again to the Circumlocution Office, and try what satisfaction he could get there. So he went back to the Circumlocution Office, and once more sent up his card to Barnacle Junior by a messenger who took it very ill indeed that he should come back again, and who was eating mashed potatoes and gravy behind a partition by the hall fire.

He was readmitted to the presence of Barnacle Junior, and found that young gentleman singeing his knees now, and gaping his weary way on to four o'clock.

'I say. Look here. You stick to us in a devil of a manner,' said Barnacle Junior, looking over his shoulder.

'I want to know –'

'Look here. Upon my soul you mustn't come into the place saying you want to know, you know,' remonstrated Barnacle Junior, turning about and putting up the eye-glass.

'I want to know,' said Arthur Clennam, who had made up his mind to persistence in one short form of words, 'the precise nature of the claim of the Crown against a prisoner for debt, named Dorrit.'

'I say. Look here. You really are going it at a great pace, you know. Egad, you haven't got an appointment,' said Barnacle Junior, as if the thing were growing serious.

'I want to know,' said Arthur, and repeated his case.

Barnacle Junior stared at him until his eye-glass fell out, and then put it in again and stared at him until it fell out again. 'You have no right to come this sort of move,' he then observed with the greatest weakness. 'Look here. What do you mean? You told me you didn't know whether it was public business or not.'

'I have now ascertained that it is public business,' returned the suitor, 'and I want to know' – and again repeated his monotonous inquiry.

Its effect upon young Barnacle was to make him repeat in a defenceless way, 'Look here! Upon my SOUL you mustn't come into the place saying you want to know, you know!' The effect of that upon Arthur Clennam was to make him repeat his inquiry in exactly the same words and tone as before. The effect of that upon young Barnacle was to make him a wonderful spectacle of failure and helplessness.

'Well, I tell you what. Look here. You had better try the Secretarial Department,' he said at last, sidling to the bell and ringing it. 'Jenkinson,' to the mashed potatoes messenger, 'Mr Wobbler!'

Arthur Clennam, who now felt that he had devoted himself to the storming of the Circumlocution Office, and must go through with it, accompanied the messenger to another floor of the building, where the functionary pointed out Mr

'How much red tape may there be, that could look round on the faces which now hem us in – for our appearance here has caused a rush from all points to a common centre – the lowering foreheads, the sallow cheeks, the brutal eyes, the matted hair, the infected, vermin-haunted heaps of rags – and say, "I have thought of this. I have not dismissed the thing. I have neither blustered it away, nor frozen it away, nor tied it up and put it away, nor smoothly said pooh, pooh! to it when it has been shown to me"?' Reprinted Pieces

Wobbler's room. He entered that apartment, and found two gentlemen sitting face to face at a large and easy desk, one of whom was polishing a gunbarrel on his pocket-handkerchief, while the other was spreading marmalade on bread with a paper-knife.

'Mr Wobbler?' inquired the suitor.

Both gentlemen glanced at him, and seemed surprised at his assurance.

'So he went,' said the gentleman with the gun-barrel, who was an extremely deliberate speaker, 'down to his cousin's place, and took the Dog with him by rail. Inestimable Dog. Flew at the porter fellow when he was put into the dog-box, and flew at the guard when he was taken out. He got half-a-dozen fellows into a Barn, and a good supply of Rats, and timed the Dog. Finding the Dog able to do it immensely, made the match, and heavily backed the Dog. When the match came off, some devil of a fellow was bought over, Sir, Dog was made drunk, Dog's master was cleaned out.'

'Mr Wobbler?' inquired the suitor.

The gentleman who was spreading the marmalade returned, without looking up from that occupation, 'What did he call the Dog?'

'Called him Lovely,' said the other gentleman. 'Said the Dog was the perfect picture of the old aunt from whom he had expectations. Found him particularly like her when hocussed.'

'Mr Wobbler?' said the suitor.

Both gentleman laughed for some time. The gentleman with the gun-barrel, considering it, on inspection, in a satisfactory state, referred it to the other; receiving confirmation of his views, he fitted it into its place in the case before him, and took out the stock and polished that, softly whistling.

'Mr Wobbler?' said the suitor.

'What's the matter?' then said Mr Wobbler, with his mouth full.

'I want to know –' and Arthur Clennam again mechanically set forth what he wanted to know.

'Can't inform you,' observed Mr Wobbler, apparently to his lunch. 'Never heard of it. Nothing at all to do with it. Better try Mr Clive, second door on the left in the next passage.'

'Perhaps he will give me the same answer.'

'Very likely. Don't know anything about it,' said Mr Wobbler.

The suitor turned away and had left the room, when the gentleman with the gun called out 'Mister! Hallo!'

He looked in again.

'Shut the door after you. You're letting in a devil of a draught here!'

Dickens' first-hand experience of the Law, both as a journalist in Doctor's Commons and as a clerk in law firms, provided him with sufficient reason for Mr Bumble to describe it as 'a ass – a idiot!' But it is in *Bleak House* when the interminable case of 'Jarndyce versus Jarndyce' achieves the status of monster capable of swallowing up generations of people who cross its path, that Dickens really gets to grips with it:

The one great principle of the English law is, to make business for itself. There is no other principle distinctly, certainly, and consistently maintained through all its

A view of Goldsmiths Buildings, the Temple, where in the novel Our Mutual Friend, *Mortimer Lightwood dwells. 'Whosoever had gone out of Fleet Street into the Temple at the date of this history, and had wandered disconsolate about the Temple until he stumbled upon a dismal churchyard, and had looked up at the dismal windows commanding that churchyard until at the most dismal window of them all he saw a dismal boy, would in him have beheld, at one grand comprehensive swoop of the eye, the managing clerk, junior clerk, common-law clerk, conveyancing clerk, every refinement and department of clerk, of Mr Mortimer Lightwood, erewhile called in the newspapers eminent solicitor.'*

narrow turnings. Viewed by this light it becomes a coherent scheme, and not the monstrous maze the laity are apt to think it. Let them but once clearly perceive that its grand principle is to make business for itself at their expense, and surely they will cease to grumble.

London Reporting

First in *Master Humphrey's Clock* and then in *The Daily News*, Dickens had attempted to produce a platform for his views about what needed to be changed. The first failed in its editorial format to capture the interest of the public, and he left *The Daily News* after seventeen issues because he felt that the railway businessmen who owned its stock, were limiting his editorial freedom. But on March 30th, 1850, Dickens launched an immediately and extremely successful periodical of 'uncompromising humanitarian radicalism' which he called *Household Words*. It promoted workers' rights, union organisation, and proper preventive measures

Took's Court, the original of Cook's Court in Bleak House*: 'On the eastern borders of Chancery Lane, that is to say, more particularly in Cook's Court, Cursitor Street, Mr Snagsby, Law Stationer pursues his lawful calling.'*

against factory accidents; it exposed religious and political hypocrisies, and worked for the reform of both the educational and prison systems.

In *Household Words*, Dickens used pure fact like never before, astutely bringing to bear irony, allegory and humour, whatever editorial tools he felt were required to present the facts and statistics to his readers in the most accessible manner. His main priority was sanitary reform – although he was very keen that the poor should be properly educated, he knew there was no chance of that until they were clean and free of disease. He employed his brother-in-law, Henry Austin, who had become Secretary of the Sanitary Commission, to provide the facts for a series of articles about water supply and refuse disposal, about the living environments of the slums from the '30s onwards. . . . The notion of slum clearance and municipal planning had barely been aired before *Household Words*.

In his journalism Dickens used information that he had gathered

165

walking, often incognito, around the worst slums in London. As an editor he had, in more than one sense, very little competition on the newsstands; it is quite certain that no editor drew upon better first-hand fact than Dickens.

Outside the magazine he lent considerable weight to sanitary reform associations and to sanitary legislation in general. In line with his abhorrence of paper pushers, red tape, and the 'philosopher' theorists, Dickens was a pragmatist.

He applied to serve as a police magistrate, commissioner or inspector. 'I think I could do good service,' he said, adding that he would enter into it with his 'whole heart'. When he wasn't taken up on the offer he turned his energies instead to a philanthropic partnership with Angela Burdett-Coutts – he, at 26, the bright ascending star, she an earnest young heiress of the Coutts banking fortune, just 24. They became the greatest of friends, and as her adviser, Dickens declared: 'Trust me that I will be a faithful steward of your bounty; and that there is no charge in the Wide World I would accept with so much pride and happiness as any such from you.'

He had always been very concerned that working and lower middle class children should be properly educated, and when in 1843, a lawyer's clerk named Samuel Starey, treasurer of the ragged school at Field Lane, Holborn, wrote to Miss Coutts for financial help, he went at Miss Coutts' request to visit the school, set on the first floor of a rotten house in the environs of *Oliver Twist*. In a letter to the Editors of *The Daily News*, he describes what he found:

It was a hot summer night; and the air of Field Lane and Saffron Hill was not improved by such weather, nor were the people in those streets very sober or honest company. Being unacquainted with the exact locality of the school, I was fain to make some inquiries about it. These were very jocosely received in general; but everybody knew where it was, and gave the right direction to it. The prevailing idea among the loungers (the greater part of them the very sweepings of the streets and station houses) seemed to be, that the teachers were quixotic, and the school upon the whole 'a lark.' But there was certainly a kind of rough respect for the intention, and (as I have said) nobody denied the school or its whereabouts, or refused assistance in directing to it.

It consisted at that time of either two or three – I forget which – miserable rooms, upstairs in a miserable house. In the best of these, the pupils in the female school were being taught to read and write; and though there were among the number, many wretched creatures steeped in degradation to the lips, they were tolerably quiet, and listened with apparent earnestness and patience to their instructors. The appearance of this room was sad and melancholy, of course – how could it be otherwise! – but, on the whole, encouraging.

The close, low, chamber at the back, in which the boys were crowded, was so foul and stifling as to be, at first, almost insupportable. But its moral aspect was so far worse than its physical, that this was soon forgotten. Huddled together on

There was no age limit for drinking and, before 1839, no licensing hours. Between them, the new beer shops and the gin palaces mopped up most of the poor classes of London, but Dickens was not censorious. He felt that the social reformer's priorities lay elsewhere: sort out the environmental pressures, sanitary conditions and repression of the poor, and the drink problem would subside.

a bench about the room, and shown out by some flaring candles stuck against the walls, were a crowd of boys, varying from mere infants to young men; sellers of fruit, herbs, lucifer-matches, flints; sleepers under the dry arches of bridges; young thieves and beggars – with nothing natural to youth about them: with nothing frank, ingenuous, or pleasant in their faces; low-browed, vicious, cunning, wicked; abandoned of all help but this; speeding downward to destruction; and UNUTTERABLY IGNORANT.

This, Reader, was one room as full as it could hold; but these were only grains in sample of a Multitude that are perpetually sifting through these schools; in sample of a Multitude who had within them once, and perhaps have now, the elements of men as good as you or I, and maybe infinitely better; in sample of a Multitude among whose doomed and sinful ranks (oh, think of this, and think of them!) the child of any man upon the earth, however lofty his degree, must, as by Destiny and Fate, be found, if, at its birth, it were consigned to such an infancy

and nurture, as these fallen creatures had!

This was the Class I saw at the Ragged School. They could not be trusted with books; they could only be instructed orally; they were difficult of reduction to anything like attention, obedience, or decent behaviour; their benighted ignorance in reference to the Deity, or to any social duty (how could they guess at any social duty, being so descarded by all social teachers but the jailer and the hangman!) was terrible to see. Yet, even here, and among these, something had been done already. The Ragged School was of recent date and very poor; but it had inculcated some association with the name of the Almighty, which was not an oath: and had taught them to look forward in a hymn (they sang it) to another life, which would correct the miseries and woes of this.

The new exposition I found in this Ragged School, of the frightful neglect by the State of those whom it punishes so constantly, and whom it might, as easily

Dickens often took his friends on voyages through such slums, visiting some of the lodging houses as he did so: he would go in quite blithely but there are reports of his companions, overpowered by the stench within, who came out into the streets to be sick.

'I wonder whether the race of men . . . could deduce such an astounding inference as the existence of a polished state of society that bore with the public savagery of neglected children in the streets of its capital city, and was proud of its power by sea and land, and never used its power to seize and save them!' The Uncommercial Traveller

and less expensively, instruct and save; together with the sight I had seen there, in the heart of London; haunted me, and finally impelled me to an endeavour to bring these Institutions under the notice of the Government; with some faint hope that the vastness of the question would supersede the Theology of the schools, and that the Bench of Bishops might adjust the latter question, after some small grant had been conceded. I made the attempt: and have heard no more of the subject, from that hour.

Strangely, in his suggestions for reform of the methods of teaching in Ragged Schools Dickens reveals the kind of strict, paternalist attitude that he disliked in others. He wanted the poor to be neat, tidy, clean and to lead good lives. 'I told her,' he says in a letter to John Forster about his dealings with Miss Coutts, 'that it was of immense importance they should be washed.' And, to *The Daily News* he suggests that there should be set limits as to the ideas that the pupils can be expected to absorb:

I have no desire to praise the system pursued in the Ragged Schools: which is necessarily very imperfect, if indeed there be one. So far as I have any means of

Ragged Schools. *'The name implies the purpose. They who are too ragged, wretched, filthy, and forlorn, to enter any other place: who could gain admission into no charity-school, and who would be driven from any church door: are invited to come in here, and find some people not depraved, willing to teach them something, and show them some sympathy, and stretch a hand out, which is not the hand of Law, for their correction . . .'*
Letters

'. . . I was first attracted to the subject, and indeed was first made conscious of [the Schools'] existence, about two years ago, or more, by seeing an advertisement in the papers dated from West Street, Saffron Hill, stating "That a room had been opened and supported in that wretched neighbourhood for upwards of twelve months, where religious instruction had been imparted to the poor." Letters

judging of what is taught here, I should individually object to it, as not being sufficiently secular, and as presenting too many religious mysteries and difficulties, to minds not sufficiently prepared for their reception.

In helping Miss Coutts to set up a reform home for prostitutes at Urania Cottage in Shepherds Bush, he issues 'An Appeal to Fallen Women' which promises help, provided they show themselves to deserve it.

You will see, on beginning to read this letter, that it is not addressed to you by name. But I address it to a woman – a very young woman still – who was born to be happy and has lived miserably; who has no prospect before her but sorrow, or behind her but a wasted youth; who, if she has ever been a mother, has felt shame instead of pride in her own unhappy child.

You are such a person, or this letter would not be put into your hands. If you have ever wished (I know you must have done so some time) for a chance of rising out of your sad life, and having friends, a quiet home, means of being useful to yourself and others, peace of mind, self-respect, everything you have lost, pray read it attentively and reflect upon it afterwards.

I am going to offer you, not the chance but the *certainty* of all these blessings, if you will exert yourself to deserve them. And do not think that I write to you as if I felt myself very much above you, or wished to hurt your feelings by reminding you of the situation in which you are placed. God forbid! I mean nothing but kindness to you, and I write as if you were my sister.

Think for a moment what your present situation is. Think how impossible it is that it ever can be better if you continue to live as you have lived, and how certain it is that it must be worse. You know what the streets are; you know how cruel the companions that you find there are; you know the vices practised there, and to what wretched consequences they bring you, even while you are young. Shunned by decent people, marked out from all other kinds of women as you walk

170

Throughout his novels Dickens exposed the mindless systems of education current in the nineteenth century. From Nicholas Nickleby *the first class in English spelling and philosophy, conducted by Squeers:*

'"We go upon the practical mode of teaching, Nickleby; the regular education system. C-l-e-a-n, clean, verb active, to make bright, to scour. W-i-n, win, d-e-r, winder, a casement. When the boy knows this out of a book, he goes and does it."'

along, avoided by the very children, hunted by the police, imprisoned, and only set free to be imprisoned over and over again – reading this very letter in a common jail you have already dismal experience of the truth.

But to grow old in such a way of life, and among such company – to escape an early death from terrible disease, or your own maddened hand, and arrive at old age in such a course – will be an aggravation of every misery that you know now, which words cannot describe. Imagine for yourself the bed on which you, then an object terrible to look at, will lie down to die. Imagine all the long, long years of shame, want, crime, and ruin that will arise before you. And by that dreadful day, and by the judgment that will follow it, and by the recollection that you are certain to have then, when it is too late, of the offer that is made to you now, when it is NOT too late, I implore you think of it and weigh it well.

There is a lady in this town who from the window of her house has seen such as you going past at night, and has felt her heart bleed at the sight. She is what is called a great lady, but she has looked after you with compassion as being of her own sex and nature, and the thought of such fallen women has troubled her in her bed.

She has resolved to open at her own expense a place of refuge near London for a small number of females, who without such help are lost for ever, and to make a HOME for them. In this home they will be taught all household work that would be

useful to them in a home of their own and enable them to make it comfortable and happy. In this home, which stands in a pleasant country lane and where each may have her little flower-garden if she pleases, they will be treated with the greatest kindness; will lead an active, cheerful, healthy life: will learn many things it is profitable and good to know, and being entirely removed from all who have any knowledge of their past career will begin life afresh and be able to win a good name and character.

And because it is not the lady's wish that these young women should be shut out from the world after they have repented and learned to do their duty there, and because it is her wish and object that they may be restored to society – a comfort to themselves and it – they will be supplied with every means, when some time shall have elapsed and their conduct shall have fully proved their earnestness and reformation, to go abroad, where in a distant country they may become the faithful wives of honest men, and live and die in peace.

I have been told that those who see you daily in this place believe that there are virtuous inclinations lingering within you, and that you may be reclaimed. I offer the Home I have described in these few words to you.

A year earlier, in 1847, he suggests in a letter to Miss Coutts that the prostitutes be shipped abroad and married off, and that a system of points be used to ensure that the fallen women continue to merit the assistance offered them:

While advances in printing made literature more available than ever before in books and periodicals, literacy was far from common. Dickens recognized this as a social evil, but did not flinch from using comic mimicry (something at which he had been particularly adept long before he became a writer) to express it: In Our Mutual Friend *Mr Boffin hires Silas Wegg as his literary advisor:*

"'Bought him at a sale," said Mr Boffin.

"Eight wolumes. Red and gold. Purple ribbon in every wollume, to keep the place where you leave off. Do you know him?"

"The book's name, Sir?" inquired Silas.

"I thought you might have know'd him without it," said Mr Boffin slightly disappointed. "His name is Decline-And-Fall -Off-the-Rooshan-Empire."'

In reference to the Asylum, it seems to me very expedient that you should know, if possible, whether the Government would assist you to the extent of informing you from time to time into what distant parts of the World, women could be sent for marriage, with the greatest hope for their future families, and with the greatest service to the existing male population, whether expatriated from England or born there. If these poor women *could* be sent abroad with the distinct recognition and aid of the Government, it would be a service to the effort. But I have (with reason) a doubt of all Governments in England considering such a question in the light in which men undertaking that immense responsibility, are bound, before God, to consider it. And therefore I would suggest this appeal to you, merely as something which you owe to yourself and to the experiment; the failure of which, does not at all affect the immeasurable goodness and happiness of the project itself.

I do not think it would be necessary, in the first instance at all events, to build a house for the Asylum. There are many houses, either in London or in the immediate neighbourhood, that could be altered for the purpose. It would be necessary to limit the number of inmates, but I would make the reception of them as easy as possible to themselves. I would put it in the power of any Governor of a London Prison to send an unhappy creature of this kind (by her own choice of course) straight from his prison, when her term expired, to the asylum. I would put it in the power of any penitent creature to knock at the door, and say For God's sake, take me in. But I would divide the interior into two portions; and into the first portion I would put all new-comers without exception, as a place of probation, whence they should pass, by their own good conduct and self-denial alone, into what I may call the Society of the house. I do not know of any plan, so well conceived, or so firmly grounded in a knowledge of human nature, or so judiciously addressed to it, for observance in this place, as what if called Captain Maconnochie's Mark System, which I will try very roughly and generally, to describe.

A woman or girl coming to the asylum, it is explained to her that she has come there for *useful* repentance and reform and means her past way of life has been dreadful in its nature and consequences, and full of affliction, misery, and despair to *herself*. Never mind society while she is at that pass. Society has used her ill and turned away from her, and she cannot be expected to take much heed of its rights or wrongs. It is destructive to herself, and there is no hope in it, or in her, as long as she pursues it. It is explained to her that she is degraded and fallen, but not lost, having this shelter; and that the means of Return to Happiness are now about to be put into her own hands, and trusted to her own keeping. That with this view, she is instead of being placed in this probationary class for a month, or two months, or three months, or any specified *time* whatever, required to earn there a certain number of *Marks* (they are mere scratches in a book) so that she may make her probation a very short one, or a very long one, according to her own conduct. For so much work, she has so many marks; for a day's good conduct, so many more. For every instance of ill-temper, disrespect, bad language, any outbreak of any sort or kind, so many – a very large number in proportion to her receipts – are deducted. A perfect Debtor and Creditor account is kept between her and the Superintendent, for every day; and the state of that account, it is in her own power and nobody else's, to adjust to her advantage. It is expressly pointed out to her, that before she can be considered qualified to return to any kind of society – even to the Society of the asylum – she must give proofs of her power of self-restraint and her sincerity, and her determination to try to shew that she deserves the confidence it is proposed to place in her.

Clearly Miss Coutts upbraided him for his attitude towards the women, for in his next letter to her, he says -

Your two objections to my sketch of a plan, I wish to offer half a dozen words upon.

1st As to Marriage. I do not propose to put that hope before them as the immediate end and object to be gained, but assuredly to keep it in view as the possible consequence of a sincere, true, practical repentance, and an altered life.

It is a very peculiar aspect of Dickens' genius that he attacks the very vices – authoritarian and patronising attitudes – that he himself has. And there are many inconsistencies in his social and political judgements too (he eventually even became disenchanted with the work of the Ragged Schools). His judgements were never formulated into a coherent system, however, and were not meant as the basis of any kind of 'thought' on his part. He was very deeply instinctive in them, attacking anything that

In and around Wych Street and Catherine Street, the very great problem of prostitution was obvious. Dickens' reaction was, to say the least, practical – ship them off to the other side of the world and find native or any other husbands for them. Fortunately he worked in tandem with the enlightened philanthropist Miss Burdett-Coutts, and together they found a middle way.

As in his philosophy of education of the poor, practical, strict and paternalistic, but determinedly against 'fire and brimstone' techniques ('I am confident that harm is done to this class of minds by the injudicious use of the Old [Testament]'), so in expounding his highly structured plan for prostitutes, he wrote: 'One great point that I try to bear in mind continually, and which I hope the clergyman will steadily remember, is, that these unfortunate creatures are to be Tempted to virtue. They cannot be dragged, driven, or frightened.'

Left:

In David Copperfield, *Martha comes to London to find refuge in anonymity, but like thousands of women in similar circumstances, is brought to ruin. Her unexpected appearance before David – as a lady of the night – leads, like many such chance events in the small world of Dickens' London, to major developments in the story:*

'My shortest way home, – and I naturally took the shortest way on such a night – was through St Martin's Lane. Now, the church which gives its name to the lane, stood in a less fine situation at that time; there being no open space before it, and the lane winding down to the Strand. As I passed the steps of the portico, I encountered, at the corner, a woman's face. It looked in mine, passed across the narrow lane, and disappeared. I knew it. I had seen it somewhere. But I could not remember where.'

threatened him which reminded him of his own past: for example, it was the religious bias of the teaching in the Ragged Schools which reminded him of the doctrinaire religious teaching of his own youth and helped cool his attitude to the schools: 'I heard a lady visitor the night I was among you propounding questions in reference to the "Lamb of God", which I most unquestionably would not suffer anyone to put to my children, recollecting the immense absurdities that were suggested to my

175

Pip, Herbert and Startop make their anxious way to Mill Pond Stairs to pick up the convict Magwitch, thence past London Bridge 'and old Billingsgate market [shown here] with its oyster boats and Dutchmen, and the White Tower and Traitor's Gate. . .' and on to Gravesend in order to put Magwitch on the Continental-bound steamer and thus effect his escape. Dickens travelled the exact route, by way of research, before writing Great Expectations.

childhood by the like injudicious catechising,' he wrote to Starey.

The Death Sentence was another point on which eventually (in two letters to the *Times*) he changed his mind: first he was against it and later in favour, though he remained set against hangings in public – perhaps still affected by the public execution of the murderer Courvoisier, which he witnessed as a young man. On the day, the condemned man emerged above a baying crowd, 'feeble and agonised . . . with ringing hands – uplifted though fettered – and moving lips as if in prayer.' The atmosphere generated by the experience – 'a ghastly night in Hades with demons' – finds expression in some of the darker moments in *Great Expectations*. Here is the piece where Pip tries to organise the escape of his benefactor, the convict Magwitch, otherwise known as Provis. The 'Judas' Compeyson, whom Pip had been surprised by years earlier when he had carried food and a file to Magwitch on the marshes, also appears, in his usual shadowy, misted, half-glimpsed state:

We were up early. As we walked to and fro, all four together, before breakfast, I

176

'"Is he there?" said Herbert.

"Not yet."

"Right! He was not to come down till he saw us. Can you see his signal?"

"Not well from here; but I think I see it. – Now, I see him! Pull both. Easy, Herbert. Oars!"

We touched the stairs lightly for a single moment, and he was on board and we were off again. He had a boat cloak with him, and a black canvas bag, and he looked as like a river-pilot as my heart could have wished.

"Dear boy!" he said, putting his arm on my shoulder as he took his seat. "Faithful dear boy, well done. Thankye, thankye!"' Great Expectations

deemed it right to recount what I had seen. Again our charge was the least anxious of the party. It was very likely that the men belonged to the Custom House, he said quietly, and that they had no thought of us. I tried to persuade myself that it was so – as, indeed, it might easily be. However, I proposed that he and I should walk away together to a distant point we could see, and that the boat should take us aboard there, or as near there as might prove feasible, at about noon. This being considered a good precaution, soon after breakfast he and I set forth, without saying anything at the tavern.

He smoked his pipe as we went along, and sometimes stopped to clap me on the shoulder. One would have supposed that it was I who was in danger, not he, and that he was reassuring me. We spoke very little. As we approached the point, I begged him to remain in a sheltered place, while I went on to reconnoitre; for, it was towards it that the men had passed in the night. He complied, and I went on alone. There was no boat off the point, nor any boat drawn up anywhere near it, nor were there any signs of the men having embarked there. But, to be sure the tide was high, and there might have been some footprints under water.

When he looked out from his shelter in the distance, and saw that I waved my hat to him to come up, he rejoined me, and there we waited; sometimes lying on the bank wrapped in our coats, and sometimes moving about to warm ourselves: until we saw our boat coming round. We got aboard easily, and rowed out into the track of the steamer. By that time it wanted but ten minutes of one o'clock, and we began to look out for her smoke.

But, it was half-past one before we saw her smoke, and soon afterwards we

saw behind it the smoke of another steamer. As they were coming on at full speed, we got the two bags ready, and took that opportunity of saying good-bye to Herbert and Startop. We had all shaken hands cordially, and neither Herbert's eyes nor mine were quite dry, when I saw a four-oared galley shoot out from under the bank but a little way ahead of us, and row out into the same track.

A stretch of shore had been as yet between us and the steamer's smoke, by reason of the bend and wind of the river; but now she was visible, coming head on. I called to Herbert and Startop to keep before the tide, that she might see us lying by for her, and I adjured Provis to sit quite still, wrapped in his cloak. He answered cheerily, 'Trust to me, dear boy,' and sat like a statue. Meantime the galley, which was very skilfully handled, had crossed us, let us come up with her, and fallen alongside. Leaving just room enough for the play of the oars, she kept alongside, drifting when we drifted, and pulling a stroke or two when we pulled. Of the two sitters, one held the rudder lines, and looked at us attentively – as did all the rowers; the other sitter was wrapped up, much as Provis was, and seemed to shrink, and whisper some instruction to the steerer as he looked at us. Not a word was spoken in either boat.

Startop could make out, after a few minutes, which steamer was first, and gave the word 'Hamburg,' in a low voice as we sat face to face. She was nearing us

'It was half-past one before we saw her smoke, and soon afterwards we saw behind it the smoke of another steamer. As they were coming on at full speed, we got the two bags ready, and took that opportunity to say good-bye to Herbert and Startop.' Great Expectations, *moments before the dramatic end to Pip's attempt to help the convict Magwitch escape.*

178

The Cupboard is Empty
To Our Sorrow
But I Hope it will
Be Full to Morrow

Throughout his work Dickens was fascinated by writing of all kinds: the huge letters of billboards, 'To Let' notices, the papers that littered the streets, the names that David Copperfield reads scratched into the school door. Like these prison cell carvings, they all seem to be telling us something more than what they literally say. In Bleak House *Mr Krook writes upon the wall for Esther: 'He went on quickly until he had formed, in the same curious manner, beginning at the ends and bottoms of the letters, the word JARNDYCE, without once leaving two letters on the wall together.'*

very fast, and the beating of her paddles grew louder and louder. I felt as if her shadow were absolutely upon us, when the galley hailed us. I answered.

'You have a returned Transport there,' said the man who held the lines. 'That's the man, wrapped in the cloak. His name is Abel Magwitch, otherwise Provis. I apprehend that man, and call upon him to surrender, and you to assist.'

At the same moment, without giving any audible direction to his crew, he ran the galley aboard of us. They had pulled one sudden stroke ahead, had got their oars in, had run athwart us, and were holding on to our gunwale, before we knew what they were doing. This caused great confusion on board the steamer, and I heard them calling to us, and heard the order given to stop the paddles, and heard them stop, but felt her driving down upon us irresistibly. In the same moment, I saw the steersman of the galley lay his hand on his prisoner's shoulder, and saw that both boats were swinging round with the force of the tide, and saw that all hands on board the steamer were running forward quite frantically. Still in the same moment, I saw the prisoner start up, lean across his captor, and pull the cloak from the neck of the shrinking sitter in the galley. Still in the same moment, I saw that the face disclosed, was the face of the other convict of long ago. Still in the same moment, I saw the face tilt backward with a white terror on it that I shall never forget, and heard a great cry on board the steamer and a loud splash in the

179

water, and felt the boat sink from under me.

It was but for an instant that I seemed to struggle with a thousand mill-weirs and a thousand flashes of light; that instant past. I was taken on board the galley. Herbert was there, and Startop was there; but our boat was gone, and the two convicts were gone.

What with the cries aboard the steamer, and the furious blowing off of her steam, and her driving on, and our driving on, I could not at first distinguish sky from water or shore from shore; but, the crew of the galley righted her with great speed, and, pulling certain swift strong strokes ahead, lay upon their oars, every man looking silently and eagerly at the water astern. Presently a dark object was seen in it, bearing towards us on the tide. No man spoke, but the steersman held up his hand, and all softly backed water, and kept the boat straight and true before it. As it came nearer, I saw it to be Magwitch, swimming, but not swimming freely. He was taken on board, and instantly manacled at the wrists and ankles.

180

The galley was kept steady, and the silent eager look-out at the water was resumed. But, the Rotterdam steamer now came up, and apparently not understanding what had happened, came on at speed. By the time she had been hailed and stopped, both steamers were drifting away from us, and we were rising and falling in a troubled wake of water. The look-out was kept, long after all was still again and the two steamers were gone; but, everybody knew that it was hopeless now.

At length we gave it up, and pulled under the shore towards the tavern we had lately left, where we were received with no little surprise. Here, I was able to get some comforts for Magwitch – Provis no longer – who had received some very severe injury in the chest and a deep cut in the head.

He told me that he believed himself to have done under the keel of the steamer, and to have been struck on the head in rising. The injury to his chest (which rendered his breathing extremely painful) he thought he had received against the side of the galley. He added that he did not pretend to say what he might or might not have done to Compeyson, but, that in the moment of his laying his hand on his cloak to identify him, that villain had staggered up and staggered back, and they had both gone overboard together; when the sudden wrenching of him (Magwitch) out of our boat, and the endeavour of his captor to keep him in it, had capsized us. He told me in a whisper that they had gone down, fiercely locked in each other's arms, and that there had been a struggle under water, and that he had disengaged himself, struck out, and swum away.

Magwitch was tried and 'for his return to the land that had cast him out', he is condemned to death, but dies naturally in prison. As a journalist, Dickens had visited Newgate prison, and recorded the experience in 'A Visit to Newgate', from which this excerpt is taken:

In one corner of this singular-looking den was a yellow, haggard, decrepit old woman in a tattered gown that had once been black, and the remains of an old straw bonnet, with faded ribbon of the same hue, in earnest conversation with a young girl – a prisoner, of course, of about two-and-twenty. It is impossible to imagine a more poverty-stricken object, or a creature so borne down in soul and body, by excess of misery and destitution. The girl was a good-looking, robust female, with a profusion of hair streaming about in the wind – for she had no bonnet on – and a man's silk pocket-handkerchief was loosely thrown over a most ample pair of shoulders. The old woman was talking in that low, stifled tone of voice which tells so forcibly of mental anguish; and every now and then burst into an irrepressible sharp, abrupt cry of grief, the most distressing sound that human ears can hear. The girl was perfectly unmoved. Hardened beyond all hope of redemption, she listened doggedly to her mother's entreaties, whatever they were: and, beyond inquiring after 'Jem,' and eagerly catching at the few halfpence her miserable parent had brought her, took no more apparent interest in the conversation than the most unconcerned spectators. God knows there were enough of them, in the persons of the other prisoners in the yard, who were no more concerned by what was passing before their eyes, and within their hearing, than if they were blind and deaf. Why should they be? Inside the prison, and out, such scenes were too familiar to them to excite even a passing thought, unless of ridicule or contempt for the display of feelings which they had long since forgotten and lost all sympathy for.

A little farther on, a squalid-looking woman in a slovenly thick-bordered cap, with her arms muffled up in a large red shawl, the fringed ends of which straggled nearly to the bottom of a dirty white apron, was communicating some instructions to *her* visitor – her daughter evidently. The girl was thinly clad, and shaking with the cold. Some ordinary word of recognition passed between her and her mother when she appeared at the grating, but neither hope, condolence, regret, nor affection was expressed on either side. The mother whispered her instructions, and the girl received them with her pinched-up half-starved features twisted into an expression of careful cunning. It was some scheme for the woman's defence that she was disclosing; and a sullen smile came over the girl's face for an instant, as if she were pleased: not so much at the probability of her mother's liberation, as at the chance of her 'getting off' in spite of her prosecutors. The dialogue was soon concluded; and, with the same careless indifference with which they had approached each other, the mother turned towards the inner end of the yard, and the girl to the gate at which she had entered.

The girl belonged to a class – unhappily but too extensive – the very existence of which should make men's hearts bleed. Barely past her childhood, it required but a glance to discover that she was one of those children, born and bred in poverty and vice, who have never known what childhood is; who have never been taught to love and court a parent's smile, or to dread a parent's frown. The thousand nameless endearments of childhood, its gaiety and its innocence, are alike unkown to them. They have entered at once upon the stern realities and miseries of life, and to their better nature it is almost hopeless to appeal, in after-times, by any of the references which will awaken, if it be only for a moment, some good feeling in ordinary bosoms, however corrupt they may have become. Talk to them of parental solicitude, the happy days of childhood, and the merry games of infancy! Tell them of hunger and the streets, beggary and stripes, the gin-shop, the station-house, and the pawnbrokers, and they will understand you.

The prison chapel is situated at the back of the governor's house: the latter having no windows looking into the interior of the prison. Whether the associations connected with the place – the knowledge that here a portion of the burial service is, on some dreadful occasions, performed over the quick, and not upon the dead – cast over it a still more gloomy and sombre air than art has imparted to it, we know not, but its appearance is very striking. There is something in a silent and deserted place of worship highly solemn and impressive at any time; and the very dissimilarity of this one from any we have been accustomed to, only enhances the impression. The meanness of its appointments – the bare and scanty pulpit, with the paltry painted pillars on either side – the women's gallery with its great heavy curtain – the men's with its unpainted benches and dingy front – the tottering little table at the altar, with the commandments on the wall above it, scarcely legible through lack of paint, and dust and damp – so unlike the rich velvet with gilding, the stately marble and polished wood, of a modern church – are the more striking from their powerful contrast. There is one subject, too, which rivets the attention and fascinates the

Newgate Exercise Yard. 'It is necessary to explain here that the buildings in the prison . . . form a square, of which the four sides abut respectively on the Old Bailey, the old College of Physicians (now forming a part of Newgate Market), the Sessions House, and Newgate Street. The intermediate space is divided into several paved yards, in which the prisoners take such air and exercise as can be had in such a place.' Sketches

gaze, and from which we may turn disgusted, horror-stricken in vain, for the recollection of it will haunt us, waking and sleeping for months afterwards. Immediately below the reading-desk, on the floor of the chapel, and forming the most conspicuous objects in its little area, is *the condemned pew;* a huge black pen, in which the wretched men who are singled out for death are placed, on the Sunday preceding their execution, in sight of all their fellow-prisoners, from many of whom they may have been separated but a week before, to hear prayers for their own souls, to join in the responses of their own burial service, and to listen to an address, warning their recent companions to take example by their fate, and urging themselves, while there is yet time – nearly four-and-twenty hours – to 'turn and flee from the wrath to come!' Imagine what have been the feelings of the men whom that fearful pew has enclosed, and of whom, between the gallows and the knife, no mortal remnant may now remain! Think of the hopeless clinging to life to the last, and the wild despair, far exceeding in anguish the felon's death itself, by which they have heard the certainty of their speedy transmission to another world, with all their crimes upon their heads, rung into their ears by the officiating clergyman!

At one time – and at no distant period either – the coffins of the men about to be executed were placed in that pew, upon the seat by their side, during the whole service. It may seem incredible, but it is strictly true. Let us hope that the increased spirit of civilisation and humanity which abolished this frightful and degrading custom may extend itself to other usages equally barbarous; usages which have not even the plea of utility in their defence, as every year's experience has shown them to be more and more inefficacious.

Leaving the chapel, descending to the passage so frequently alluded to, and crossing the yard before noticed as being allotted to prisoners of a more respectable description than the generality of men confined here, the visitor arrives at a thick iron gate of great size and strength. Having been admitted through it by the turnkey on duty, he turns sharp round to the left, and pauses before another gate; and having passed this last barrier, he stands in the most terrible part of this gloomy building – the comdemned ward.

The press-yard, well known by name to newspaper readers, from its frequent mention (formerly, thank God!) in accounts of executions, is at the corner of the building, and next to the ordinary's house, in Newgate Street, running from Newgate Street, towards the centre of the prison, parallel with Newgate Market. It is a long narrow court, of which a portion of the wall in Newgate Street forms one end, the gate the other. At the upper end, on the left hand – that is, adjoining the wall in Newgate Street – is a cistern of water, and at the bottom a double grating (of which the gate itself forms a part) similar to that before described. Through these gates the prisoners are allowed to see their friends; a turnkey always remaining in the vacant space between during the whole interview. Immediately on the right is a building containing the press-room, day-room, and cells; the yard is on every side surrounded by lofty walls, guarded by *chevaux de frise;* and the whole is under the constant inspection of vigilant and experienced turnkeys.

In the first apartment into which we were conducted – which was at the top of a staircase, and immediately over the press-room – were five-and-twenty or thirty prisoners, all under sentence of death, awaiting the result of the recorder's report – men of all ages and appearances, from a hardened old offender with swarthy face and grizzly beard of three days' growth, to a handsome boy not fourteen years old, of singularly youthful appearance even for that age, who had been condemned for burglary. There was nothing remarkable in the appearance of these prisoners. One or two decently-dressed men were brooding with a dejected air over the fire; several little groups of two or three had been engaged in conversation at the upper end of the room, or in the windows; and the remainder were crowded round a young man seated at a table, who appeared to be engaged in teaching the younger ones to write. The room was large, airy, and clean. There was very little anxiety or mental suffering depicted in the countenance of any of the men; – they had all been sentenced to death, it is true, and the recorder's report had not yet been made; but we question whether there

'They led him through a paved room under the court, where some prisoners were waiting till their turns came, and others were talking to their friends, who crowded round a grate which looked into the open court.' Oliver Twist

184

was one man among them, notwithstanding, who did not *know* that, although he had undergone the ceremony, it never was intended that his life should be sacrificed. On the table lay a Testament, but there were no signs of its having been in recent use.

In the press-room below were three men, the nature of whose offence rendered it necessary to separate them, even from their companions in guilt. It is a long, sombre room, with two windows sunk into the stone wall, and here the wretched men are pinioned on the morning of their execution, before moving towards the scaffold. The fate of one of these men was uncertain; some mitigatory circumstances having come to light since his trial, which had been humanely represented in the proper quarter. The other two had nothing to expect from the mercy of the Crown; their doom was sealed, no plea could be urged in extenuation of their crime, and they well knew that for them there was no hope in this world. 'The two short ones,' the turnkey whispered, 'were dead men.'

The man to whom we have alluded, as entertaining some hopes of escape, was lounging at the greatest distance he could place between himself and his companions, in the window nearest the door. He was probably aware of our approach, and had assumed an air of courageous indifference; his face was purposely averted towards the window, and he stirred not an inch while we were present. The other two men were at the upper end of the room. One of them, who was imperfectly seen in the dim light, had his back towards us, and was stooping over the fire, with his right arm on the mantel-piece, and his head sunk upon it. The other was leaning on the sill of the farthest window. The light fell full upon him, and communicated to his pale, haggard face and disordered hair an appearance which, at that distance, was perfectly ghastly. His cheek rested upon his hand; and, with his face a little raised, and his eyes wildly staring before him, he seemed to be unconsciously intent on counting the chinks in the opposite wall. We passed this room again afterwards. The first man was pacing up and down the court with a firm military step – he had been a soldier in the foot-guards – and a cloth cap jauntily thrown on one side of the head. He bowed respectfully to our conductor, and the salute was returned. The other two still remained in the positions we have described, and were motionless as statues.

A few paces up the yard, and forming a continuation of the building, in which are the two rooms we have just quitted, lie the condemned cells. The entrance is by a narrow and obscure staircase leading to a dark passge, in which a charcoal stove casts a lurid tint over the objects in its immediate vicinity, and diffuses something like warmth around. From the left-hand side of this passage, the massive door of every cell on the story opens; and from it alone can they be approached. There are three of these passages, and three of these ranges of cells, one above the other, but in size, furniture, and appearance they are all precisely alike. Prior to the recorder's report being made, all the prisoners under sentence of death are removed from the day-room at five o'clock in the afternoon, and locked up in these cells, where they are allowed a candle until ten o'clock; and here they remain until seven the next morning. When the warrant for a prisoner's execution arrives, he is immediately removed to the cells, and confined in one of them until he leaves it for the scaffold. He is at liberty to walk in the yard; but both in his walks and in his cell, he is constantly attended by a turnkey, who never

The Old Bailey, 1865. 'From the rail before the dock, away into the sharpest angle of the smallest corner in the galleries, all looks were fixed upon one man – the Jew.' Oliver Twist

leaves him on any pretence whatsoever.

We entered the first cell. It was a stone dungeon, eight feet long by six wide, with a bench at the further end, under which were a common horse rug, a Bible, and Prayer-book. An iron candlestick was fixed into the wall at the side; and a small high window in the back admitted as much air and light as could struggle in between a double row of heavy, crossed iron bars. It contained no other furniture of any description.

SKETCHES

Dickens' sensitivity to the shocking realities of the society in which he lived seems to reach a climax in society's orchestration of the elimination of one of its own. 'Conceive the situation of a man spending his last night on earth in his cell,' the piece from *Sketches* continues. In his novels one character alone merits taking into the ghastly reality of that situation – the merry old gentleman himself, 'such an out and outer,' Dickens said of him as he pondered his fate, 'that I don't know what to make of him.'

The court was paved, from floor to roof, with human faces. Inquisitive and eager eyes peered from every inch of space. From the rail before the dock, away into the sharpest angle of the smallest corner in the galleries, all looks were fixed upon one man – the Jew. Before him and behind: above, below, on the right and on the left: he seemed to stand surrounded by a firmament, all bright with gleaming eyes.

He stood there, in all this glare of living light, with one hand resting on the wooden slab before him, the other held to his ear, and his head thrust forward to enable him to catch with greater distinctness every word that fell from the presiding judge, who was delivering his charge to the jury. At times, he turned his eyes sharply upon them to observe the effect of the slightest feather-weight in his favour; and when the points against him were stated with terrible distinctness, looked towards his counsel, in mute appeal that he would, even then, urge somthing in his behalf. Beyond these manifestations of anxiety, he stirred not hand or foot. He had scarcely moved since the trial began; and now that the judge ceased to speak, he still remained in the same strained attitude of close attention, with his gaze bent on him, as though he listened still.

A slight bustle in the court recalled him to himself. Looking round, he saw that the jurymen had turned together, to consider of their verdict. As his eyes wandered to the gallery, he could see the people rising above each other to see his face: some hastily applying their glasses to their eyes, and others whispering to their neighbours with looks expressive of abhorrence. A few there were, who seemed unmindful of him, and looked only to the jury, in impatient wonder how they could delay. But in no one face – not even among the women, of whom there were many there – could he read the faintest sympathy with himself, or any feeling but one of all-absorbing interest that he should be condemned.

As he saw all this in one bewildered glance, the death-like stillness came again, and looking back, he saw that the jurymen had turned towards the judge. Hush!

They only sought permission to retire.

He looked, wistfully, into their faces, one by one, when they passed out, as though to see which way the greater number leant; but that was fruitless. The jailer touched him on the shoulder. He followed mechanically to the end of the dock, and sat down on a chair. The man pointed it out, or he would not have seen it.

He looked up into the gallery again. Some of the people were eating, and some fanning themselves with handkerchiefs; for the crowded place was very hot. There was one young man sketching his face in a little note-book. He wondered whether it was like, and looked on when the artist broke he pencil-point, and made another with his knife, as any idle spectator might have done.

In the same way, when he turned his eyes towards the judge, his mind began to busy itself with the fashion of his dress, and what it cost, and how he put it on. There was an old fat gentleman on the bench, too, who had gone out, some half

'"Is the young gentleman to come too, Sir?" said the man whose duty it was to conduct them. "It's not a sight for children, Sir."' Oliver Twist and Mr Brownlow are admitted into the prison lodge prior to visiting Fagin – the 'snared beast' – in the death cell.

an hour before, and now come back. He wondered within himself whether this man had been to get his dinner, what he had had, and where he had had it; and pursued this train of careless thought until some new object caught his eye and roused another.

Not that, all this time, his mind was, for an instant, free from one oppressive overwhelming sense of the grave that opened at his feet; it was ever present to him, but in a vague and general way, and he could not fix his thoughts upon it. Thus, even while he trembled, and turned burning hot at the idea of speedy death, he fell to counting the iron spikes before him, and wondering how the head of one had been broken off, and whether they would mend it, or leave it as it was. Then, he thought of all the horrors of the gallows and the scaffold – and stopped to watch a man sprinkling the floor to cool it – and then went on to think again.

At length there was a cry of silence, and a breathless look from all towards the door. The jury returned, and passed him close. He could glean nothing from their faces; they might as well have been of stone. Perfect stillness ensued – not a rustle – not a breath – Guilty.

The building rang with a tremendous shout, and another, and another, and then it echoed loud groans, then gathered strength as they swelled out. like angry thunder. It was a peal of joy from the populace outside, greeting the news that he would die on Monday.

The noise subsided, and he was asked if he had anything to say why sentence of death should not be passed upon him. He had resumed his listening attitude, and looked intently at his questioner while the demand was made; but it was twice repeated before he seemed to hear it, and then he only muttered that he was an old man – an old man – an old man – and so, dropping into a whisper, was silent again.

The judge assumed the black cap, and the prisoner still stood with the same air and gesture. A woman in the gallery uttered some exclamation, called forth by this dread solemnity; he looked hastily up as if angry at the interruption, and bent forward yet more attentively. The address was solemn and impressive; the sentence fearful to hear. But he stood, like a marble figure, without the motion of a nerve. His haggard face was still thrust forward, his under-jaw hanging down, and his eyes staring out before him, when the jailer put his hand upon his arm, and beckoned him away. He gazed stupidly about him for an instant, and obeyed.

They led him through a paved room under the court, where some prisoners were waiting till their turns came, and others were talking to their friends, who crowded round a grate which looked into the open yard. There was nobody there, to speak to *him;* but, as he passed, the prisoners fell back to render him more visible to the people who were clinging to the bars: and they assailed him with opprobrious names, and screeched and hissed. He shook his fist, and would have spat upon them; but his conductors hurried him on, through a gloomy passage lighted by a few dim lamps, into the interior of the prison.

Here, he was searched, that he might not have about him the means of anticipating the law; this ceremony performed, they led him to one of the condemned cells, and left him there – alone.

He sat down on a stone bench opposite the door, which served for a seat and bedstead; and casting his blood-shot eyes upon the ground, tried to collect his thoughts. After a while, he began to remember a few disjointed fragments of

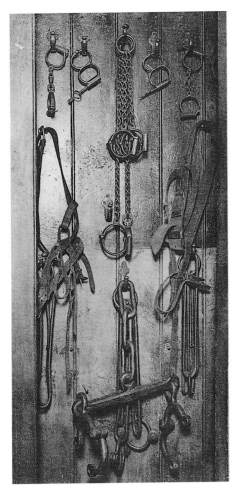

Manacles, Newgate Prison. 'We were at Newgate in a few minutes, and we passed through the lodge where some fetters were hanging up on the bare walls among the prison rules, into the interior of the jail.' Great Expectations

Left:
Newgate Prison, an emblem of 'the guilt and misery of London'.

what the judge had said, though it had seemed to him at the time, that he could not hear a word. These gradually fell into their proper places, and by degrees suggested more: so that in a little time he had the whole, almost as it was delivered. To be hanged by the neck, till he was dead – that was the end. To be hanged by the neck till he was dead.

As it came on very dark, he began to think of all the men he had known who had died upon the scaffold; some of them through his means. They rose up, in such quick succession, that he could hardly count them. He had seen some of them die, – and had joked too, because they died with prayers upon their lips. With what a rattling noise the drop went down; and how suddenly they changed, from strong and vigorous men to dangling heaps of clothes!

Some of them might have inhabited that very cell – sat upon that very spot. It was very dark; why didn't they bring a light? The cell had been built for many years. Scores of men must have passed their last hours there. It was like sitting in a vault strewn with dead bodies – the cap, the noose, the pinioned arms, the faces that he knew, even beneath, that hideous veil. – Light, light!

At length, when his hands were raw with beating against the heavy door and walls, two men appeared: one bearing a candle, which he thrust into an iron candlestick fixed against the wall: the other dragged in a mattress on which to pass the night; for the prisoner was to be left alone no more.

Then came night – dark, dismal, silent night. Other watchers are glad to hear the church-clocks strike, for they tell of life and coming day. To the Jew they brought despair. The boom of every iron bell came laden with the one, deep, hollow sound – Death. What availed the noise and bustle of cheerful morning, which penetrated even there, to him? It was another form of knell, with mockery added to the warning.

The day passed off. Day? There was no day; it was gone as soon as come – and night came on again; night so long, and yet so short; long in its dreadful silence, and short in its fleeting hours. At one time he raved and blasphemed; and at another howled and tore his hair. Venerable men of his own persuasion had come to pray beside him, but he had driven them away with curses. They renewed their charitable efforts, and he beat them off.

Saturday night. He had only one night more to live. And as he thought of this, the day broke – Sunday.

It was not until the night of this last awful day, that a withering sense of his helpless, desperate state came in its full intensity upon his blighted soul; not that he had ever held any defined or positive hope of mercy, but that he had never been able to consider more than the dim probability of dying so soon. He had spoken little to either of the two men, who relieved each other in their attendance upon him; and they, for their parts, made no effort to rouse his attention. He had sat there, awake, but dreaming. Now, he started up, every minute, and with gasping mouth and burning skin, hurried to and fro, in such a paroxysm of fear and wrath that even they – used to such sights – recoiled from him with horror. He grew so terrible, at last, in all the tortures of his evil conscience, that one man could not bear to sit there, eyeing him alone; and so the two kept watch together.

He cowered down upon his stone bed, and thought of the past. He had been wounded with some missiles from the crowd on the day of his capture, and his head was bandaged with a linen cloth. His red hair hung down upon his bloodless

face; his beard was torn, and twisted into knots; his eyes shone with a terrible light; his unwashed flesh crackled with the fever that burnt him up. Eight – nine – ten. If it was not a trick to frighten him, and those were the real hours treading on each other's heels, where would he be, when they came round again! Eleven! Another struck, before the voice of the previous hour had ceased to vibrate. At eight, he would be the only mourner in his own funeral train; at eleven –

Those dreadful walls of Newgate, which have hidden so much misery and such unspeakable anguish, not only from the eyes, but, too often, and too long, from the thoughts, of men, never held so dread a spectacle as that. The few who lingered as they passed, and wondered what the man was doing who was to be hanged tomorrow, would have slept but ill that night, if they could have seen him.

The condemned cell: 'It was a stone dungeon, eight feet long by six wide, with a bench at the further end, under which were a common horse rug, a Bible, and Prayer-book. An iron candlestick was fixed into the wall at the side; and a small high window in the back admitted as much air and light as could struggle in between a double row of heavy, crossed iron bars. It contained no other furniture of any description.' Sketches

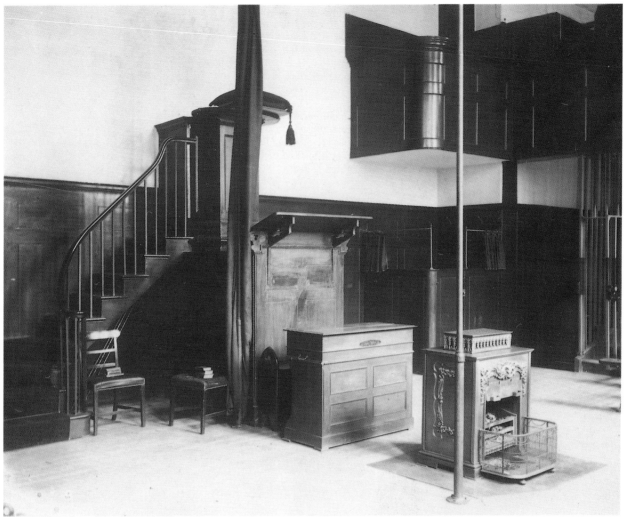

The pulpit and condemned pew in Newgate Prison Chapel. 'There is one subject, too, which rivets the attention and fascinates the gaze . . . the condemned pew; a huge black pew, in which the wretched men who are singled out for death are placed.' Sketches

From early in the evening until nearly midnight, little groups of two and three presented themselves at the lodge-gate, and inquired, with anxious faces, whether any reprieve had been received. These being answered in the negative, communicated the welcome intelligence to clusters in the street, who pointed out to one another the door from which he must come out, and showed where the scaffold would be built, and, walking with unwilling steps away, turned back to conjure up the scene. By degrees they fell off, one by one; and, for an hour, in the dead of night, the street was left to solitude and darkness.

The space before the prison was cleared, and a few strong barriers, painted black, had already been thrown across the road to break the pressure of the expected crowd, when Mr Brownlow and Oliver appeared at the wicket, and presented an order of admission to the prisoner, signed by one of the sheriffs. They were immediately admitted into the lodge.

'Is the young gentleman to come too, sir?' said the man whose duty it was to conduct them. 'It's not a sight for children, sir...'

Day was dawning when they again emerged. A great multitude had already assembled; the windows were filled with people, smoking and playing cards to beguile the time; the crowd were pushing, quarrelling, joking. Everything told of life and animation, but one dark cluster of objects in the centre of all – the black stage, the cross-beam, the rope, and all the hideous apparatus of death.

'The condemned man emerged, 'feeble and agonised . . . with ringing hands – uplifted though fettered – and moving his lips as if in prayer.'